P9-DFM-674

Theological Foundations

Concepts and Methods for
Understanding Christian Faith

Theological Foundations

Concepts and Methods for
Understanding Christian Faith

J.J. Mueller, SJ, et al.

Saint Mary's Press®

The publishing team included Leslie M. Ortiz, general editor; John B. McHugh, director of college publishing; prepress and manufacturing coordinated by the prepublication and production services departments of Saint Mary's Press.

Cover image by Scala / Art Resource, NY.
Interior background images by PhotoDisc, Inc.

Copyright © 2007 by Saint Mary's Press, Christian Brothers Publications, 702 Terrace Heights, Winona, MN 55987-1318, www.smp.org. All rights reserved. No part of this book may be reproduced by any means without the written permission of the publisher.

Printed in the United States of America

7000

ISBN 978-0-88489-920-4

Library of Congress Cataloging-in-Publication Data

Mueller, J. J. (John J.)
      Theological foundations : concepts and methods for understanding
Christian faith / J.J. Mueller.
            p. cm.
Includes index.
ISBN 978-0-88489-920-4 (pbk.)
            1. Theology. I. Title.

BT75.3.M84 2007
230—dc22

                                            2007028252

About the Authors

J.J. Mueller, SJ, PhD
Fr. Mueller holds a PhD in historical and systematic theology from the Graduate Theological Union at Berkeley. His interests are Christology and social responsibility.

Ronald Crown, DPhil, MSLS
Dr. Crown holds a DPhil in theology (New Testament studies) from the University of Oxford and an MS in library science from the University of Kentucky.

Bernhard A. Asen, PhD
Dr. Asen holds a PhD in biblical languages and literature from Saint Louis University. His particular interests are the prophets and the Psalms.

James A. Kelhoffer, PhD
Dr. Kelhoffer holds a PhD in New Testament and early Christian literature from the University of Chicago. His interests are the New Testament and the early Church.

Brian D. Robinette, PhD
Dr. Robinette holds a PhD in theology from the University of Notre Dame. His primary interests are Christology and theological anthropology.

Daniel Finucane, PhD
Dr. Finucane holds a PhD in historical theology from Saint Louis University. His interests include ecclesiology and foundational theology.

Jay M. Hammond, PhD
Dr. Hammond holds a PhD in historical theology from Saint Louis University. His interests include Medieval Christianity, Franciscan thought, and sacramental theology.

Barbara W. Blackburn, PhD
Dr. Blackburn holds a PhD in historical theology from Saint Louis University. Her interests are moral theology and the theology of death and suffering.

J. A. Wayne Hellmann, OFM Conv, ThD
Dr. Hellmann holds his doctoral degree in historical and systematic theology from Ludwig-Maximilian Universität in Munich, Germany. His interests are the study of St. Francis of Assisi, the Franciscan spiritual tradition, and the application of theology to social justice.

Ronald Modras, DrTheol
Dr. Modras holds a doctorate in theology from the University of Tubingen in Germany. His interests include interreligious dialogue and Jewish-Christian relations.

John Renard, PhD
Dr. Renard holds a PhD in Islamic studies from the Near Eastern Languages and Civilizations Department of Harvard University. Since 1978, he has been teaching courses in Islam and other major non-Christian traditions as well as comparative theology at Saint Louis University.

Angelyn Dries, OSF, PhD
Dr. Dries holds a PhD in historical theology from the Graduate Theological Union at Berkeley. Dr. Dries is the Danforth Chair of Theology at Saint Louis University. Her areas of interest include world Christianity and the modern missionary movement.

Acknowledgements

Thank you to the following people who advised the publishing team through discussion, class testing of the manuscript, student focus groups, or review of this work in progress:

Anthony Amodeo, Reference and Instruction Librarian, Loyola Marymount University, California

Jason Bourgeois, PhD, Quincy University, Illinois

Ulrike R. M. Guthrie, MA, independent scholar, Maine

Alan D. Krieger, Theology Librarian, University of Notre Dame, Indiana

Mari Heidt, PhD, Marquette University, Wisconsin

Harriet A. Luckman, PhD, College of Mount Saint Joseph, Ohio

Michael McClymond, PhD, Saint Louis University, Missouri

Ruben Rosario-Rodriguez, PhD, Saint Louis University, Missouri

Daniel Scholz, PhD, Cardinal Stritch University, Wisconsin

Paul Wadell, PhD, Saint Norbert College, Wisconsin

Maureen Walsh, graduate student, Georgetown University, Washington, DC

Table of Contents

The Structure of the Content and Its Relationships

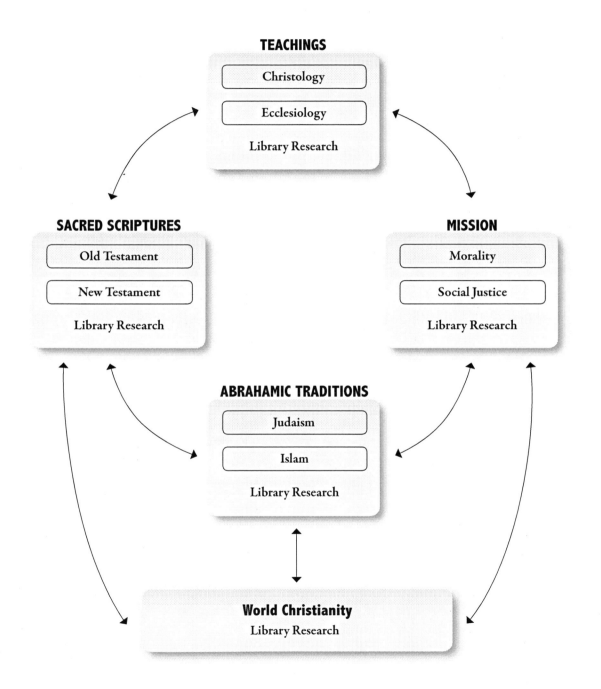

TEACHINGS

Christology

Ecclesiology

Library Research

SACRED SCRIPTURES

Old Testament

New Testament

Library Research

MISSION

Morality

Social Justice

Library Research

ABRAHAMIC TRADITIONS

Judaism

Islam

Library Research

World Christianity
Library Research

Introduction
From the Editor
J.J. Mueller, SJ, PhD

What Is Theology?

When we ask the question, "What is theology?" the word's etymology offers us helpful insight. The word *theology* comes from the Greek and means "God-talk" (*theos* = "God"; *logos* = "word"). Hence, theology describes *what* we do: We talk about God. Better yet, we have conversations about God. Theology is communal; it belongs to the life of faith in the ongoing Christian community, stemming from the revelation of Jesus two-thousand years ago. Theology also describes the methods we use when we talk about God. Anselm of Canterbury (d. 1109) defined theology as "faith seeking understanding," and we would add, "so that understanding deepens our faith, which means understanding and acting in pursuit of our goal, which is loving God and neighbor as Jesus did." We do not find the word *theology* in other religious traditions (e.g., Hinduism, Buddhism, Judaism, Islam); it is, however, the word used in the Christian tradition. Besides the generic sense of "talk about God," it has developed a specific sense as an academic discipline with a body of writing, methods, interpretations, subdisciplines, and so on. (This same specificity occurs in academic disciplines with generic names, such as English, history, philosophy, and medicine.)

Purpose of This Book

This book is about how to successfully study theology. Nothing is foreign to this pursuit of theology and, because theology pursues the deepest questions of being authentically human in God, why should there be any limit? Absolutely everything is grist for the theological mill. As an academic discipline, theology is not insular, exclusive, or a foreigner in the academy; it is in conversation with the best results, discoveries, and methods of every academic discipline's pursuit of truth. Theology takes up the most important questions for every human being, such as what is the meaning and purpose of life, death, suffering, family, person, society, structures, governance, poverty, and wealth? It takes up cosmic questions as well: Why am I here? Why is this planet spinning in this galaxy among billions of other galaxies? What if there is intelligent life elsewhere? Why is there a universe at all? What is it all about?

Theology above all recognizes that we live in God's Mystery and that we cannot answer all these questions adequately but that there is purpose to being here in this universe. The Christian believes what Jesus said and did and in what he asked of his followers: to love God above all things and our neighbor as ourselves. God is love.

Audience

This book is intended primarily for college students; however, it is also for people of the Catholic faith and other Christian denominations; people of other religious traditions; and people who are of no particular tradition but who are seekers. All are welcome to sit at the theological table.

This book provides a solid foundation. The text is designed for both people with little or no background in theology and those with quite a bit who seek a solid explanation of the subdisciplines involved. It is designed as a "first book," to be read all at once or by individual chapters chosen to introduce theological material pertinent to a particular course. In reading each chapter, students will receive an overview of the subdisciplines of theology. They will come to understand terms, concepts, vocabulary, and the development of the tradition through the ages and across cultures. Students will build a basic understanding of the whole of theology through its parts. They will be capable of building upon this base immediately, as well as be able to relate new material to this foundation.

Organization of the Book

This book is broken into ten chapters or subdisciplines of theology. These chapters are then grouped into five parts based upon similarities among the methods used for study in the subdisciplines. Read chronologically, the book moves from the revelation found in scripture to a discussion of global Christianity. However, the book is flexible in that each chapter is able to stand alone as a self-contained lesson on a particular theological discipline or topic. The chapters can be read in any order, grouped together, or read from front to back, according to the desires of the instructor.

Unique to this introductory theology text is the incorporation of a significant library research component. Later in this introduction, a section titled "From the Reference Librarian" will introduce the basic library skills students need for academic study. Each chapter then ends with an additional "From the Reference Librarian" section that focuses on the subject matter of that chapter and builds upon the basic skills from the introduction. Each section concludes with a list of the library skills introduced to that point. In that sense, the library sections are cumulative. However, each of these library research discussions is essentially an elaboration of the basic skills dealt with in the introduction, which allows students to read the chapters out of sequence.

We have deliberately included library research as an important component of studying theology because the skills of library research are not simply a matter of locating information (important as that is) but also a matter of evaluating the quality of the information found. Theological inquiry should be truly informed and not merely a matter of opinion (although theology by its nature involves having opinions); that is, the student of theology should be well equipped to determine the authoritativeness of theological statements and to pursue theological truth in an educated manner.

Arrangement of Each Chapter

Each chapter within the text begins with an introduction from the editor, and then the area specialty or subdiscipline of theology is presented by an expert in that area, followed first by questions about the text to make sure the subject matter is understood and then by questions for discussion that require reflection on the subject matter. The chapters conclude with the integrated research component, "From the Reference Librarian." The student will learn electronic research skills for use in libraries and on the Internet. Most importantly, this research component will provide an understanding of what the skills are, why they work, and how to adjust them to get the desired results. The skills learned are useful not only in the study of theology but also in the study of every academic discipline.

Learning for Living

Chapter 4 of John's gospel tells a story of Jesus meeting a Samaritan woman at a well. Samaritans and Jews did not generally mingle; hostility seemed the social norm. By Jewish law, Jesus should never have been alone with the woman, let alone talked to her, but he did. They engaged in dialogue, and the topic was the water in the well and drinking from it. As they conversed, the woman found that Jesus gradually opened her innermost soul. She finally ran to her fellow Samaritans and excitedly proclaimed, "He told me everything I have ever done." The Samaritans believed her and went off to see this "Jesus" person, inviting him to stay with them, which Jesus did for two days. The extended stay resulted in many more Samaritans coming to believe, and they then said to the woman, "It is no longer because of what you said that we believe, for we have heard for ourselves, and we know that this is truly the Savior of the world" (Jn 4:42).

To put it in today's context, they said thanks to their "teacher" (the Samaritan woman), and these students (the Samaritans from the village) said: "We have now found out for ourselves. Thank you for helping us, directing us, giving your experience . . . but we know now for ourselves that God encountered us, and we know God through Jesus. We will live in this relationship and know it will change how we live."

To be a college student is to come to see for yourself, experience and decide for yourself the truths of life, and open your heart to this Mystery.

A Student's Perspective about Theology in College

There was only one barrier between my desire to continue studying theology and actually officially declaring it as my major: what seemed to be all of society. One common theme I heard over and over was that to major in theology was not practical. It seemed that for most, a college education simply meant a good job on graduation. "Practical" meant financially secure, and theology was not the way to get there. Yet, as I sat with the children at Missionaries of Charity and eventually spent time with those at the Juvenile Detention Center just blocks from campus, nothing could have seemed more practical than what I was doing. I was learning about the world, about how people lived on a daily basis. I learned about racism, sexism, and economic disparity. These were lessons on the world, and I wanted more of them despite the excruciating questions these lessons brought up. On top of this, I began to have a true admiration for great thinkers. The theology faculty members at my university were gifted people and devoted theologians. These were people with thought processes and ways of life that somehow made a difference in the lives of the people around them.

Just as I grew to respect and admire the theology faculty, I found myself having similar feelings about my fellow students. These were great people who have since gone on to do amazing things. I quickly realized the high caliber of students choosing theology. These were not people floating through school. They wanted to learn, and they taught me a lot. I am forever grateful for that group and the many other students I met.

While clearly I am thankful for having chosen a theology major, I would be remiss if I suggested everyone should become a theology major. I do believe a basic understanding of some fundamental theological issues would serve every person along the journey of life. Theology is a means to an end, and that is how to live. I hold these words as mine: "Students, in the course of their formation, must let the gritty reality of this world into their lives, so they can learn to feel it, think about it critically, respond to its suffering and engage it constructively. They should learn to perceive, think, judge, choose, and act for the rights of others, especially the disadvantaged and the oppressed."[1]

Whatever you choose to study, I suggest you take this concept to heart. Go beyond your books and get to know the world, really get to know it. Travel. Volunteer. Immerse yourself in the world and especially with the poor who know the reality better than anyone. Most importantly, realize that the world is in desperate need of people who are willing to think and who are able to think well. I firmly believe a background in theology can create such people.

You are now the budding theologian, and I welcome you to join me on this journey. Walk with me. Argue with me. Live with me. Experience with me. Reflect with me. Let us do all of these things together, falling in love with the questions themselves. Maybe someday, a long time from now, we will realize that while we never discovered all the answers, we did nurture ourselves to journey with God in and through this world (Thomas Gill, BA, 2005, Saint Louis University).

From the Reference Librarian
A Practical Guide to Doing Research
Ronald Crown, DPhil, MSLS

The purpose of this introduction is to acquaint you with some basic library research skills you will need for the study of theology. Call it "Using the Library 101." The editor and authors of this text believe that learning how to use a library is an important part of studying theology—or any other subject for that matter (and the library skills you will learn can be applied to any subject, not just theology). The reason library skills are important is that part of becoming an educated person is not just learning things but *learning how to learn* things. Truly educated people are not just those who know more than they did before they received an education but those who also know how to continue learning after they have left school. Questions about the Christian faith—theological questions—do not necessarily disappear just because you have taken a course in theology or graduated from college, so learning how to learn (or how to study) a subject is just as important as learning the subject itself. Knowing how to use the resources of a good library is an important part of your ability to learn and study on your own.

So how does the library fit into learning how to learn? And, more importantly, how does the library fit into learning *after* you have learned how to learn? While you are in college, the library functions somewhat as a supplement to the expert knowledge communicated by your professors and gleaned from textbooks. After you leave college, a library can, in effect, replace professors and textbooks as your main, regular source of specialized knowledge on almost any subject. You will be fortunate indeed if, after leaving college or university, you live in the vicinity of a good library—assuming that you know how to use it.

So how do you learn how to learn theology? Or rather, where does the library (and the librarian) come into learning how to learn? All that we say about library skills and research techniques in this book boils down to two key elements:

Skill Key #1

Use the library's reference collection to begin your research.

> ## Skill Key #2
>
> ### Use the library's catalog to locate sources of information.

Perhaps these statements strike you as too obvious to mention (especially Skill Key #2—how else are you going to find something in the library?), but everything you will learn in this book about using the library is an elaboration of one of these two key elements. Moreover, these two elements relate closely because, as we shall see, knowing how to make proper use of the reference collection can make using your library's catalog a whole lot easier.

A third skill should also receive mention:

> ## Skill Key #3
>
> ### Use the library's collection of online databases and printed periodical indexes to identify articles in magazines and scholarly journals.

This is indeed an important library skill, but we will not be spending much time with it in this textbook for the following reasons:

1. The philosophy of library instruction (or "information literacy") underlying this book is that of a "curriculum-integrated" approach. Instead of trying to present all of the library skills you might possibly need or use, we are assuming your library skills will continue to develop as you proceed through the course of your studies. In particular, as your knowledge and expertise in a subject area increase, the library skills you will need will become more sophisticated as well. Learning the library skills presented in this book will provide you with a solid basis for the more advanced library skills you will need later on—much as an introductory course in a subject area provides a foundation for further study.

2. Because this text is an introduction to studying theology, the focus of the research discussions will be on the initial stages of research, which usually involve the use of the library's reference collection (Skill Key #1). By way of contrast,

periodical indexes and databases often include material beyond the level and scope of an introductory course.

3. The main principle behind Skill Key #2, the distinction between a "keyword" search and a search using subject headings, is one that also applies to searches in article databases. Instructors and librarians who wish to include Skill Key #3 as part of a course should be able to do so based on the foundations presented in this book.

Starting with the Reference Collection—Skill Key #1

So, let's begin at the beginning of the research process. You have a topic in which you are interested, and you want to begin to learn more about it. Why should you start with the reference collection?

Answering that question requires a short digression. At the most basic level, the library provides a collection of various types of resources to use in learning about any subject (we usually think of books and journals, but the collection can also include material in other formats, such as microfilm or microfiche; special collections, such as private papers, diaries, and letters; art objects; music scores or sound recordings; video and film collections; and, more recently, digital formats). The problem in any library is how to find what you want or need (not always the same thing), and the larger the library and the greater variety of information sources offered, the more important is the ability to locate it. The library has to be more than a mere collection of "stuff" (unlike most of our personal "libraries"). A good library constitutes an organized system of knowledge, the purpose of which is to make it easier for you to study any subject. This is true of all academic libraries, large or small (even small academic libraries can seem intimidating). There is a "method in the madness," and learning what that method is and how to make it work for you is what this section and the research sections of subsequent chapters are all about.

Student: How is the library organized?

The organization of an academic library involves several principles, but at this point, we will concern ourselves with one that is often overlooked but is fundamental—the division of the collection into two main parts: a reference collection and a circulating collection (this is oversimplified because there may be other divisions of the library, such as special collections, that we are ignoring for the time being). For many, perhaps most, people, the distinction between the two parts of the collection is simply the books you cannot check out and those you can, but there is more to it than that.

A reference collection, of course, contains reference books. As the word *reference* suggests, a reference book is a book that you "refer" to; that is, you use it to look up something. We have all used dictionaries to look up the meaning (or spelling or etymology) of a word; dictionaries are one excellent example of a reference work. (And remember that word *dictionary*—you are going to see it a lot, and its meaning will not always be what you would think.) No one sits down to read a dictionary from cover to cover; one refers to it. Another obvious example of a reference work is an encyclopedia. Most people do not (normally) read an encyclopedia from cover to cover but refer to a particular article or section that pertains to the topic of interest. You may be familiar with encyclopedias such as *World Book*, *Encyclopedia Britannica*, *Collier's*, and so forth. These are general-knowledge encyclopedias intended to cover the broad scope of human knowledge. The *American Heritage Dictionary of the English Language*, fourth ed., defines an encyclopedia as "a comprehensive reference work containing articles on a wide range of subjects . . . usually arranged alphabetically." Different general-knowledge encyclopedias cover "a wide range of subjects" with varying degrees of comprehensiveness, but they are alike in that the aim of such an encyclopedia is to provide basic knowledge about the subjects covered. That gives us the first reason for starting research in the reference collection: Use reference works to get a basic orientation—get your feet wet, so to speak—with regard to your topic.

But there is another, equally important reason for starting with the reference collection. This second reason is that the vast majority of the encyclopedias, especially in academic libraries, are subject-specific encyclopedias. You may have noticed that I omitted (indicated by the ellipses " . . . ") part of the dictionary definition of an encyclopedia. Here is the complete definition as given by the dictionary, with the omitted phrase in italics: "A comprehensive reference work containing articles on a wide range of subjects *or on numerous aspects of a particular subject*, usually arranged alphabetically."

Note the following encyclopedia titles:

The Routledge Encyclopedia of Philosophy, ten vols.

The Encyclopedia of Ethics, three vols.

The Encyclopedia of Bioethics, five vols.

The Encyclopedia of Human Behavior, four vols.

The Encyclopedia of Psychology, eight vols.

The Freud Encyclopedia, one vol.

The Encyclopedia of the Enlightenment, four vols.

The Dictionary of American History, ten vols.

The Encyclopedia of the United States in the Nineteenth Century, three vols.

Each of these encyclopedias focuses on a particular subject to the exclusion of everything else. Subject-specific encyclopedias thus have two important advantages over general-knowledge encyclopedias: First, a subject-specific encyclopedia will often devote more space to a particular topic, providing you with a more detailed introduction to it. Second, a subject-specific encyclopedia will often include coverage of specialized topics for which a general-knowledge encyclopedia simply has no room. Not only can you often find more-detailed information in a subject-specific encyclopedia, but you can also find information on topics not covered in a general-knowledge encyclopedia. As even introductory-level college courses involve technical subject matter beyond the level of "general" knowledge, the use of subject-specific encyclopedias is imperative.

You may have noticed one other thing as you scanned through the list of encyclopedias. Some of them cover broad subject-specific areas (philosophy, psychology, American history), while others cover a subset of those fields: ethics (subset of philosophy), Freud (subset of psychology), and the American Revolution (subset of American history). This brings us to the important matter of the "scope" of an encyclopedia.

To explore further this idea of the "scope" of encyclopedias, look at the following three subject-specific theological encyclopedias:

The Encyclopedia of Christianity, five vols.

The Encyclopedia of Early Christianity, two vols.

Augustine through the Ages: An Encyclopedia

These three encyclopedias, beginning with the first, cover an increasingly narrow range of subject matter—from the entirety of Christianity to a particular historical period of Christianity (the early Church) to a particular individual prominent in the early Church (Saint Augustine).

The scope of subject-specific encyclopedias can vary in other important ways. For example, besides being limited chronologically to a particular period of history (as in the *Encyclopedia of Early Christianity*), an encyclopedia can be limited geographically (the *Dictionary of Christianity in America*). The scope of an encyclopedia also varies with respect to whether it includes biographical articles or not. For example, the *Oxford Dictionary of the Christian Church* includes articles on persons, but the *New Dictionary of Theology* does not. This is important to know because one of the ways of studying theology is to study theologians. (Note, too, that entire encyclopedias can be biographical in that they are devoted to a single individual; see the previous examples on Freud and Saint Augustine.) The scope of an encyclopedia can also vary depending on the approach taken to the subject. Broadly speaking, theology can be approached either historically (i.e., the history of theology) or systematically (the study of theological concepts isolated from any historical context, often called "doctrinal" or "fundamental" theology). The scope of the following two encyclopedias with respect to this distinction is clearly indicated by their titles:

Dictionary of Historical Theology
Dictionary of Fundamental Theology

Unfortunately, encyclopedia titles are not always so clear. The title *New Dictionary of Theology* does not give you much help when it comes to determining whether it treats theology historically or systematically or both.

Review #1

Let's review what we have learned so far. The reference collection is a distinct part of the library, separated from the rest of the library collection in order for you to use it to acquire basic knowledge about a subject before venturing into the mass of information contained in the library's general collection. The reference collection is comprised mostly of subject-specific encyclopedias whose scope can vary in different ways for any particular subject. Based on what we know now, we can elaborate on the first key element of using libraries.

Skill Key #1

Use the library's reference collection to begin your research.

   a) Use a subject-specific encyclopedia to acquire specialized knowledge about a subject.

   b) Use a subject-specific encyclopedia whose scope is appropriate for both your topic and the approach you want to take to that topic.

Student: But how am I supposed to know which subject-specific encyclopedia to use? And how can I tell if its scope is appropriate?

In the first place, we do not expect you to be able to answer such questions yet. Part of the purpose of this textbook is to give you the knowledge to help you answer such questions. Each chapter of this book is about a particular subfield within the broad field of theology. Accordingly, the research section at the end of each chapter will begin by introducing and discussing the use of reference tools whose subject matter and scope are appropriate for researching topics related to that chapter. In addition, the reference collection is based in what is usually called the "Reference Department" (or, more recently, the "Information Commons," "Public Services," or some similar designation), which is where you can find a reference librarian who can provide assistance concerning appropriate encyclopedias to use. All academic libraries have reference librarians whose primary function is to help people locate the resources they need. A reference librarian is formally trained in library research methods and has usually spent a great deal of time becoming familiar with the library's collections, especially the reference collection. Often, reference librarians are themselves subject specialists with advanced degrees (master's or PhDs). Usually, the librarian will be able to guide you quickly to the reference tool best suited to your specific request. Reference librarians may spend part of their working day at a reference desk, where they are available to anyone with a question about library research. They are usually available by appointment also. Check with your own library to find out what specific research services it provides. As you become more familiar with library resources and research techniques, you will come to rely less on the reference librarian's assistance and more on your own knowledge and abilities; that is, you will become an independent learner.

However, just knowing you should start with an encyclopedia in the reference collection will not do you any good unless you also understand how to make the best use of an encyclopedia. Suppose you have found a subject-specific encyclopedia of an appropriate scope for your topic. If you are like most people using an encyclopedia, you find an article on your topic, read it, and thereby acquire the basic knowledge you need as a foundation for further research. Most people have then finished with the encyclopedia. However, many encyclopedias (and most of the good ones) have certain features that can be of great use to you, especially if you are using the encyclopedia to begin the process of research. To enable you to exploit fully the resources of an encyclopedia, in later chapters of this book we will look at such features of encyclopedias as cross-references, indexes, and synoptic outlines of contents. Right now, we will focus on the one feature of encyclopedias that will help take the research process beyond the encyclopedia—the bibliography that lists additional sources on a topic and appears at the end of the encyclopedia article. (If there is no bibliography at the end of the article, try a different encyclopedia.) In addition to the bibliography listing sources you might use to further your research, the book titles found there can guide you to resources in your library's collection that may not be listed in the bibliography. The use of encyclopedias as access points gives us yet another reason to start research in the reference collection and explains why, in addition to being a repository of basic knowledge, the reference collection is separate from the rest of the library's collection. The reference collection provides the means by which you find your way into the rest of your library's collection.

How does it do that? Think about how you normally find out what is in a library. You search the library's catalog using one of the three main types of library searches: by author, by title, or by subject. Searching by an author's name (usually in the form "last name, first name") or by book title is straightforward. However, if you are interested in a particular subject but do not know either the title of a book on that subject or the name of an author who has written on the subject, you are left with the third alternative—subject searching. Subject searching is somewhat more complicated than searching by author or title because it involves the use of a specialized vocabulary called "subject headings." Subject headings are assigned to books by catalogers for the precise purpose of enabling library users to find books on particular subjects. Most academic libraries in the United States use the specialized subject vocabulary developed by the Library of Congress and published in a multivolume, frequently revised and updated series called the *Library of Congress Subject Headings* (abbreviated *LCSH*, frequently revised and updated in part because books keep appearing on subjects that did not exist in the past, for example, books about computers or the Internet).

Look at the following sample adapted from the *LCSH* (twenty-ninth ed.) that shows the beginning of the entry for the subject heading "Theology." You will notice that not only is "Theology" a subject heading but it also appears with subdivisions ("Theology—Methodology") and even with sub-subdivisions ("Theology—History—20th Century").

Theology (*May Subd Geog*)
    [BR-BX]
    UF Christian theology
    Theology—19th century
        [Former heading]
        Theology—20th century
        [Former heading]
        Theology, Christian
    BT Christianity
        God
    RT Religion
    SA *subdivision* Theology *under individual*
        monastic and religious orders and
        under uniform titles of sacred works,
        e.g., Jesuits—Theology; Bible—Theology
    NT Apologetics
        Church
        Natural theology
        Negative theology
        Theology, Doctrinal
        Theology, Practical
[...]
    —History
    ——Early church, ca. 30–600
        UF Theology—Early church, ca.
        30–600
            [Former heading]

——**Middle Ages, 600–1500**
   UF Theology—Middle Ages,
   600–1 500
      [Former heading]
   Theology—12th century
      [Former heading]
   Theology—15th century
      [Former heading]
——**16th century**
   UF Theology—16th century
·   *[Former heading]*
——**17th century**
   UF Theology—17th century
      [Former heading]
——**18th century**
   UF Theology—18th century
      [Former heading]
——**19th century**
   UF Theology—19th century
      [Former heading]
——**20th century**
   UF Theology—20th century
      [Former heading]
—**Methodology**
   [BR118]
   UF Propaedeutics (Theology)
      Theology—Propaedeutics
   NT Storytelling—Religious aspects—
      Christianity

Subject headings can also be qualified by adjectives and appear in an inverted form ("Theology, Doctrinal"); this is so that other subject headings beginning with the word "Theology," referring to other types of theology (e.g., "Theology, Practical"), and related to various kinds of theology will appear in alphabetical sequence. Therefore, subject headings for something as simple and straightforward as "Theology" can be quite complex and not exactly intuitive. (Here is one example of a nonintuitive subject heading: books on "stupidity" used to be cataloged with the subject heading "Inefficiency, intellectual," although the subject heading has now been changed to "Stupidity.") So how do you determine the correct form of subject heading, especially in those cases where the subject heading may be expanded with subdivisions or may simply not be intuitive? This is where the bibliography from your encyclopedia article becomes important.

Let's illustrate this with an example. After reading the chapter of this text that discusses Christology, you are interested in the rise of heretical Christological views in the early Church. Instead of just guessing the subject heading for books on that topic, find a subject-specific encyclopedia whose scope is appropriate for the topic. Since you have not read the chapter on Christology yet, your reference librarian should be able to direct you to the *Encyclopedia of Early Christianity* if you ask for assistance. After pulling the volume off the shelf, look up "Heresy" and then take note of the bibliography at the end of the article:

Bibliography
H.E.W. Turner, *The Pattern of Christian Truth* (London: Mowbray, 1954); W. Bauer, *Orthodoxy and Heresy in Earliest Christianity* (Philadelphia: Fortress, 1971; orig. German ed., 1934); E.P. Sanders et al., eds. *Jewish and Christian Self-Definition*, 3 vols. (Philadelphia: Fortress, 1980–1982); H.O.J. Brown, *Heresies: The Image of Christ in the Mirror of Heresy and Orthodoxy from the Apostles to the Present* (Garden City: Doubleday, 1984); A. Le Boulluec, *La Notion d'heresie dans la Litterature grecque IIe-IIIe siecles*, 2 vols. (Paris: Etudes Augustiniennes, 1985); J. O'Grady, *Heresy: Heretical Truth or Orthodox Error: A Study of Ea3 Christian Heresies* (Longmead: Element, 1985); M. Desjardins, "Bauer and Beyond: On Recent Scholarly Discussions of *Hairesis* in the Early Christian Era," *SCent* 8 (1991):65–82; A.M. Ricter, "'Orthodoxy,' 'Heresy' and the Unity of the Church in Pre-Constantinian Times," SP 24 (1993):316–330; E. Junod, "De la Necessite et de l'utilite des heresies selon Origene (Contre Celse II,

12–13)," *Orthodoxie et heresie dans l'eglise ancienne* (Geneva: Revue de theologie et philosophie, 1993), pp. 101–124; SEC (1993), *Vol. 4: Orthodoxy, Heresy, and Schism in Early Christianity*; A. J. Hultgren, *The Rise of Normative Christianity* (Minneapolis: Fortress, 1994).
(Adapted from the *Encyclopedia of Early Christianity*, second ed., vol. 1.)

Because all the titles appear in the bibliography, you already know they are about your topic (even if the title of the book does not clearly indicate it; see *The Pattern of Christian Truth* and compare the title *Orthodoxy and Heresy in Earliest Christianity*), so it does not matter which one you choose to identify subject headings. Armed with this bibliographic information, you then search your library catalog using one of the titles from the bibliography. If, for example, you searched for *The Pattern of Christian Truth*, the catalog record would look something like this (if your library does not own this book, you could try another title from the bibliography):

Author	Turner, H. E. W. (Henry Ernest William), 1907–
Title	The pattern of Christian truth : a study in the relations between orthodoxy and heresy in the early church / H. E. W. Turner.
Published	New York : AMS Press, 1978.
Description	xvi, 508 p. ; 23 cm.
Series	Bampton lectures; 1954.
Note	Reprint of the 1954 ed. published by A. R. Mowbray, London, which was issued as Bampton lectures, 1954.
Bibliography	Includes bibliographical references and indexes.
Subjects	Theology, Doctrinal—History—Early church, ca. 30–600. Heresies, Christian—History—Early church, ca. 30–600.

Note the two subject headings assigned to this book; one of them—"Heresies, Christian—History—Early church, ca. 30-600"—appears to be exactly what you need for this topic. This subject heading informs us that the book is about the history of heresy in the early Church and that the period of the early Church extends from approximately the year 30 CE to approximately the year 600 CE (ca. is an abbreviation for the Latin word *circa*, which means "approximately").

In most library catalogs, you do not have to re-enter your search once you have a subject heading; you can simply click on the highlighted subject heading to produce a list of related subject headings:

<u>Heresies Christian History Early Church Ca 30–600—</u>	
<u>24 Related Subjects</u>	24
Heresies Christian History Early Church Ca 30–600	64
Heresies Christian History Early Church Ca 30–600	
Historiography 2005	1
Heresies Christian History Early Church Ca 30–600 Sources	4

The first line indicates there are twenty-four other subject headings related to "Heresies, Christian—History—Early Church ca. 30–600" in this catalog, and the second line shows there are sixty-four books listed with that subject heading (results will obviously vary from library to library). Already, you have expanded the range of sources available to you far beyond those listed in the encyclopedia. What's more, you are also able to find books on the topic written after 1997, the publication date of the *Encyclopedia of Early Christianity*. Look at the publication dates of the following titles from the sixty-four listed:

1   A Companion to Second-Century Christian "Heretics"/edited by Antti Marjanen & Petri Luomanen.   2005

Location	Call #	Status
Pius Stacks	BT1319 .C65 2005	DUE 09-19-06

2   Irenaeus' Use of Matthew's Gospel in Adversus Haereses/by D. Jeffrey Bingham.   1998

Location	Call #	Status
Pius Stacks	BR65.I74 B46 1998	NOT CHECKD OUT
Pius Stacks	BR65.I74 B46 1998 c.2	NOT CHECKD OUT

3   Lost Christianities : The Battles for Scripture and the Faiths We Never Knew/Bart D. Ehrman.   c2003

Location	Call #	Status
Pius Stacks	BS2840 .E4 2003	NOT CHECKD OUT

4   Pauline Christianity : Luke—Acts and the Legacy of Paul/by Christopher Mount.   2002

Location	Call #	Status
Pius Stacks	BS2589 .M68 2002	NOT CHECKD OUT

The other subject heading that appeared in the catalog record for *The Pattern of Christian Truth*—"Theology, Doctrinal—History—Early Church ca. 30-600"—represents a broader subject range than "Heresies, Christian"; for one thing, it will certainly encompass orthodox Christian thinking. For another, not just Christology but any theological topic, such as those considered in this text—ecclesiology, sacraments, and so on—could be included within the scope of a book with this subject heading. However, since the heading potentially includes Christian heresies within its range, a book with that subject heading could still be at least partly about Christian heresy. The only way to tell is to examine the book itself. Using a broader subject heading is one way to adjust your search strategy if your first attempt with a subject heading does not produce results (as in a smaller library with a less-extensive collection on the subject of heresy in the early Church).

Student: What if my library doesn't own the *Encyclopedia of Early Christianity*?

You can always ask your librarian to help you find an appropriate encyclopedia for your topic, and there is one encyclopedia you can use as a "fallback" to research almost any theological topic, the *New Catholic Encyclopedia* (*NCE*), second ed., published in 2003; some libraries may still have the first edition published in 1967, which will also work.

Let's see how researching the topic of early Christian heresy in the *NCE* compares with what we found in the *Encyclopedia of Early Christianity* (*EEC*). The *NCE* is a general encyclopedia in the sense that it covers a range of subjects, not simply theology or Church history but also science, literature, public affairs, and so on. However, because it was produced by Catholic scholars for those with an interest in Catholic subjects specifically, the coverage of theological topics is more extensive than that normally found in a general encyclopedia. You will notice the difference in scope between the *NCE* and the *EEC* by observing that the article on heresy in the *NCE* includes not only a section on the "Patristic Era" (i.e., the early Church) but also a section on the "Middle Ages and After." It contains additional articles on "Heresy (Canon Law)" and "Heresy, History of," with their respective foci on the Church-law aspects of heresy and the history of heresy and heretics, respectively. The amount of basic information in the *NEC* specifically on early Christian heresy may vary from that in the *EEC*, but you can use the bibliography in the same way to help you find your way through the library catalog. The following is the bibliography from the end of the *NCE* article on heresy:

Bibliography: 1. BROSCH. *Das Wesen der Haresie* (Bonn 1936). H. E. W. TURNER. *The Pattern of Christian Truth* (London 1954). K. RAHNER, *On Heresy* (New York 1964). M. MEINERTZ, "οχίομα und αἵρεσιζ im N.T." *Biblische Zeitschrift* 1 (1957) 114-118. J . DE GUIBERT. "La Notion d'heresie chez Saint Augustin." *Bulletin de literature ecclesiastique* 11 (1920) 368–382. G.W. H. LAMPE. ed., *A Patristic Greek Lexicon* (Oxford 1961–) fasc. I. p. 51. A. LANG, "Der Bedeutungswandel der Begriffe 'fides' und 'haeresis' und die dogmatische Wertung der Konzilsentscheidungen von Vienne und Trient." *Munchener theologische Zeitschrift* 4 (1953) 133–146. (From the *New Catholic Encyclopedia*, second ed., vol. 6.)

Notice that the title *The Pattern of Christian Truth* also appears in this bibliography. You should notice some other things as well. First, there is no order to the way titles are listed in the bibliography (as was the case with the bibliography from the *EEC*). The listing of an encyclopedia bibliography may be alphabetical, chronological, or, as in the two bibliographies we have looked at, in no particular order. Second, the most recent title listed in the *NCE* bibliography was published in 1964 (even though the encyclopedia was published in 2003). That should certainly be an indication that you should use the titles from this bibliography to find more up-to-date books and not be limited to the titles in the bibliography itself.

Review #2

Let's again take a moment to review. Catalogers assign subject headings to books to enable you to find books on the subject in which you are interested. This information is included in the catalog record and is searchable. All library catalogs (whether electronic or not) provide for this kind of subject searching, but being able to search the library catalog by subject depends upon knowing the correct subject heading. Although subject headings can be complicated or nonintuitive, the use of bibliographic information from an encyclopedia article on a subject makes it easy to identify the appropriate subject heading. In addition, because subject headings (like encyclopedias) vary in scope, it is possible to adjust a search strategy by choosing a broader or narrower subject heading.

We can now further expand on the two key elements of using libraries:

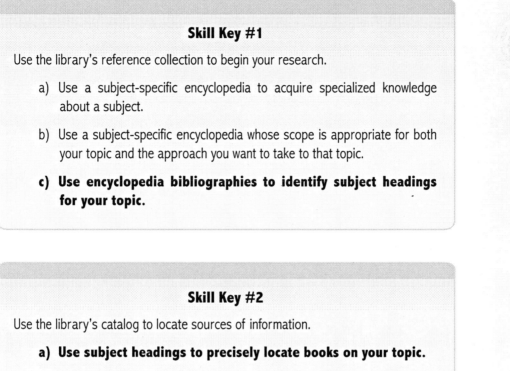

Skill Key #1

Use the library's reference collection to begin your research.

a) Use a subject-specific encyclopedia to acquire specialized knowledge about a subject.

b) Use a subject-specific encyclopedia whose scope is appropriate for both your topic and the approach you want to take to that topic.

c) Use encyclopedia bibliographies to identify subject headings for your topic.

Skill Key #2

Use the library's catalog to locate sources of information.

a) Use subject headings to precisely locate books on your topic.

b) Use subject headings whose scope fits your topic as closely as possible, then adjust your search with a broader or narrower subject heading as necessary.

Using Keyword Searching to Identify Subject Headings

In addition to using encyclopedia bibliographies, there is another way to identify subject headings: The advent of electronic library catalogs has made it possible to search the catalog by "keyword." Keyword searching is sometimes called "natural-language" searching because this type of search simply looks for words wherever they appear in the catalog record. Keywords are simply any words (or brief phrases) that may appear in a book title, in the author's name, in a subject heading, in notes added to the record by a cataloger, or in tables of contents. (Precisely which parts of a catalog record are included in a keyword search may vary from library to library.) Thus, it is possible to search for a book on a subject simply by typing in some keywords related to that topic. You might get results with a word in the book's title, for example, or maybe even a subject heading. The problem is determining which keywords to use by thinking of terms you would expect to find in the title or table of contents (many electronic library catalogs now include tables of contents) of a book on a particular subject. If we continue our example using the subject of heresy in the early Church, we might try a combination of keywords such as "early," "church," and "heresy." (There are many other possibilities; indeed, that is part of the problem—there are so many possibilities with a keyword search.) We can type the following as our search statement (the use of "AND" ensures that all three words will be present in any record retrieved):

early AND church AND heresy

Keyword searching can complicate your search by bringing up irrelevant material. The following record was among those retrieved by such a search. All of the aforementioned keywords appear in this record, but the book has nothing to do with the topic of heresy in the early Church. We have highlighted our search terms.

Author	Como, David R., 1970–
Title	Blown by the Spirit : Puritanism and the emergence of an Antinomian Underground in pre-Civil-War England / David R. Como.
Published	Stanford Calif. : Stanford University Press, 2004.

Location	Call #	Status
Pius Stacks	BR757 .C68 2004	NOT CHECKD OUT

Table of contents

9   Two Strains Crossed: Hybrid Forms of English Antinomianism   325

10 Ultra-Antinomianism?   381

11 Forging Heresy: Mainstream Puritans and Laudians on Antinomianism   392

    Epilogue: 1640 and Beyond   415

    Conclusion   432

App. A   The Influence of Familism in Seventeenth-Century England   457

App. B   Familist Extracts from the Diary of Edward Howes (British Library, Sloane MS. 979)   469

App. C   Truth and Fiction in the Archives: Sources, Source-Skepticism, and the Sport of Heresy-Hunting   474

App. D   Schedule of Errors Alleged Against Roger Bearley, 1616/17   482

App. E   Letter of John Eachard, 1631   486

    Bibliography   491

    Index   505

Description	xii, 513 p. ; 24 cm.
Bibliography	Includes bibliographical references (p. [491]–503) and index.
Subjects	Antinomianism—England—History—17th century.
	Puritans—England—History—17th century.
	England—Church history—17th century.

Compare that with the following catalog record. This book is actually about the topic of heresy in the early Church (see part 2 in the Table of Contents) but would not have shown up in our keyword search. The keyword search requires that all the search terms be present; in the case of this record for *Lost Christianities*, "early" and "church" appear (both, as it happens, in the subject heading) but not "heresy" (although "heresies" does and is highlighted).

Author	Ehrman, Bart D.
Title	Lost Christianities : The Battles for Scripture and the Faiths We Never Knew/Bart D. Ehrman.
Published	New York : Oxford University Press, c2003.
Location	Call #	Status
Pius Stacks	BS2840 .E4 2003	NOT CHECKD OUT

Table of Contents

    Preface

    Major Christian Apocrypha Discussed, Dates and Contents

    Introduction: Recouping Our Losses   1

Description	xv, 294 p. : ill. ; 25 cm.
Bibliography	Includes bibliographical references (p. 259-287) and index.
Subjects	Apocryphal books (New Testament)—Criticism, interpretation, etc.
	Heresies, Christian—History—**Early church**, ca. 30–600.
	Church history—Primitive and **early church**, ca. 30–600.

Of course, we could include both the singular and plural forms of "heresy" in our search, but then we should do the same for all the terms in our search. And how many other keywords must we use to find exactly what we want in the catalog?

Here is another record that would have been retrieved by a keyword search on "early," "church," and "heresy" (although it was necessary to scan through two or three dozen titles):

Title	Orthodoxy, heresy, and schism in early Christianity / edited with introductions by Everett Ferguson.
Published	New York : Garland, 1993.
Description	xvi, 354 p. ; 24 cm.
Series	Studies in early Christianity ; v. 4.
Note	One paper in French.
Bibliography	Includes bibliographical references.
Subjects	Church history—Primitive and early church, ca. 30–600.
	Theology, Doctrinal—History—Early church, ca. 30–600.
	Heresies, Christian—History—Early church, ca. 30–600.

After seeing that this book is indeed about the desired subject, we can now readily identify the precise subject heading to use. So, the problem with using keywords is that (1) it is highly likely that, although keyword searching can retrieve relevant material, it will also retrieve a large amount of irrelevant material (see *Blown by the Spirit* in the earlier example), which you then have to wade through to find what you want; and (2) it is highly likely that you will miss relevant material (such as *Lost Christianities*). Notice, however, the one thing that appears for all the books actually about the subject of heresy in the early Church—the presence of the subject heading "Heresies, Christian—History—Early Church, ca. 30–600." Ultimately, a keyword search can lead to an appropriate subject heading and thus can be a useful way to identify such subject headings.

Whether you use an encyclopedia bibliography to identify subject headings in your library catalog or simply do a keyword search, *the use of subject headings remains the most precise way to ensure that you will find material about your subject*. Keyword searching can be a useful technique if you use it to identify subject headings in order to focus your search. The less time you spend sifting through irrelevant material, the more time you will have to spend on your research.

We can now add another point to the second key element of using the library:

Skill Key #2

Use the library's catalog to locate sources of information.

a) Use subject headings to locate precisely books on your topic.

b) Use subject headings whose scope fits your topic as closely as possible, then adjust your search with a broader or narrower subject heading as necessary.

c) As an alternative to using encyclopedia bibliographies, use keyword searching to identify subject headings for your topic.

Using "Concise" Dictionaries

Each specialized field of knowledge has its own technical vocabulary of words that appear only in the context of that field of study or words that are used with other subjects but have a distinctive meaning when used in a particular field. You may have come across several unfamiliar terms as you read this chapter, for example, words like *patristic, Christological,* or *heresy.* The word *Christological* is usually found in a theological context, while the word *heresy* can be used in relation to other subjects. You could, of course, simply look up the meaning of unfamiliar terms in a standard dictionary, but just as there are subject-specific encyclopedias, there are also subject-specific dictionaries to help with understanding the specialized vocabulary of a field of knowledge. Such subject-specific dictionaries do what all dictionaries do—provide basic definitions (and sometimes, brief discussions) of the technical vocabulary of the field.

The following are the titles of three standard concise dictionaries for theology. If your library does not have at least one of these, ask the librarian to show you an alternative title.

Donald K. McKim. *Westminster Dictionary of Theological Terms.* Louisville, KY: Westminster John Knox Press, 1996.

Gerald O'Collins, SJ, and Edward G. Farrugia, SJ. *A Concise Dictionary of Theology.* Revised and expanded ed. Mahwah, NJ: Paulist Press, 2000.

Geoffrey Parrinder. *A Concise Encyclopedia of Christianity*. Oxford, UK: Oneworld, 1998.

Complete Review

Your repertoire of library skills has expanded as follows:

Skill Key #1

Use the library's reference collection to begin your research.

    a) Use a subject-specific encyclopedia to acquire specialized knowledge about a subject.

    b) Use a subject-specific encyclopedia whose scope is appropriate for both your topic and the approach you want to take to that topic.

    c) Use encyclopedia bibliographies to identify subject headings for your topic.

    d) Use a concise subject-specific dictionary to look up the specialized vocabulary of a particular field.

Skill Key #2

Use the library's catalog to locate sources of information.

    a) Use subject headings to locate precisely books on your topic.

    b) Use subject headings whose scope fits your topic as closely as possible, then adjust your search with a broader or narrower subject heading as necessary.

    c) As an alternative to using encyclopedia bibliographies, use keyword searching to identify subject headings for your topic.

We will add to this list throughout the book. You might want to copy these onto a piece of paper or notebook for your next trip to the library.

As we proceed through the rest of this textbook, we will continue to build on the two key elements of using the library, which will help you become a lifelong learner. You know enough now to begin your journey of discovery in theology and in the library. Don't forget, if necessary, to ask the librarian for help.

Student: Why can't I just use the Internet to do all my academic research?

The Internet is a wonderful thing. In fact, many library resources (such as library catalogs) are available on the Internet for searching by anyone. But there is an important distinction to be made between the electronic resources provided by your library (which may be available on the Internet), such as library catalogs, article databases, electronic books, and so on, and things that are simply "out there" on the World Wide Web. The electronic resources provided by your library have been selected specifically for the purpose of academic research. Therefore, they can be regarded as suitable for academic research, with no questions asked. Obviously, there is much on the Internet that has not been evaluated by any librarian or included in any library collection, so it is important that you learn to evaluate carefully the quality of any Internet source you may want to use or cite in academic work (that is another part of learning how to learn). We will have more to say on this in a later chapter. At this point, we only want to emphasize that the library represents a great deal of expense and effort to provide high-quality sources of information for your use. Using the resources the library provides means you can spend less time asking yourself whether a source is sufficiently authoritative for academic research.

The Process of Research

A final word about research: Research is not a series of mechanical steps to be followed. Doing research is, in part, a matter of knowing where to look for what you want to find, but before you know where to look, you must know where you can look, that is, what kinds of resources are available. That is why this book focuses on the basic library skills of using a reference collection and searching the library catalog. Exactly which library skill you employ in any given situation will depend on the precise nature of the question you are asking. Sometimes your research will begin and end with reading an encyclopedia article or simply looking up the meaning of an unfamiliar word or phrase. At other times, you will need to do more in-depth research and make use of several library skills. There will often be more than one way to approach researching a topic. The library skills you learn in this book will give you options. If one thing does not work, try an alternate approach. After all, it would not be called "research" if you knew exactly where you were going (and how you were going to get there) from the beginning. If you get stuck, the reference librarian is always there to assist you.

Endnotes

[1] Adapted from an address given by Fr. Peter Hans Kolvenbach, SJ, at Santa Clara University in 2000: "The Service of Faith and the Promotion of Justice in American Jesuit Higher Education." Available online at http://www.scu.deu/news/attachments/kolvenbach_speech.html

I

THE SACRED SCRIPTURES AND CHRISTIAN THEOLOGY

1

The Old Testament

From the Editor

Have you ever seen movies, read books, or heard stories about people who lost their memory and, as a result, also lost their identity? Who we are is unveiled in time by our earliest environment of family, then by what we do, experiences we have, choices we make, and their consequences. Each of us is born in the middle of the human story, not the beginning. Before people wrote, they told stories about themselves and the meaning of life as they experienced it. At some point, they began to record their memories and what they believed about how to live and what was important in writing. Those memories were largely based on their religious experiences. First orally transmitted and then in writing, the record provided an identity for those people. In the major religious traditions of the world, we refer to the most significant oral traditions and written records as Sacred Texts. They are handed down to help shape the people of current and future generations, called humanity. Sacred Texts therefore hold a special place in a community because they talk about the God–Human relationship and who we are, why we are here, and what we are about.

Theology (lit., "talk about God") is faith seeking understanding, or we can say now it is the "memory" of a faith community seeking God, finding God, and handing down that knowledge and wisdom, so others can know the truth of this encounter with God and its essential role in being human. We do not simply repeat a text; it is alive in the community as a resource to find God, point to God, live in God, and be formed by God.

We begin this book at the beginning with the sacred memory, the Sacred Texts of Christianity, in order to understand who, what, and why this community of believers has come to be. We will find out why Christianity has incorporated the Jewish Sacred Text as part of the Christian Sacred Texts—an important part of the tradition not only for Christians but, as we shall see later, also for Muslims in their Sacred Texts, called "the Qur'an." And remember, while we are investigating what theology is and does, we do not want to lose sight of the great theme of theology: you, me, humanity, creation, and God together. No one and nothing is left behind.

At the end of this chapter, we will begin our librarian's component, which will help you find more information, knowledge, and understanding of many topics that arise in this chapter, other chapters, and in the future. It is a skill needed to free us up to pursue knowledge in the many sources in and outside of the discipline of theology.

The Old Testament
Bernhard A. Asen, PhD

The Hebrew Bible, Called by Christians the "Old Testament"

My maternal grandfather was a great storyteller. Over the years, I have told and retold many of his stories to family and friends. He was fond of talking about his youth and his life on the farm. He sang songs and recited poetry, told riddles, and recited limericks. I have also found out from my mother and other family members that many of Grandpa's stories were precisely that—stories. "Some of them had a kernel of truth," my mother once told me, "but most of them were greatly embellished!"

Sometime in the second century BC, a man named Jesus, son of Eleazar son of Sirach of Jerusalem, wrote an introduction to a book he says was written by his grandfather, Jesus Ben Sira.

> Many great teachings have been given to us through the *Law and the Prophets and the other [books]* that followed them, and for these we should praise Israel for instruction and wisdom. . . . So my grandfather Jesus, who had devoted himself especially to the reading of the *Law and the Prophets and the other books* of our ancestors, and had acquired considerable proficiency in them, was himself also led to write something pertaining to instruction and wisdom so that by becoming familiar also with his book those who love learning might make even greater progress in living according to the law.
>
> You are invited therefore to read it with goodwill and attention, and to be indulgent in cases where, despite our diligent labor in translating, we may seem to have rendered some phrases imperfectly. For what was originally expressed in Hebrew does not have exactly the same sense when translated into another language. Not only this book, but even the *Law itself, the Prophecies, and the rest of the books* differ not a little when read in the original. [emphasis added]

This introduction to the book of Sirach (also known as the Wisdom of Jesus son of Sirach, and Ecclesiasticus) gives us some valuable information about the collection of books that circulated among the Jewish community some two-hundred years before the beginning of the Christian era. Three times, Ben Sira's grandson tells us his grandfather was devoted to reading the "Law and the Prophets and the other books." Here, we may have the earliest reference to the division of the Hebrew Bible into three parts: the Law, the Prophets, and the Writings. When referring to these three parts of their Bible, the Jewish people, who are often referred to as the "People of the Book," use the Hebrew words for Law (*Torah*), Prophets (*Nebiim*), and Writings (*Kethubim*). By adding the vowel "a" between the first and second letters of these words (*TNK*) they form an acronym—*TaNaK*. Even today, Jews still refer to their Bible by this acronym. The Tanak is also known as the Jewish Testament, the First Testament, and, by most Christians, the Old Testament (OT). The word *Old* is to be understood in the sense of prior, first, or venerable, not outdated or superseded by the New or Christian Testament.

Ben Sira's grandson tells us further that he translated his grandfather's book from Hebrew into Greek and that when you translate from one language into another, the "books differ not a little when read in the original." The Tanak was originally written in Hebrew, although some small portions (e.g., Dan 2:4b–7:28) are written in Aramaic.

Also beginning around the second century BC, the Tanak was translated into Greek. This translation is known as the Septuagint and is frequently abbreviated by the Roman numerals LXX. (According to an ancient tradition, seventy-two scholars translated the Tanak in seventy-two days. The number was rounded off to seventy.)

It is important to note that while Sirach's grandson refers to the "Law, Prophets and other books," the Jewish people do not consider the Book of Sirach to be part of the Tanak. The book was included, however, in the LXX. By the time Sirach was translated, Greek had replaced Hebrew as the dominant language of the ancient world. The leaders of the Jewish community at that time did not consider books written in Greek to be inspired by God. Consequently, some books that were part of the LXX were not included in the Tanak. Jews and Protestants refer to the following books, or parts of books, as apocryphal (their meaning is "hidden" or obscure), but Roman Catholics refer to them as deuterocanonical (added later to the collection or canon of inspired writings):

1 and 2 Esdras

The Wisdom of Solomon (follows Song of Songs)

1 and 2 Maccabees

The Letter of Jeremiah (chapter 6 of Baruch)

Tobit (follows Nehemiah)

Sirach (Ecclesiasticus) (follows The Wisdom of Solomon)

Susanna (chapter 13 of Daniel)

The Prayer of Manasseh

Baruch (follows Lamentations)

Judith (follows Tobit)

The Prayer of Azariah and the Song of the Three Jews (follows Daniel 3:23; verses 24–90)

Bel and the Dragon (chapter 14 of Daniel)

Additions to Esther (follows Esther)

As stated, the Jews did not include these writings in the Tanak, not only because they were written in Greek but also because they were not widely read or used. But why do Protestants refer to these books as apocryphal, while Roman Catholics refer to them as deuterocanonical? In order to answer this question, we need to move forward in history to the fourth century AD, when Latin became the dominant language of the Roman Empire. From approximately 390–405 AD, Jerome (342–420), who was a great scholar, saint, and linguist, moved to the Holy Land to translate the Christian scriptures from their original languages into the growingly popular Latin, the language of the people of the fourth-century Roman Empire, which he did; it is called the Vulgate. He relied on both the Hebrew and Greek texts for his translation but placed a higher value on the Hebrew language and decided to follow the order of books in the Tanak rather than in the LXX. The books not included in the Tanak were considered apocryphal.

Centuries later, when Martin Luther (1483–1546) translated the Bible into German, he also followed the order of books in the Tanak and placed these writings in a separate section still known today as the Apocrypha. Luther, following the lead of Jerome, considered these books important for history and spiritual edification but not canonical, inspired, or useful for establishing Church doctrine. In response to Luther and the Reformation, the Council of Trent (1545) officially declared for the Roman Catholic Church that these books were not apocryphal but deuterocanonical.

You may have noticed that the division of Law, Prophets, and Writings referred to in the introduction to Sirach places the prophetic books in the middle of the collection. However, if you look at your English translation of the Bible, you will no doubt find that the prophets are not in the middle but at the end of the

Tanak. The last book of the Tanak is Second Chronicles, but the last book of most English translations of the Bible is the book of the prophet Malachi, which ends with the words, "Lo, I will send you the prophet Elijah before the great and terrible day of the Lord comes. He will turn the hearts of parents to their children and the hearts of children to their parents, so that I will not come and strike the land with a curse" (4:5–6).

In order to understand this positioning, we once again need to jump ahead hundreds of years into the Christian era. Whereas the Jewish people saw the prophets as the prime interpreters of the Torah, Christians saw the prophets as foreshadowing or hoping for the future coming of Jesus. In the New Testament (NT) gospels, John the Baptist is referred to as "Elijah who is to come" (Mt 11:14; 17:9–13; Mk 6:14–15; Lk 1:17), mentioned by the prophet Malachi. According to the gospel writers, John the Baptist prepared the way for Jesus, whom Christians confess as the Christ. Christ is not Jesus' last name but a Greek translation of a Hebrew word *meshiach* ("messiah"), which means "anointed one." In 1 Samuel 10:1, we read that "Samuel took a vial of oil and poured it on [Saul's] head, and kissed him; he said, 'The Lord has anointed you ruler over his people Israel.'" From that time on, when kings ascended to the throne, they were considered "anointed ones" (messiahs). As we will see later, it was with Saul's successor, David, that the word *messiah* took on special, even technical, meaning.

The Jews believed that through David's descendants, his kingship would last forever, and from David's day to this day, the Jewish people expect the coming of the new and final David, the Messiah. Christians, however, believe that Jesus is the "Messiah, the Son of David, the son of Abraham" (Mt 1:1).

Though the Jewish people have great respect for the NT, they do not need it to live out their faith. Christians, however, need the Tanak to properly understand Jesus because the word *messiah* (*Christos* in Greek) is thoroughly grounded in the history and tradition of the Tanak. Christians must never lose sight of the fact that without "the Old Testament, the New Testament would be an incomprehensible book, a plant deprived of its roots and destined to dry up and wither" (The Pontifical Biblical Commission, 2002, p. 211).

An influential Jewish scholar named Martin Buber (1878–1965) once addressed a group of priests and said, "What is the difference between Jews and Christians? We all await the Messiah. You believe He has already come and gone, while we do not. I therefore propose that we await Him together. And when He appears, we can ask him: were You here before?" Then he paused and added: "And

I hope that at that moment I will be close enough to whisper in his ear, 'For the love of heaven, don't answer'" (Wiesel, 1995, 354–355).

As we proceed now to look at the various divisions of the Tanak, we need to keep in mind that, like my grandfather's stories, the stories contained in the Law, Prophets, and Writings are diverse kinds of literature. Many of the stories record actual events that can be corroborated by extrabiblical history and literature, but many of them are based on legends, remnants of ancient myths, songs, and hymns that may never have actually happened but that contain important and enduring "kernels of truth."

Tanak Division 1—Torah: Words of Instruction

The first division of the Tanak is the Torah. *Torah* is often translated into English as "law" but more properly means "teaching" or "instruction." In the broadest sense, the entire Tanak is teaching and instruction. More narrowly defined, the Torah refers to the books of Genesis, Exodus, Leviticus, Numbers, and Deuteronomy. These books are known as the Pentateuch ("five scrolls"). The Jewish tradition also calls them the "Five Books of Moses" because, according to Jewish tradition, Moses was the author of these books.

However, through many centuries, it has become clear to Jewish and Christian scholars that the Pentateuch was not the work of Moses or of any one particular author but is rather a compilation of a variety of authors and literary sources.

Already in the seventeenth century, Jewish scholar Baruch Spinoza (1632–1677) and Christian scholar Richard Simon (1638–1712) began to question the Mosaic authorship of the Pentateuch. However, it was not until the nineteenth century that a formal hypothesis developed concerning the formation of the Pentateuch. A German scholar, Julius Wellhausen (1844–1918), developed what has come to be known variously as the "Documentary," "Source," or "JEDP Hypothesis," which argues that the Pentateuch is a compilation of four primary anonymous sources. Though the hypothesis has been and continues to be questioned and refined, it is still accepted by contemporary scholarship as a valuable analytical method for studying the Pentateuch. The anonymous sources are as follows:

J   This author prefers to refer to Israel's God by the name *Yahweh* ("Lord"). The Yahwist's literary style is down-to-earth, picturesque, and fond of what are known as anthropomorphisms (placing human qualities on God). For example, the Lord walks "in the garden at the time of the evening breeze" (Gen 3:8) and "made garments of skins for the man [Adam] and for his wife, and clothed them" (3:21).

E   Known as the Elohist source, this author prefers to use the name *Elohim* ("God"). In the Hebrew language, *Elohim* is plural in form but singular in meaning. The Elohist sees God as more transcendent than does the Yahwist and emphasizes God's communication through dreams (Gen 28:10–22).

D   The *Deuteronomist* ("second law") is concerned with issues relating to Israel's law code and the importance of Israel's covenant relationship with Yahweh. Most scholars today consider the book of Deuteronomy to be the heart of the Pentateuch.

P   The *Priestly* source emphasizes God's holiness, the importance of worship, the sacrificial system, times, seasons, and genealogies. (cf. Gen 1:1—2:4; or Gen 5:1–32)

Precisely when these sources were written is still the subject of considerable debate. Many of the stories were first passed on orally from generation to generation. Various redactors (editors) along the way provided additional information and commentary until finally, sometime after the Babylonian exile (586 BC), the sources came together into the form we have today.

Genesis: Origins and Ancestry

The first book of the Torah (Pentateuch) is Genesis. It can be divided into two major sections: Chapters 1–11 are known as the Primeval History (the word *primeval* refers to "origins," "beginnings") because they deal with the creation of the cosmos and human beings, the alienation of human beings from God, and the destruction of the world through the great flood, followed by a new beginning and the start of civilization. Chapters 12–50 were once referred to as the Patriarchal History (a patriarch is a man who is head of a family or group). However, more recently—and more accurately—these chapters have been called the Ancestral History because men and women played equally crucial roles in Israel's history and tradition.

The Tanak contains two accounts of the creation of "the heavens and the earth" (Gen 1:1). The first (Gen 1:1—2:4) is assigned to the Priestly (P) writer of the Pentateuch. As you read it, you will discover that it is progressive and repetitious and that the transcendent God "speaks" the world and humanity out of chaos into existence. It is as though the author wanted to provide people with a creation creed or a confession that could be used in worship or in teaching.

When God says, "Let *us* make humankind in *our* image, according to *our* likeness" (Gen 1:26, emphasis added), God is addressing all the heavenly beings, inviting them to become involved in the creative process. Christians believe that the fullness of the Godhead (Father, Son, and Holy Spirit) was involved in creation. However, the Trinity was not on the mind of the Priestly writer.

Other nations around Israel also had creation stories filled with gods, goddesses, and heavenly beings. One of these stories, the Enuma Elish, or Babylonian creation story, dates as far back as 2300 BC and has some interesting parallels to the P creation story. For example, both stories speak about chaos, and both follow a similar pattern of the creative process. The major and decisive difference between the two stories is that the Enuma Elish involves many gods (polytheism), while Israel's God is "most high over all the earth" and "exalted far above all gods" (Ps 97:9).

This transcendent God also created male and female human beings simultaneously. When you read Genesis 1:26 carefully, you will observe that one gender is not created before the other. God first creates human beings and then differentiates them according to gender. The Hebrew word used here for "human being" is *'adam* and includes both male and female.

In the second creation story (Gen 2:4b—3:24), the J writer of the Pentateuch sees the Lord God (Yahweh Elohim) as very down-to-earth. In fact, the man (*ha-'adam*) is formed from "the dust of the ground" (*'adamah*) (Gen 2:7). There is a Hebrew play on words here (*'adam, 'adamah*), where God is imaged as a potter who shapes clay. Later (2:21–22), the woman is "built" or "constructed" from the man's rib. Though the man was created first, the woman, we are told, was to be a "helper," a "partner" (2:18), not a subordinate. They were created in relation, not in competition, to one another.

The man and the woman lived in a primeval garden where they had access to all the fruit of the trees except the fruit of the tree of the knowledge of "good and evil" (Gen 3:5) that was in middle of the garden (3:3). Created in relationship but also with the freedom to choose, the man and the woman *both* decided to eat from the forbidden tree. In so doing, they overstepped the bounds of being creatures. They wanted, rather, to become "know-it-alls"—gods themselves. Theologians refer to this as the "Fall" and to the couple's decision as the "originating" or "original sin," which led to their expulsion from the garden and God's decision to keep the first couple from eating "from the tree of life . . . and liv[ing] forever" (3:22).

Like the P creation story, another ancient text sheds some interesting light on J's Fall narrative. In one version of a document known as the Mesopotamian

(Babylonian) *Gilgamesh Epic* (720–612 BC), the hero, Gilgamesh, searches for a plant that will give him everlasting life. However, on his return home after he finds the plant, a snake steals it and then the snake sheds its skin. The ancients saw this as a sign of immortality.

From here on, the primeval history of humanity becomes increasingly estranged from the creator God. Brotherly rivalry (Cain and Abel) leads to violence and finally to murder (Gen 4:1–15). The world's violence and corruption increase to the point where God decides to send a great flood to destroy the earth (Gen 6—8:19). Just as there were other accounts of creation in the ancient world, so also there were other flood stories. The Babylonian *Gilgamesh* and *Atrahasis* epics share a number of similarities with the biblical flood account. The primary difference in the biblical account is that the "Lord sits enthroned over the flood; the Lord sits enthroned as king forever" (Ps 29:10). God then makes a covenant with Noah promising that the world will never again be destroyed by the mighty waters (Gen 8:20—9:17) and places the rainbow in the sky as the sign of that promise. Civilization begins anew, but human corruption and alienation from God continue (Gen 9:18–28). The primeval history ends with the story of the Tower of Babel (Gen 11:1–9), where human beings once again attempt to become like God by building a tower that reaches to heaven. God confuses their speech into babbling, however, which means that they cannot understand one another and have to stop the construction of their tower. Thus, Genesis explains the beginning of many languages and nations. This biblical word for confusing speech (*Babel*) has entered the English language as the word *babble*, often referring to the nonsense speech of babies.

The Ancestral History

Genesis 12–50 recounts the stories of the founders of God's people, especially Abraham, Isaac, Jacob, Joseph, and their wives and families. The three major themes in the ancestral history all revolve around the word *promise*:

Promise of land

Promise of many descendants

Promise of a continuing relationship with God (covenant)

However, the ancestors repeatedly face what seem to be insurmountable obstacles to the fulfillment of these promises.

In Genesis 12:1–3, Abram ("mighty father") is told by the Lord, "Go from your country and your kindred and your father's house to the land that I will show you. I will make of you a great nation, and I will bless you, and make your name great, so that you will be a blessing. I will bless those who bless you, and the one who curses you I will curse; and in you all the families of the earth shall be blessed."

The obstacle, however, is that we are told in Genesis 11:30 that Abram's wife, Sarai, "was barren; she had no child." Fearing that the promise of many descendants (Gen 15:5) will not be fulfilled, Sarai decides to help the promise along, so she gives Abram her slave-girl, Hagar, so as to produce an heir. Hagar gives birth to Ishmael (which means "God has heard"), but Ishmael will not be the heir. God tells Abraham (Abram) that Sarah (Sarai) will bear a son and his name will be Isaac (Gen 17:19). With names changed from Abram and Sarai to Abraham ("father of a multitude") and Sarah ("princess") (Gen 17:5, 15), the birth of Isaac is announced in Genesis 18. Sarah laughs at the prospect of bearing a child at age 90, but God has the last laugh when Isaac ("laughter") is born (Gen 21:1–7).

While Genesis 16 and 21 are the only accounts in the Tanak concerning Hagar and Ishmael, it is important to point out that God also promises Hagar (Gen 21:18) and Abraham that Ishmael will be blessed, fruitful, exceedingly numerous, and the father of twelve princes and a "great nation" (Gen 17:20). According to the Islamic tradition, which traces its religious heritage back to Abraham, Abraham and Hagar are buried near the Ka'aba in the Grand Mosque in Mecca, and Ishmael, not Isaac, is Abraham's number-one son. Furthermore, when Abraham dies at age 175, we are told that *both* his sons, "Isaac and Ishmael buried him in the cave of Machpelah" (Gen 25:9).

After Abraham passes the supreme test of faith through his willingness to offer his "only son" (Gen 22:2), the Lord once again reaffirms the promise to Abraham to make his offspring "as numerous as the stars of heaven and as the sand that is on the seashore" (Gen 22:17). Abraham obeyed the Lord's command because he submitted himself to God (the word *Islam*, by the way, means "submission") and trusted that the Lord would "provide" (Gen 22:8, 14).

The realization of this promise of many descendants, however, requires now that Isaac and his beautiful wife, Rebekah, also have children. However, the same obstacle that confronted Sarah now confronts Rebekah; she is unable to bear children. Isaac prays to the Lord, who responds by allowing Rebekah to conceive not one but two children, Esau and Jacob, who represent two nations: Israel (Jacob) and Edom (Esau) (Gen 25:23).

Esau is the firstborn and, according to ancient custom, should receive his father's blessing, as well as the lion's share of the family inheritance. During their birth, however, Jacob (which means "the one who supplants") grabs his brother

Esau by the heel and tries to pull him back into the womb so that Jacob will be the firstborn (Gen 25:26). Jacob is unsuccessful, but it will not be his last attempt to gain the right of the firstborn. Rivals from the beginning, Jacob manages to swindle Esau out of his birthright in exchange for a bowl of stew (Gen 25:29–34) and later, with his mother Rebekah's help, tricks Esau out of father Isaac's blessing (Gen 27).

At odds with Esau, Jacob then embarks on a series of journeys that include several encounters with the Lord. The first encounter comes through a dream at Bethel ("house of God"), where the Lord introduces himself to Jacob as the "God of Abraham your father and the God of Isaac" (Gen 28:13) and then reiterates the ancestral promise to Jacob that "the land on which you lie I will give to you and to your offspring; and your offspring shall be like the dust of the earth . . . and all the families of the earth shall be blessed in you and in your offspring" (Gen 28:13–14).

Jacob meets and falls in love with Rachel, daughter of his uncle Laban, and works seven years for her hand in marriage (Gen 29:20) but is tricked into marrying Leah instead and then has to work another seven years before marrying Rachel (Gen 29:27–28).

Rachel, like Rebekah and Sarah before her, was barren, but "God remembered Rachel, and God heeded her and opened her womb. She conceived and bore a son . . . and she named him Joseph" (Gen 30:22–24).

Jacob's next decisive encounter with the Lord occurs at a place called Peniel ("face of God"), where a "man" (perhaps an angel, perhaps the Lord) wrestled with Jacob until daybreak (Gen 32:24). Refusing to let the "man" go, Jacob says, "I will not let you go, unless you bless me" (Gen 32:26). Jacob is asked his name, responds, and is then told, "You shall no longer be called Jacob, but Israel, for you have striven with God and with humans, and have prevailed" (Gen 32:27–28). And so Jacob becomes Israel ("the one who strives with God"), the father of the twelve tribes that will make up the nation known as Israel.

Jacob next meets his estranged twin, Esau, and upon seeing him is so moved that he says, "[F]or truly to see your face is like seeing the face of God" (Gen 33:10). At the end of the Jacob story, the rival brothers are reconciled and, like Ishmael and Isaac before them, together bury their father, Jacob (Gen 35:29).

The final chapters of the ancestral history (Gen 37–50) recount the story of Joseph and his rivalry with his brothers. Not only do the brothers resent that Joseph is their father Jacob's favorite, but also they are put off by Joseph's dreams and, on first reading, his superior attitude. The brothers initially plot to kill Joseph but instead decide to sell him into servitude in Egypt, where, ironically, through his ability to interpret dreams, Joseph will rise to power, be reconciled with his brothers, and eventually save his entire family from famine. In the end, Jacob journeys to Egypt and settles in the land of Goshen. The book of Genesis ends with Joseph's words to his brothers, restating the promise to Abraham that "God will surely come to you, and bring you up out of this land to land that he swore to Abraham, to Isaac, and to Jacob" (Gen 50:24). Joseph dies and is "placed in a coffin in Egypt." The very last word of Genesis, "Egypt," prepares the way for the remaining books of the Torah.

World of the Patriarchs

Covenant and Law

Whereas the ancestral history emphasizes the promise of children and becoming a great nation, the books of Exodus, Leviticus, Numbers, and Deuteronomy emphasize the promise and importance of the land and the ongoing relationship between the God of the promise and the children of the promise.

The dominant figure in Exodus is Moses. When the book of Exodus opens, we read that "a new king arose over Egypt, who did not know Joseph" (Ex 1:8). This Egyptian king or Pharaoh thought that he was divine; indeed, the Nile River was considered the birthplace of the Egyptian gods. Fearful that the "Israelite" people were becoming too numerous, the Pharaoh overworks the people but finds that they continue to multiply. The Pharaoh then embarks on a program of genocide, demanding, "Every boy that is born to the Hebrews you shall throw into the Nile, but you shall let every girl live" (Ex 1:22). The scene is set for a struggle between Israel's God and the Pharaoh of Egypt, who thinks he *is* God. We will see a somewhat similar struggle in the NT when King Herod responds to Jesus' birth with what has been called the "Slaughter of the Innocents" (Matthew 2:16–18).

Moses, rescued as a baby by Pharaoh's daughter from certain death in the Nile (Ex 2:1–10), will rise to become, along with Abraham and David, one of the three most revered figures in Israel's history. In what is frequently referred to as Moses' "call narrative," God reveals himself as the "God of your father, the God of Abraham, the God of Isaac, and the God of Jacob" (Ex 3:6) and also as Yahweh (Ex 3:13–15). In the Hebrew language, *Yahweh* is actually a form of the verb "to be" ("I am that I am"), and this emphasizes that Israel's God is a dynamic, active, "verbal" God who intervenes on behalf of his people.

Though reluctant, Moses accepts Yahweh's call, repeatedly confronts the Pharaoh to let the Israelite people out of Egypt, and finally, through a series of plagues beginning with turning the Nile to "blood" (Ex 7:14–25) and ending with the death of the firstborn of the Egyptians (Ex 12:29–32), where the angel of death passes over God's people (Passover, Ex 12:1–28), they leave Egypt and bondage. This image of exodus from bondage to freedom brought about by God has remained a strong image and motivating force for many peoples, cultures, and religious traditions.

The next major event in the journey to the Promised Land is known as the Sinai Covenant. Like the covenants with Noah and Abraham, this covenant contains a promise *from* God, but it also contains a promise of the people *to* God. When Moses and the people arrive at Mount Sinai, God says: "Now therefore, if you obey my voice and keep my covenant, you shall be my treasured possession out of all the peoples. Indeed, the whole earth is mine, but you shall be for me a priestly kingdom and a holy nation" (Ex 19:5).

This covenant is conditional. It involves keeping God's law as set forth in the Decalogue, or Ten Commandments (Ex 20:1–17; Deut 5:6–21). These commandments were not understood as clubs hanging over people's heads but as tokens of love. *If* you love me, God is saying in the Ten Commandments, there are certain things that you will and will not do for me and for others. The descendants of Abraham, like Abraham himself, are called to obey (trust) that the Lord will provide.

There were two basic kinds of law in the ancient world, apodictic (absolute) and casuistic (case) law. Apodictic law is expressed in the formula, "You shall not," and casuistic law in the formula, "If you do *x*, then *y* will be the consequence." With the exceptions of the casuistic commands to keep the Sabbath day (Ex 20:8) and honor one's parents (Ex 20:12), the remaining commandments are apodictic.

In addition to the Ten Commandments, which are referred to as moral or ethical law, the Tanak also contains other law codes that pertain to matters of worship, sacrifice, and the observance of important festivals, especially the festivals of Unleavened Bread and Passover.

The entire book of Leviticus is devoted to laws that concern holiness. What is known as the Holiness Code (Lev 17–26) emphasizes what the people are to do to be that "holy nation" that God called them to be in Exodus 19:5.

The Book of Numbers recounts the journey of God's people through the wilderness and prepares them for their entrance into the land. Numbers contains many fascinating stories about encounters with other people and nations, among them the story of Balaam and his talking donkey (Num 22).

Many scholars today would consider the Book of Deuteronomy to be the heart of the Torah. It emphasizes the importance of the covenant and how Moses was a "prophet in Israel . . . whom the Lord knew face to face. He was unequaled for all the signs and wonders that the Lord sent him to perform . . ." (Deut 34:10).

Tanak Division 2—Nebiim: Words of Judgment and Salvation

The second major division of the Tanak is known as the "Prophets." It includes the books called the Former Prophets (Joshua, Judges, 1–2 Samuel, 1–2 Kings), the Major Prophets (Isaiah, Jeremiah, Ezekiel), and the Book of the Twelve or Minor Prophets (Hosea, Joel, Amos, Obadiah, Jonah, Micah, Nahum, Habakkuk,

Zephaniah, Haggai, Zechariah, Malachi). These books are called "Minor" not because they are less important but simply because they are shorter. The books of the Former Prophets, together with Deuteronomy, are known as the Deuteronomistic History (DtrH). Taken as a whole, these books narrate the history of Israel from the death of Moses to the Babylonian Exile in 586 BC. The DtrH centers on and expands the continuing covenant relationship between God and the people.

The books of Joshua, Judges, Samuel, and Kings recount the Israelites' entrance into and settlement of the land of Canaan. Once settled on the land, the people become increasingly convinced that in order to become a "great nation" (Gen 12:2), they need to be "like other nations" (1 Sam 8:5). Consequently, they demand to have a king to rule over them. Though reluctant, and not before warning the people what they are asking for, God grants their request (1 Sam 8:4–22).

Israel's first king, Saul, is anointed (remember that the Hebrew word for "anointed one" is *meshiach*) by Samuel (1 Sam 10:1). Popular and well intentioned, Saul is rejected by God because of disobedience (1 Sam 13:8–15; 1 Sam 15) and replaced by a man after God's "own heart" (1 Sam 13:14). That man is David, who, along with Abraham and Moses, numbers among the three most important figures in the Tanak. David is also popular and well intentioned, and he, too, is disobedient. However, unlike Saul, David is not rejected but given a promise that his dynasty will last forever.

After he is anointed king of all Israel, makes Jerusalem the capital, and defeats the Philistines (2 Sam 5), David decides to build the Lord a "house" for the Ark of the Covenant, the ancient symbol of the Lord's presence with Israel (2 Sam 7). In return, the Lord tells David, through the prophet Nathan, that the Lord will make David a "house" (2 Sam 7:11).

> When your days are fulfilled and you lie down with your ancestors, I will raise up your offspring after you, who shall come forth from your body, and I will establish his kingdom. He shall build a house for my name, and I will establish the throne of his kingdom forever. I will be a father to him, and he shall be a son to me. When he commits iniquity, I will punish him. . . . But I will not take my steadfast love from him, as I took it from Saul. . . . Your house and your kingdom shall be made sure forever before me; your throne shall be established forever. (2 Sam 7:12–16)

In these words, we have what is known as the Davidic covenant or succession narrative. David's kingly line will continue in perpetuity. From this point on in Israel's history, it is believed that the anointed one (messiah) will come from David's line. Even though David commits adultery with another man's wife (Bathsheba) and then has the man (Uriah) killed, David is not rejected as king (2 Sam 11).

Once again, the prophet Nathan comes to David. However, this time he comes with a story that exposes David's sin. David then admits what he did and repents (2 Sam 12:7–15). In the end, while David is never rejected by the Lord as was Saul, his "house" is constantly plagued by sibling rivalry, rebellion, dysfunction, and death.

David's successor, Solomon, builds the temple that David wanted to build (1 Kings 6:1–38) and becomes known for his wisdom and wealth. However, Solomon's love for building leads to overtaxation, and his marriages to foreign women lead to idolatry and apostasy. When Solomon's son, Rehoboam, ascends the throne, the people ask him to "lighten the hard service of your father and his heavy yoke that he placed on us" (1 Kings 12:4). Rather than relent, however, Rehoboam responds, "My father disciplined you with whips, but I will discipline you with scorpions" (1 Kings 12:11).

The people of the north, led by Jeroboam (922–901 BC), rebel against Rehoboam, and the once-united monarchy of David and Solomon splits into two. From then on, the north, with its capital in Samaria, was known as Israel, and the south, with its capital in Jerusalem (the City of David), was known as Judah. Israel continued its rebellion until it was defeated by the Assyrians in 722 BC, and Judah fought until it fell to the Babylonians in 586 BC.

During the history of these two separate kingdoms, we have a succession of individuals known as prophets whose messages contain both judgment and salvation:

a) The prophets of the Assyrian period include Amos, Hosea, Micah, Isaiah of Jerusalem, Joel, Nahum, and Zephaniah.

b) The prophets of the Babylonian and later Persian periods include Jeremiah, Habakkuk, Obadiah, Ezekiel, Second and Third Isaiah, Haggai, Zechariah, Malachi, and Jonah.

Though sometimes understood as predictors of the future, these prophets were much more proclaimers of God's covenant responsibilities for specific times and places—just as in our own era we can mention certain religious and political leaders who speak out on behalf of social justice and the preservation of the environment. While there are some predictive elements in prophecy, they are not primary. For the prophets, the future was not one-hundred or five-hundred years down the road but tomorrow, next week, next year. For the Jewish people, the prophets are the prime interpreters of the Torah. Because God had chosen Israel, the people had a special responsibility to be that "holy nation" mentioned in Exodus 19:5.

Prophetic oracles are usually introduced by what is known as the prophetic messenger formula: "Thus says the Lord. . . ." The oracles often proclaimed judgment not only on the nations but also on Israel and Judah. In the prophet Amos are a series of oracles against foreign nations that charge them with what we today might refer to as "war crimes" (Am 1:1–2:3). However, in the oracles against Judah and Israel (Am 4:4–8), the crimes are not war crimes but crimes against God's own people that, among other things, include rejection of the Torah (2:4), selling the "righteous for silver, and the needy for a pair of sandals" (2:6), and trampling the "heads of the poor into the dust of the earth" (2:7).

According to Amos, it was precisely because Israel was God's people and should have known better that they would be judged harshly: "You only have I known of all the families of the earth; therefore I will punish you for all your iniquities" (Am 3:2). All of the worship and sacrifice in the world are insufficient if the poor and downtrodden are not cared for or worse, are pushed aside.

For Amos, and for the prophets as a whole, perhaps no two words are more important than *justice* and *righteousness*. While the precise meaning of these words must be defined in the specific context of each prophet, Amos sums it up well when he says:

> I hate, I despise your festivals, and I take no delight in your solemn assemblies. Even though you offer me your burnt offerings and grain offerings, I will not accept them; and the offerings of well-being of your fatted animals I will not look upon. Take away from me the noise of your songs; I will not listen to the melody of your harps. But let justice roll down like waters, and righteousness like an ever-flowing stream. (Am 5:21–24)

As important as worship and sacrifice are, they cannot replace taking care of the most marginalized and least powerful in the community. This also includes care for the land itself and is the basis of our contemporary concern for the environment.

But there were also those times when the prophets spoke oracles of salvation. Stern and firm as he was, even the prophet Amos looked forward to a time of salvation:

> . . . when the one who plows shall overtake the one who reaps, and the treader of grapes the one who sows the seed; the mountains shall drip

sweet wine, and all the hills shall flow with it. I will restore the fortunes of my people Israel. . . . I will plant them upon their land, and they shall never again be plucked up out of the land that I have given them, says the Lord your God. (Am 9:13–15)

Isaiah of Jerusalem looked forward to a time when the Lord would "judge between the nations, and shall arbitrate for many peoples; they shall beat their swords into plowshares, and their spears into pruning hooks; nation shall not lift up sword against nation, neither shall they learn war any more" (Isa 2:4).

This same oracle is found also in Micah 4:3 and, sarcastically, in Joel 3:10, where the prophet tells them to go ahead, "[b]eat your plowshares into swords, and your pruning hooks into spears," it will not matter if you do because in the end it is the Lord who will judge the nations. It is the Lord who is "a refuge for his people, a stronghold for the people of Israel" (3:16).

In a series of poems found in Isaiah 40–55, the prophet speaks about a "servant" who will suffer great sorrow (Isa 53) but whose "anguish . . . shall make many righteous, and he shall bear their iniquities" (Isa 53:11). It is not clear whether the servant is an individual or the people as a whole—though Christians have traditionally interpreted this servant as referring to Jesus. What is clear is that this servant was wounded for the people's transgressions and crushed for their iniquities and that by the servant's bruises, the people would be healed (Isa 53:5).

And in Judah's darkest hour, the prophet Jeremiah looked forward to a new covenant with the house of Israel and the house of Judah:

The days are surely coming, says the Lord, when I will make a new covenant with the house of Israel and the house of Judah. It will not be like the covenant that I made with their ancestors when I took them by the hand to bring out of the land of Egypt—a covenant that they broke, though I was their husband, says the Lord. But this is the covenant I will make with the house of Israel after those days, says the Lord: I will put my law [Torah] within them, and I will write it on their hearts; and I will be their God, and they shall be my people. (Jer 31:31–33)

Tanak Division 3—Kethubim: Words of Wisdom

The third and final division of the Tanak is the Kethubim, or the "Writings." The material in this division is more varied than that found in the Torah and Nebiim. The Writings contain history (1–2 Chronicles, Ezra, Nehemiah), songs (Psalms), proverbs (Proverbs), love poetry (Song of Songs), laments, praise (Lamentations, Psalms), hero/heroine stories (Ruth, Esther, Daniel 1–6), and what is known as "wisdom literature" (Job, Ecclesiastes).

While poetry can be found throughout the Tanak, the Writings contain some of Israel's most elegant and prayerful poetry. Hebrew poetry, like poetry generally, has some defining characteristics. One important characteristic of Hebrew poetry is what is known as parallelism. In *synonymous* parallelism, a similar, complementary statement in the second line follows a statement in the first line. For example, "The heavens are telling the glory of God; and the firmament proclaims his handiwork" (Ps 19:1). *Antithetical* parallelism occurs when a second line makes an opposite statement from the first line: "The Lord watches over the way of the righteous, but the way of the wicked will perish" (Ps 1:6). In *synthetic* parallelism, the thought of the first line is expanded in the second line: "O Lord, do not rebuke me in your anger, or discipline me in your wrath" (Ps 6:1).

The Book of Psalms contains 150 poems that give God praise, lament, extol the Davidic monarchy, and thank God for many acts of individual and communal deliverance. Well over one-third of these 150 songs are laments, either of individuals or of the community. Because the Israelites did not formulate a specific belief in an afterlife until the post-exilic period (after 586 BC), it was important for God to come to help individuals and the community *now*, not in some future life beyond this one.

This life was to be lived fully but also wisely. The wise person is the one whose "delight is in the law of the Lord" and who "meditates" on that law "day and night" (Ps 1:2). The words of wisdom found in the Writings emphasize that the just will be rewarded and the unjust punished. "The Lord watches over the way of the righteous, but the way of the wicked will perish" (Ps 1:6). "Therefore walk in the way of the good, and keep to the paths of the just. For the upright will abide in the land, and the innocent will remain in it; but the wicked will be cut off from the land, and the treacherous will be rooted out of it" (Prov 2:20–22).

At the same time, however, Job, who was said to be "blameless and upright, one who feared God and turned away from evil" (Job 1:1), suffered the devastating loss of his seven sons, three daughters, and all his wealth and possessions. Later, struck with "loathsome sores" over his entire body (Job 2:7), Job cannot understand why he suffers. In the midst of his pain and distress, three "wise" friends (Eliphaz, Bildad, and Zophar) come to visit him and offer the traditional words of wisdom that Job must have done something wrong to deserve such punishment. "Think now," asked Eliphaz, "who that was innocent ever perished? Or where were the upright cut off?" (Job 4:7). Nevertheless, Job persists in his innocence and in the end is invited by the Lord to consider the mystery of creation, where Job comes to realize that he "uttered what [he] did not understand, things too wonderful for [him], which [he] did not know" (Job 42:3). Job then "repent[s] in dust and ashes" (Job 42:6) and receives "twice as much as he had before" (Job 42:10). A further challenge to traditional wisdom is found in the Book of Ecclesiastes (*Qoheleth* ["the Preacher"] in Hebrew), where the author says:

> When I applied my mind to know wisdom, and to see the business that is done on earth, how one's eyes see sleep neither day nor night, then I saw all the work of God, that no one can find out what is happening under the sun. However much they may toil in seeking, they will not find it out; even though those who are wise claim to know, they cannot find it out. (Eccl 8:16–17)

In the end, similar to Job, Qoheleth concludes that the meaning of life is to "Fear God, and keep his commandments; for that is the whole duty of everyone. For God will bring every deed into judgment, including every secret thing, whether good or evil" (Eccl 12:13–14).

While many factors contributed to Job and Qoheleth's challenge to traditional wisdom, surely the most important factors were the loss of the land, the Temple, and the Davidic monarchy after 586 BC. Though Cyrus the Persian allowed the Jews to return to their homeland in 539 BC, things would never be the same again, and further, even greater, suffering was on the horizon.

After Alexander the Great (356–323 BC) conquered the Persians, the Jews came under the power and influence of Hellenism (Greek culture and religion). Hellenism fascinated many Jews, especially the young. Many others, however, saw it as a threat to their traditions and to their faith. The first six chapters of Daniel are stories of how Daniel and his three friends remained loyal to the Lord even though they served in a foreign court. In this "time between," often called the intertestamental period, it was important to serve "the living God" (Dan 6:20, 26) and not idols of metal, wood, or stone.

Alexander's successors became increasingly ruthless in their attempts to force the Jews to assimilate. In 167 BC, a tyrannical ruler named Antiochus IV Epiphanes tried to wipe out the Jewish faith by banning people from having copies of the Torah, preventing worship on the Sabbath, and forcing people to worship Zeus.

In an act that has come to be known as "the abomination of desolation," Antiochus sent his soldiers into the Temple in Jerusalem in 167 BC, where they slaughtered a pig (considered an "unclean" animal by Jews) on the altar and erected a statue of Zeus (1 Macc 1:41–64). These abominable acts led to the Maccabean revolt, where Judas (known as Maccabeus, "the hammer") and his brothers zealously fought off the merciless Hellenizers and in December of 164 BC were victorious over Antiochus's soldiers and cleansed the Temple. This cleansing is known to this day in Judaism as Hanukkah (Dedication).

During this period of intense persecution, the Jews needed assurance once again that the promises made to Abraham would be fulfilled. A new kind of literature appeared during this period. It is known as "apocalyptic" literature. Its primary purpose was to provide people hope in the midst of despair. The word *apocalyptic* comes from the Greek language. Its basic meaning is "to reveal" or "uncover." What apocalyptic literature reveals is how God will ultimately be victorious over evil and establish his kingdom forever.

Daniel 7–12 provides us with the only complete example of apocalyptic literature in the Tanak. Written during the dark days of the Maccabean struggle against Hellenism, the author has a night vision where he sees,

> . . . one like a human being [literally in Hebrew: "Son of Man"] coming with the clouds of heaven. And he came to the Ancient One and was presented before him. To him was given dominion and glory and kingship, that all peoples, nations, and languages should serve him. His dominion is an everlasting dominion that shall not pass away, and his kingship is one that shall never be destroyed. (Dan 7:13–14)

The "one like a human being" is a heavenly figure to whom God would give everlasting rule. This figure would become very important as history moved closer to the beginning of the Christian era.

In the Christian NT, the expression "Son of Man" is one of a number of Christological titles applied to Jesus. In the NT gospels, the phrase "Son of Man" occurs over eighty times and, importantly, is used only by Jesus. The words are also found in Acts 7:56 (Stephen's martyrdom) and in Revelation 1:13, where the author, similar to Daniel, sees "one like the Son of Man." The NT Book of Revelation is Christian apocalyptic literature. In order to understand this often misused and abused book, it is important to read it against the background of its Jewish apocalyptic roots, where previous ideas and language are drawn upon and established: for example, visions (heavenly court convened), images (beasts, angels, plagues, harvest), phrases (names for God, horns of animals, seals, books, cities), numbers ("seven" as perfect number), and colors ("white" is heavenly). Even here, we can see the need to understand the OT in order to understand the NT.

Another reason the period between the Tanak and the NT is so important is because many ideas developed that were not present previously in the tradition. For example, the only explicit reference we have to a belief in life after death in the Tanak is found in Daniel 12:2: "Many of those who sleep in the dust of the earth shall awake, some to everlasting life, and some to shame and everlasting contempt." Prior to this time, it was believed that when people died, they went to Sheol, the place of the dead. Furthermore, in this intertestamental period, there is an increasing interest in angels and demons not present elsewhere in the Tanak. The deuterocanonical Book of Tobit is an angelophany where the angel Raphael ("God heals"), disguised as a man, Azariah ("the Lord heals"), accompanies a young man named Tobias on a fascinating journey that involves exorcism of a demon (Asmodeus) and a miraculous healing of blindness.

Belief in life after death, angels, and demons, along with many other beliefs, became increasingly important and had enormous impact on the writers of the NT. As we said at the beginning of this chapter, Christians must never lose sight of the importance of the Tanak for understanding the NT, for without the Tanak, the NT would be an incomprehensible book, "a plant deprived of its roots and destined to dry up and wither."

My grandfather often said, "I should write a book." He never did. I could have written a book as well but had only a few brief pages to introduce you to the "People of the Book," their incredible stories and enduring faith that God,

> . . . will swallow up death forever. . . . wipe away the tears from all faces, and the disgrace of his people he will take away from all the earth, for the Lord has spoken. . . . This is the Lord for whom we have waited; let us be glad and rejoice in his salvation. (Isa 25:7–9)

Christians, too, are "People of the Book." They believe that God's Messiah was enfleshed in the life, death, and resurrection of Jesus the Christ, and they too wait "with eager longing" (Rom 8:19) for the time when God "will wipe every tear from their eyes. Death will be no more; mourning and crying and pain will be no more, for the first things have passed away" (Rev 21:4, cf. Isa 25:7–9).

Let us await the Messiah together!

Questions about the Text

1. What does *Tanak* mean? What are its three divisions?

2. What does *Torah* mean?

3. What do the sources J-E-D-P mean?

4. Explain the Sinai Covenant and its conditions.

5. Who were the first three kings of Israel?

6. To what historical event does the feast of Hanukkah refer?

7. What does the word *apocalyptic* mean?

Questions for Discussion

1. How might the threefold arrangement of the books of the Tanak influence one's understanding of the concept of the Messiah?

2. What are some of the important theological themes of the Torah? Why do you consider them important?

3. If prophecy is primarily proclamation and not prediction, how can people be "prophetic" in today's world?

4. What do you think it means to live life not only fully but also wisely?

5. Why do you think apocalyptic literature is sometimes used to frighten people rather than to provide them with hope?

For Further Study

General

Berlin, Adele, and Marc Zvi Brettler, eds. *The Jewish Study Bible: Jewish Publication Society. Tanakh Translation*. New York: Oxford University Press, 2004.

This translation reflects contemporary biblical scholarship as well as the richness of the Jewish tradition. It contains excellent notes and informative essays on the history of Jewish interpretation of the Tanak.

Brown, Raymond, E., SS, Joseph A. Fitzmyer, SJ, and Roland E. Murphy, O. Carm., eds. *The New Jerome Biblical Commentary*. Englewood Cliffs, NJ: Prentice Hall, 1990.

This one-volume commentary on the entire Bible is compact and comprehensive. It is highly respected by biblical scholars from various Christian denominations.

Lysik, David A., ed. *The Bible Documents: A Parish Resource.* Chicago: Liturgy Training Publications, 2001.

This is a handy collection of some of the Catholic Church's most important documents concerning the interpretation of scripture.

Miller, John, W. *How the Bible Came to Be: Exploring the Narrative and Message.* New York: Paulist Press, 2004.

This book is an exploration of the formation and history of the biblical canon.

The Pontifical Biblical Commission. *The Jewish People and Their Sacred Scriptures in the Christian Bible.* Boston: Pauline Books & Media, 2002.

Wiesel, Elie. *Memoirs: All Rivers Run to the Sea.* New York: Alfred A. Knopf, 1995.

Introductory

Anderson, Bernhard W., and Katheryn Pfisterer Darr. *Understanding the Old Testament.* Abridged fourth ed. Englewood Cliffs, NJ: Prentice Hall, 1998.

This one-volume introduction complete with photos, maps, and chronologies can be read by all those interested in the OT, regardless of religious persuasion.

deSilva, David A. *Introducing the Apocrypha: Message, Context and Significance.* Grand Rapids, MI: Baker Academic, 2002.

This book introduces the OT apocrypha and shows how many of these Jewish writings were used by the authors of the NT.

Wisdom Literature

Fiorenza, Elisabeth Schüssler. *Wisdom Ways: Introducing Feminist Biblical Interpretation.* Maryknoll, NY: Orbis Books, 2001.

This volume is an introduction to feminist biblical studies and interpretation using wisdom as the departure point.

Murphy, Roland E. *The Tree of Life: An Exploration of Biblical Wisdom Literature*. Second ed. Grand Rapids, MI: William B. Eerdmans, 1996.

An accessible, clear, and concise introduction to the wisdom books of the OT.

The Prophets

Miller, John W. *Meet the Prophets: A Beginner's Guide to the Books of the Biblical Prophets*. New York: Paulist Press, 1987.

This introduction to the biblical prophets attempts to bridge the gap between the meaning of the message then and now.

Jewish Apocalyptic Literature

Collins, John J. *The Apocalyptic Imagination: An Introduction to the Jewish Matrix of Christianity*. New York: Crossroad, 1987.

This is an introduction to Jewish apocalyptic literature in its historical context.

From the Reference Librarian
Researching Bible Topics—Old Testament

Student: What kinds of topics can I study for the Old Testament?

A lot, no doubt, but to get a handle on the question, let's try to categorize them. One category of topic is biographical. Is there a particular figure (Abraham, Moses, David, etc.) that you would like to study in depth? Another category would include subjects related to the Bible's "world of thought" and would include researching such biblical and theological concepts as "righteousness," "faith," or "covenant," or such biblical phenomena as "prophecy," "wisdom literature," "apocalyptic," and so on. Yet another category might be topics relating to the historical world of the Bible. This would include the study of the geographical setting of scripture, including archaeological investigation, daily life and customs, and so on. There is much more, but perhaps this is enough to get you started.

Whatever your topic is, remember your starting point is as follows:

Skill Key #1

Use the library's reference collection to begin your research.

a) Use a subject-specific encyclopedia to acquire specialized knowledge about a subject.

b) Use a subject-specific encyclopedia whose scope is appropriate for both your topic and the approach you want to take to that topic.

Student: What subject-specific reference sources should I use to study the Old Testament?

A number of reference works are devoted entirely to the Bible. A standard encyclopedia on the Bible usually found in academic libraries is the following title:

David Noel Freedman, ed. *The Anchor Bible Dictionary*. 6 vols. New York: Doubleday, 1992.

Don't let the word *dictionary* in the title throw you off. This is an exhaustive encyclopedia containing articles on almost any topic imaginable relating to the Bible (both Old and New Testaments). All articles have bibliographies, usually listing both books and journal articles.

Some reference sources focus even more narrowly on the OT alone or on parts of it. For example, your library may own the following title devoted entirely to the five books of Moses:

> T. Desmond Alexander and David W. Baker. *Dictionary of the Old Testament: Pentateuch*. Downers Grove, IL: InterVarsity Press, 2003.

Another type of reference tool, usually called a Bible dictionary or handbook, may also be useful. Bible dictionaries are usually one volume, so the articles will be shorter than those you will find in the *Anchor Bible Dictionary*. The following titles are representative of this type of reference tool; your librarian can suggest alternatives if your library does not own either one.

> Paul Achtemeier, ed. *The HarperCollins Bible Dictionary*. Rev. ed. San Francisco, CA: Harper, 1996.

> David Noel Freedman, ed. *Eerdmans Dictionary of the Bible*. Grand Rapids, MI: William B. Eerdmans, 2000.

Since, as you have already learned, study of the Bible entails the use of a number of technical terms (Tanak, Torah, Pentateuch, etc.), the following example of a concise dictionary, as described in the introductory chapter, will be helpful for quickly looking up the meaning of an unfamiliar term or expression:

> Richard N. Soulen and R. Kendall Soulen. *Handbook of Biblical Criticism*. Third ed., rev. and expanded. Louisville, KY: Westminster John Knox Press, 2001.

The one-volume Bible dictionaries may also be helpful for definitions.

Although almost all of the reference tools just listed will be helpful with specifically theological topics, some reference tools (including the two listed next) focus entirely on the theology of the Bible. Such reference tools usually contain articles on terms actually appearing in the Bible and theological concepts based on those terms.

> Donald E. Gowan. *The Westminster Theological Wordbook of the Bible*. Louisville, KY: Westminster John Knox Press, 2003.

Carroll Stuhlmueller, ed. *The Collegeville Pastoral Dictionary of Biblical Theology*. Collegeville, MN: Liturgical Press, 1996.

Kevin J. Vanhoozer et al., eds. *Dictionary for Theological Interpretation of the Bible*. Cambridge, UK: Baker Academic, 2005.

Finally, another type of useful reference tool is a Bible atlas. Understanding the geographical setting of the biblical story is crucial to grasping the significance of the overall biblical narrative. If your library does not own one, ask the librarian if there is something similar available.

Collegeville Atlas of the Bible. Collegeville, MN: Liturgical Press, 1998.

Yohanan Aharoni and Michael Avi-Yonah. *The Macmillan Bible Atlas*. Third ed. rev. New York: Macmillan, 1993.

James B. Pritchard. *The Harper Concise Atlas of the Bible*. New York: HarperCollins, 1991.

Remember also that it is possible to begin research of almost any topic, including the Bible, using the *New Catholic Encyclopedia* (described in the introductory chapter). You can find articles for all three types of topics mentioned, including OT figures (such as Abraham, Moses, or David) or other aspects of the OT that you have read about in this chapter (e.g., see "Pentateuchal Studies," vol. 11, pp. 88–100, for a much lengthier discussion of the documentary hypothesis) or about important theological topics (such as righteousness, prophecy, etc.).

Student: How do I research individual books of the Bible?

One more way of studying the Bible is to study each individual book, asking several questions: Who wrote it? When was it written? Why was it written? What situation was being addressed? What were the historical circumstances behind the writing of the book? What does the book (or certain sections of it) mean?

We will use this type of topic to illustrate the second of the key elements of using the library.

Skill Key #2

Use the library's catalog to locate sources of information.

a) Use subject headings to locate precisely books on your topic.

You can, of course, find articles on individual books of the Bible in almost all of the reference sources listed previously. The bibliographies from these reference sources as described in the introductory chapter will lead you to the appropriate subject heading(s) for a biblical book, but subject headings for the Bible have a unique format, so it will be worthwhile to see how they are formed.

Subject headings for OT books always begin with the root "Bible O T" (the "O T" stands for "Old Testament") and follow the pattern that follows. (Be sure to put a space between the "O" and the "T.")

Search Format:

Subject heading "root"	Name of book
Bible O T	Genesis
Bible O T	Isaiah

As you will discover in the next chapter, the format for books of the NT is the same, with the exception of the use of "N. T." (for "New Testament") instead of "O. T." We will have more to say about subject headings for biblical books in the next chapter. For now, you should have a good grasp of the importance of using a subject-specific encyclopedia.

Student Tasks

1. Ask your reference librarian to show you where the Bible encyclopedias are located.

2. Select a book from the OT and use the correct form of subject heading to search your library catalog for books about it.

[Note: Most college and many public libraries allow electronic access to their catalog through the Internet. That convenience allows a student to work from home, dorm, or other places. This can be useful and makes your computer a terminal connected to the library resources.]

2

The New Testament and Other Early Christian Literature

From the Editor

Imagine a favorite beautiful lake, where the water is fresh, fish abound, and gentle streams empty in and out. For all the change and motion, somehow the lake seems to always be the same. That's much the way the Christian Bible is. It is a resource that gives life, changes and flows into people's lives, yet seems to remain the same. The Sacred Scriptures are a living resource that informs, dwells in, and challenges the lives of Christians.

The Christian Sacred Texts are contained in what is called the Bible. The heart of the Bible is the revelation of God in Jesus the Christ, by his words and actions, which are contained in the New Testament (NT). Just as we learned that different types of writings make up the Old Testament (OT), so too the NT, which consists of gospels and letters to communities by various authors. Why some writings were included in the Bible and others were not is an interesting scholarly topic of theology—we will see some discussion of it in the following chapters.

The role of the Christian Bible as a source for theology is central because Jesus is the center of the Christian revelation in God. "God-talk" (*theology*) for believing Christians relies on the historical event of Jesus that is alive today. The Bible talks about the experience of God as Christians; what it is, does, invites, challenges, and requires; and how the early communities understood and lived it, and sometimes did not.

For Christians, the Sacred Texts provide a resource to nourish the soul, to celebrate religious events and moments, to understand their relationship with God, and many other purposes. Theology brings its Sacred Texts to bear on its best understanding of God and God's ways and how to respond. Theology, through scripture scholars, continually seeks to better understand the Sacred Texts, especially in their language, time, place, and context. That said, the focus is still on the lived experience of Christians throughout the world, who live and proclaim the message with their lives. Only when the Sacred Scriptures as the revelation of God come alive through living Christians, in word and deed— in relationships, self, and creation—is the relationship with God alive and active.

This second chapter will provide an understanding of the significant relationship of the NT and other Christian literature to theological investigation and how such investigation is done. It will also conclude our section on Sacred Texts and prepare us for the remainder of the book. The significance of this chapter will become more evident as we see it used in the rest of the book.

The New Testament and Other Early Christian Literature

James A. Kelhoffer, PhD

Overview: The Early Christians and Their Writings

Four Gospels, One Jesus, and Luke's "Many" Witnesses

The author of the gospel according to Luke begins by telling us that he consulted with "many" earlier writings and eyewitness accounts about Jesus:

> Since many have undertaken to set down an orderly account of the events that have been fulfilled among us, just as they were handed on to us by those who from the beginning were eyewitnesses and servants of the word, I too decided, after investigating everything carefully from the very first, to write an orderly account for you, most excellent Theophilus, so that you may know the truth concerning the things about which you have been instructed. (Lk 1:1–4)

Sometimes I wonder what happened to all those "many" other writings and witnesses. Doubtless, some of them are reflected in the writings that comprise our NT. Early Christians, such as the author of Luke, would eventually produce quite a number of narratives about Jesus and the early Church, letters, and other writings as witnesses to their faith, their experiences as followers of Jesus, and their attempts to form nurturing communities. Several of these writings came to be included in the NT; others were not.

This short introduction to the NT has three main parts. Part 1 briefly mentions the twenty-seven writings included in the NT, as well as several other early Christian writings that date to the first or early-second centuries. Part 2 considers the four NT gospels (Matthew, Mark, Luke, and John) and what these four authors emphasize in their accounts of Jesus' public ministry and death. Part 2 also discusses where written gospels came from and introduces a comparative approach to the gospels and their sources. Part 3 looks at letters that the early Christians wrote to each other and focuses on the apostle Paul's letter to the Galatians. Because most of the NT writings are letters, this section offers some guidelines on how to read early Christian letters.

What Is the New Testament (and What Is It Not)?

The NT is a collection of twenty-seven of the earliest Christian writings. Christians today (whether Roman Catholic, Orthodox, or Protestant) receive these twenty-seven writings as their Second or New(er) Testament of scripture.

In the chapter on the OT, we saw that the Hebrew Bible/Tanak/OT includes different kinds (or genres) of literature—the Law, the Prophets, and the Writings. The NT likewise contains different literary genres. In addition to the four narratives about Jesus (commonly referred to as "gospels"), there is one narrative about the earliest church (Acts), twenty-one letters (or writings with at least some characteristics of an ancient Greek letter), and one apocalypse. These writings were composed between approximately 50 CE and 120 CE and may be summarized as follows:

1. Historical narratives: Five writings total (the four gospels and Acts). For the sake of simplicity, this chapter refers to the four narratives about Jesus as "gospels." The first three gospels—Matthew, Mark, and Luke—are oftentimes referred to as the Synoptic gospels because of the large amount of overlapping materials. (In Greek, *synoptic* means "seen together" [= *optic* + *syn*].) The Fourth Gospel, or gospel according to John, is distinguished from the Synoptic gospels by its theological emphases and extensive sections on Jesus' discourses and miracles. In addition to these four narratives about Jesus, the Acts of the Apostles offers a selective history of the earliest church. The author of the gospel of Luke also wrote the Acts of the Apostles. These two volumes together are commonly referred to as Luke-Acts and in terms of their length comprise approximately one-fourth of the NT.

2. Letters: Twenty-one writings total. Thirteen of the NT letters are attributed to the apostle Paul. Of these thirteen, seven are known today as the undisputed Pauline letters (Romans, 1 Corinthians, 2 Corinthians, Galatians, Philippians, 1 Thessalonians, Philemon) because virtually all scholars are persuaded that Paul did in fact write them. The undisputed Pauline letters date to the 50s CE and are the earliest surviving Christian writings. The other six NT letters attributed to Paul are commonly called the Deutero-Pauline letters (a "second" [= *deutero*] group of Pauline letters), since many scholars doubt that Paul himself wrote them (2 Thessalonians, Colossians, Ephesians, 1 Timothy, 2 Timothy, Titus). The last three Deutero-Pauline letters are oftentimes called the Pastoral Epistles. The eight other NT letters (or letter-like writings) were

either written anonymously or attributed to other apostolic figures, such as Peter. They are the book of Hebrews and the seven Catholic or General Epistles (James, 1 Peter, 2 Peter, 1 John, 2 John, 3 John, Jude).

3. Apocalypse: The Revelation of John is the only NT example of this genre. In the chapter on the OT, you read about apocalypses and both the similarities and differences of this genre to the OT prophets.

So, in terms of the number of writings, most of the NT is comprised of letters (twenty-one out of twenty-seven) from a Church leader such as Paul to an early Christian community. Since the NT includes the works of different authors and different literary genres, you may find it helpful to think of the NT as a library of early Christian writings rather than as a single "book."

In addition to these twenty-seven writings, we either possess or know something about numerous other writings by the first generations of Christians. The following list offers other examples of early Christian historical narratives, letters, and apocalypses.

1. Other early Christian historical narratives include the gospel of *Thomas*, the gospel of *Peter*, the *Infancy Gospel of Thomas*, the *Protevangelium of James*, the gospel of the *Ebionites*, the gospel of the *Nazareans*, the gospel according to the *Hebrews*, one writing (possibly two) known as the gospel of *Truth*, the *Acts of Paul and Thecla*, and the *Martyrdom of Polycarp*.

2. Other early Christian letters include a lost letter of *Paul to the Church at Corinth* (mentioned in 1 Cor 5:9); *3 Corinthians* (a second-century writing known not to be written by Paul); seven letters of Ignatius, a bishop and martyr from Antioch in Syria; *1 Clement*; the *Didache* or *Teaching of the Twelve Apostles*; Polycarp's letter to the Philippians; and the *Letter of Barnabas*.

3. Two other early Christian apocalypses are the *Shepherd of Hermas* and the *Apocalypse of Peter*.

When did the Church decide upon the NT as a collection of (only) twenty-seven particular writings? The short answer is that this was a complicated process and took several centuries. In fact, the earliest surviving document listing the NT's twenty-seven writings (and no others) as comprising the authoritative Christian NT comes from a single (albeit influential) bishop in Egypt, Athanasius of Alexandria, in the year 367 CE. What this means is that if you were a follower of Jesus in the early centuries of the Church, you may well have heard some—but most likely not all, or even many—NT writings read in your church community. You may also have come into contact with any number of other early Christian writings as well.

Why Is the New Testament Written in Greek?

All the NT writings were written in ancient Greek—not Hebrew (the primary language of the Jewish scriptures), Aramaic (the mother tongue of most Palestinian Jews, including Jesus), or Latin (the main language in the western parts of the Mediterranean, such as Italy, North Africa, and Spain). More specifically, the writings of the NT are in the *Koine* ("common") dialect of ancient Greek. After the conquests of Alexander the Great (who died in 323 BCE and over three centuries before the birth of Jesus), *Koine* Greek had become the standard language for commerce in most cities in the eastern parts of the Mediterranean, including Syro-Palestine. *Koine* Greek remained a common language in the Greek East even after Roman rule spread to these eastern regions during the second and first centuries BCE. The ancient Mediterranean world included numerous different languages, cultures, and ethnic groups. Within this multicultural milieu, the writers of the NT, like so many of their non-Christian neighbors, chose the "common" dialect of Koine Greek for their written communications.

In addition, most citations of the Jewish scriptures in the NT are from the OT in a Greek translation known as the Septuagint (LXX). You read about the Septuagint in the last chapter. The "Bible" of many early Christian communities was the OT in Greek.

What Does "New Testament" Mean?

The term *New Testament* can also be translated as "new covenant." Three NT writers—the author of Luke, the apostle Paul, and the author of Hebrews—refer to the "new testament/covenant" to differentiate between the relationship that God established with the Jewish people, as related in the Torah, and the extension of that relationship to all humanity in Jesus Christ (Lk 22:20; 1 Cor 11:25; 2 Cor 3:6a; Heb 7:22, 8:6–13, 9:15, 12:24). For example, the apostle Paul writes that God "has made us competent to be ministers of a new covenant[/testament]" (2 Cor 3:6a). Paul also mentions "the old covenant[/testament]" (2 Cor 3:14), and the author of

Hebrews refers to "the first covenant[/testament]" (Heb 9:1, 15, 18). As we read in the last chapter, the possible connotation that the Jewish scriptures are some-how "old(er)" need not suggest to us today that the "new covenant/testament" has outdated or superseded the first covenant/testament. Although this is apparently the view of certain early Christian writings, such as Luke-Acts, early Christian lit-erature reflects a variety of views toward Jews and the Jewish scriptures.

Early Christian Gospels

Each of the four gospels offers distinctive information about Jesus, his public min-istry, death, resurrection, and significance. We shall first survey the main emphases in Matthew, Mark, Luke, and John, and then consider from where these writings about Jesus came. When we look at the sources the gospel authors used and ex-amples of how they edited their sources, we can learn much about these authors' theology and recognize the points about Jesus that they especially wished to em-phasize to their communities.

What Are the Main Themes of Mark, Matthew, Luke, and John?

Mark

Each of the NT gospels deserves to be read for its distinctive characterization of Jesus. In each gospel, you will notice certain themes that are not emphasized as much—or at all—in the other gospels. For example, the earliest of the three Syn-optic gospels, the gospel of Mark, follows three prominent themes:

1. Secrecy about Jesus' messianic identity

2. The disciples' lack of understanding about Jesus and his teachings

3. The suffering of Jesus

Here is an example of the first theme in connection with a miracle of Jesus:

He [Jesus] took her by the hand and said to her, "*Talitha cum*," which means, "Little girl, get up!" And immediately the girl got up and began to walk about (she was twelve years of age). At this they were overcome with amazement. He strictly ordered them that no one should know this, and told them to give her something to eat. (Mk 5:41b–43)

Next follows an example of the second theme, or the disciples' lack of understanding:

> But when they saw him [Jesus] walking on the sea, they thought it was a ghost and cried out; for they all saw him and were terrified. But immediately he spoke to them and said, "Take heart, it is I; do not be afraid." Then he got into the boat with them and the wind ceased. And they were utterly astounded, for they did not understand about the loaves, but their hearts were hardened. (Mk 6:49–52)

It is not until the middle of Mark's narrative that Jesus starts to reveal that he will suffer and die, the third theme:

> Then he [Jesus] began to teach them that the Son of Man must undergo great suffering, and be rejected by the elders, the chief priests, and the scribes, and be killed, and after three days rise again. He said all this quite openly. And Peter took him aside and began to rebuke him. But turning and looking at his disciples, he rebuked Peter and said, "Get behind me, Satan! For you are setting your mind not on divine things but on human things." (Mk 8:31–33)

You may have noticed that this last passage ties together two different themes in Mark—Jesus' suffering and the obtuseness of one prominent disciple, namely Peter.

Matthew

Although the gospel of Matthew shares many points in common with the gospel of Mark, it gives its own particular presentation of Jesus. One theme we may not expect to find in Matthew is Jesus' affirmation of the Mosaic Law (Torah) to his followers:

> Do not think that I have come to abolish the law or the prophets; I have come not to abolish but to fulfill. For truly I tell you, until heaven and earth pass away, not one letter, not one stroke of a letter, will pass from the law until all is accomplished. Therefore, whoever breaks one of the least of these commandments,

Assignment

Let me offer you an invitation. I encourage you to read all of Mark in a single sitting, looking for the three themes of secrecy, misunderstanding, and suffering. Ask yourself how the author of Mark weaves them together to offer his audience an overall picture of Jesus' healing ministry, interactions with disciples, and death. While reading Mark, you may notice additional, less-prominent themes in this gospel and find it helpful to consider how these complement Mark's main themes. Of these three main themes of secrecy, misunderstanding, and suffering in Mark, only the suffering of Jesus emerges as a prominent theme in the other NT gospels.

and teaches others to do the same, will be called least in the kingdom of heaven; but whoever does them and teaches them will be called great in the kingdom of heaven. For I tell you, unless your righteousness exceeds that of the scribes and Pharisees, you will never enter the kingdom of heaven. (Mt 5:17–20)

At the end of this passage, the scribes' and Pharisees' "righteousness" is regarded positively as a goal that Jesus' true followers must achieve and then surpass, in order to "be called great in the kingdom of heaven." This points to an element of conflict or competition between Matthew's community and (other) Jews who do not follow Jesus (or who do not follow Jesus in the way that the author of Matthew prescribes). Such conflict is further underscored by Matthew's depiction of Jesus as entering "*their* synagogue" (Mt 12:9) to heal a man who had a withered hand. Compare the parallel passage in Mark 3:1, which reads "*the* synagogue." Mark does not distinguish, as Matthew does, between Jesus' followers and those associated with a synagogue.

Such differentiation from the synagogue can likewise be seen in two of Matthew's references to the disciples' missionary activities. During his lifetime, the Matthean Jesus commands a limited outreach only toward Jews: "Go nowhere among the Gentiles, and enter no town of the Samaritans, but go rather to the lost sheep of the house of Israel" (Mt 10:5b–6). By contrast, at the very end of this gospel, Jesus sanctions a universal mission to all nations:

Go therefore and make disciples of all nations, baptizing them in the name of the Father and of the Son and of the Holy Spirit, and teaching them to obey everything that I have commanded you. And remember, I am with you always, to the end of the age. (Mt 28:19–20)

In Matthew's community, making disciples and "teaching them to obey everything" Jesus commanded apparently included keeping the Mosaic Law (Torah), which according to Matthew 5:17–20 will never pass away. We therefore find in Matthew's narrative an attempt to bring together several contrasting themes and emphases, including missions to Jews and Gentiles and the importance of the Torah.

Luke

The third Synoptic gospel, Luke, also has its own distinctive themes and emphases. Most scholars agree that, different from the other three gospels, the gospel of Luke displays a special interest in establishing his version of Jesus' story among other ancient Greco-Roman and Jewish historical narratives. Luke makes this aim evident in his prologue (Lk 1:1–4, discussed previously), where he claims that his account will start at the beginning, be based on eyewitness reports, investigate with accuracy, and focus on the truth. These four claims can be found at the beginning of many Hellenistic and early Roman period histories. Luke wanted dignified, intellectual readers like Theophilus (Lk 1:3; Acts 1:1), the person to whom his book is addressed, not just to learn miscellaneous interesting details concerning Christian origins but also to be persuaded that his version of the events offered the "truth" about what actually took place. For Luke, earlier written sources (such as Mark and the common source known as Q, discussed shortly) were extremely valuable but required the skillful hand of a trusted historian for ordering and interpretation.

In addition to supplementing Mark with numerous fascinating stories about Jesus' birth and childhood and the birth and teachings of Jesus' role model, John the Baptist, Luke also highlights, among other things, the inclusion of women among early followers of Jesus and concern for the poor. Much more so than Matthew or Mark, Luke's gospel highlights women who traveled with Jesus. Yet despite the additional attention women receive in this gospel, scholars today debate whether Luke's depictions of women are actually more positive than those in Matthew or Mark. Two passages in particular inform this debate:

> Soon afterwards he went on through cities and villages, proclaiming and bringing the good news of the kingdom of God. The twelve were with him, as well as some women who had been cured of evil spirits and infirmities: Mary, called Magdalene, from whom seven demons had gone out, and Joanna, the wife of Herod's steward Chuza, and Susanna, and many others, who provided for them out of their resources. (Lk 8:1–3; cf. Mk 15:41)

> Now as they went on their way, he entered a certain village, where a woman named Martha welcomed him into her home. She had a sister named Mary, who sat at the Lord's feet and listened to what he was saying. But Martha was distracted by her many tasks; so she came to him and asked, "Lord, do you not care that my sister has left me to do all the work by myself? Tell her then to help me." But the Lord answered her, "Martha, Martha, you are worried and distracted by many things; there is need of only one thing. Mary has chosen the better part, which will not be taken away from her." (Lk 10:38–42)

In particular, Luke 10:38–42 seems to imply Jesus' rejection of the notion that a woman must assume a subordinate, servile role within the household.

Concerning the rich and the poor in this gospel, Jesus warns about those who "store up treasures for themselves but are not rich toward God" (Lk 12:21) and about the future punishment awaiting such people: "But woe to you who are rich, for you have received your consolation. Woe to you who are full now, for you will be hungry. Woe to you who are laughing now, for you will mourn and weep" (6:24–25). Likewise, only in Luke does Jesus instruct the "very rich" ruler to sell "all" that he owns (Cf. Lk 18:22–23||Mk 10:21–22||Mt 19:21–22).

John

For his themes and emphases, the author of the gospel of John acknowledges that he writes in order to inspire faith in Jesus: "Now Jesus did many other signs in the presence of his disciples, which are not written in this book. But these are written so that you may come to believe . . . " (Jn 20:30–31a); the author of the Fourth Gospel also provides figurative "I am" sayings of Jesus, as well as a prologue (Jn 1:1–14) emphasizing the role of Jesus the Word in creation:

> I am the bread of life. Whoever comes to me will never be hungry, and whoever believes in me will never be thirsty. . . . I am the living bread that came down from heaven. Whoever eats of this bread will live forever; and the bread that I will give for the life of the world is my flesh. (Jn 6:35, 6:51)

> In the beginning was the Word, and the Word was with God, and the Word was God. He was in the beginning with God. All things came into being through him, and without him not one thing came into being. (Jn 1:1–3a)

You may find it helpful to read the entire Johannine prologue (Jn 1:1–18) and reflect on how this passage compares with the presentations of Jesus in the Synoptic gospels, especially the genealogies (Mt 1:1–17; Lk 3:23–38; cf. Mk 1:2–4).

By now you may agree that a person reading, for example, Mark in light of Matthew's narrative (or vice versa), would likely miss many important details in Mark (or Matthew). It is important to approach each gospel individually in order to gain an appreciation for its author's overall theological concerns. Having surveyed each of these gospels separately, in the following sections we shall consider the origin of written gospels about Jesus and the oral and written traditions behind the NT gospels in relation to one another.

From Jesus to the Gospels: Where Did the Gospels Come From?

The four narratives about Jesus' life, ministry, and passion attributed to Matthew, Mark, Luke, and John were originally written anonymously and were, moreover, not called "gospels" by their authors. NT authors consistently use the Greek term *gospel* for oral proclamation of the "good news." By the middle of the second century, the term *gospel* was added to gospel manuscripts as a literary designation for these writings, characterizing them as a written summary of the "good news" of Jesus. Also in the second century, names were attached to these writings, presumably to distinguish between different written gospels in Christian communities that possessed more than one gospel. Although the gospel authors chose not to indicate much about themselves in their writings, from careful study of these writings we can learn much about what they thought about Jesus and his significance.

Concerning *when* the gospels were written, we can work forward from an approximate date for the crucifixion of Jesus (30 CE). You have already read that the earliest surviving Christian writings are the apostle Paul's seven undisputed letters, which date to the 50s CE. Most scholars date Mark's gospel to around 70 CE because of its likely reference to the first Roman-Jewish War (66–73 CE), which culminated in the destruction of Jerusalem and the Jewish temple:

> Do you see these great buildings? Not one stone will be left here upon another; all will be thrown down. . . . But when you see the desolating sacrilege set up where it ought not to be (let the reader understand), then those in Judea must flee to the mountains. (Mk 13:2, 14)

The gospels of Matthew and Luke were written after Mark and might be dated between 75 CE and 85 CE, and John, probably toward the end of the first century in the 90s or early in the second century. One thing this means is that four (or more) decades passed between the lifetime of Jesus (30 CE) and the earliest surviving written gospels about Jesus (Mk, 70 CE). This is one reason that the author Luke, in the passage with which this discussion began, acknowledges having made use of "many" written sources and eyewitness testimonies (Lk 1:1–4). What Luke explicitly acknowledges was most probably true for the other three NT gospels as well.

The circulation of oral traditions about Jesus for decades prior to—and, indeed, after—the emergence of written gospels can explain a number of the similarities among these four gospels. For example, we read in all four accounts that Jesus was crucified under Pontius Pilate (the Roman Prefect of Judea, 26–36 CE) on a Friday at the time of the Jewish festival of Passover (the celebration of the

Exodus and subsequent covenant with Yahweh in Sinai) (Mt 26:2; Mk 14:16; Lk 22:15; Jn 19:14). Despite these similarities, the Synoptics and John have developed these details into different narratives. Mark and the other two Synoptic gospels present Jesus celebrating the Passover on Thursday evening with his disciples the day before the crucifixion (for example, Mk 14:12–25). Yet in the Fourth Gospel, Jesus does not celebrate the Passover with his disciples because he is arrested prior to the Passover, which in John's account falls on Friday (not Thursday, as in the Synoptics). Another disparity concerns the timing of the crucifixion: Did it commence in the morning or the middle of the day? According to Mark 15:25, it begins around 9:00 a.m., but in John 19:14–16, it starts shortly after 12:00 p.m. The telling and retelling of stories about Jesus by his followers over several decades prior to the writing of gospels about Jesus can account for many such similarities and differences.

The Synoptic Problem (I): What Is It, and Can It Be Solved?

The Synoptic Problem addresses the need to account for both the similarities and the differences among the gospels of Matthew, Mark, and Luke. How can there be so much overlapping material about Jesus' life, ministry, and death, yet such distinctive and even contradictory points in each gospel? The most widely accepted solution to the Synoptic Problem has two main parts. Acknowledged by nearly all scholars today, the first part posits that the author of Mark wrote first and was used as a source by the authors of Matthew and Luke. Building on this hypothesis of Markan priority, we can learn much about the theology of Matthew and Luke by looking at what they chose to incorporate, edit, or leave out from Mark. Let's consider representative examples from Matthew and Luke. To see the differences, we will start with the Markan source.

You have read that secrecy is a prominent theme in Mark. Mark 6:47–52 relates how Jesus' disciples were in a boat on the sea when they saw Jesus walking on water. Earlier, this chapter touched upon the disciples' reaction:

> . . . they thought it was a ghost and cried out; for they all saw him [Jesus] and were terrified. But immediately he spoke to them and said, "Take heart, it is I; do not be afraid." Then he got into the boat with them and the wind ceased. And they were utterly astounded, for they did not understand about the loaves, but their hearts were hardened. (Mk 6:49b–52)

Matthew includes some of this material from Mark 6:47–52 but takes it in a decidedly different direction:

... they were terrified, saying, "It is a ghost!" And they cried out in fear. But immediately Jesus spoke to them and said, "Take heart, it is I; do not be afraid." Peter answered him, "Lord, if it is you, command me to come to you on the water." He said, "Come." So Peter got out of the boat, started walking on the water, and came toward Jesus. . . . When they got into the boat, the wind ceased. And those in the boat worshiped him, saying, "Truly you are the Son of God." (Mt 14:26b–29, 32–33)

Notably, Matthew passes over in silence Mark's depiction of the disciples' hard-heartedness and instead presents the apostle Peter as joining Jesus in walking on water. Matthew's Jesus does not censure the disciples for their obstinacy. Instead, the disciples acknowledge Jesus as God's Son (Mt 14:33). One thing that Matthew's editing of this Markan passage reveals is that Matthew is not merely a passive recipient of earlier gospel traditions. Rather, Matthew is an active author who finds his own creative theological voice through editing Markan (and other) materials available to him.

Let's consider our second example of editing, this time from the gospel of Luke. Luke subtly edits material from Mark concerning the end of the world. In both the Markan and Lukan versions, Jesus speaks about what will happen in "this generation," that is, during the lifetime of Jesus' contemporaries. Let's look at the two texts together:

Mark 13:30	Luke 21:32
Truly I tell you, this generation will not pass away *until all these things* have taken place.	Truly I tell you, this generation will not pass away until *all things* have taken place.

With the exception of omitting one Greek word (*tauta*, a demonstrative pronoun meaning "these"), the Lukan version is essentially the same as that in Mark. But do the two verses in Mark and Luke mean the same thing?

In Mark 13:30, the occurrence of "all these things" within a generation of Jesus' death includes colossal and observable changes in the heavens and the appearance of the Son of Man:

But in those days, after that suffering, the sun will be darkened, and the moon will not give its light, and the stars will be falling from heaven, and the powers in the heavens will be shaken. Then they will see "the Son of Man coming in clouds" [cf. Dan 7:13–14] with great power and glory.

Then he will send out the angels, and gather his elect from the four winds, from the ends of the earth to the ends of heaven. (Mk 13:24–27)

You may recall from the beginning of this chapter that the author of Luke made use of eyewitnesses for his gospel and, by implication, was not an eyewitness or a follower of the earthly Jesus. Luke wrote at some time after Mark, when the expectation of Mark 13:24–30 had not been realized. Luke eliminates this difficulty by removing a single word, *these*, from Mark 13:30. In Luke 21:32, "all things" is less specific than "all these things" (Mark 13:30) and need not be taken as a reference to Jesus' prediction of the End, as in the gospel of Mark.

We find a similar example of Luke's editing of Mark to teach about the end of the world in Mark 9:1 and Luke 9:27:

Mark 9:1	Luke 9:27
There are some standing here who will not taste death until they see that the kingdom of God *has come with power*.	There are some standing here who will not taste death before they see the kingdom of God.

In Mark's narrative, the "coming" of God's kingdom may be interpreted in light of Mark 13:24–30, which predicts the coming of the Son of Man within "this generation." By deleting "has come with power" (Mk 9:1), Luke 9:27 makes no such claim. In Luke's theology, seeing "the kingdom of God" (Lk 9:27) and "all things" taking place (21:32) is open to any number of interpretations and does not denote that the time of the End is near, as Mark 9:1 and 13:24–30 do. To be sure, Luke does expect Jesus to return at some future point (for example, Lk 12:35–48; Acts 1:11), just not as soon as Mark's narrative implies.

The Synoptic Problem (II): What Is the Sayings Source "Q"?

The last section introduced the first part of the solution to the Synoptic Problem accepted by most scholars today: The hypothesis of Markan priority posits that Mark wrote first and that his gospel was used as a source in Matthew and Luke. The second part of the solution to the Synoptic Problem builds on the hypothesis of Markan priority and notes that the authors of Matthew and Luke made use of Mark differently. Because neither Matthew nor Luke reflects the other's particular editing of Markan materials, most scholars infer that Matthew and Luke wrote independently of one another.

Despite the independence of Matthew and Luke, these two gospels share in common approximately two hundred verses that do not occur in Mark. Two hundred verses is a substantial amount of material that most likely would not have survived for decades in independent oral traditions until the writing of Matthew and Luke. Since Matthew and Luke wrote independently of one another and share so much non-Markan material in common, most scholars are persuaded that in addition to Mark's gospel, they made use of one or more other written sources. In German-language NT scholarship, the word *Quelle* ("source") designates this non-Markan source material preserved in Matthew and Luke. The existence of this other source material ("Q") in Matthew and Luke is the second part of the solution to the Synoptic Problem. Matthew's and Luke's extensive borrowing from Mark and Q accounts for many of the similarities among the three Synoptic gospels.

In addition to materials from Mark and Q, it is likely that at least some passages contained only in Matthew came from pre-Matthean sources (M) and, likewise, that Luke made use of written sources not reflected in Mark or Matthew (L). The four-source hypothesis—encompassing Mark, Q, M, and L—offers the most complete explanation for why the Synoptic gospels contain so much overlapping material and also how each of these three gospels offers distinctive materials.

Why Are Only Three of the Gospels "Synoptic"? The Synoptics and John

One thing that this short introduction to the NT will not attempt to resolve is the relation of the Fourth Gospel to the Synoptics. Scholars are not of one mind on this issue. If one posits that John borrowed from one or more of the Synoptic gospels, it is necessary to explain why this author offers such a different characterization of Jesus, as compared with those in the Synoptics. On the other hand, maintaining the independence of John vis-à-vis the Synoptics runs into the difficulty of explaining points where John overlaps with the Synoptics. Examples of similar gospel materials in John and one or more of the Synoptics include Jesus' feeding of the five thousand (Jn 6:1–14; Mk 6:30–44); the healing of a Roman official's son (Jn 4:46–53; compare the healing of the centurion's child or slave in Q/Lk 7:1–10 and its parallel in Q/Mt 8:5–13); and especially numerous parts of the passion of Jesus in John 18–19. Whereas nearly all scholars study the Synoptics within the framework of Markan priority and a strong majority is persuaded by the "Q" hypothesis, there is not a consensus today concerning a possible literary relationship between the Synoptics and John.

Keeping in Touch: Early Christian Letters

This chapter's third and final section focuses primarily on early Christian letters. We will present this section in two parts. Part 1 will consist of the following:

1. Some principles for reading an early Christian letter

2. Applying these to the apostle Paul's letter to the Galatians

Building on the discussion of Galatians, in part 2 we will consider:

1. How the book of Acts depicts Paul's opponents and the unity of the Church

2. Understandings of faith and works in Paul and two other NT authors

3. Three NT authors' perspectives on living as a Christian within the Roman Empire

Part 1: Principles of Interpretation

Principles for Reading Early Christian Letters

Think about the last time you received a letter. Was it from a parent, a boyfriend or girlfriend, a friend from high school, or someone else? What prompted the person to write to you at this particular point in time? The following are questions you ask intuitively when a letter (or some other form of communication, such as an e-mail or an instant message) arrives:

a) Author: Who wrote it? What do I know about this person that will help me understand his/her communication?

b) Audience: To whom did they write? What is my relationship to the author? Is this a personal letter to me or an advertisement, mass mailing, or spam that others receive as well?

c) Opponents: What persons, practices, or beliefs does the author oppose? Are the author's opponents non-Christian Jews, Greco-Roman polytheists, or Christians with a different theology or understanding of Jesus?

d) Purpose: What led the author(s) to write this letter to me (us) now? What response does the author expect and encourage from me?

You can learn much about the twenty-one NT letters—and, indeed, all of the NT writings—by studying them with these questions in mind. Before you read further, let me invite you to read the NT book of Galatians, which is one of the apostle Paul's undisputed letters. Make a list of what Galatians reveals about its author, audience, and occasion, as well as Paul's opponents. After you have done this for Galatians, you can pose the questions outlined in this section to other NT letters. The following paragraphs offer a few remarks concerning each of these four areas in Galatians.

Application of Principles

Paul the Author. As was standard practice in ancient Greek letters, Paul's letter to the Galatians, territory in what is now Turkey, begins by identifying its author: "Paul an apostle—sent neither by human commission nor from human authorities, but through Jesus Christ and God the Father, who raised him from the dead—and all the members of God's family who are with me" (Gal 1:1–2). In this letter's opening statement, Paul assumes his authority as an apostle sent by God. Later in Galatians, we will learn that Paul's Christian opponents disputed whether God had in fact commissioned Paul to proclaim the good news to the gentiles.

Paul also recalls an earlier time in his life when his zealousness for his Jewish faith led him to persecute the Church:

> You have heard, no doubt, of my earlier life in Judaism. I was violently persecuting the church of God and was trying to destroy it. I advanced in Judaism beyond many among my people of the same age, for I was far more zealous for the traditions of my ancestors. But when God, who had set me apart before I was born and called me through his grace, was pleased to reveal his Son to me, so that I might proclaim him among the Gentiles, I did not confer with any human being, nor did I go up to Jerusalem to those who were already apostles before me, but I went away at once into Arabia, and afterwards I returned to Damascus. (Gal 1:13–17)

Paul was not one of Jesus' original twelve disciples (cf. Acts 7:57–8:1; 9:1–31; 22:1–21; 26:2–23). Scholars today debate whether Paul's first encounter with the risen Jesus represents a particular "calling" within Paul's Jewish faith or a "conversion" to a different religion. This question is part of a larger debate about when Judaism and Christianity became separately defined religions.

Later in this letter, Paul recalls that he was the one who led the Galatians to faith in Jesus and that they received God's Spirit and beheld miracles that Paul performed when they came to believe (Gal 3:1–5). From Galatians and Paul's other letters, we also learn something about Paul's ministry as a traveling evangelist. Paul used letters as a way to stay in touch and address problems in those congregations he was not able to visit as often as he may have wished.

Galatian Audience.   Throughout this letter, Paul expresses concern that the Christians in Galatia have rejected—or are about to reject—the good news that Paul had earlier proclaimed to them:

> I am astonished that you are so quickly deserting the one who called you in the grace of Christ and are turning to a different gospel—not that there is another gospel, but there are some who are confusing you and want to pervert the gospel of Christ. (Gal 1:6–7)

In particular, Paul worries that the Galatians may have believed that becoming circumcised was required for all male converts to Christianity. Although circumcision for men was prescribed in the Jewish Law (Torah) and common in Judaism and in several other cultures in the ancient Near East, the practice was quite unpopular in Greco-Roman society. At the time Paul wrote Galatians, his Greco-Roman audience appears to have been pulled in three different directions: Should they continue to affirm Paul's teaching; embrace a different version of the good news from other Christian missionaries, including circumcision; or return to their former polytheistic religion(s)? In the following passage, Paul reflects concern about the last of these possible reactions:

> Formerly, when you did not know God, you were enslaved to beings that by nature are not gods. Now, however, that you have come to know God, or rather to be known by God, how can you turn back again to the weak and beggarly elemental spirits? How can you want to be enslaved to them again? You are observing special days, and months, and seasons, and years. I am afraid that my work for you may have been wasted. (Gal 4:8–11)

Elsewhere in this letter, Paul uses the metaphor of a mother's pain in childbirth to describe his anguish and concern for this congregation's spiritual well-being (Gal 4:19–20).

Paul's Christian Opponents.   Early in this letter, Paul offers the hypocrisy of the apostle Peter, referred to as Cephas, as an example of his current opponents' untenable theology:

> But when Cephas came to Antioch, I opposed him to his face, because he stood self-condemned; for until certain people came from James, he

used to eat with the Gentiles. But after they came, he drew back and kept himself separate for fear of the circumcision faction. And the other Jews joined him in this hypocrisy, so that even Barnabas was led astray by their hypocrisy. But when I saw that they were not acting consistently with the truth of the gospel, I said to Cephas before them all, "If you, though a Jew, live like a Gentile and not like a Jew, how can you compel the Gentiles to live like Jews?" (Gal 2:11–14)

In Paul's theology, there is only one people of God made up of Jews and Gentiles, whether circumcised or uncircumcised, men or women, enslaved or free (Gal 3:27–28).

Yet the early Church included some followers of Jesus who believed that the covenant of circumcision given to the patriarch Abraham in Genesis 17 had created divisions in humanity—divisions that remained even after the time of Jesus. In Galatians, Paul claims that those who embraced this position and, accordingly, opposed his theology included the apostle Peter and James (Jesus' brother, not an apostle and mentioned in Mark 6:3). It is important to underscore that Galatians reflects an inner-Christian debate over the relationship of the good news of Jesus Christ to the OT. From this letter, we do not learn about a conflict between Christianity and Judaism. Instead, we see sincere followers of Jesus with different understandings struggling to work out important theological positions some twenty years after the death of Jesus. Such conversations continue in the Church today as well, for example, on matters like euthanasia, abortion, divorce, sexuality, women, and money.

Purpose. Now that we understand something about the author, audience, and opponents in Galatians, Paul's purpose for writing this letter to this particular congregation at this point in time becomes clear: Paul responds to the theology of his Christian opponents in an effort to reassure the Galatians of the legitimacy of their belief in the good news that Paul had proclaimed to them. It is easy to understand why Paul's tone is so urgent in this letter. Rival Christian missionaries had come to Galatia, undermined Paul's authority, and challenged certain aspects of Paul's theology, including the notion that God accepts people because of their faith, or belief, in Jesus regardless of whether they are circumcised. Paul's opponents would have agreed with him concerning the importance of faith in Jesus but responded that faith should lead Jesus' followers to respect the continued validity of the covenant of circumcision that the Lord made with Abraham in Genesis. Paul's opponents would likely have found common ground with the author of

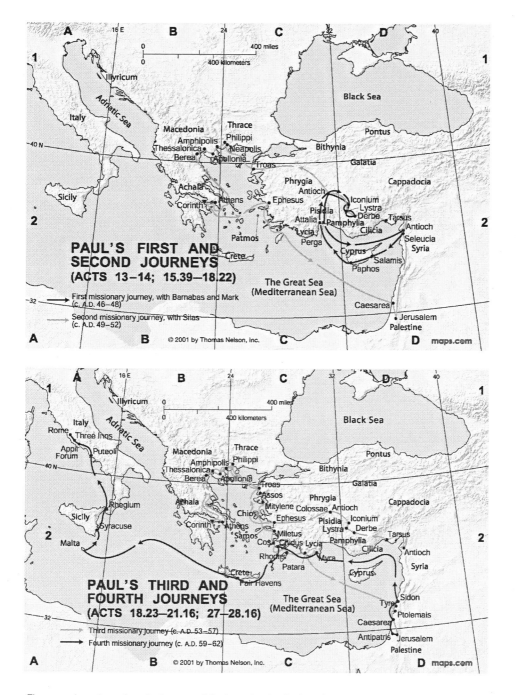

PAUL'S FIRST AND SECOND JOURNEYS
(ACTS 13–14; 15.39–18.22)

First missionary journey, with Barnabas and Mark (c. A.D. 46–48)

Second missionary journey, with Silas (c. A.D. 49–52)

© 2001 by Thomas Nelson, Inc.   maps.com

PAUL'S THIRD AND FOURTH JOURNEYS
(ACTS 18.23–21.16; 27–28.16)

Third missionary journey (c. A.D. 53–57)

Fourth missionary journey (c. A.D. 59–62)

© 2001 by Thomas Nelson, Inc.   maps.com

The maps shown here chart the journeys of Paul as related in the Acts of the Apostles. While scholars argue that the chronology and details of the journeys as told in Acts in inaccurate (as will be discussed in the pages that follow), the images shown here provide a visual reference to Luke's telling of the history.

Matthew, who you will recall assumes that followers of Jesus will keep the Law (Mt 5:17–20; 28:19–20).

Part 2: Placing Paul in Converstaion

Acts of the Apostles : Paul's Opponents and the Unity of the Church

The preceding pages have examined Paul's letter to the Galatians and given attention to what this letter reveals about its author, audience, occasion, and opponents. The remaining sections of this chapter build on this discussion of Galatians by examining three related topics. These are (1) Paul's opponents and the unity of the Church in Acts; (2) understandings of faith and works in the NT letters of Ephesians and James; and (3) the Christian as a part of the Roman Empire, according to Paul's letter to the Church at Rome, the epistle of 1 Peter, and the Revelation of John. Giving attention to these three topics helps us to see to what extent these theological discussions, like the matter of circumcision, remained living and unresolved issues in the early Church during, and after, the time of Paul.

Although in Galatians Paul identifies his opponents as rival Christian leaders, another early Christian author would portray differently this same crisis over circumcision. Writing several decades (or more) after Paul, the author of Luke-Acts presents Paul's primary opponents not as Church leaders but as non-Christian Jews. Luke's selective history of the early Church, the Acts of the Apostles, characterizes Jewish antagonists to the Pauline mission as follows:

> But when the Jews saw the crowds, they were filled with jealousy; and blaspheming, they contradicted what was spoken by Paul. . . . Thus the word of the Lord spread throughout the region. But the Jews incited the devout women of high standing and the leading men of the city, and stirred up persecution against Paul and Barnabas, and drove them out of their region. So they shook the dust off their feet in protest against them, and went to Iconium. (Acts 13:45, 49–51)

You can find additional allegations of persecution of the Pauline mission by Jews in Acts 17:5–7; 17:13; 18:12–17, 21:27–28; 23:12–15; 24:1–2; 25:2b–5. In contrast to Galatians the Acts of the Apostles never mentions that Paul had to defend himself against the accusations of Christian opponents, let alone rival Christian leaders. Most scholars regard the earlier witness of Paul as the more reliable account.

In the understanding of the author of Acts, the Church was unified and dealt with the question of circumcision rather easily. In Acts, it is the apostle Peter (not Paul) who first converts Gentiles and allows the male converts to remain uncircumcised (Acts 9:32—11:18). When Church leaders meet to discuss the matter, James, the Lord's brother, affirms Peter's and Paul's labors among the Gentiles (Acts 15:13–21). How does this picture of a unified, harmonious Church compare with Galatians 2:11–14, where Paul opposes Peter (Cephas) to his face after James had sent spies to Antioch to report on Paul's missionary work among the Gentiles? Such differences between Acts, on the one hand, and Galatians and Paul's other undisputed letters, on the other hand, support the inference that Acts was likely written a generation or two after Paul by an author who had not personally known Paul or read Paul's letters.

Faith and Works in Paul, Ephesians, and James

In Galatians, Paul responds to his opponents' accusation that not requiring the Mosaic Law (Torah), including circumcision, will lead to lawless conduct by followers of Jesus. The rationale for this accusation seems to be that if the Law is set aside as a guide for human behavior, there will be no limits or absolute ethical requirements governing the Christian life—much like some today believe that if a strict or narrow interpretation of the Bible is not followed (e.g., based on particular scriptures about women's rightful behavior or corporal punishment), our society will go to "hell in a hand basket." In response, Paul offers freedom in Christ as an opportunity to serve one's fellow believers and thereby govern ethical conduct: "For you were called to freedom, brothers and sisters; only do not use your freedom as an opportunity for self-indulgence, but through love become slaves to one another" (Gal 5:13). For Paul, works of the Mosaic Law are entirely unnecessary:

> Yet we know that a person is justified not by the works of the law but through faith in Jesus Christ. And we have come to believe in Christ Jesus, so that we might be justified by faith in Christ, and not by doing the works of the law, because no one will be justified by the works of the law. (Gal 2:16)

Another of Paul's undisputed letters, Romans, likewise states: "For we hold that a person is justified by faith apart from works prescribed by the law" (Rom 3:28).

Paul's teachings on faith and works in response to a particular crisis did not put an end to the issue in the early Church. The subject comes up, for example, in the letter to the Ephesians. The theology of Ephesians differs at several points from that reflected in the seven undisputed letters of Paul. For this reason, nearly all scholars believe that a later student or admirer of Paul wrote Ephesians. That is why Ephesians is classified among the NT's six Deutero-Pauline letters. An example of the distinctive theology in Ephesians concerns faith and works:

> For by grace you have been saved through faith, and this is not your own doing; it is the gift of God—not the result of works, so that no one may boast. For we are what he [God] has made us, created in Christ Jesus for good works, which God prepared beforehand to be our way of life. (Eph 2:8–10)

The apostle Paul could have agreed with the statement that salvation is God's gift to humanity and is "not the result of works." Yet the notion that believers are "created in Christ Jesus for good works" is not a part of Paul's theological vocabulary in Galatians or the other undisputed Pauline letters. At the time of the Galatian crisis, Paul was too busy confronting works of the Law (Torah) to reflect on the importance of works in general for followers of Jesus.

Another NT letter, James, likewise reflects an interest in faith and works. James is one of the Catholic or General Epistles. Different from Ephesians but like Galatians, James reflects a polemical context and criticizes the position of certain other Christians:

> What good is it, my brothers and sisters, if you say you have faith but do not have works? Can faith save you? If a brother or sister is naked and lacks daily food, and one of you says to them, "Go in peace; keep warm and eat your fill," and yet you do not supply their bodily needs, what is the good of that? So faith by itself, if it has no works, is dead. (Jas 2:14–17)

Like Ephesians, the epistle of James refers to "works" but not specifically to works prescribed in the Mosaic Law. More than anything, James addresses how the faithful should live in a manner consistent with what they believe.

These three early Christian authors—Paul, the author of Ephesians, and the author of James—tell us about conversations and, at times, debates over the relative importance of faith and works in the Christian life. Such conversations are a necessary part of forming any religious community and continue today among Christians and people of other religions.

Living as a Christian within the Roman Empire

The previous section mentioned Paul's concern about the allegation that his theology could lead to lawlessness and any number of moral excesses (Gal 5:13). In his later letter to the Church at Rome, Paul again addresses this concern:

> I appeal to you therefore, brothers and sisters, by the mercies of God, to present your bodies as a living sacrifice, holy and acceptable to God, which is your spiritual worship. Do not be conformed to this world, but be transformed by the renewing of your minds, so that you may discern what is the will of God—what is good and acceptable and perfect. (Rom 12:1–2)

The metaphor of a "living sacrifice" envisions believers who voluntarily limit their freedom because they have received God's mercy and now wish to offer themselves to God's service. In the following chapter of this letter, Paul expands upon this teaching about the believer's ethical conduct to include principles for living within the (totalitarian) Roman Empire:

> Let every person be subject to the governing authorities; for there is no authority except from God, and those authorities that exist have been instituted by God. Therefore whoever resists authority resists what God has appointed, and those who resist will incur judgment. For rulers are not a terror to good conduct, but to bad. Do you wish to have no fear of the authority? Then do what is good, and you will receive its approval; for it is God's servant for (your) good. . . . Pay to all what is due them—taxes to whom taxes are due, revenue to whom revenue is due, respect to whom respect is due, honor to whom honor is due. (Rom 13:1–4a, 7)

Likewise, 1 Peter, one of the Catholic Epistles, offers a similar exhortation to live as peaceful citizens under the authority of Rome:

> For the Lord's sake accept the authority of every human institution, whether of the emperor as supreme, or of governors, as sent by him to punish those who do wrong and to praise those who do right. For it is God's will that by doing right you should silence the ignorance of the foolish. As servants of God, live as free people, yet do not use your freedom as a pretext for evil. Honor everyone. Love the family of believers. Fear God. Honor the emperor. (1 Pet 2:13–17)

According to Paul and the author of 1 Peter, then, Christians are expected to make every effort to live within the constraints of the Roman Empire. Both authors maintain that the faithful must seek to live within that society without conforming to it.

By contrast, the NT's only apocalypse, the Revelation of John, views Rome as fundamentally hostile to the people of God:

> I saw a woman sitting on a scarlet beast that was full of blasphemous names, and it had seven heads and ten horns. The woman was clothed in purple and scarlet, and adorned with gold and jewels and pearls, holding in her hand a golden cup full of abominations and the impurities of her fornication; and on her forehead was written a name, a mystery: "Babylon the great, mother of whores and of earth's abominations." And I saw that the woman was drunk with the blood of the saints and the blood of the witnesses to Jesus. (Rev 17:3–6)

John thus identifies Rome with Babylon, the enemy of the ancient Israelites. Interestingly, the author of 1 Peter can likewise refer to Rome as "Babylon" (1 Pet 5:13) without expressing alarm about the danger that, according to Revelation, Rome poses to the Church.

Cultural and other differences have led sincere believers to variant experiences within a particular culture. Such was clearly the case for Paul and the author of 1 Peter, who accepted life within Roman society, and the author of Revelation, who viewed Rome as fundamentally corrupt and looked forward to the time of her downfall (Rev 18:1–4). In the centuries following these writings, numerous Christian authors attempted to address what it meant to live within Roman society, which at times could be hostile toward the Church. Following the rise of the first Christian emperor Constantine in the early fourth century, the question would have to be redefined to consider whether the Empire now led by a Christian emperor was too friendly toward certain expressions of Christianity and too severe toward others, not to mention Jews and polytheists as well.

Summary

In this chapter, we have learned that early Christians wrote historical narratives about Jesus (gospels) and the early Church, apocalypses, and letters. Twenty-seven of these writings, composed between approximately 50 CE and 120 CE, came to be included in the NT. The NT is written in the *Koine* ("common") dialect of ancient Greek, which was the common language in most cities in the eastern parts of the Mediterranean after the conquests of Alexander the Great. Each of the four NT gospels presents a distinctive picture of Jesus. One reason for the differences among these gospels is that their authors borrowed from various oral and written traditions and wrote decades after the crucifixion.

Twenty-one of the NT writings are letters. When reading an early Christian letter, it is helpful to ask what the letter reveals about its author, audience, opponents, and purpose. Despite their many points of agreement, the NT writings also highlight differences and even divisions in the early Church on matters such as circumcision, the relative unity of the earliest Church, the importance of faith and works, and living as a Christian within the Roman Empire.

Questions about the Text

1. How many writings are there in the NT? What are the three main divisions?

2. What are the two categories for the authorship of the Pauline letters, and why are there two?

3. What themes do we find in Mark's gospel? In Matthew's? In Luke's? In John's? Why are they important?

4. What is the "Synoptic Problem"? Describe the hypotheses used by most scripture scholars to explain it.

5. What are the four principles for reading an early Christian letter? Why are they important to follow?

6. What is the tension between faith and good works that Paul found in the early Church? How do you evaluate this tension today?

Questions for Discussion

1. Why does it or does it not make sense to refer to the NT as a single "book"? How might the metaphor of the NT as a library of much of the earliest surviving early Christian literature be helpful and accurate?

2. Scholars today debate whether Paul's encounter with the risen Jesus represents a particular "calling" within Paul's Jewish faith or a "conversion" from Judaism to a dif-

ferent religion. What do you think? Do you regard your own religious experiences as more of a calling or a conversion? Or have you experienced elements of both?

3. Galatians and Acts offer two different pictures of the early Church—one divided and the other unified. If you grew up in the Church (or some other religious community), which of these resonates with your experience of your religious community?

4. How important is faith to your understanding of God? How important are works as an expression of your faith?

5. Romans 13 and 1 Peter 2 instruct the early Christians to submit to the governing Roman authorities. Can you think of a time when you would be unwilling to submit to your government? Can you think of any circumstances under which you would agree with the Revelation of John and characterize a totalitarian regime as worthy of God's judgment and destruction? What happens when Christians today have different views about how to respond to the policies of a particular government?

For Further Study

New Testament

Ehrman, Bart D. *The New Testament: A Historical Introduction to the Early Christian Writings*. Third ed. New York: Oxford University Press, 2003.

This book provides an excellent introduction to the NT and some two dozen other early Christian writings.

Holmes, Michael W., ed. *The Apostolic Fathers*. Grand Rapids, MI: Baker, 1989.

This affordable volume offers short introductions and English translations of fifteen of the earliest extracanonical Christian writings, known today as the "Apostolic Fathers" (Barnabas; the Didache; the seven letters of Ignatius of Antioch; Polycarp, Philippians; the Martyrdom of Polycarp; 1 Clement; 2 Clement; the Shepherd of Hermas; and Diognetus).

Jefford, Clayton N. *Reading the Apostolic Fathers: An Introduction*. Peabody, MA: Hendrickson, 1996.

This volume offers helpful chapter-long introductions to the Apostolic Fathers.

Koester, Craig R. *Revelation and the End of All Things*. Grand Rapids, MI: William B. Eerdmans, 2001.

In providing commentary on the NT's apocalypse, the Revelation of John, this author engages certain popular contemporary approaches to Bible prophecy and interpretations of apocalyptic literature, such as in the *Left Behind* novels.

Powell, Mark Allan. *Fortress Introduction to the Gospels*. Minneapolis, MN: Fortress, 1998.

This text includes chapters on the historical Jesus and the origins of written gospels, the four NT gospels, and other early Christian gospels.

Roetzel, Calvin. *The Letters of Paul: Conversations in Context*. Fourth ed. Louisville, KY: Westminster John Knox, 1998.

This is a survey of the apostle Paul's Hellenistic and Jewish cultural contexts, the thirteen NT letters attributed to Paul, and models of interpreting Paul's theology, legacy, and significance.

From the Reference Librarian
Researching Bible Topics—New Testament

As you continue to develop your research skills from the foundation of chapter 1, remember the basic starting point and Skill Key #1 to unlock research:

Skill Key #1

Use the library's reference collection to begin your research.

a) Use a subject-specific encyclopedia to acquire specialized knowledge about a subject.

b) Use a subject-specific encyclopedia whose scope is appropriate for both your topic and the approach you want to take to that topic.

Student: So what reference tools are available for studying the New Testament?

Many of the reference tools mentioned at the end of the previous chapter, such as the *Anchor Bible Dictionary*, can be used for researching NT topics since they cover the entire Bible—both Old and New Testaments. However, several reference tools are devoted entirely to the NT, among which are the following:

Craig A. Evans and Stanley E. Porter, eds. *Dictionary of New Testament Background*. Downers Grove, IL: InterVarsity Press, 2000.

Joel B. Green and Scot McKnight, eds. *Dictionary of Jesus and the Gospels*. Downers Grove, IL: InterVarsity Press, 1992.

Gerald F. Hawthorne and Ralph P. Martin, eds. *Dictionary of Paul and his Letters*. Downers Grove, IL: InterVarsity Press, 1993.

Ralph P. Martin and Peter H. Davids, eds. *Dictionary of the Later New Testament and Its Developments*. Downers Grove, IL: InterVarsity Press, 1997.

The first three titles focus on specific NT writings: the four gospels, the Pauline epistles (including the Deutero-Pauline letters), and the remaining writings of the NT. These volumes contain articles on each of the NT writings covered as well as important theological topics (e.g. "kingdom of God," "messianic secret," "eschatology") raised by the content of those writings. The fourth title in the list is not tied to particular writings of the NT but is "concerned with archaeology, geography, historical figures, political institutions, historical events, peoples and culture."

Another type of reference tool commonly used in Scripture study is a concordance. A concordance lists all the occurrences of a particular word in the order in which they appear in the Bible. For example, if you are interested in the use of the word *hope*, you might encounter a list such as the following.

HOPE‡ (187) [HOPED, HOPEFUL. HOPELESS, HOPES, HOPING]

Ru	1:12	Even if I thought there was **h** for me.
2Ki	6:33	Why should I **h** in the LORD any longer?"
1Ch	29:15	on the earth are like a shadow, and there is no **h**.
Ezr	10:2	but even now there is **h** for Israel in spite of this.
Job	3:9	let it **h** for light, but have none;
	4:6	and the integrity of your ways your **h**?
	5:16	So the poor have **h**, and injustice shuts its mouth.
	6:19	caravans of Tema look, the travelers of Sheba **h**.
	7:6	and come to their end without **h**.
	8:13	the **h** of the godless shall perish.
	11:18	And you will have confidence, because there is **h**:
	11:20	and their **h** is to breathe their last."
	13:15	I have no **h**; but I will defend my ways to his face.
	14:7	"For there is **h** for a tree, if it is cut down.
	14:19	so you destroy the **h** of mortals.
	17:15	where then is my **h**? Who will see my **h**?
	19:10	and I am gone, he has uprooted my **h** like a tree.
	27:8	the **h** of the godless when God cuts them off.
	41:9	Any **h** of capturing it will be disappointed:
Ps	9:18	nor the **h** of the poor perish forever.
	33:17	The war horse is a vain **h** for victory.
	33:18	on those who **h** in his steadfast love,

33:22   O LORD, be upon us, even as we **h** in you.

39:7   My **h** is in you.

42:5   and why are you disquieted within me? **H** in God;

(From *NRSV Concordance Unabridged*, Kohlenberger, ed., Grand Rapids, MI: Zondervan, 1991.)

Note that you may need to take alternate forms of a word into consideration (hoped, hopeful, etc.); some are listed at the beginning of the list, but not all concordances do this. Also, make sure that you use a concordance that matches the English version of the Bible you are using (the reference librarian can help you find the right concordance). This is because different English translations may use different English words to translate the same Hebrew or Greek word.

Student: How do I refine my use of Library of Congress subject headings?

The second key element of using the library is this:

Skill Key #2

Use the library's catalog to locate sources of information.

a) Use subject headings to locate precisely books on your topic.

b) Use subject headings whose scope fits your topic as closely as possible, then adjust your search with a broader or narrower subject heading as necessary.

In the previous chapter, you learned that subject headings for OT books follow a particular format: Bible O T [name of book]. Subject headings for NT books follow the same format, but "N T" is used (for "New Testament") in place of "O T" as the "root" of the subject heading. (Again, make sure to put a space between the "N" and the "T.")

Search Format:

Subject heading root	Subdivision
Bible NT	[name of book]
Bible NT	Matthew
Bible NT	Romans
Bible NT	Corinthians 1st

These are very broad subject headings and, in fact, may be too broad for the particular topic you want to pursue. Remember, you want to use subject headings to locate precisely books on your topic. One way of focusing a subject search more precisely is by adding subdivisions to the basic "root" subject heading for any particular biblical book (this applies to OT books also). Two of these additional subdivisions are standard and often useful. Examine the following subject headings that include the subdivisions "Criticism, interpretation, etc." or "Commentaries."

Search Format:

Subject heading root	Subdivision 1	Subdivision 2
Bible NT	Matthew	Criticism, interpretation, etc.
Bible NT	Matthew	Commentaries
Bible OT	Genesis	Criticism, interpretation, etc.
Bible OT	Samuel 1st	Commentaries

Student: What do these subdivisions mean, and how can I use them to focus my subject search?

Let's begin with the "Criticism, interpretation, etc." addition to the Library of Congress subject heading root. Look at the following titles whose catalog records are reproduced here, all of which have the subject heading "Bible NT Matthew—Criticism, interpretation, etc." Now look at the box "Subjects" on the left, then follow to the right to see other subject headings and subdivisions that you can use to refine your search.

Author	Weber, Gerard P., 1918–
Title	Breaking open the gospel of Matthew: the Sermon on the Mount / Gerard P. Weber and Robert L. Miller.
Published	Cincinnati, Ohio : St. Anthony Messenger Press, c1998.
Subjects	Bible. N.T. Matthew—Criticism, interpretation, etc.
	Sermon on the mount.

Author	Head, Peter M.
Title	Christology and the synoptic problem : an argument for Markan priority / Peter M. Head.
Published	Cambridge ; New York : Cambridge University Press, 1997.
Subjects	Bible. N.T. Mark—Criticism, interpretation, etc.
	Bible. N.T. Matthew—Criticism, interpretation, etc.
	Jesus Christ—History of doctrines—Early church, ca. 30–600.
	Synoptic problem.

Author	Brown, Jeannine K., 1961–
Title	The Disciples in narrative perspective : the portrayal and function of the Matthéan Disciples / Jeannine K. Brown.
Published	Atlanta, GA : Society of Biblical Literature, c2002.
Subjects	Jesus Christ—Disciples.
	Bible. N.T. Matthew—Criticism, interpretation, etc.
	Apostles.

Author	Barton, Stephen C
Title	Discipleship and family ties in Mark and Matthew / Stephen C. Barton.
Published	Cambridge ; New York : Cambridge University Press, 1994.
Subjects	Jesus Christ—Family.
	Jesus Christ—Views on the family.
	Bible. N.T. Mark—Criticism, interpretation, etc.
	Bible. N.T. Matthew—Criticism, interpretation, etc.
	Christian life—Biblical teaching.

Author	Luomanen, Petri, 1961–
Title	Entering the kingdom of heaven : a study on the structure of Matthew's view of salvation / Petri Luomanen.
Published	Tübingen : Mohr Siebeck, c1998.
Subjects	Bible. N.T. Matthew—Criticism, interpretation, etc.
	Salvation—Biblical teaching.

Author	Menninger, Richard E., 1948–
Title	Israel and the church in the Gospel of Matthew / Richard E. Menninger.
Published	New York : P. Lang, c1994.
Subjects	Bible. N.T. Matthew—Criticism, interpretation, etc.
	Jesus Christ—Messiahship.
	Church—Biblical teaching.
	Israel (Christian theology)—Biblical teaching.

Law (Theology)—Biblical teaching.
Jewish Christians—Palestine.
Jewish Christians—History—Early church, ca. 30–600.
Judaism (Christian theology)—Biblical teaching.

Author Luz, Ulrich.
Title **The theology of the Gospel of Matthew / Ulrich Luz ; translated by J. Bradford Robinson.**
Published Cambridge ; New York : Cambridge University Press, 1995.
Subjects Bible. NT Matthew—Theology.
Bible. NT Matthew—Criticism, interpretation, etc.

You can see that the subject heading "Bible NT Matthew—Criticism, interpretation, etc." encompasses a variety of topics related to the gospel of Matthew, ranging from a broad treatment of the theology of Matthew to a specific theme (Christology, the disciples, salvation, etc.) or even a specific passage (Sermon on the Mount in Matthew 5–7). Using the subdivision "Criticism, interpretation, etc." allows you to view a variety of topics related to the biblical book you want to study and to identify even more precise subject headings.

The other subdivision mentioned is "Commentaries," and it refers to a specific format. Commentaries on Scripture are simply explanations of the meaning of the biblical text that follow the order of the text, beginning with chapter 1, verse 1 and proceeding to the last verse of the last chapter. This type of book is useful for studying specific passages or even individual verses within a book.

Commentaries come in all varieties. Some are aimed at a popular audience, some are aimed at biblical scholars (and require a knowledge of ancient languages such as Greek and/or Hebrew), and others fall somewhere in between. You will probably have to look at a particular commentary to determine whether you can use it.

One kind of commentary that is often very useful, especially for undergraduates, is called a "one-volume commentary." This simply means that commentaries on all of the books of the Bible are contained in one volume. Such commentaries are, obviously, not as detailed as a one-volume commentary written on just one book but are, for that very reason, less technical and easier for nonspecialists to use. The following one-volume commentary was produced by Roman Catholic biblical scholars, but your library may own several others that are just as useful.

> *The New Jerome Biblical Commentary*. Englewood Cliffs, NJ: Prentice Hall, 1990.

Unlike most one-volume commentaries produced by Protestant scholars, this volume also contains a commentary on the deuterocanonical books. (What does *deuterocanonical* mean? How can you find out?)

Another type of subject search is a search for books on a person, some individual mentioned in the Bible. The format usually followed when searching for persons as subjects is the same as that used when searching for persons as authors, "last name, first name." However, since persons mentioned in the Bible do not have "last names," at least not in the sense we are accustomed to, a descriptive phrase, as illustrated by the examples for both Old and New Testament persons that follow, is often added to the name to make clear to whom the search is referring.

Search Format:

Name	Descriptive phrase(s)
Abraham	Biblical patriarch
Moses	Biblical leader
Isaiah	Biblical prophet
Saul	King of Israel
Matthew	The apostle, Saint
Luke	Saint
Paul	The apostle, Saint

By now, you should have a good grasp of the basics of library research, including using the reference collection both to obtain basic information about your topic and as a way to lead you into the rest of the library collection and using subject headings in the library catalog to search with precision for books in your library. In subsequent chapters, we will further elaborate on these techniques.

Student Tasks

For each of the following tasks, look for books published within the last fifty years.

1. Go to your library and locate a dictionary of the NT.

2. Select a book from the NT and use the correct form of subject heading to search your library catalog for books about it.

3. Find a commentary on the book you have selected.

    Format = Bible NT [name of book] Commentaries

4. Find a book that deals with a particular topic or aspect of the NT writing.

    Format = Bible NT [name of book] Criticism, interpretation, etc.

5. Find books about a person in the NT, using the Library of Congress format: [Name Descriptive phrase]. What subdivisions appear with the subject heading for that person?

II

CHRISTOLOGY AND ECCLESIOLOGY: FOLLOWING CHRIST IN A COMMUNITY OF THE HOLY SPIRIT

3

Christology—"Who Do You Say That I Am?"

From the Editor

To confirm one's response to the question, "Who are you?" one is typically asked for photo identification, often a driver's license. I have yet to come across anyone who likes his or her photo. One reason is that the camera takes a three-dimensional image and changes it to two dimensions, which distorts and flattens the real person. Successful painters and film and television stars, among others, learn to convincingly communicate through flat, two-dimensional mediums. A second reason for not liking the ID photo is that it says nothing really important about who the person is. If I know the person, I might say that what is most important about her is that she is lovable and loving, generous, thoughtful, and kind; has a great sense of humor; is sensitive, caring, peace-filled, honest, intelligent, insightful, and dedicated—a wonderfully unique individual.

The same can be said about Jesus the Christ. Though we cannot sit down with him and learn from him in person because time and history necessarily keep us at a distance so that in some respects Jesus "flattens" out like a photo, we have available a great deal of material about him in the Bible from which to draw. This material comes from those who knew him, followed him, and experienced him; it tells of those who met him and whose plans changed radically after encountering him.

Theology tries to "thicken" or flesh out these sources and resources, allowing us the knowledge and freedom to find this same Jesus of Nazareth in our lives today. This has been part of the legacy of Christianity from the start: People asking questions in order to deepen their faith, or as Anselm might say, "Faith seeking understanding."

Christology is at the heart of finding the answer to the identity question: Who is Jesus? This chapter takes us through three sources to thicken our understanding of who this Jesus really is and how he was perceived by others in his time and history, so we can learn for ourselves how to recognize, encounter, and enter into a unique relationship with the real Jesus. We will begin with the source of our knowing, which is a narrative or story, and see how its purpose is to tell us something crucially important about Jesus' call to salvation in God right now.

Christology—"Who Do You Say That I Am?"

Brian D. Robinette, PhD

The Question

In a turning point in his ministry, Jesus asks his disciples a question that seems innocent enough yet has remained the fundamental question for Christology ever since. Jesus and his ministry had developed quite a reputation by this point. He had numerous followers, both near and far, and perhaps just as many enemies. The question probably seemed a matter of information gathering, an attempt to discern the "beat on the street": "Who do people say that I am?" (Mk 8:27). Jesus' disciples reply with a variety of answers: "John the Baptist; and others, Elijah; and still others, one of the prophets" (8:28). Jesus follows up with a more pointed and personal question, one that, like many of his questions, discloses not only something fundamental about himself but also something fundamental about the one whom he addresses: "But who do *you* say that I am?" (8:29a, emphasis added).

Peter ventures a reply that seems to represent the thought of the gathered disciples: "You are the Messiah" (Mk 8:29b). Peter seems to know quite well the meaning of his statement. Jesus is the "anointed one" of Israel (derived from the Hebrew *masiah*), the one who will deliver God's covenanted people from exile and bondage, the one elected by God to finally reestablish the unity and independence of Israel from Roman imperial domination, a leader like King David, who, 1,000 years earlier, was also hailed as God's "anointed one" for his legendary religious, political, and military leadership. But Jesus never confirms Peter's reply. Imagine the disciples' surprise, then, as Jesus tells them not to tell anyone about him. Imagine their puzzled looks as he proceeds to tell them that the "Son of Man" will suffer and be rejected by Israel's leaders, that he will be killed and rise after three days. No wonder Peter "took him aside and began to rebuke him" (8:32b). How could Jesus possibly be Israel's messiah if he was to endure rejection and humiliation? What kind of bizarre liberation could come from such demonstrable defeat? Indeed, what has messiahship to do with suffering and death? Now imagine the disciples' shock when Jesus responds to Peter's rebuke with his own: "Get behind me, Satan! For you are setting your mind not on divine things but on human things" (8:33).

Christology begins with a question: "Who do you say that I am?" and is the attempt to answer the question of Jesus' ultimate identity and purpose. In more precise terms, Christology is the systematic study of Jesus of Nazareth, the one called the "Christ" (*christos* is Greek for the Hebrew *masiah*): his mission and person, his relationship to God, his ultimate significance for humanity. As the story in Mark's gospel so poignantly reveals, thinking Christologically often challenges our assumptions. It requires attention to paradox and surprise. The fact that one no less than Peter, Jesus' closest disciple and leader of the primitive Christian movement, could get it wrong (while getting it right) indicates the challenge before us. For Peter was correct: Jesus is the messiah, the "anointed one" of God, but *not* in the way Peter (and so many of his contemporaries) imagined the messiah to be. Like the blind man who is healed just before this startling exchange (Mk 8:22–26), Peter is blind to Jesus' true messianic mission. In fact, Jesus regards Peter's vision as a dangerous illusion and temptation, hence, the strong rebuke. What Jesus wants Peter and his disciples to "see" is a reversal of assumptions and values: "For those who want to save their life will lose it, and those who lose their life for my sake, and for the sake of the gospel, will save it" (8:35).

In this chapter, we shall learn to think Christologically and to discover how the story of Jesus' life, death, and resurrection provides the basic theological framework for understanding his identity and mission. We will begin by examining the life-story of Jesus of Nazareth and how, in light of their powerful Easter experiences, the disciples and other early Christians began a process of interpreting that story in daring theological terms. We shall also explore how the later Christological doctrines, or official teachings of the Church, particularly those of the fourth and fifth centuries CE, continue to provide indispensable "grammatical rules" to assist Christians as they speak about Jesus, his relationship to God, and his significance for humanity. Throughout our study, we shall identify three touchstones that structure all Christological reflection:

1. All Christology derives from *story*.

2. All Christology is rooted in an experience of *salvation*.

3. All Christology springs from the conviction that in Jesus Christ the *presence of God* has been revealed and has taken hold of the world in an unprecedented way.

The Story Begins: Jesus of Nazareth and the Kingdom of God

Election and Eschatology

Jesus was a storyteller. He told fantastic stories, strange stories, stories that liberated and enlightened, stories that confused and upset. As a first-century Palestinian Jew living in a storytelling culture, Jesus lived by stories. Most of all, he lived (and died) by Israel's primary narrative.

As we have seen in the previous chapters, the people of Israel told and retold the story of Exodus and the covenant. Their self-understanding was shaped by a faith that God had acted decisively in history to liberate their Hebrew ancestors from slavery and Egyptian imperial domination, establishing them as a free people now beholden to their liberator God in mutual fidelity. As God promised to love and protect the Hebrew people, so they promised proper worship and ethical activity as codified in the Law (Torah). Freedom *from* slavery and bondage (Exodus) implied a freedom *for* a committed community of faith and justice (the covenant). Throughout their subsequent history, from the time of the united kingdom under kings Saul, David, and Solomon (1022–922 BCE) to the time of devastation and exile during the Babylonian period (587–537 BCE), the people of Israel—and especially the prophets—viewed their fortunes as tied to their faithfulness to the covenant. In times of crisis, the prophets proclaimed messages of grief, judgment, and conversion, calling upon their people and leaders to return to the covenant with God in order to avert disaster. Often, the prophets cited social and economic injustices as reasons for their internal hardships and vulnerabilities to outside forces, for example, the Assyrians, the Babylonians, and, during Jesus' time, the Romans. And often, with their messages of judgment and radical critique came messages of hope for a future when God, just as in the time of Exodus, would bring an end to all that afflicted them.

If we are to understand how the larger pattern and the individual stories of Jesus' life make sense, we must see them as reflecting this broader historical and narrative context. There are two structural features about this context. The first is a theology of election. The people of Israel, including Jesus, resolutely believed that God had a unique destiny for them, a belief that in and through their specific history as a people, God's character was revealed and the original purposes for humanity disclosed. As part of God's covenant with Israel, the people were also God's "elect," marked with a distinctive responsibility to be a "light to the peoples"

(Isa 51:4). The second structural feature is a particular theology of history, or what we call "eschatology." *Eschatology* literally means the "study of the last things," that is, the study of history's ultimate future. Jesus passionately believed, as did many of his contemporaries, that God would soon bring about a fulfillment of Israel's history, a decisive resolution to the all-too-present realities of suffering, alienation, brokenness, and oppression. Theirs was an "eschatological imagination"—a worldview that imagined and yearned for a final future fulfillment of creation and history, for human well-being, for lasting peace and justice. The God of life and death, of past, present, and future, would soon bring about a new and final Exodus in a way that would not just involve Israel, but because of Israel's special role in salvation history, it would also be a fulfillment for *all* people. It is important that we keep these two aspects in mind, particularly as we consider Jesus' specific focus on the people of Israel in his mission. Unquestionably, his mission is for Israel, but because it is for *Israel*, it is also for all humanity. Election (particularity) and eschatology (universality) go hand in hand.

As one might expect, this eschatological imagination was especially robust during times of historical crisis. During Jesus' time, Israel lived under the oppressive rule of the Romans. The once-independent nation of Israel was occupied by the external and "pagan" forces of an empire that seemed to many Jews very much like the Egyptians who had enslaved their ancestors more than twelve-hundred years earlier. While the Romans allowed the Jews to practice their religion, run their Temple, and keep many of their customs, the burdensome taxation, ubiquitous military presence, and overall powerlessness to function as an independent nation with its own king provided more than enough evidence to any Jew that God's deliverance was needed. Consequently, several Jewish groups yearned for, spoke of, and, in some cases, fought for a future in which Israel would be internally healed of religious and social divisions and freed from the external forces of oppression.

For many, these were necessarily linked. For example, there were those who imagined that what Israel needed most of all was an internal reformation and purification so that God would deliver Israel from its enemies. The Pharisees held this view, as did John the Baptist, Jesus' immediate predecessor and mentor, though he differed from the Pharisees in many ways. As the requirements for God's coming rule and solution to Israel's desperate circumstances, John preached total moral conversion and purification, ritually enacted by water baptism. Other groups, such as the Zealots, openly spoke of a military solution, in which Israel would throw off the yoke of oppression by force. Still others, like the Sadducees, the priestly and aristocratic class who ran the Temple in Jerusalem, and who had much at stake in keeping the peace with Rome so that the Temple might continue to function as Israel's religious and symbolic center, tended to maintain the status quo and compromise with Roman authorities. As we shall see, sometimes they actively cooperated with Roman leaders to identify and remove potential threats of religious and political unrest as a matter of security.

As should be clear by now, during Jesus' time there was little distinction between religion and politics. Whereas we tend to separate these terms, in the ancient world, religious practice was rarely a private matter but instead was bound up with all dimensions of human life, including the social, economic, and political. Only if we keep this in mind will we be able to fully grasp why Jesus was so threatening to so many parties, why he was killed, and why his message and ministry continue to be a powerful force for religious and social transformation today. However, we will not understand the particular mission and person of Jesus unless we also understand his historical context, his eschatological imagination, and the way he emerges as a distinctive voice in the diverse landscape of first-century Judaism. Jesus' message of the "Kingdom of God" will resonate with all that we have examined thus far, but it will also provide a strikingly different alternative to the solutions just outlined. His is a story with an unexpected twist.

Proclamation of the Kingdom of God

"The time is fulfilled, and the kingdom of God has come near; repent, and believe in the good news" (Mk 1:14). These words in Mark's gospel inaugurate Jesus' public ministry. We need to examine several features of this bold proclamation to gain a better appreciation of Jesus' mission.

"*The time is fulfilled.*" Jesus' imagination was eschatological, possessed by the singular idea that Israel's story was coming to fulfillment. The future is now; God is doing something new and groundbreaking under our very noses. "[*T*]*he kingdom of God has come near.*" God's rule is overtaking human history in an unprecedented way to bring about final healing and liberation, that is, "salvation." The Kingdom of God is an event that is happening. It is "at hand," in the immediate future, but it is also, in a very real sense, "now." It is both present and future, or as theologians commonly put it, "already and not yet."

If we can keep these two aspects in a state of tension, we will be able to grasp something of the dramatic character of Jesus' stories, actions, and mission. "[*R*]*epent, and believe in the good news.*" The coming Kingdom of God demands a decision, a reaction—conversion. This call to repentance quite literally means to "turn about-face," to go the opposite direction. Whereas we tend to think of repentance as a matter of apologizing for personal sins, repentance meant for Jesus the changing one's entire worldview: how one perceives, thinks, speaks, and acts. Jesus is summoning people to a new and radical way of life, one convicted by and committed to the "gospel" or "good news" that God is presently doing and will soon complete.

But what is this "Kingdom of God," and what makes it "good news"? While it is the central symbol of his ministry, Jesus never strictly defines the "Kingdom of God" in the way one might a philosophical category or scientific principle. The reason for this is at least two-fold. First, the "Kingdom of God" is symbolic: It cannot be defined any more than "God" or "love" or "beauty" can be adequately defined. One must use multiple metaphors and analogies to even begin disclosing something of the richness of what is meant. For this reason, Jesus constantly uses stories, and most often parables, to speak of this extraordinary reality. He says, for example, that the Kingdom of God is like the tiny mustard seed that grows beyond anyone's imagination to become larger than other bushes. The Kingdom of God is a gift and a fullness of God encountering us in ways that may initially seem humble but will eventually exceed our expectations.

Second, the "Kingdom of God" for Jesus is not merely an "idea" but a concrete reality that comes about through action, divine and human. It is something that is performed, something to be realized or made real in and through the cooperative activity of God and humanity. Jesus does not merely preach this reality; he lives it, enacts it, and summons others to do likewise, and this is exactly why it is "good news." For in his ministry of physical, spiritual, and social healing, of establishing peace and justice among people, he is seeking to bring about God's ultimate plan of well-being or salvation for humanity. Story alone is capable of capturing something of the dramatic revolutions in human affairs that the Kingdom of God would bring about.

But what is "good news" for some may seem challenging and even offensive to others. Jesus' Sermon on the Mount, for example, is a bold proclamation of liberation for the poor and oppressed, for those who are meek, who mourn and hunger, who are merciful and make peace, "for theirs is the kingdom of heaven" (Mt 5:1–7:29). What is presently the situation of despair and alienation for many will soon be flipped upside down and turned inside out. Things are *not* what they are supposed to be, and God is doing something about it, says Jesus.

Along with this emancipatory message comes a message of confrontation and judgment. Those who maintain social and religious distinctions of "insider" and "outsider," and those who stand to benefit from the way things are—the privileged, the elite, the powerful, and the persecutors—stand under judgment and a call to total conversion. It is perfectly understandable that Jesus' ministry attracted just as many enemies as it did followers. His was a polarizing ministry in many ways, though he ultimately sought reconciliation between groups of people who stood in opposition to each other as part of a religious, social, and political system binding them in interminable conflict. One of Jesus' most well-known parables (the parable of the Good Samaritan) illustrates the point.

Asked by a scholar of the law what he must do to inherit eternal life, Jesus in turn asks the scholar to summarize the law. The scholar responds, "You shall love the Lord your God with all your heart, and with all your soul, and with all your strength, and with all your mind, and your neighbor as yourself" (Lk 10:27). Jesus responds, "You have given the right answer; do this, and you will live" (v. 28). Apparently unsatisfied, the scholar further pursues the question and asks Jesus, "And who is my neighbor?" (v. 29). With this question, Jesus has the opportunity to drive his point home. The question about "neighbor" has everything to do with the Kingdom of God, so Jesus tells a story that begins quite conventionally. (Parables often begin with an ordinary scene, only to suddenly explode into paradox and surprise.)

A man falls victim to robbers and is left half-dead. A priest happens to be walking by. Here, we might expect the priest to do something magnanimous. A priest is surely our model of holiness, but the priest passes by on the opposite side, as does the Levite after him. (Levites were subordinate Temple officials.) At this point in the story, the listener might actually suspend judgment about this ostensible breach of justice because the priest and Levite were required by the law not to touch the body of a corpse (and the man surely must have appeared dead). According to ritual purity laws, touching the body of a corpse would make them ritually impure to carry out their religious duties in the Temple.

The next to come along is the Samaritan. The Samaritan people, situated between Jerusalem to the south and Galilee to the north, were considered an "outsider" group, Jewish by ethnicity but heretical in their practices. They had become independent from mainstream Judaism about four-hundred years earlier and had developed their own scriptures, worship practices, and sacred spaces. Often vilified for their heterodox ways, they were a ritually "unclean" people. Yet this Samaritan, despite whatever unorthodox beliefs he may have held, actually performs the reality of the Kingdom. As the parable puts it, he is "moved with pity" at the sight of the wounded, naked man (Lk 10:33). In Hebrew, the word *compassion* refers to that "gut feeling" one has when deeply moved by a feeling of care and love. Importantly, it is just this kind of reaction metaphorically ascribed to God prior to the Exodus: "I have observed the misery of my people who are in Egypt; I have heard their cry on account of their taskmasters. Indeed, I know their sufferings" (Ex 3:7). Moved by God's own compassion for the dispossessed, the Samaritan performs the very thing one would expect from the priest and Levite. He pours oil and wine over the wounds, bandages them, and takes the man to a place of rest, even promising the innkeeper he will come back to pay whatever is further needed in restoring the man's health (Lk 10:34–35). There is surprising excess to the gift. The Kingdom of God comes by way of reversing and even overflowing expectations.

"Which of these three, do you think, was a neighbor to the man who fell into the hands of the robbers?" Jesus asks (Lk 10:36). Jesus turns the tables, and now the questioner is the one questioned. The legal scholar, faced by the parable, responds in the only sensible way: "The one who showed him mercy" (v. 37a). "Go and do likewise," says Jesus (v. 37b), concluding a repartee that, with a few swift verbal strokes, dismantles the questioner's assumptions about demarcating lines of ritual purity and the groups distinguished by them. It is not that Jesus rejects the Law, for he seeks to fulfill it (Mt 5:17). Jesus is outraged by how the Law had been used as a weapon and source of division, when its original purpose was to bring reconciliation between people. The Law, and many of Israel's central symbols, especially the Temple, as we shall see, had been co-opted by the powerful and elite for self-aggrandizement. "Do not judge, so that you may not be judged. . . . how can you say to your neighbor, 'Let me take the speck out of your eye,' while the log is in your own eye?" (Mt 7:1, 4). Woe to those who occupy places of privilege. Woe to those who place heavy demands (religious and economic) on the people. Woe to the hypocrites obsessed with obtaining personal purity by way of separating themselves from sinners (see Mt 23:1–36). "The greatest among you will be your servant. All who exalt themselves will be humbled, and all who humble themselves will be exalted" (Mk 23:11).

Miracles

Along with the sayings of comfort and judgment recorded by the gospels, we also find many deeds whereby Jesus symbolically enacts something of the reality of God's Kingdom. All four gospels relate numerous episodes of Jesus healing persons bearing physical and spiritual affliction. While modern people may have difficulty with these stories, consigning them to an archaic or "mythological" way of thinking long superseded by modern science, there is little question that acts of a miraculous character were ascribed to Jesus during his lifetime.

If we are to fully appreciate the miracles in the gospels, we cannot simply view them as a suspension of nature's laws in a kind of holy magic show or as proof of Jesus' divinity. Rather, the miracles disclose God's Kingdom in a unique way, for by them God brings about healing for people in the reality of their concrete situation, in their bodies and private suffering, and often openly giving them dignity by restoring them to their community (for example, lepers, sick, blind, deaf). Jesus' ministry is all-encompassing and holistic, transforming ordinary people in the socially isolating experience of suffering. Often, people who suffer from some kind of physical infirmity also suffer from it socially and spiritually. Perhaps you have personally witnessed or even experienced how a chronic disease or disability can isolate a person from social groups, even those that are supposed to be the most inclusive and nurturing. The conventional wisdom of Jesus' time tended to view physical infirmity as a visible sign of impurity, as though disease and disability were manifestations of personal sin. Consequently, those suffering from chronic disease and dysfunction were often excluded from participating fully (if at all) in Jewish religious life. Jesus rejected this arrangement outright. "As [Jesus] walked along, he saw a man blind from birth. His disciples asked him, 'Rabbi, who sinned, this man or his parents, that he was born blind?' Jesus answered, 'Neither this man nor his parents sinned; he was born blind so that God's works might be revealed in him'" (Jn 9:1–3).

As Jesus touches and heals the "untouchables"—the leper, the woman with a hemorrhage, the demoniac boy, the man with a withered hand—he simultaneously restores to them those social and spiritual relationships that in many cases had been denied them from birth. Jesus does not explain evil; he simply confronts it. The leper is healed and told to present himself to the Temple (Mk 1:40–45). The paralytic's sins are forgiven, just as he is given his health (2:1–12). The Gerasene demoniac condemned to roaming night and day among the tombs is healed and told to return to his family (Mk 5:1–20). The crippled woman stands up and praises God (Lk 13:10–13). The mute person is given the capacity of speech (Mt 9:32–34). "Great crowds came to him, bringing with them the lame, the maimed, the blind, the mute, and many others. They put them at his feet, and he cured them, so that the crowd was amazed when they saw the mute speaking, the maimed whole, the lame walking, and the blind seeing. And they praised the God of Israel" (Mt 15:30–31).

The New Testament (NT) describes such events as "acts of power" (*dynamis*) or "signs" (*semeion*), whereby Jesus directly confronts the palpable forces of evil in its diverse and mysterious manifestations. A miracle, theologically understood, is the dramatic in-breaking of God's rule into the world in order to restore human beings to that physical, social, and spiritual wholeness intended for them from the beginning of creation. Evil and suffering represent the antikingdom and are emphatically not God's will for humanity. Miracles are therefore filled with eschatological significance: fragmentary realizations of God's ultimate future of well-being for human beings and thus part of the overarching narrative that Jesus is proclaiming and manifesting in his ministry.

Table Fellowship

In addition to his proclamation and miracles of healing, Jesus symbolically enacts the reality of the Kingdom through his inclusive "table fellowship." Though it might be difficult to grasp this in our contemporary context of supermarkets, microwaves, and "fast food," in the ancient world, and in ancient Judaism in particular, eating and sharing a meal was an intimate act charged with wide-ranging social and religious significance. Indeed, the table functioned as a kind of microcosm of Jewish society and practice. For a first-century Jew, an array of purity laws and customs regulated all aspects of eating—what one ate and when, how it was to be eaten and with whom, and so on. While such laws and customs can promote an appreciation for the sacredness of meal, they could also (and frequently did) become a source of division between those regarded ritually "clean" and "unclean."

As we have already noted, for certain prominent groups in first-century Judaism (and here we may point to the Pharisees as an example), a conception of holiness prevailed that fostered a sense of distinction and even separation from other (ritually impure or "unclean") groups through the rigorous adherence to laws and ancestral customs. However, it is just this comprehensive "purity system" that Jesus consistently challenges as a false path for Israel, and nowhere more forcefully than in his table fellowship of shocking hospitality to and inclusivity of the sinner and outsider. "When the scribes of the Pharisees saw that he was eating with sinners and tax collectors, they said to his disciples, 'Why does he eat with tax collectors and sinners?' When Jesus heard this, he said to them, 'Those who are well have no need of a physician, but those who are sick; I have come to call not the righteous but sinners'" (Mk 2:16–17).

Just as in the parables of the lost sheep, the lost coin, and the prodigal son (see Lk 15), Jesus' mission is not intended primarily for those who imagine they are already righteous before God but for the outcast and unclean. By including sinners at the table, Jesus is quite deliberately enacting a story alternative to the one told by those who anticipate Israel's deliverance through the heroic and self-justifying adherence to a purity system. "Listen to me, all of you, and understand: there is nothing outside a person that by going in can defile, but the things that come out are what defile" (Mk 7:14–15).

To be sure, Jesus is passionately interested in moral and spiritual conversion. One need only survey the difficult sayings and precepts scattered throughout the gospels to become aware of the true demands of discipleship, but the kind of conversion Jesus envisions is one that, instead of resulting in opposition between groups according to degree of purity, results in lasting reconciliation between them. God's coming Kingdom precisely means the dismantling of "insider" and "outsider" suspicion and rivalry. Jesus' meal practices therefore anticipate God's ultimate future for humanity, where all are welcome to the eschatological banquet, even (and especially) those who appear to have received no formal invitation. Importantly, it is just this understanding of inclusion and reconciliation at the table that informs the early Church's practice of Eucharist.

Confrontation at the Temple and the Question of Jesus' Authority

While much more could be said about Jesus' public ministry, we must now turn our attention to the culminating developments of Jesus' life that led to his death—and the apparent failure of his mission.

It should be obvious by now that Jesus was a dangerous man—dangerous because he preached empowering messages of hope to the marginalized and oppressed; he was reputed to heal persons of physical affliction, even forgiving them of their sins; he boldly challenged many of Israel's religious leaders to radical conversion; he was associated with John the Baptist, who had recently been beheaded by the local Roman ruler Herod; and some publicly hailed him as the "messiah" who would deliver Israel from Roman domination. As if all this were not enough to lead to a tragic end, like so many prophets before him, Jesus did something that, perhaps more than any other single act, sealed his fate. To more fully grasp the dramatic significance of this act, both historically and theologically, an understanding of its context is crucial.

The time was the annual Passover celebration, and the place, Jerusalem. The Passover celebration commemorated Israel's primary narrative, the Exodus. As thousands of Jews streamed into Jerusalem for this central religious holiday, the atmosphere was electric and volatile. As might be expected, the Roman military presence in Jerusalem during this religious/national holiday was greatly intensified, for the Exodus was not merely a memory of the distant past but a live hope among Jews for future emancipation from their Roman occupiers. Therefore, as all manner of pilgrims entered David's city, including those groups like the Zealots who openly spoke of a military overthrow of their oppressors, the slightest gesture of revolution was swiftly met by Rome's brutally efficient military. That Jesus and his followers entered Jerusalem under these combustible circumstances probably made him a marked man, but then Jesus engages in a provocative act at the very epicenter of the Jewish world:

> Then they came to Jerusalem. And he entered the temple and began to drive out those who were selling and those who were buying in the temple, and he overturned the tables of the money changers and the seats of those who sold doves; and he would not allow anyone to carry anything through the temple. He was teaching and saying, "Is it not written, 'My house shall be called a house of prayer for all the nations'? But you have made it a den of robbers." And when the chief priests and the scribes heard it, they kept looking for a way to kill him; for they were afraid of him, because the whole crowd was spellbound by his teaching. (Mk 11:15–18)

The Temple area was the public square of Jerusalem, the place where pilgrims would have first arrived to exchange currency and buy animals for sacrifice. In this symbolic act, Jesus challenges the Temple system as such and in particular, its aristocratic and priestly administrators, the Sadducees. Jesus was certainly not alone in criticizing the Temple system. Numerous Jewish groups were deeply troubled by how the Sadducees compromised with Roman authorities for the sake of self-preservation and privilege, not to mention the heavy taxation for its upkeep. As Jesus overturns the money-changing tables and disrupts the buying and selling in the Temple's perimeter, he forces to a halt the entire apparatus surrounding this central symbol. In effect, Jesus is saying the Temple no longer effectively mediates the presence of God for Israel. It is thoroughly corrupt, a "den of robbers."

Though Jesus' authority was frequently questioned throughout his ministry, this striking elevation in prophetic rhetoric especially provoked his opponents. As Mark relates in a succeeding passage, "The chief priests, the scribes, and the elders came to him and said, 'By what authority are you doing these things?'" (11:27–28) Who is this Jesus who challenges the Temple in this way, who presumes to authoritatively interpret the Law, who dares to forgive sins, who recklessly associates with the unclean, thus confusing what ought to be meticulously distinguished? Who is this who draws disciples unto himself—twelve, no less, to symbolize the number of Israel's tribes? What manner of man is this who would speak on behalf of Israel's God in this way?

Although Jesus (as portrayed in the Synoptic gospels) rarely speaks of his own person in any explicit or formal way—Jesus does not, for example, describe himself as the "second person of the Trinity" or "one in being with the Father," as later Church doctrines will—it becomes progressively clear in the converging pattern of his sayings and deeds that Jesus presumes to personally embody the reality of God in a unique and powerful way, as though the message of the Kingdom of God were directly and inseparably related to him, its messenger. He speaks and acts with an unprecedented authority. As scandalous as it may be, particularly within a monotheistic context, it becomes increasingly difficult to avoid identifying the person of Jesus with the God he reveals. With this move in our reflection, we are beginning to discover from the "ground up," that is, from the history and life-story of the man from Nazareth, who he ultimately is. That is to say, we are now thoroughly engaged in a process of Christological discovery, one that with the ensuing events of his death and resurrection will reach its decisive point of departure.

Crucifixion, Death, and Resurrection

In the passage previously cited, we read that following the incident at the Temple, various Jewish authorities sought to have Jesus killed. The provocation proved too much, especially given the context of Rome's zero-tolerance policy toward potential insurgency. Jesus is arrested and brought to stand trial before the Sanhedrin, a formal judicial assembly of chief priests, elders, and scribes. Various allegations are made against him, including blasphemy, messianic ambition, and threats against the Temple (Mk 14:53–65). Whatever the ultimate motivation for the Sanhedrin's handing over of Jesus to the Romans, perhaps foremost among them was the desire to quell any potential uprising that would result in a devastating response by Rome—not unlike what eventually happened forty years later when the Temple was destroyed (70 CE) to suppress a civil war. Assigning blame for Jesus' death is a delicate matter, but about this we can be quite clear: Both Jewish and Roman authorities were involved in Jesus' brutal execution. If Jesus had already aroused significant opposition among the powerful and elite within Israel, enough that some of them wanted Jesus dead, the fact that he was crucified indicates Roman involvement because crucifixion was a specifically Roman form of torture and execution reserved for non-Roman citizens. It was intended to be gruesome theatre, orchestrated to instill terror and compliance among an occupied populace.

With cruel irony, Jesus died on a cross with a plaque above his head inscribed with these words, "The King of the Jews." The so-called "anointed one" of Israel died a criminal's death. The Kingdom of God had not come, it seemed, but suffered demonstrable defeat as its chief messenger hung naked from a cross. Panic and fear set in among the disciples as they fled, leaving only the women to mourn at the tomb.

Now, had the story ended here, the man from Nazareth would be little more than a footnote in history. Jesus was certainly not the only Jew to be crucified, nor was he the only one hailed as Israel's "messiah." But Jesus' story does not end here, for not only will his once-dispersed and despairing group of disciples continue to tell the story of his life and death, but they also will begin proclaiming with boundless enthusiasm a most unlikely twist in its telling: that God raised this crucified Jesus from the dead, vindicated him in his messianic mission, and revealed him as "Lord." What is more, his death and resurrection grant salvation—the forgiveness of sins, a new freedom from the power of violence and death, and a sure hope in the future that all creation will attain its ultimate destiny. A passage from Acts 2 concisely and powerfully frames the essence of the early Church's proclamation. Here, as Peter addresses the people of Israel, he is able to "see" what was only obscure to him during Jesus' public ministry:

> "You that are Israelites, listen to what I have to say: Jesus of Nazareth, a man attested to you by God with deeds of power, wonders, and signs that God did through him among you, as you yourselves know— this man, handed over to you according to the definite plan and foreknowledge of God, you crucified and killed by the hands of those outside the law. But God raised him up, having freed him from death, because it was impossible for him to be held in its power. . . . This Jesus God raised up, and of that all of us are witnesses. . . . Therefore let the entire house of Israel know with certainty that God has made him both Lord and Messiah, this Jesus whom you crucified." . . . Peter said to them, "Repent, and be baptized every one of you in the name of Jesus Christ so that your sins may be forgiven; and you will receive the gift of the Holy Spirit." (Acts 2:22–24, 32, 36, 38)

At the beginning of this chapter, we observed that "thinking Christologically" requires an imagination open to paradox and surprise. That which appears to be utter failure becomes God's victory. This Jesus, who died not out of some masochistic death wish but because of his solidarity with the outsider, the unclean, and the sinner, becomes himself an outsider and a victim, one cursed as a common criminal. In other words, Jesus dies very much as a consequence of the life he led, and to the very end, even as he breathes his last, he offers peace and reconciliation to those who accuse and murder him. "Father, forgive them; for they do not know what they are doing" (Lk 23:34).

In this pattern of total self-giving love, even unto death, Jesus enacts a life-story that entails the reversal of conventional values. Authority comes not from domination but from humility; power is not manipulative but empowers others; authentic life results not from pursuing self-interest but dying to self. "Whoever wants to be first must be last of all and the servant of all" (Mk 9:35). Jesus' messianic vocation is not, therefore, a pursuit of a military revolution or the establishment of mighty fortresses but a vocation whose fundamental characteristic is living life wholly for the Other. "'You shall love the Lord your God with all your heart, and with all your soul, with all your mind, and with all your strength.' . . . [and] 'You shall love your neighbor as yourself.' There is no other commandment greater than these" (Mk 12:30–31). "No one has greater love than this, to lay down one's life for one's friends" (Jn 15:13).

Jesus' resurrection from the dead is not a kind of reward for a life well lived, nor is it merely a happy ending to an otherwise tragic story. It is an event filled with tremendous significance for understanding who God is and the destiny God has for human beings. By raising Jesus from the dead, God is revealed as one who sides with the outsider and marginalized, as one who provides an ultimate hope for the victimized and oppressed. God is the God of life and death, and no power or threat can vanquish the divine will of well-being for humanity. However, just as God is revealed as a God for the oppressed, the resurrection of Jesus is also an offer of forgiveness and grace. In the passage from Acts 2 previously cited, Peter declares that by raising Jesus from the dead, those who crucified him (and by extension, all who say "No" to God's Kingdom) are given the opportunity to be fully reconciled to God. Having become victim to the violent rejection of God's will for humanity, Jesus is raised victorious as God's ultimate "Yes." God's love for humanity is so excessive and tenacious that even though Jesus, commended by God to Israel, is rejected and crucified as a criminal, God raises him from the dead as the ultimate gift of life. As Saint Paul puts it, "And he died for all, so that those who live might live no longer for themselves, but for him who died and was raised for them. . . . So if anyone is in Christ, there is a new creation: everything old has passed away; see, everything has become new!" (2 Cor 5:15, 17).

How did the disciples come to believe in this "newness," and what specific meaning does resurrection language possess for Christians? This early Christian proclamation stands upon two pillars. The first was the discovery of the empty tomb by the women followers of Jesus. By itself, the empty tomb does not necessarily imply Jesus' resurrection. It remains an ambiguous sign, as there are many possible reasons why it might have been empty, including the possibility that the disciples stole Jesus' body (see Mt 27:62–66). The second pillar is the tradition of resurrection appearances in which Jesus reveals himself to his disciples as one who has triumphed over death. The accounts are varied, as a cursory examination of the gospels demonstrates.

Despite their diversity, however, they all agree on two basic points. First, the risen Jesus who appeared to the disciples is the self-same Jesus of Nazareth, not some apparition or hallucination. The gospels insist that Jesus, after his death and by the power of God, manifests himself in a way that is not the result of human imagination. The encounter comes from "beyond" them. Second, while this is the self-same Jesus of Nazareth the disciples knew and loved before his death, he is also transformed into a state of existence that is different from ordinary space–time existence. Jesus does not simply come back to life, as though he returns to his premortem life. Resurrection does not mean resuscitation; it means transformation—transformation into a manner of life that exceeds our capacity to imagine.

We may put it this way: Jesus' resurrection is both in full continuity with his historical existence and in discontinuity to the extent that he has passed through death and been given a life no longer susceptible to corruptibility. Jesus' total human existence has reached its final and eternal fulfillment in God, and it is just this fulfilled life with God for which human beings are made. Jesus' resurrection is the future of all creation, a future already present. The Kingdom has come in the very person of Jesus.

The Story Continues: The Christology of the New Testament Church

Understandably, the early Christian proclamation was met with resistance and/or misunderstanding. The gospels themselves relate that the disciples only gradually understood the nature and significance of this event. Nevertheless, once the

Ministry of Jesus

conviction set in, it completely revolutionized their imagination. As the disciples continued to tell and retell the remarkable events they witnessed, they began to see Jesus' life, death, and resurrection as the ultimate revelation of God to humanity. This process of telling the story is an act of Christology. Recalling the definition provided at the outset of this chapter, Christology is the attempt to formally articulate Jesus Christ's mission and identity, his relationship to God, and his significance for humanity. In the NT, several Christological statements and patterns attempt to say something important about his identity and mission. Let us briefly examine three.

Jesus as "Lord" (*Kyrios*)

Early on in the primitive Christian movement, Jesus was hailed as Israel's "messiah" and "Lord." In Greek, these words are *christos* and *kyrios* respectively. Importantly, Christians attributed to Jesus titles such as these in the context of worship—while they gathered in community to remember Jesus' deeds, death and resurrection; as they prayed through and rediscovered the scriptures; as they ritually enacted Jesus' last supper with his disciples before his death, and so on. The earliest Christians very much experienced the presence of the risen Christ among them, even singing hymns to him in a way that, from an outsider's point of view, might seem as though they regarded him as God. This is not to say that the earliest Christians had yet developed a specific vocabulary to speak of Jesus as "God," but the evolution of early Christian language and practice shows an unmistakable and steady process of coming to precisely this conclusion.

By hailing Jesus as "Lord," the earliest Christians were not just acknowledging Jesus' authority as God's true emissary in the world, and thus one to whom his disciples owed allegiance, but they were also saying something about Jesus' exalted status after his death. By raising him from the dead, God has triumphed over chaos, violence, and death. Jesus is "Lord" of creation, sovereign in human history, sovereign among the world's powers, be they social, political, or religious. Paul summarizes this conviction in one of his letters as he writes that, although many people allege and worship other gods, "for us there is one God, the Father, from whom are all things and for whom we exist, and one Lord, Jesus Christ, through whom are all things and through whom we exist" (1 Cor 8:5–6). One cannot help but notice the closest relationship between "God" and "Jesus" in this passage. Though explicitly monotheistic, both the "Father" and the "Lord Jesus Christ" *together* are sovereign over creation and human history.

Death and Resurrection/Exaltation Christology

In his letter to the Philippians, Paul quotes an early hymn that epitomizes a second Christological pattern. It too tells a story but does so in a condensed narrative format, rich with meaning and mystery:

Let the same mind be in you that was in Christ Jesus, who, though he was in the form of God, did not regard equality with God as something to be exploited, but emptied himself, taking the form of a slave, being born in human likeness. And being found in human form, he humbled himself and became obedient to the point of death—even death on a cross. Therefore God also highly exalted him and gave him the name that is above every name, so that at the name of Jesus every knee should bend, in heaven and on earth and under the earth, and every tongue should confess that Jesus Christ is Lord, to the glory of God the Father. (Phil 2:5–11)

Notice here the pattern of "descent" and "ascent." Jesus, though in the "form of God," empties himself (*kenosis*) and becomes the lowliest of the lowly, taking on a life of complete self-expenditure for others, even unto death on a cross. In Jesus, God's shocking humility is expressed. God's "power" is of the sort that it identifies with the powerless, itself becoming utterly vulnerable to the violent resistance of God's own creation. The "descent" is one of love. Yet, precisely because of this self-expenditure for others, God "raised him high" and gave Jesus the "name that is above every name." He "ascends" to the very honor of God the Father so that all should acknowledge Jesus Christ's lordship over creation. The pattern here echoes the very subversion and paradox we find in so many of Jesus' parables. Powerlessness becomes true power; humility becomes might; lowliness and service become transcendence and eminence. As Paul puts it elsewhere: "For God's foolishness is wiser than human wisdom, and God's weakness is stronger than human strength" (1 Cor 1:25). Jesus is God's living parable—his life, death, and resurrection the very embodiment of divine wisdom and love.

Wisdom and Logos Christology

A third Christological pattern exhibits what is sometimes described as "high Christology." Its counterterm is "low Christology." These spatial images are helpful when talking about Jesus as divine (high) and human (low). This Christological pattern begins by characterizing Jesus' ultimate identity and mission in relationship to the eternal wisdom of God, even before Jesus' historical existence. Let us look briefly at two notable examples.

He [Jesus] is the image of the invisible God, the firstborn of all creation;
For in him all things in heaven and on earth were created, things visible and invisible, whether thrones or dominions or rulers or powers—all things have been created through him and for him. He himself is before

all things, and in him all things hold together. . . . For in him all the fullness of God was pleased to dwell, and through him God was pleased to reconcile to himself all things, whether on earth or in heaven, by making peace through the blood of his cross. (Col 1:15–20)

Much could be said about this dense passage, but we must limit ourselves to just a few observations. First, this passage, also an early Christian hymn, draws deep from the well of Israel's wisdom tradition, as can be found in such OT writings as Proverbs, the Book of Wisdom, the Book of Sirach, Job, and many of the Psalms. What is distinctive about this Christological pattern is the way it speaks of Jesus as the personal embodiment of God's wisdom: the same wisdom originally bringing forth creation, the same wisdom responsible for order and beauty in the cosmos, the wisdom that inspires all human wisdom. As the "image of the invisible God," Jesus is the earthly and historical manifestation of divine transcendence. In Jesus, the fullness of God dwelt, reconciling humanity to God through the self-sacrifice of Jesus on the cross. Divine solidarity and forgiveness are together offered to humanity in his life, death, and resurrection. Because Jesus so thoroughly manifests God's original plan for creation, it is possible to say that all things were created in, through, and for him. Jesus is the completion of all creation. The future of creation is eschatologically realized *in* him.

Second, as an instance of "high Christology," this passage speaks of Jesus' ultimate identity by highlighting his preexistence. The exalted status of Jesus as "Lord" of creation revealed to his disciples after his resurrection is the identity Jesus always possessed, not only throughout his life but even prior to his historical existence, prior to creation itself. What God accomplished in and through Jesus Christ was God's plan for humanity all along. Jesus' ultimate identity and origin are not afterthoughts to creation but found in the heart of the eternal God.

This style of Christological reflection is even more explicit in the Prologue of John's gospel:

In the beginning was the Word [*Logos*], and the Word was with God, and the Word was God. He was in the beginning with God. All things came into being through him, and without him not one thing came into being. . . . He was in the world, and the world came into being through him; yet the world did not know him. He came to what was his own, and his own people did not accept him. But to all who received him . . . he gave power to become children of God . . . And the Word [*Logos*] became flesh and lived among us, and we have seen his glory, the glory as of a father's only son, full of grace and truth. (Jn 1:1–3, 10–12, 14)

The Greek word *Logos* used here, translated as "Word," bears important philosophical and theological implications for the history of Christology. John's gospel consciously weaves Jewish and Greek philosophical thought to describe Jesus as both the decree of God's will for humanity and the incarnation of the divine intelligence. In Stoic philosophy, the *Logos* is the intelligent and creative power bringing forth and sustaining creation. By poetically portraying the *Logos* as "becoming flesh" and "dwelling among us," John's gospel articulates a mature theology of incarnation, where the divine and preexistent Son of God enters into the world out of love in order to save it from sin, disorder, and darkness. As such, we find here a bold ascription of divinity to Jesus Christ, the same sort of ascription found later in John's gospel as it relates the apostle Thomas' reaction to encountering the risen Jesus: "My Lord and my God!" (Jn 20:28).

In answer to the question "Who is Jesus?" the gospel of John weaves poetry and narrative, Jewish and Greek thought, to say something that marks both the culmination of a process of Christological reflection in the NT and the indispensable foundation for all later Christian doctrine: He is the Son of God; the preexistent Wisdom of God become human; God's eternal Word who entered the world, was crucified, and rose to reveal God's saving love and glory.

Faithfully Interpreting the Story: The Christological Councils

Our final task in thinking Christologically is to understand something of the nature and purpose of the later Christological doctrines of the Church, particularly from the fourth and fifth centuries CE. To do so, let us review where we are now with the three touchstones that are our "grammatical rules" for properly speaking about Jesus, his relationship to God, and his significance for humanity.

The Three Christological Touchstones

All Christology derives from story.

Christian revelation is not primarily concerned with the production of abstract propositions about the nature of reality but with the telling and retelling of a story of salvation. God reveals God's self in the dramatic unfolding of historical events—in the story of Israel and, in a more focused and definitive way for Christians, in the life, death, and resurrection of Jesus Christ. Jesus' life is not just a parable lived out in the context of Israel's story but also one that reshapes and fulfills that context.

All Christology derives from an experience of salvation.

In Jesus, the earliest Christians encountered the liberating and forgiving love of God in a way that surprised and overwhelmed them. In the particulars of Jesus' life-story, God broke through the power of death with new life, overcame violent rejection with peace, and met sin with an unexpected offer of forgiveness. Formal reflection upon this experience of salvation is what Christian theology calls "soteriology." (*Sōtērion* in Greek means "deliverance.") As we have seen in our study, soteriology and Christology are closely related, and both are rooted in the story of Jesus' life, death, and resurrection. It is from the experience of salvation that the earliest Christians came to worship Jesus and more clearly understand his relationship to God. As Christians called to mind all that Jesus had said and done and what God had done for Jesus by raising him from the dead, they experienced the presence of the risen Christ among them. From this communal context of worship emerged a reflective process that would produce oral traditions, hymns, titles, epistles, prayers, and textual portraits that together form the basic linguistic and conceptual materials for all subsequent Christology.

All Christology derives from the conviction that in Jesus, God's presence in the world has taken hold in an unprecedented way.

This presence was so powerful that the earliest Christians felt compelled to ask this fundamental question: Who must Jesus be if in him salvation has come about? Put somewhat differently: If, in Jesus, God has been revealed in a new and decisive way, who, in the final analysis, is this Jesus? This line of questioning proceeds from what Jesus "does" to his "person," or his "being." To employ a technical term, we are moving here from a functional consideration to an *ontological* one. (*Ontology* in philosophy is the study of "being.") In the former case, we reflect upon Jesus' work of proclaiming and bringing about the good news of salvation, that is, the Kingdom of God. In the latter case, we reflect upon the "being" or "person" who in fact mediates this salvation. The fundamental logic of all Christology, one whose development we can trace in the NT, moves toward the affirmation of Jesus as God in human form. In Jesus, it is God who personally enters into human affairs.

The Council of Nicea (325 CE)

Such a conclusion creates a host of challenging questions, particularly within the context of monotheistic belief. For example, how is it possible to affirm that Jesus is somehow God while avoiding the undesirable conclusion that there are two gods? If we adopt John's language, namely that Jesus is the *Logos* become flesh, is this *Logos* to be thought of as God properly speaking or some lesser divinity? And how is it possible, if at all, for Christians to affirm that God "becomes" something when Christians also affirm that God is eternal and unchanging? Though these questions seem technical and perhaps unimportant, they actually created conflict and confusion within the Christian movement as it spread across the Mediterranean world and increasingly interacted with Greco-Roman culture and thought. Such confusion ultimately led to the need for Christian theologians and bishops to provide a conceptual framework to speak properly and consistently about Jesus' identity. This occurred at the Council of Nicea in 325 CE, a council convoked by the Emperor Constantine near his new city of Constantinople (Istanbul), and only twelve years after he declared Christianity a legal religion in the empire.

Precipitating this important council was the controversy sparked by the priest and theologian Arius (d. 336 CE). Arius argued that the only philosophically respectable and consistent position for Christians to hold was that the *Logos* is not eternal like the Father but created. While it is true that the gospel of John describes the *Logos* as preexisting the creation of the world, this does not preclude claiming that the *Logos* is created by God the Father as the first and greatest of all creations. Only the Father is eternal; everything else is by definition a creature. In point of fact, argued Arius, God is utterly simple in being and unchanging. If, as Christians say, the *Logos* "became" human, we have already admitted that the *Logos* is not eternal and unchanging like the Father. In the end, the *Logos* is created, even though it is the greatest of all creations. As Arius was fond of putting it, "There was a time when the *Logos* was not."

If, from one point of view, Arius's position could claim a certain degree of philosophical coherence, it could not quite account for the way in which Christians actually encountered God (and not some lesser divinity) in Jesus Christ. By saying that the *Logos* was not God properly speaking but only a creature, Arius could not adequately explain how the "fullness of God" dwelt in Jesus, to refer to the previous passage from Philippians, or how the *Logos* was both "with God" in the beginning and "was God," as John's prologue reads. The need to clarify matters in view of Arius's public and influential campaign became increasingly evident, so a council of bishops and theologians in Nicea addressed the matter in a way that would produce a formal confession of faith, one still recited today in the form of the "Nicene Creed" among the vast majority of Christians around the world. Couched in the middle section of this creed, we find a series of statements that directly respond to Arius's challenge. In particular, the creed states that Jesus is not created but eternally flows from the inexhaustible creativity of the Father (he is "eternally begotten of the Father"). Moreover, Jesus Christ, as the eternal Son of the Father, shares in the Father's very divinity. He is "one in being" (*homoousias*) with the Father.

While these statements are indeed technical, let us understand what they ultimately mean. By saying that Jesus Christ is "true God from true God" and "one in being" with the Father, the Nicene Creed is saying that in Christ, the very reality of God is available in a remarkably intimate and personal way. Jesus is God's self-expression in the world. The difference between the positions of Arius and the Council of Nicea might be illuminated by means of an analogy. If, on my wedding day, I sent someone close to me to stand at the altar with my bride, let us say my best friend who knows more about me and is closer to me than anyone else, someone I trust implicitly and for whom I have the deepest respect, still his presence would be only a substitute for mine. Though he may speak for me and have authorization to stand in my place, his presence would still not be me. And just imagine the reaction of my bride—assuming I still had a bride! The difference between Arius and the Council of Nicea is analogous in this respect: The council is claiming that God's very self is encountered in Christ, not just a creature of elevated status, not a proxy. Jesus is the personal manifestation of God in the world in such a way that we can exclaim, as did Thomas, "My Lord and my God!"

From the Council of Constantinople (381 CE) to the Council of Chalcedon (451 CE)

Perhaps understandably, this ascription of divinity to Jesus Christ led to an opposite problem, one that existed as early as the first century but would eventually require the Church to make a clarifying and corrective doctrinal statement almost 125 years after Nicea. In the decades following the council, debate raged over how to understand the relationship between the humanity and divinity in Jesus Christ himself. If the Church believes that he is "one in being with the Father," does this mean he is still human? If so, in what way? Such questions became pressing because some so emphasized Jesus' divinity that it became difficult to account for his humanity. The bishop Apollinaris (d. ca. 390) of Laodicea, just south of the major Christian city of Antioch on the Mediterranean coast of Syria, intended to be faithful to the Nicene definition but ended up claiming that Jesus was a kind of "mixture" of humanity and divinity. Though Jesus possessed the body of a human, Apollinaris argued, his soul and mind were totally divine. To put it somewhat crudely, the *Logos* essentially inhabited the shell of a human body, somewhat like a driver sitting inside and operating a car.

The chief problem with this approach, however, is that it makes Jesus no longer fully human. He only possesses the appearance of being human when in fact his inner makeup and consciousness are divine. Such a view would hardly satisfy the NT's insistence that Jesus was in every way like a human being, except sin (Phil 2:5–8; Heb 4:15). Moreover, it contradicts an axiom that had prevailed in Christian theology for some time, an axiom that flows out of a fully developed theology of the incarnation: "What has not been assumed is not saved." What this phrase means is that God saves humanity by assuming (or personally taking on) all aspects of the human condition with the purpose of transforming and elevating humanity toward its ultimate fulfillment. If Jesus were without a human soul, then we are left with the absurd conclusion that the human body has been saved but not the human soul. Salvation is the transformation of the whole person, so the logic goes, not just a part of the person.

Such were the counterarguments of Apollinaris's opponents. And, in fact, Apollinaris's position was formally rejected by the Council of Constantinople in 381. However, among those who opposed Apollinaris in order that Jesus' full humanity might be protected, some quite publicly introduced other kinds of errors that would eventually require clarification. For example, a bishop from Constantinople named Nestorius (d. ca. 451) so emphatically insisted on distinguishing Jesus' divine and human natures that he could not properly account for the unity of Jesus' person. This became particularly evident as Nestorius argued that Mary, the mother of Jesus, was not the "mother of God" (*Theotokos*), as she was celebrated to be in Christian hymns at the time, but only the mother of Jesus' humanity. For Nestorius, this distinction was necessary to safeguard the integrity of each nature. Unfortunately, this solution only created the opposite problem of suggesting that in Jesus Christ there are two distinct persons, one divine and one human. The confusion this unseemly conclusion produced required yet another definition for the Church to articulate, which is just what the Council of Chalcedon set out to do in 451.

The formal definition of the Council of Chalcedon reads as follows:

[We teach believers] to acknowledge one and the same Son, our Lord Jesus Christ,

at once complete in Godhead and complete in manhood, truly God and truly man, consisting also of a reasonable soul and body;

of one substance ["one in being"] with the Father as regards his Godhead,

and at the same time of one substance ["one in being"] with us as regards his manhood;

like us in all respects, apart from sin;

as regards his Godhead, begotten of the Father before the ages,

but yet as regards his manhood begotten, for us and for our salvation, of Mary the Virgin, the God-bearer [*Theotokos*]. . . .

The distinction of natures being in no way annulled by the union,

but rather the characteristics of each nature being preserved and coming together to form one person.

This statement affirms that Jesus Christ is fully human and fully divine, not partly one or the other, contrary to Apollinaris. Moreover, the human ("manhood") and divine natures are united in one person, the one Jesus Christ, so that it is proper to say, contrary to Nestorius, that Mary is the God-bearer, or *Theotokos*. She does not just bear the humanity of Jesus but the whole person of Jesus Christ. The implication of Nestorius's position would lead to an intolerable split between Jesus' humanity and divinity. Chalcedon stresses the unity of his person.

In sum, then, in Jesus Christ, the fullness of God is expressed in human form. He not only most fully and definitively reveals God to human beings, but he also reveals the fulfillment of the human person. He is humanity at its most actualized, precisely *because* he is united with God. As a human person, he is "God-with-us," *Emmanuel* (Mt 1:23).

Conclusion: The Neverending Question

The councils of Nicea and Chalcedon provided an enduring conceptual framework for Christology for over fifteen-hundred years. As a summary expression of the Church's mature faith in Jesus Christ, they function like a set of grammatical rules to assist Christians in properly understanding and speaking of the mission and identity of Jesus Christ. As doctrines, they do not replace the story of Jesus found in the NT; rather, they serve to establish the parameters by which Christians may continue to read, interpret, and reflect upon that story without falling into critical errors.

Yet, "thinking Christologically" is an ongoing and dynamic activity. Although these conciliar statements are fundamental to Christian faith, they should not replace the activity of actually doing Christology. Every generation of Christians is charged with the task of asking the question, "Who do you say I am?" Whether asked in the first or twenty-first century, this question invites new insights and unexpected perspectives upon God and humanity. As we have seen, it is just the sort of question that may radically challenge and even transform a person's perception of the world and way of life. Perhaps appropriately, then, we end this chapter with a series of questions that ask students new to theology to continue thinking Christologically in their own context.

Questions about the Text

1. What are the three touchstones that structure Christological reflection?

2. What does the word *Christ* mean?

3. What does the word *eschatological* mean?

4. What does the "Kingdom of God" mean?

5. What word and its meaning are conveyed in the image at the beginning of John's gospel?

6. What was the theological concern at the Council of Nicea? At the Council of Chalcedon? Explain the development that lead from Nicea to the conclusions at Chalcedon.

Questions for Discussion

1. This chapter argues that "thinking Christologically" frequently challenges our assumptions about Jesus and God. As you read this chapter, what aspects of Jesus' ministry and his revelation of God most challenge your own assumptions?

2. Who are today's "Samaritans"?

3. Why, historically speaking, did Jesus die? Why are these historical factors theologically significant?

4. After reading the section on miracles, do you think miracles happen today? Have you experienced or do you know about anything along this line of human experience?

5. Do you think people today have a harder time appreciating Jesus' humanity or his divinity? Why?

6. What are some of the ways Jesus' life-ministry can continue to be a powerful force for social transformation today?

For Further Study

Christology

Alison, James. *Knowing Jesus*. London: SPCK, 1993.

Borg, Marcus J. *Meeting Jesus Again for the First Time: The Historical Jesus and the Heart of Contemporary Faith*. New York: HarperSanFrancisco, 1994.

Brown, Raymond E. *An Introduction to New Testament Christology*. New York: Paulist Press, 1994.

Johnson, Elizabeth A. *Consider Jesus: Waves of Renewal in Christology*. New York: Herder & Herder/Crossroad, 2002.

Kasper, Walter. *Jesus the Christ*. Trans. V. Green. New York: Paulist Press, 1976.

Lane, Dermot. *The Reality of Jesus*. New York: Paulist Press, 1976.

Loewe, William P. *The College Student's Introduction to Christology*. Collegeville, MN: The Liturgical Press, 1996.

Norris, Richard. *The Christological Controversy*. Philadelphia: Fortress Press, 1980.

Pelikan, Jaroslav. *Jesus through the Centuries: His Place in the History of Culture*. New Haven, CT: Yale University Press, 1985.

Senior, Donald. *Jesus: A Gospel Portrait*. New York: Paulist Press, 1992.

Thompson, William M. *The Jesus Debate: A Survey and Synthesis*. New York: Paulist Press, 1985.

Wright, N. T. *The Challenge of Jesus: Rediscovering Who Jesus Was and Is*. Downers Grove, IL: InterVarsity Press, 1999.

The passages from the Councils of Nicea and Chalcedon are taken from *Documents of the Christian Church*, ed. Henry Bettenson, second ed. (Oxford: Oxford University Press, 1963).

From the Reference Librarian
Researching Theological Topics—Christology

Once again, we start at the beginning.

Skill Key #1

Use the library's reference collection to begin your research.

a) Use a subject-specific encyclopedia to acquire specialized knowledge about a subject.

b) Use a subject-specific encyclopedia whose scope is appropriate for both your topic and the approach you want to take to that topic.

Let's begin this time by addressing further the matter of the scope of an encyclopedia. In this chapter, you have encountered the names of several persons who figured prominently in the development of Christological views in the Church. Therefore, you may want to conduct further research on a particular person, such as Athanasius or Apollinaris. One important way that encyclopedias vary in scope is the inclusion (or not) of biographical articles. Because not all encyclopedias include such articles, you will obviously want to use one that does for this kind of research. Conversely, if you are researching a concept or idea, you should know that some reference works contain only biographical articles and are therefore of no use to you in this case. If you are researching an event (such as a church council), then the reference tool you use must include historical coverage; not all reference works do. Finally, some comprehensive reference works try to include all these types of entries; often (but not always), these are multivolume encyclopedias.

Let's start with research on a person. The first question in determining the appropriate encyclopedia to use is simply "What person am I researching?" If your interest is in the Christological views of Paul or one of the NT gospel writers, for example, you could use one of the reference tools listed at the end of the chapter on the NT. However, if you want to research one of the early Church fathers, such as Athanasius or Apollinaris, you must turn to some other tool, one whose scope extends beyond the NT. Here are some examples:

Patrick W. Carey and Joseph T. Lienhard, eds. *Biographical Dictionary of Christian Theologians*. Westport, CT: Greenwood Press, 2000.

As indicated by the title, this is limited to biographical entries only and covers all eras of Church history.

Trevor A. Hart. *The Dictionary of Historical Theology*. Grand Rapids, MI: William B. Eerdmans, 2000.

The title offers a hint about the scope of this reference work; it offers coverage of persons and events (history) but not much on concepts (there are no entries on *homoousias*, *kenosis*, or *Logos*, for example).

Adrian Hastings, ed. *The Oxford Companion to Christian Thought*. Oxford: Oxford University Press, 2000.

This "companion" includes coverage of all the types of subjects mentioned previously: persons, events, concepts. In this case, *companion* is synonymous with *dictionary* or *encyclopedia*; however, the use of *companion* in the title may also indicate a collection of longer essays on broader topics as opposed to a dictionary-type collection of shorter, more focused entries that are alphabetically arranged.

E.A. Livingstone, ed. *The Oxford Dictionary of the Christian Church*. Third ed. rev. Oxford: Oxford University Press, 2005.

This dictionary also includes coverage of all types of subjects.

As it happens, three out of these four reference works have entries/articles for both Athanasius and Apollinaris. However, *The Oxford Companion to Christian Thought* has an entry for Athanasius but none for Apollinaris. (Remember, in a one-volume work that tries to cover the entire range of Church history, sometimes something has to be left out.) So, if your interest is in Apollinaris, the following question may arise.

Student: What if there is no article on the person I'm researching?

This is the appropriate point to further expand our repertoire of basic library skills as follows.

Skill Key #1

Use the library's reference collection to begin your research.

a) Use a subject-specific encyclopedia to acquire specialized knowledge about a subject.

b) Use a subject-specific encyclopedia whose scope is appropriate for both your topic and the approach you want to take to that topic.

c) Use encyclopedia bibliographies to identify subject headings for your topic.

d) Use a concise subject-specific dictionary to look up the specialized vocabulary of a particular field.

e) Use an encyclopedia's index to locate information on subjects (including person) for which there is no separate article.

Never give up on a reference work if you do not find an article specific to your topic. Information on your subject may be "buried" somewhere in an article on some other subject. The editors of the *Companion to Christian Thought* have thoughtfully prepared for such an eventuality by providing an index of names at the back of the book that "contains only the names of people who do *not* [emphasis added] have their own entry, and is intended to supplement the full list of articles...." Browsing through this index, you would find an entry for "Apollinaris (of Laodicea)" with cross-references to six other articles in the volume.

Apollinaris (of Laodicea)

Chalcedon, Council of;

Decetism; Greek

Theology; Incarnation;

Monophysitism;

Nestorianism

(From *Oxford Companion to Christian Thought*, Adrian Hastings, ed. Oxford: Oxford University Press, 2000.)

These include articles on "Chalcedon, Council of," "Docetism," "Incarnation," and "Monophysitism," all of which would be relevant to the topic of Christology. This underscores the importance of digging a little deeper when you do not find what you are looking for right away. The point is this: *Always check to see if an encyclopedia has an index (and what kind of index it has).*

The index will also be of importance for the books you find in the library catalog. Let's say you are looking for books on Athanasius and his views of Christology. After using an encyclopedia bibliography to provide an access point to the catalog, you may have discovered a book with a subject heading like the following (note again the descriptive phrase added to the name):

Search Format:

Last Name	Descriptive phrase	Subdivision 1
Athanasius	Saint, Patriarch of Alexandria, d. 373	Contributions in Christology

Such "Contributions in . . ." subdivisions often appear after the names of persons as subject headings and indicate the contributions made by those individuals in whatever field is then specified. Obviously, the subject heading shown would indicate a book precisely on your topic of interest—the Christological views of Athanasius—and a book devoted entirely to that topic, so this subject heading certainly fulfills the recommendation we have made to "use subject headings whose scope fits your topic as closely as possible." (The Library of Congress has recently started to do away with the "Contributions in . . ." subdivision. However, many libraries, especially those with a significant theology collection, continue to use this subdivision because it enables researchers to locate specific books about theologians who have a large number of books written about them, for example, Thomas Aquinas or Martin Luther. If your library catalog does not use the "Contributions in . . ." subdivision, you can accomplish the same thing by combining two or more subject headings in a single search. This search technique will be presented in chapter 5.)

Remember, however, that another part of the recommendation is to "adjust your search with a broader or narrower subject heading as necessary." One example of why that may be necessary is that a book does not have to be entirely about Athanasius's views on Christology in order to contain information on that subject. Look at the following titles located by a subject search on Athanasius, Saint, Patriarch of Alexandria, d. 373, none of which has the "Contributions in Christology" subdivision.

Khaled Anatolios. *Athanasius: The Coherence of his Thought*. London: Routledge, 1998.

Michael E. Molloy. *Champion of Truth: The Life of Saint Athanasius*. Staten Island, NY: Alba House, 2003.

Alvyn Pettersen. *Athanasius*. Milwaukee, WI: Morehouse Publishing, 1995.

Now I have to let you in on one of those little secrets your professors do not want you to know. Did you ever wonder how they have time to read all those books and articles they list in bibliographies of the works they write? The truth is they do not read everything in those lists. (Maybe a few have, but they are rare.) What they do is try to find the parts of books that are relevant to what they are writing. They do that using one of two features every book intended for use by serious students should have—a table of contents and a subject index.

For example, the book *Champion of Truth*, by Molloy, lists the following two chapters in its table of contents:

Chapter 2: The Arians

Chapter 3: The Council of Nicea

Based on what you have read in this chapter, you should recognize that you are likely to find out most of what the author has to say on the topic of Athanasius and Christology in these two chapters. Molloy also includes a bibliography at the end of the book, providing you with more potential source material. However, the fact that there is no index in this book should tell you something about its intended audience—namely, an audience not interested in using an index. This, plus the fact that the book is only 136 pages and the publisher specializes in "popularized" treatments of theological subjects (you will learn to notice these kinds of things, or the librarian will often know), should tell you that the book is aimed at a general, not a scholarly, audience. There is nothing wrong with that, but it may be important to know, especially if your instructor wants you to use more-scholarly works. On the other hand, such "popular" treatments are often easier to understand and helpful for the student just beginning theological study.

In another example, the book *Athanasius: The Coherence of His Thought*, by Anatolios, lists only four chapters in its table of contents. Each chapter title includes the phrase "the Relation between God and Creation." None of the four chapter titles makes it clear where in the book Athanasius's Christological views are discussed. Fortunately, this book was published by an academic publisher and is equipped with an index. (You are not expected to know which publishers are academic, popular, or some mixture of the two; if you want to know, the librarian can help.)

In Anatolios's index, you will find numerous page references under "Christ, doctrine of" in the index. You will also find subdivisions under "Christ, doctrine of," such as "'appropriation' model," "human body of," "human soul of," and "*Logos-sarx* model." You will also see cross-references to other entries in the index, such as "incarnation" or "redemption." The point is that you want to make the most-efficient use of your time by using the index to focus precisely on your topic.

Christ, doctrine of 2, 37, 67–84,
138–61, 212 n. 9;
"appropriation" model 38, 80,
82–3, 141–55, 160, 174–5;
Human body of 47, 63, 70–8,
159; human soul of 2, 77–8,
127–8, 169, 201–2, 206, 226
n. 116; *Logos-sarx* model 70–3;
predication model 80–4, 140–6,
150, 226 n. 121; suffering of
78–84, 143–55; *see also* incarnation, redemption
(From Khaled Anatolios, *Athanasius: The Coherence of His Thought*. London: Routledge, 1998.)

Student: What if I am interested in a more modern understanding of Christology?

Once again, it is a matter of starting with an encyclopedia whose scope encompasses a modern systematic treatment of Christology. The following standard reference titles all include such treatment and are likely to be found in Catholic college and university libraries.

Joseph A. Komonchak, Mary Collins, and Dermot A. Lane, eds. *The New Dictionary of Theology*. Wilmington, DE: Michael Glazier, Inc., 1987.

Wolfgang Beinert and Francis Schüssler Fiorenza. *Handbook of Catholic Theology*. New York: Crossroad, 1995.

The following reference work combines both historical and systematic coverage. Note that what is distinctive of this reference tool is that most articles have the same five-fold structure: (1) biblical background, (2) history of theology, (3) Church teaching, (4) ecumenical perspectives, and (5) systematic reflections.

René Latourelle and Rino Fisichella, eds. *Dictionary of Fundamental Theology*. New York: Crossroad, 1994.

The scope of an encyclopedia can vary in yet other ways. For example, one important aspect of the scope of an encyclopedia that includes historical coverage is the range of its chronological coverage. Most of the reference tools mentioned to this point cover the entire range of Church history, but note the chronological limitation indicated by the following title:

Everett Ferguson, ed. *Encyclopedia of Early Christianity*. Second ed., 2 vols. New York: Garland Publishing, 1997.

To determine precisely what belongs to the period of the "early Church" (what year it ends and another period begins), you need to read the preface or introduction to the encyclopedia.

Another encyclopedia might cover all periods of Church history yet focus on one particular aspect of the history:

Leslie Houlden, ed. *Jesus in History, Thought, and Culture: An Encyclopedia*. 2 vols. Oxford, UK: ABC-CLIO, 2003 (also published as *Jesus: The Complete Guide*. New York: Continuum, 2005).

Such titles as these, by narrowing the scope of coverage, offer treatment of more subjects and more-detailed treatment of those subjects than a reference work encompassing all of Christian history and theology. Both of these more narrowly focused encyclopedias would be appropriate for studying Christology.

By now, you should have a good grasp of not just the importance of an encyclopedia's scope but also the kinds of questions involved in determining that scope. Does an encyclopedia include biographical coverage? Historical coverage? Coverage of systematic concepts? Is it limited chronologically or in some other way?

Student Tasks

1. Find an encyclopedia article on a theologian who was important for the development of Christology. Identify a particular theological idea or concept associated with that theologian and find an encyclopedia article on it (you may have to use a different encyclopedia).

2. Find an encyclopedia article relevant to some aspect of Christology (for example, one of the Christological titles such as "Lord" or "son of God," or background articles such as "Kingdom of God," "election," "eschatology," "wisdom," or "*Logos*"). Find an article on one theologian whose name you come across in the article (you may have to use a different encyclopedia).

3. Find an encyclopedia article on one of the ecumenical councils where Christological issues were discussed in the early Church. Identify and find an additional article on either an important theological concept (other than Christology in general) discussed during the council or a theologian who was prominent at the council (you may have to use a different encyclopedia).

4. Locate one book on Christology with an index and browse through it, examining the way it presents various topics in the book. What topic, from all those included, would you like to pursue? Can you find an encyclopedia article on it?

4

The People of God: The Church

From the Editor

When a child comes into the world, she usually receives a family name. The child belongs, is family, and shares in its reality, and without the child, the family may not exist some day. This child will carry the family forward into the future. Parents, siblings, grandparents, aunts, uncles, and the communities that surround them assume a necessary responsibility and obligation to nurture, care for, provide for, and love this child, as well as instruct her in the ways of living.

Being a Christian is analogous: It means belonging to a family, being truly identified as one of the family—one belongs. One even receives a new family name with the identity—Christian. This person now belongs to God through Jesus with the rest of the Christian family and is responsible and obligated to love God and neighbor and do all this implies.

Ecclesiology is the area of theology that studies living in the Church as a member of the Church's family—its history, variety, structures, and decisions; its past, present, and future. The source of it all, like a stone thrown into a still pond that sends ripples out in every direction, is God, who sent us Jesus Christ, gave us the Holy Spirit, and invited us into this familial love relationship as disciples.

To examine two-thousand years of Christian tradition, even briefly, is something that cannot be done here fully. What we can do is provide understanding of some key foundational theological concepts. We will go back to the early sources of the Church in scripture, with an eye on its structures and strategies for living in the world and proclaiming the gospel. We will see the role that scripture took as well. Then we will examine important understandings of some of the decisions in history and their ramifications for today and perhaps tomorrow.

One lesson we have entered into and that will continue to be demonstrated in the rest of the chapters is that the Church is always in motion, alive and seeking to follow Christ in true discipleship; thus, its theological investigation is never finished. To put it simply, because theological knowledge is an investigation that is always seeking understanding, the more that theologians know, the more there is *to* know.

The People of God: The Church

Daniel Finucane, PhD

An Image

Imagine sitting at the edge of large, peaceful pond. Into the water drops a stone. From the spot where it enters, ripples slowly spread out across the surface. Expanding waves swell to lift whatever is in their path. On the water, floating twigs and living things react and move. Fish and other creatures in the pond feel the effects. Some objects on the surface that are touched form new ripples that spread along their own courses. Expanding circles carry the record of an unexpected event that moves both the water and the things that live in its depths.

The event that we find at the beginning of the Christian Church is a person—the Christ-Event (life–death–resurrection). In the earliest description we have of the Church, we hear preaching—news of Jesus of Nazareth alive and then risen—done by his followers. This event/message is called the *kerygma*, a Greek word meaning "proclamation" or "announcement." In a striking turnaround, the same people who ran away to save their lives when Jesus was arrested and killed are described in Jerusalem shortly after, calling Jesus the Christ (*Messiah* in Hebrew) and the Lord of all creation. Looking back on their own scriptures, they describe Jesus Christ as a stone rejected by other builders who has become a cornerstone for a new living building—a gathering together of people (see Ps 118:22, Mk 12:10, 1 Pet 2: 4–8). In the pond metaphor, the risen Jesus is the stone that enters the waters of human history and sends ripples through the centuries.

Each person who joins himself or herself to Jesus Christ in baptism (from the Greek word *baptismo*, "to immerse") adds new ripples. Saint Paul writes that we become part of Christ himself (1 Cor 12:12–13). As Jesus draws people into a living body, richer, larger, more complex waves of movement are created. Christ's ongoing presence and message grow in depth and strength.

What Then Is the Church?

We begin with the etymology of the root word for the insights it gives us. Originally, the Christians borrowed from the Hebrew word *kahal*, which meant those who were "assembled and assembling in the Lord." The Greek word used by early Christians was *ekklesia*, which meant "assembly" and which became *ecclesia* in Latin. This word is still heard in the Romance ("Roman" or Latin-based) languages of Spanish (*iglesia*), French (*eglise*), and Italian (*chiesa*). When the Christian faith spread to northern Europe, emphasis was placed on assembling "in the Lord's (house)" (Greek = *kyriakon*), which became in German, *kirche*; and in English, *church*. In these etymologies, the key point is that it is an assembly that continues to gather for the purpose of worship of the Lord. In the academic discipline of theology, the study of the Church is called "ecclesiology."

We now move to the traditional definition of *church*, which is offered in the *Catechism of the Catholic Church*: "In Christian usage, the word *church* designates the liturgical assembly, but also the local community or the whole universal community of believers. These three meanings are inseparable" (#752). But why this gathering? What is it called to do? How are these people connected to each other and to later generations? As we follow the story of the Church, we will concentrate on its basic roots. A full look at Church history would include discussion of the way the Church leadership follows a hierarchy of offices. We would find too that many Christian communities have expressed their identity as a community of disciples. As Saint Paul reminds us, there are many gifts in this body of Christians (1 Cor 12:4–11).

How the Ripples Started

As we reflect on how the Christ-Event sends ripples through history, we can find no better place to begin than the scriptural passage in Acts (2:1–47) that has since ancient times shown the Church, those who are immersed with Christ, what their common birth looked like and what it meant. In first-century Jerusalem, after Jesus ascends into heaven and the Holy Spirit is poured out upon the disciples on the feast of Pentecost (which coincided with the Jewish holy festival of the first fruits of the grain harvest in the spring, sometimes called the feast of "weeks" and called in Greek the "fiftieth" [Ex 23:14–17]), the apostle Peter emerges from the upper room and addresses a crowd made up of people from all over the known world, telling them of God's breathtaking work, how it is described by the prophets, and how it is meant to spread. When Peter is asked by his hearers, "What happens next?" we can see how the impact of the *kerygma* begins to play out in their lives:

> Now when they heard this, they were cut to the heart and said to Peter and to the other apostles, "Brothers, what should we do?" Peter said to them, "Repent, and be baptized every one of you in the name of Jesus Christ so that your sins may be forgiven; and you will receive the gift of the Holy

Spirit. For the promise is for you, for your children, and for all who are far away, everyone whom the Lord our God calls to him." And he testified with many other arguments and exhorted them, saying, "Save yourselves from this corrupt generation." So those who welcomed his message were baptized, and that day about three thousand persons were added. They devoted themselves to the apostles' teaching and fellowship, to the breaking of bread and the prayers. Awe came upon everyone, because many wonders and signs were being done by the apostles. All who believed were together and had all things in common; they would sell their possessions and goods and distribute the proceeds to all, as any had need. Day by day, as they spent much time together in the temple, they broke bread at home and ate their food with glad and generous hearts, praising God and having the goodwill of all the people. And day by day the Lord added to their number those who were being saved. (Acts 2:37–47)

Waves of later generations will be moved by the gospel; they too will be shaped by arguments and exhortations. They too will be challenged by corruption and shaped by communal life. When they succeed in handing on what they have received, it will be because they devote themselves together to the breaking of the bread. The foundations for the Church are in place early on, developing in structures and forms we recognize today.

The Church Is a Paradox

As an ongoing event related to the Christ-Event, the Church is always a combination of stability and movement. It is a place for believers to recognize each other and take strength from coming together. It is also where believers gather so they can be sent out. The Church is where the Spirit of God creates us and moves us. Vatican Council II teaches:

When the work which the Father gave the Son to do on earth (cf. Jn 17:4) was accomplished, the Holy Spirit was sent on the day of Pentecost in order that he might continually sanctify the Church, and that, consequently those who believe might have access through Christ in one Spirit to the Father (Eph 2:18). He is the Spirit of life, the fountain of water springing up to eternal life (cf. Jn 4:47; 7:38–39). . . . Guiding the Church in the way of all truth (cf. Jn 16:13) and unifying her in communion and in the works of ministry, he bestows upon her varied hierarchic and charismatic gifts, and in this way directs her; and he adorns her with his fruits (cf. Eph 4:11–12; 1 Cor 12:4; Gal 5:22). (*Lumen Gentium* 4)

This modern description of the Holy Spirit in the Church is nothing more than a modern expression—the latest ripple—of the early insight of Saint Paul:

> Now there are varieties of gifts, but the same Spirit; and there are varieties of services, but the same Lord; and there are varieties of activities, but it is the same God who activates all of them in everyone. To each is given the manifestation of the Spirit for the common good. (1 Cor 12:4–7)

An Ongoing Vision for the *Ekklesia*

The event of the pouring out of the Holy Spirit of God at Pentecost sets out a vision and a mandate; from the start, the Church gathers diverse people. Central to this story is the message that unity is built in diversity. Saint Paul writes that we need each other in order to be the Body of Christ. We all have gifts or charisms (the Greek word *charis* means "grace"). These gifts are given for all who embrace Christ and are given the Holy Spirit. What is rippling in the Church? The presence of the Spirit of God, to enliven, to inspire different talents, and yet, to unify.

The Second Vatican Council takes up the root meaning of *ekklesia* when it emphasizes the biblical image of the Church as "The People of God." It is tempting to think of the Church in terms of its leaders, to see the Church as the pope and the bishops, but the council reminded us that the Church is everyone gathered. Recalling the words of 1 Peter 2:9–10, the council describes followers of Christ as "a chosen race, a royal priesthood, a holy nation . . . who in times past were not a people, but now are the People of God" (see *Lumen Gentium* 9).

This is a people who live in and change the world with the gospel message. Vatican II captures that activity with another image: We are a Pilgrim Church (see *Lumen Gentium* 48). Pilgrims are people who are going somewhere. They seek a destination. They travel a certain way. The less baggage they carry, the better. The better their sight and sense of direction, the better they understand their journey, and the better they know their companions, the more effective they are in meeting challenges and arriving at their new home.

Starting with the group that Jesus chose to follow him and sent to spread the good news of the reign of God coming near, the apostles themselves, the Church has had to face a paradoxical challenge. In order to be true to the apostolic message, it has had to adapt and reexamine its structures and practices. In the unfolding generations, bishops, understood as successors to the apostles, preached the gospel and brought unity to the Church by rehearsing its story. Over the years, the Church has gathered these leaders into councils to respond to new controversies and deepen the Church's understanding of the gospel. When it traveled to new lands and learned to speak new languages, Christianity remained true to its mandate to preach to all nations, and in doing so, it became inculturated. The Church expresses the face of Christ in the features and manner of each group that embraces the gospel. In baptism, the Eucharist, the leadership of bishops, the basic creeds, and the canon of scripture, the identity of the Church is preserved and at the same time evolves and moves as a living tradition. Pope John XXIII expressed this basic way of life in the Church when he opened the Second Vatican Council in 1962 with the words, "The substance of the ancient doctrine of the deposit of faith is one thing, and the way in which it is presented is another" (Abbott, 1966, 715). He challenged the council fathers to take up the work of *aggiornamento* (to bring "up to date") to bring the gospel to the modern world. To do so, he wanted to throw open the doors to the world. The council soon invited Catholic women to attend, as well as people of other Christian denominations and other experts from around the world. Pope John's successor, Pope Paul VI, and other council leaders worked to deepen the Roman Catholic Church's cooperation with other Christians, as well as with women and men from other religious traditions. This bore fruit most notably in the council's document on ecumenism (*Unitatis Redintegratio*) and its document on the Church and non-Christian religions (*Nostra Aetate*).

We will take up Pope John's challenge again in this chapter. Our first task is to understand how the Church has "rippled" through history as a living tradition and how the Church can continue and deepen those ripples today.

After That First Day

How *has* the Church adapted and grown in Christ? Two significant challenges faced the first generations of Christians.

In the Church's earliest years, the followers of Jesus were a subgroup of Judaism. Jesus, his apostles, and his other early followers were Jewish. After experiencing Jesus alive in the resurrection, his followers continued to worship God in the Temple and obey the Jewish Law. They kept kosher and observed the Sabbath on the last day of the week. They also believed Jesus was the Christ, the fulfillment of God's promise; he was Lord over death, the Messiah, and the fulfillment of the

Law. On the first day of the week, they met in their homes to break bread and experience Jesus present with them. Eventually, Gentiles were attracted to the new group. The question arose, "Did these people need to become Jews to be followers of Christ?" After significant turmoil (see Acts 15:1–29, Gal 5:2–12), the young Christian community, led by the arguments of Saint Paul, accepted the fact that baptism, rather than circumcision (the male rite of entrance into the Judaic covenant), made a Christian person a son or daughter of God (Gal 3:26–29). The book of Acts describes how the apostles met in Jerusalem in 49 CE, in what is the first recorded council, to argue the issue. In the process, the Jewish subgroup developed a new sort of relationship to its mother religion, Judaism, and stepped out into the world as a new way of following God. (Early on, the movement was, in fact, called "the Way" [see Acts 9:2, 22:4].)

As the first generation of Christians gave way to the next wave of believers, another challenge met them. The early Church believed Jesus was going to return soon to complete the work of the reign of God. The oldest text from the New Testament (NT), the first letter of Paul to the Thessalonians, illustrates how sure they were that Jesus' return would be in their own lifetimes (see 1 Thess 4:13–5:11). Yet, many Christians began to die. The apostles, the foundational witnesses to the resurrection, began to pass away before the return of the Lord. Eventually, the community realized it was going to be around for a while. With this shift in expectation about the time of Jesus' return, the community developed a new strategy for passing on the teachings of Jesus. Written gospels were compiled that carried the parables, healings, and sayings of Jesus, along with the narrative of his life, death, and resurrection. A new strategy for carrying the tradition was created.

A Historical Resource

In this chapter, we cannot take on every important challenge Christians have faced over twenty centuries or look at every development that has helped create the contemporary Church, nor can we go into all the new questions that arise in every age where "faith seeks understanding." An example of an ancient and yet ongoing example of how the Church expresses a living tradition is found in the creeds, said weekly at the Sunday services of many different Christian communities. (Later, we will suggest more topics from Church history that those who are interested in further study can pursue.)

Christians from a wide variety of denominations recite a creed (Lat., *credo* = "I believe"). The one Catholics pray after the scriptural readings of the Mass is

Second Ecumenical Council, 381 CE
Fifth Ecumenical Council, 553 CE
Sixth Ecumenical Council, 680 CE

Fourth Ecumenical Council, 451 CE

Rome

Constantinople

Chalcedon

Nicea

First Ecumenical Council, 325 CE
Seventh Ecumenical Council, 787 CE

Ephesus

Early Ecumenical Councils

Third Ecumenical Council, 431 CE

Jerusalem

© 2007 by Saint Mary's Press®

Early Councils

called the Nicene Creed. It is named for the Council of Nicea (325 CE). It would probably be more accurate to call it the Nicene-Constantinople Creed because the Council of Constantinople in 381 was still working on it. The Councils at Ephesus (431) (the third council, met in the Greek seaboard city where Paul labored and the traditional home of Saint John the Evangelist) and Chalcedon (451) (the fourth council, nearby the city nearly opposite Constantinople in Asia Minor) met later to handle other key issues.

We should point out that some changes in the Catholic version of the Creed came even later, in the Middle Ages. The "filioque" phrase, the addition of the words "and the son," is one of the causes in the split between Catholic and Orthodox churches in 1054. This phrase remains both a source of tension and a theological discussion between these churches.

All this illustrates the point that the Creed was written in a concise way to clarify what the Church believed and to unite the people in that belief. Creeds functioned therefore less like a sermon and more like an archeological treasure site. Different layers of the past are preserved in them, and we find pieces of events and arguments embedded in them. The Church has used and adapted many different forms of its creeds through the centuries. From the beginning, these statements of belief were proclaimed when the Christian service called "Eucharist" was celebrated and when the community came together for baptisms. The Church's unity in Christ was thus expressed in many places and voices.

The odd thing is that though we may have heard this creed often and even recited it recently, we may not actually listen to the words. We now focus on the text itself as an example of Living Tradition. Try to read it as if it were the first time:

The Nicene Creed

We believe in one God, the Father, the Almighty,
maker of heaven and earth, of all that is seen and unseen.

We believe in one Lord, Jesus Christ, the only Son of God,
eternally begotten of the Father,
God from God, Light from Light, true God from true God,
begotten, not made, one in Being with the Father.
Through him all things were made.
For us and for our salvation he came down from heaven:
by the power of the Holy Spirit
he was born of the Virgin Mary, and became man.
For our sake he was crucified under Pontius Pilate;
he suffered, died, and was buried.
On the third day he rose again in fulfillment of the Scriptures;
he ascended into heaven and is seated at the right hand of the Father.
He will come again in glory to judge the living and the dead,
and his kingdom will have no end.

We believe in the Holy Spirit, the Lord, the giver of life,
who proceeds from the Father and the Son.
With the Father and the Son he is worshipped and glorified.
He has spoken through the Prophets.
We believe in one holy catholic and apostolic Church.
We acknowledge one baptism for the forgiveness of sins.
We look for the resurrection of the dead,
and the life of the world to come. Amen.

Using the archaeological image, a good place to start our investigation is to ask what elements strike us as odd or interesting. What sticks out? What sounds unusual? What differs from our usual expectations or expressions? What is said in a way we do not normally say things?

Digging around in the Creed

Several phrases might be strange. "Seen and unseen" is not the way we usually talk. We are dealing with beliefs though, with spiritual claims, so the idea behind it might make sense. We do know realities (love, trust, character) that are not visible in the same way as loaves of bread or a flowing river.

Statements about Jesus stand out too. Several are strung together: "eternally begotten of the Father, God from God, Light from Light, true God from true God, begotten, not made, one in Being with the Father." Peter did not use this language in Acts 2. This is philosophical and theological language. It is language that early Christians wrestled with for years before agreeing. That in itself is an important realization. We are not in the sacred city of Jerusalem anymore. Our excavation of the Creed has taken us to secular cultures in the four greatest cities of the Mediterranean world, great because of their trade, commerce, art and architecture, and cultural diversity: Athens, Rome, Antioch, and Alexandria.

To do justice to the Creed or even to this one portion, we must probe its history, trace the events, debates, councils, theologians, and bishops who hammered out what ended up being accepted by the churches as the expression of their faith. Whole books have been written to tell this story. We do not have the space to retrace it here. (Some texts that go into detail will be suggested later.) We can offer a glimpse, however, of some key steps in the Creed's development and see where the Church's faith rests and how it has worked to arrive at that resting place.

The Nicene Creed's wording is inculturated; it comes from a particular past and looks to the present and future, striving to be faithful to the revelation of Jesus and its meaning in developing new contexts. In what has been a pattern throughout Christianity, new arguments were raised by Christians interacting with the current world and in particular with Greek culture and philosophy. At the same time, it has to be said that culture raises questions and challenges the Christian community. Not everyone was happy that such cultural influences were taken into the Church. Tertullian (c. 160–220) was a native of Carthage in Africa, who received a solid pagan education, became a lawyer, lived in Rome, converted at about age 35 to Christianity, and then became a priest and theologian. He wanted to protect the faith from dangerous secular meddlers and asked a question that never quite goes away, "What does Athens have to do with Jerusalem?" Or, to put it another way, what does secular culture have to do with Christianity? Mostly the answer given by Christians in the next unfolding centuries was, "a lot." The gospel would eventually travel not just through Greek thought but also through the Roman Empire and many other cultures. In our day, it continues to travel in new encounters in Africa, China, India, Russia, Indonesia, and Brazil, just to mention the largest populations today. The Church will be wherever humans are tomorrow as well, perhaps even to new places beyond the earth. Therefore, the question continues, and answers are sought.

A Question of Substance

The phrase "one in Being with the Father" relates the meaning of a key word: *consubstantial.* Passages in the NT claim Jesus to be divine. Others emphasize how human he was. Figuring out how these two claims could both be asserted and interrelated, and doing so in ways that did not lose one or the other claim, confuse them, or try to hybridize them, was difficult.

In addressing the Christological questions, authors of the Nicene documents began using a word that was not part of the scriptural accounts but that did address the questions raised about the scripture's message in their Greek philosophical climate. Jesus was described as *homoousios* with God. *Consubstantial* is the related term in Latin. A good translation is "of the same stuff" ("same substance"). Making this wording official (that is what councils do in resolving debates—they resolve to say things deliberately, officially) was the big decision with which not everyone was happy. The concern was about introducing a word not found in the NT and whether the Church would be preserving the same message if it used a nonbiblical language such as philosophy.

The Nicene Creed reflects the results of debates over wording. Each Sunday, millions of Christians say that Jesus was "one in Being with the Father." Should the phrasing matter? The Church found that the central message, the *kerygma,* was at stake. We claim Jesus is the "same stuff" (substance) as God—that he is fully divine. He is also *homoousios* with humanity. Jesus is the "same human stuff" (substance) as us—he is fully human. This is emphasized later in the Creed, where Mary is mentioned. People were arguing over whether the divine somehow outweighed the human. The Council of Ephesus brought Jesus' mother into the debates, calling Mary, *Theotokos,* "God-bearer," and in that word they identified Jesus as divine while insisting that he was a human son as well, reinforcing that he was born of Mary and is the same as us (human).

The Christological controversies within the councils of the fourth and fifth centuries illustrate that trying to understand God in human words is complex and imperfect. At the same time, by choosing words carefully, we can get closer to the truth of what we experience and understand about God. Our words cannot say everything, but they matter tremendously.

In the messy process of clarifying the wording of the Creed, the Church used an old tool in a new way. Liturgical creeds, used originally at baptisms and the Eucharist, were adapted to speak as clearly as possible about whom Jesus is. Hence, the questions raised by Greek culture could not be understood nor the truth of it conveyed by repeating phrases from scripture. The Church took a significant step in introducing Greek terms, in a Christian way, that lend additional insights into its understanding of faith. At the same time, the Church found that other cultures held important resources in themselves to carry the original message authentically. Hence, the paradox is that change could be part of remaining truly unchanged in the traditional understanding of Jesus.

Tradition

When the apostles were gone, the churches they left behind assumed responsibility for passing on the gospel through history. This handing down is the ongoing creating of tradition. The Latin word *tradere* means "to hand on." For example, when a young bride uses something passed down from her great-grandmother as part of her wedding gown or when we eat a Thanksgiving meal of turkey, we are continuing traditions. In a theological context, *tradition* means to remain connected and empowered by the original Christ-Event through history. Some examples that show how central this handing on was for the identity of the community occur in Luke 1:1–2, 1 Corinthians 11:23, and 2 Timothy 2:2.

When we study ecclesiology, history is in a sense the laboratory part of the course. We use reports issued from time to time, like the Creed, to investigate the Church's earlier experiences. From the early Church's struggles to express itself in new and different cultures while keeping the same gospel message it received from the beginning, we gain a lesson for own times; we face the same process and challenges.

History can also show us that handing on the tradition can be costly, as the following story in our tradition tells us through the martyr Saint Polycarp.

The Story of Polycarp

Can you remember an elderly person in your life whom you loved and respected, who told you stories from the past about people, life, or events? Most of us have people in our lives who tell us these stories—a grandmother, an older neighbor, or a friend. After a while, we may realize that we have heard the same story quite a few times. We might even be able to tell the story or finish parts of it. Over time, we realize these repeated stories stayed with us, set our values, and helped fashion our identities. They become more precious, and we cherish them for the transmission of life they nurtured. And as we grow, we often sit around with others and retell these stories: "Do you remember the time . . . ?"

In the second century, there lived an old man named Polycarp, who for decades had been a cornerstone of the Church in Smyrna. He was bishop there in a time of persecution by the Romans. Christians were given the opportunity to avoid torture and death by renouncing their faith; if they did so, they received a written certificate acknowledging that they were willing to obey the civil religion and bend their knees to the emperor. Roman officials knew that leaders like Polycarp were prime targets to change others.

When soldiers came to arrest Polycarp, they too felt a deep respect for this old, saintly man. He fed them a meal, asking them for time to pray before leaving with them, and they let him pray for two hours. The account that comes down to us from his followers, "The Martyrdom of Saint Polycarp," describes him being led away, sitting on an ass, reminiscent of the ride taken by Jesus into the town where he was crucified. The soldiers tried to talk Polycarp into calling Caesar "Lord," so they could leave him alone to die eventually in his own bed, but he refused. At his trial, the proconsul instructed him to take the oath and gain his freedom. Polycarp replied that he could not now stop serving his savior and Lord of eighty-six years. The proconsul warned then of the wild animals and the fire that were awaiting Polycarp. The give-and-take between this bishop, his accusers, and the crowd is a stirring story of faith (and a vivid illustration of the Greek word *martyr*, or "witness" to the faith).

The description of Polycarp's last moments tells of him surrounded by fire yet not destroyed by it, evoking the scene of Shadrach, Meshach, and Abednego from the book of Daniel (3:19–97). Eventually, he was stabbed with a dagger to end his life. One of the strangest elements in the story is the description of the smell coming from the fire that surrounded Polycarp, which witnesses said was like bread baking and like incense. This account of the martyrdom of Polycarp connects him in the most direct way possible to Christ. Rather than leave this Lord for another, the old man became Christ. His body became like Eucharistic bread; his destruction was like the incense that brings our prayers to God. What reasons could we ever have for waxing poetic in the face of an execution? In the martyrs, the early Church recognized the cost of true discipleship—the whole self. After eighty-six years of prayer, Polycarp knew where his strength was. His witness would be a powerful influence on later generations; the blood of the martyrs is the seed of the Church.

As we can also see in the story of Polycarp, the Christian community preserves its memory through its continuous tradition linking us back to Jesus and forward to every new challenge. Remember the ripple image with which we began this chapter? Tradition is the Christ-Event, as the rock entering into the water of time, sending waves outward to every new generation. The record of the ripples is tradition as it unfolds in history, which we examine next.

History Is Central

Christianity shapes and is shaped by the historical context in which we live. Indeed, at the root of our understanding of ecclesiology is our realization and our claim that God acts in history; God deals directly with the created universe. We have not been abandoned but are in relationship to God.

Christianity's Jewish roots teach us that this universe is, as God declares after each day's work at Creation, a good place. Not everyone in the ancient world (or now) could believe this message, and it is easy to understand why. Before adequate nutrition, antibiotics, decent clothing and shelter, indoor plumbing, safe childbirth, and a wealth of other developments, life was short and hard for most people (and even today, life remains difficult and too short for many in our world). Into this difficult world, first Judaism and then Christianity brought an amazing message: The world is worth living in and caring about. As difficult as its problems are, it is worth caring for and fixing. In theological terms, it is worth redeeming. Salvation belongs to this world.

The Church's worldview shares these Jewish roots. One of the most famous verses in the NT, seen sometimes on banners at sporting events, is John 3:16: "For God so loved the world that he gave his only son." The Christian's worldview is rooted in the incarnation of Jesus Christ. Jesus is God and human in one person. Those who followed Jesus in first-century Galilee found God at work. This person who was every bit as human as they were also embodied something striking and unique. The same God whose work they found in Abraham, in Moses, in David, in the prophets, in the temple, in the Torah and the other scriptures was at work in this Jesus from Nazareth. He came preaching the "reign of God," and they were drawn to him, enthralled, wondering, trying to understand what that reign was. Yet, frightened and disappointed, they fled and deserted him at his death. He was arrested by those who were quite sure that whatever reign this new "king" was building, it was a threat to their own power.

The Church is an unlikely story. God acted in Jesus; Jesus acts in the Church. The actions of the Church are in the hands of normal human beings. God leaves incredibly important responsibilities in flimsy, fickle hands.

As we live in the present, we do not just look to the past. Through diverse Christian communities, even through different approaches to our common tradition, we can form powerful visions for the future. Our journey is shared as the Church also serves people of other religious traditions and all humanity as integral to its vision in Christ. Within this global service to humanity, Vatican II provides us with a powerful vision of Christ, who is present in the Church and his Body and who is revealed in the actions of the Church and its sacraments (Lat., *sacramentum* = "the sign"), the topic of chapter 5 (see *Lumen Gentium* 1–8). Our strengths and our troubles are linked to Christ in the sacraments, to the sacrament of his Church, just as the weaknesses and strength of the disciples were linked to Jesus. Just when his disciples were most at a loss for what he had meant, when their hopes were crushed with his death, they experienced him alive again. Because of what God did in Jesus, raising him to life, these followers who were lost were changed. They exploded with hope.

Is Competition Good for Us?

To illustrate where that hope took them, we will look at one development from the early Church in some detail. First, recall the theme of Peter's Pentecost speech and the Nicene Creed. They both emphasize the paramount teaching that God is Lord and in charge in the world. We will examine how the early Church forged its vision of the world in terms of creation and "the world to come" by arguing it out with their worldview competitors.

We can put the challenge this way: Is competition good for the community of the Church? Should we compete over theological wording? Think of how athletes train for a contest. They prepare for a goal they want to reach. Discipline and effort help them deepen their understanding of who they are. Other types of challenges may not be competitive in the sense of creating a contest with another. Some may pit us more deeply against our self or our previous accomplishments. Consider how a musician or a painter evolves in her craft, with new projects deepening and exploring her insights and expressions. What can competition in theology accomplish?

Gnosticism: Who Knows Best?

To illustrate how a deeper understanding of the gospel message can come through real historical struggles, it may be useful to look at how some people shook up the Christian churches with new and different beliefs. A major competitor for the early Christian church was Gnosticism. More accurately, we should refer to Gnosticisms in the plural because various versions of this religion developed. Certain teachings were common to the many forms, however. *Gnosis* is a Greek work meaning "knowledge." If you say the English word *know* out loud, you will hear and be pronouncing the first syllable of the original Greek sound, because *know* comes from this Greek etymology. Gnostics claimed a special form of knowledge. It made their worldview and their groups esoteric. Some special leaders had the knowledge of God and the way to salvation. Those who wanted a share in it had to come to those who had this special knowledge. Gnostics created a select group of "insiders."

What was the different worldview of these challengers? In addition to having some Jewish influences, Gnosticism was rooted in the thought of the Greek philosopher Plato (427–347 BCE), who taught that the physical world was derived from a larger reality. The spiritual, the world of the mind, was what was most real; the material world was an imperfect copy of what was original and true. In Gnostic thought, the spiritual and material were pushed even farther apart to form a dualism where the spirit and the gods or God were seen as good, while the body and things of the earth were definitely bad. A human being was understood as a regrettable combination of the divine and earthly; the Gnostics thought that in a human, a divine spark of the larger Godhead had been trapped in a body. The goal was to release the spark again and thereby escape this world. Consequently, Gnostics performed austere practices like fasting and refraining from sex.

Christian Gnosticism?

A form of Christian Gnosticism developed when people within this worldview adopted and then adapted certain teachings about Jesus. It is with their understanding of the resurrection in particular that we can see the difference between Gnostics taking on Christian terminology and the original Christians proclaiming the message about what happened to Jesus.

A Gnostic text from the late second century, called "The Treatise on Resurrection," describes how Jesus in his resurrection made himself into "an imperishable Aeon." Jesus becomes a form of light—again. In this "spiritual resurrection," Jesus "swallows up" the psychic dimension of the person, as well as the bodily dimension. He has no use for the earth or worldly things. The Gnostic description of Jesus adapts him to the views already held in their worldview. Should Christians have been concerned about new ideas and interpretations? How do Christians know whether these teachings draw us away from our central beliefs? Do these questions and distinctions matter? Right here in this discussion, we can see the significant and important role theology has: It is faith seeking understanding so as to find God. The Christian community has taken a stance that authentic understanding of God's revelation matters, judgments follow and matter, and our commitment to enter into relationship with God matters—to Christians individually and to their embrace of neighbors everywhere. The simple bottom line is that God also gave us the gift of understanding as one important way to learn from God. So we ask again from a theological perspective: Do these questions and conclusions matter to Christians?

What Should We Make of Competition?

Should their audiences then (and should we now) not be open to all new ideas? This is a perennial question. Certainly, a Christian response should be thoughtful. Then and now, intelligent hearers would want to listen to both sides and think about what was true in the messages. Nevertheless, it is legitimate to ask which differences matter.

The Gnostics preached the gospel of a heavenly, spiritual resurrection for Jesus. However, the gospels of Matthew, Mark, Luke, and John describe Jesus' resurrected body as new and transformed but still very much a body. Jesus still eats with his friends. Could Gnostic and Christian messages both be right? At stake here is an understanding, and a claim, of how God deals with the world and the humans in it. In one view, the Gnostics saw the world as a place to be shunned. True knowledge led humans out of it to a better place beyond. Real transformation got past the merely human to make a person into a new being, a new sort of divine light, that could leave this ugly world behind. Christians, on the other hand, claim that God loves the world. The resurrection of Jesus, and through it the possibility of human transformation, is linked to the world now. Jesus does not redeem us at the expense of our being human. He redeems us in our humanity, fulfilling it. He is the same stuff as we are. When we become one with him, we become more of who we are.

The Plot Thickens

People in the second century and people in our own time have argued about what readings can deliver the true message of the Christ-Event. We will spend a little more time here with a leading Gnostic to see how his competing ideas led to clarification about texts Christians were using to understand Jesus. The Gnostics' new perspective on the gospel left out something central to the original message.

A key character in the confusion created by the Gnostic challenge is a man named Marcion (d. 160), a wealthy shipowner who was excommunicated for immorality by his father, who was a bishop. Marcion then set himself up in Rome. This second-century Gnostic leader with his own agenda pushed for a reform of the Christian message, arguing that the Church should move along the trajectory Saint Paul began, distinguishing Christian faith from its Jewish roots. Marcion insisted on a small core of Christianity based on love (i.e., Christian scriptures) instead of anything to do with Law (*Tanak* or Old Testament). He insisted, moreover, that the apostles and disciples misunderstood Jesus' message and that only Saint Paul truly understood it. Marcion argued that the Church should leave behind what he saw as an inadequate understanding of God embedded in the Jewish scriptures. He rejected outright these Jewish writings, and he recommended selected Christian texts: certain writings of Paul and a version of Luke's gospel that emphasized the Gentile mission. He wrote brief introductions to his selected texts, and some of those are the only writings of his that we have today.

The churches throughout Christianity reacted to what Marcion had done and rejected his narrowly selected collection of writings. They focused more carefully on texts they had been reading, works that carried a fuller presentation of the original tradition. Therefore, in reaction to Marcion, the original complete text of Luke was used. Instead of using one gospel in isolation, the complementary perspectives of the gospels of Matthew, Mark, and John were included as well to give the best understanding of Jesus, of his incarnation, life, death, and resurrection. The churches' canon of scripture emphasized that Marcion was too limiting. (The word *canon* means a "measuring stick," like a foot-long ruler by which something can be measured. The canon is a "rule" for deciding which sacred texts are authentic to the genuine faith tradition and therefore should be included in the Church's reading and worship.)

In selecting the texts that would present his message, Marcion left out Christian sources that said something different from what he was preaching. At stake for the Gnostics and Christians of the second century, and at stake in this century and the future, were conflicting claims about gospel texts and their relationship to Christ. The early Christian Church asserted that the resurrection was of a certain type, expressed in the "canonical" gospels but not in others (e.g., the gospel of Thomas or the gospel of Peter). An important stance went hand in hand with this choice of gospels. The Church claimed not only that this message was true but also that it was what the original witnesses to Jesus' resurrection had experienced. Whether someone chooses to believe a different gospel or not is one issue. Another one significant for historical argument is that the message claimed by the Church in selecting its gospels was the original message. The others were innovations that tried to bring in a new angle on the original gospel but in doing so changed its very identity.

This sort of plot seems to continue to thicken through history. Do we think Gnosticism is dead, buried, and forgotten? Aware or not, contemporary fans of certain Gnostic ideas and texts sometimes criticize the Church for dismissing or hiding other gospels. Why was the gospel of Thomas left out of the canon? Fans of the popular novel *The Da Vinci Code* or the movie *Stigmata* are intrigued by several questions: Did the Church hide the real gospels? Did it hide the truth? Did it not want competition? To answer these questions, we must consider that the Church was identifying its roots—it was maintaining the very meaning of its message. The universal Church recognized that the Gnostic's message did (and does) say something different from what the Church knew to be true. The result of the confusion brought by Marcion is ironic in light of modern questions about the canon. The Christian community found that Marcion was too narrow. The Gnostics see the truest reality as ultimately "spiritual." On the other hand, an incarnational understanding of Jesus, the Church, and creation sees things in a more sophisticated, holistic way.

Does this mean that new ideas cannot be heard? Should we avoid thinking about what others propose? Of course not. By all means, we should read the texts over which the Church argued. There has not been much of a cover-up, really. The "alternate" gospels have been translated and available in libraries and bookstores for decades. The best strategy for those either in the Church or outside of it who are intrigued by the debates is to do enough studying to see what all the arguing was about.

Studying Tradition

When we pay attention to something as important as the wording of the Creed, we are pulled directly into a concern for history and tradition. God started this revelation long before we were here. In our opening image, we saw the beginning of the "ripple effect" of the Christ-Event—the preaching of the apostles, the birth of the Church, and the ongoing life of this community that moves into each era with news that God is alive in the world.

In the Creed, we have found archaeological treasures where the early Church met challenges. We turn now to another resource that the Creed carries through history—one that shows how the Church can continue to meet new challenges in every era.

As the Church moved through the centuries and interacted with different ideas and cultures, it came to recognize a set of criteria for understanding when developments were legitimate or not. These criteria also are embedded in the Creed. In a line that specifies what sort of church we believe in, it is described as being one, holy, catholic, and apostolic. These have traditionally been called the "marks of the Church." They identify how the Church continues to evolve as a living tradition.

The Marks (Signs) of the Church

One

Unity has been a concern of the Church from the start. John's gospel vividly expresses Jesus' concern for unity among his followers. In the Last Supper scene in John 17:1–26, Jesus prays that the disciples will be one, just as the Father and Jesus are one. Early on, foundational practices and structures of the Church were emphasized to create unity; the Eucharist, the bishop, the creeds, arguments over doctrine, councils, and the canon of the Christian scriptures all served the oneness of the Church.

Holy

Christians are baptized into Christ himself. Each Christian is to become him. Orthodox Christianity has expressed this vividly; Christ became human so that humans could become divine. Holiness is sometimes visible, sometimes not. The most dramatic image of this mark is martyrdom.

Catholic

The Greek word *katholikos* is often translated as "universal," yet its root meaning is more accurately given as "throughout the whole." The word *catholic* expresses a dynamic image; it is like the biblical image of yeast that enlivens a whole mass of dough. It is like our ripple metaphor, where the gospel spreads outward in ever-expanding spheres of influence. In the early centuries, when new ideas about Christ's divinity and humanity were debated, the struggle was to see whether innovative expressions would spread and be accepted widely. Would churches throughout different areas and cultures find the newly developed theologies to be legitimate growths of understanding? *Homoousios* ("same nature" as God) became accepted. Marcion's canon did not. The strategy of calling all the churches (represented by their bishops) to come together in councils to argue these points came from the understanding that a "catholic" development would be proven to be from the Spirit of God, if the Church moved toward a *consensus fidelium* ("consensus of the faithful")—an agreement among all believers.

Apostolic

An apostle is one who is sent. In Christian usage, it refers to those witnesses of the risen Christ who were sent to spread the gospel to the rest of the world. The role of "the Twelve" came from the fact they were witnesses to an original event (see Acts 1: 15–26).

This criterion asks whether an expression or practice is connected to the original message. Has growth come from the deepest roots? Early on, apostolicity attached itself to particular cities where the seeds of the gospel were planted first: (1) Jerusalem was the birthplace of the Church. (2) Antioch, a port to the north, was the launching spot for missionary journeys of Paul and others. In this city, the followers of Jesus Christ were first called "Christians" (see Acts 11: 26). (3) Alexandria, long a place of scholarship and culture and the home of a large Greek-speaking Jewish community, became the home of an early thriving church, a place for theological scholarship. (4) Rome was the seat of the empire, the place from which persecutions were launched yet ironically then the place where the blood of the martyrs became seeds for faith. From the earliest generations of the Church, Rome was venerated as the place where Peter and Paul were killed, and it held a prominence among other churches. (5) A fifth city, originally Byzantium and renamed Constantinople (and now called Istanbul, in Turkey), became the "New Rome" in Christendom when the emperor Constantine moved his capital there from Rome in the fourth century. A rich mix of leadership, study, and controversy over the apostolic faith became part of its heritage.

When the Church faces challenges today, when it faces difficulties from within or from outside its community, it still finds its solutions and strength most clearly by embracing unity, holiness, catholicity, and deep apostolic roots. The marks of the Church have served in the past to balance and shape its growth. They are the criteria by which we can be guided today.

The image of the ripple effect continues through history, and we see it when looking back through the tradition. We can put it this way: If the apostle Peter, the preacher from the first-century Pentecost that gave birth to the Church, were to return today, would he recognize what began with that first sermon? As it spread through the major cities of the Roman Empire, through Greek culture, and later through human nations and cultures on all the continents of the world, the *ekklesia* has shown the same recognizable patterns of the original structure provided by God to the first hearers of the gospel. The ripples that flow from that event have a distinct shape and pattern of that Christ-Event. If Peter returned, I think he would recognize the Church today in continuity with his preaching.

What Do the Marks of the Church Mean Today?

We might ask how these criteria challenge the contemporary Church to embrace its full identity.

Unity

What sort of issues cause problems in a parish? In a denomination? Between different denominations? Do poor and wealthy churches often work together? Do different denominations? Practical work can unite. Hungry people do not usually quibble about who made the soup. What can be done to overcome factions in a community?

Holiness

What does holiness look like today—an act of service, an apology, a donation of time and money? Do we stand with someone in trouble, even if it means embarrassment? In a culture charged with materialistic values, what forms does holiness take? What does holiness say to violence? Do we ever let humor diffuse a situation so that we overcome the temptation to take ourselves too seriously?

Catholicity

Are there areas where we would rather the gospel's influence not go? In what situations would we rather not be reminded of our calling? Can we let our own views be questioned by the humanity of others? Are we able to give a reason, explanation, or lived example for what we think and believe?

Apostolicity

Who do we look to as authorities? Are there elderly women and men we trust and look to for advice? Are there children who, by example, show us God's presence? Why did people like Pope John Paul II, Martin Luther King Jr., Mother Teresa of Calcutta, Billy Graham, and Desmond Tutu from South Africa draw crowds from different continents that numbered in the millions or hundreds of thousands?

To address both historical and contemporary issues, we have resources in the experiences and wisdom of scripture and tradition, in the strategies and structures that have been created through human efforts and the work of the Holy Spirit. The Church has drawn on the insights of Church leaders and of the whole people of God. In the document on the Church called *Lumen Gentium* ("Light of all peoples"), we find the council fathers' description of the particular role of the laity today:

> Christ is the great prophet who proclaimed the kingdom of the Father both by the testimony of his life and by the power of his word. Until the full manifestation of his glory, he fulfills this prophetic office, not only by the hierarchy who teach in his name and by his power, but also by the laity. He accordingly both establishes them as witnesses and provides them with the appreciation of the faith (*sensus fidei*) and the grace of the word (cf. Acts 2:17–18; Rev 19:10) so that the power of the Gospel may shine out in daily family and social life. (#35)

Conclusion: Leaving a Lot Out

The ripples of the Christ-Event are concentric, moving outward in directions we could not have known, controlled, or predicted. The variety of people and places, events and rituals, movements and eras that are connected to the Christian message over its two-thousand years of history make the task of understanding the Church daunting. Anyone with any familiarity with the Church will ask how we can stop our story now in the fifth century. What about the next fifteen-hundred years? What about the structures and challenges we see today? What about the many unrecognized and unsolicited contributions of women? How do we begin to explain or evaluate the messages that claim to speak for Christ and his Church? Storefront churches and towering cathedrals, white-robed popes stepping off jets, polished TV preachers asking for money, arguments over how much religion should influence public life and politics—all of these images come into our living room, unless we turn them off with our remote control. The problems that hurt the Church come from both outside and inside. Can we find common ground for diverse groups of Orthodox Christians, Protestants, and Roman Catholics, as well as Copts, Armenians, Syrian Christians, and others?

What we have studied here does not stop in the fifth century, or ever. It shows that we have the resources to take up these difficult issues. The Church has faced major challenges of identity and crisis, and it has not only survived but flourished. Extraordinary charisms have been drawn out of the ordinary human members of the Body of Christ by the movement of God's own Spirit. By striving for unity and holiness, embracing catholicity that ripples even through troubled historical waters, and rooting itself in the apostolic faith that connects us to the movement of the Spirit in Jerusalem at the first Pentecost, the Church can face the modern world too. In fact, much work lies ahead. It is our hope that readers of this introduction to the Church's history will embrace the challenges facing the Church today and look through the other "ripples" of its history for the lessons we still need to learn.

Vatican II's *Pastoral Constitution on the Church in the Modern World* renews the Church's mandate with the words, "The joy and hope, the grief and anguish of the people of our time, especially of those who are poor or afflicted in any way, are the joy and hope, the grief and anguish of the followers of Christ as well" (*Gaudium et Spes* 1). Our calling is clear: Our *ekklesia*, our gathering as the People of God in the Holy Spirit, is enough to make us the presence of Christ in the world.

Student Activity 1: Starting at the Beginning:
The Church in Acts

Our oldest account of the Christian Church is in the second chapter of the NT's book of Acts. In the middle of Jerusalem, Jesus' followers, who a few hours before were hiding in a closed room, spilled into the streets and started talking in different languages, called "tongues." Some people who encountered them thought they were crazy. If we examine this story carefully, we find a description not of a random collection of followers but of a communion, a distinct sort of community (*communio* in Latin, *koinonia* in Greek). Even in the beginning, after the resurrection, we see a group with a structure and a mission to others.

You are invited now to do a theological reading of the passage Act 2:1–47. It is not long but, as we will see, it is rich in content and has huge implications for Christianity itself. To set the stage briefly, this group preaches the Good News of Jesus Christ—the gospel—right after the Pentecost event, sometimes called "the birthday of the Church." In order to understand the passage and its points better, use the following questions. This is good practice in thinking "theologically."

Questions

1. Who are the principle actors in this scene? Who are all these people in the city? Who are the prophets quoted in Peter's speech?

2. How is unity described in this passage (consider verses 1, 3, 4, 32, 36, 41, 42, 44)? What is the main message? What is the reaction of the crowd? Are there different reactions?

3. When do the people ask, "What are we supposed to do with this?"

4. Where does the group meet daily? Why two places? Why both places?

5. Why are the people astounded?

6. How does the Jewish background of the apostles and their audience shape the preaching and the responses?

7. How is the involvement of God portrayed in this passage?

8. Where does the energy come from to make the gospel message public?

9. Why does the Holy Spirit allow people to hear the message in their own languages?

Writing a Theological Reflection

After thinking through this passage and talking about it with others, it is useful to collect your impressions by writing them down. Using a one-page format or a journal entry, discuss the main impact of the passage. Give some thought to the issues it presents about the nature of the Church. Consider what other questions the passage raises that you did not have before.

Student Activity 2: A Classroom Exercise for Exploring Contemporary Ecclesiology

Avery Dulles's book, *Models of the Church*, has been an important influence on ecclesiological discussions since Vatican II. His original five models of the Church as institutional, mystical communion, sacrament, herald, and servant can help people identify their own connection to the Church as well as challenge each person to take seriously charisms and tasks in the Church to which they may not have given as much attention. In a later edition of his book, Dulles introduced a sixth model, the community of disciples, which he sees as drawing all the models into common ecclesiological reflection. The following exercise can engage classroom discussion and individual reflection.

Arrange the class into five groups. Each one should prepare and then present a basic description of one of Dulles's models of the Church. The advantages and disadvantages or strengths and weaknesses of each model should be discussed. Each group should be prepared to ask the next group a question or two. Either a sixth group can be chosen at the beginning to present the communion of disciples model, or each group can be asked to respond to the sixth model, saying how it enhances its own group's understanding of the nature of the Church. (If groups are chosen at random, for example, by students "counting off," students may then have to explore a model for which they are not naturally or initially supportive or knowledgeable. At the end of the exercise, students can be invited to offer a thought or two from their own point of view.)

Extended discussions of each of Dulles's models can be found in his own text and in a number of sites on the Internet.

Questions about the Text

1. What are the etymologies for the word *Church*? What do they indicate to others about the Church?

2. What is the definition of the word *Church*?

3. Where does the word *creed* come from? What is its purpose?

4. What is meant by the Latin-derived word *consubstantial* and its Greek counterpart *homoousios*? Why is the concept important?

5. Who is Polycarp, and why is he referred to in this chapter?

6. What does the word *Gnosticism* mean, and what is it all about?

7. What are the four marks of the Church? What do they mean today?

Questions for Discussion

1. What do you think of when you use the word *church*?

2. Write your own creed of what you believe. If doing this exercise with others, share your creeds with each other.

3. What role does culture play in the creeds? Can there be a creed that is not enculturated? How would that be done?

4. Do you know someone personally or have you read about someone who in some ways exemplifies fidelity as Polycarp did?

5. Gnostics move to special knowledge. What other special ways might people use to form religions?

6. What do you think are examples of the four marks of the Church that witness to its true identity in God?

For Further Study

Chapter Themes

Abbott, Walter M., ed. *The Documents of Vatican II*. Trans. Joseph Gallagher. New York: Herder & Herder, 1966.

Brown, Raymond E. *The Churches the Apostles Left Behind*. Mahwah, NJ: Paulist Press, 1984.

Doyle, Dennis M. *The Church Emerging from Vatican II: A Popular Approach to Contemporary Catholicism*. Revised ed. New London, CT: Twenty-Third Publications, 2002.

A wide array of contemporary topics is discussed in an engaging style. The book follows the organization and agendas of two documents from Vatican II: *Lumen Gentium* and *Gaudium et Spes*.

Dulles, Avery. *Models of the Church*. Expanded ed. New York: Image Books, 1987.

Dulles discusses different ways to discuss and understand the church as institutional, mystical communion, sacrament, herald, and servant. He elaborates advantages and disadvantages of such models and ties them together with a final model, the community of disciples.

Happel, Stephen and David Tracy. *A Catholic Vision*. Minneapolis, MN: Fortress Press, 1984.

In this look at the churches following the NT period, the author writes consciously of the need for ecumenical reflection.

McGonigle, Thomas D., and James F. Quigley. *A History of the Christian Tradition: From Its Jewish Origins to the Reformation*. Mahwah, NJ: Paulist Press, 1988.

———. *A History of the Christian Tradition: From the Reformation to the Present*. Mahwah, NJ: Paulist Press, 1996.

These two volumes are an overview of Church history that presents the main events, people, and issues that continue to influence the Church today.

The Creed

Johnson, Luke Timothy. *The Creed: What Christians Believe and Why It Matters*. New York: Image Books, 2004.

Marthaler, Bernard L. *The Creed: The Apostolic Faith in Contemporary Theology*. Revised ed. New London, CT: Twenty-Third Publications, 1992.

Gnosticism

Robinson, James M., Gen. Ed. *The Nag Hammadi Library in English*. Revised ed. New York: HarperSanFrancisco, 1990.

Reference Works

Brown, Raymond E., et al. *The New Jerome Biblical Commentary*. Revised ed. Upper Saddle River, NJ: Prentice Hall, 1989.

Cross, F. L., et al. *The Oxford Dictionary of the Christian Church*. Third revised ed. Oxford, UK: Oxford University Press, 2005.

From the Reference Librarian
Researching Using the Internet—Ecclesiology

According to Dr. Finucane, you can find on the Internet "extended discussions" of the various "models" of the Church developed by Avery Dulles. Because this information comes from a professional, you know that these discussions must be worthwhile, but how do you find them?

On the day this was written, I "Googled" the following—Avery Dulles Models of the Church—and retrieved over 59,000 hits. (You might also try this search with other search engines, such as Yahoo!, Dogpile, etc. Note the variety in the number of hits with each search engine.) One reason for the large number of hits is that Internet search engines only do one kind of searching—keyword. For example, many of the 59,000 hits are simply from lists of used books for sale from sites such as Amazon.com and so on. Such sites are of no use to you. Unlike using Library of Congress subject headings in your library catalog, there is no way to search the Internet with precision for what you want, in this case, a discussion of Dulles' ideas about ecclesiology.

Student: How do I use the Internet in my research?

Tip #1

Carefully evaluate the quality of any Internet source you intend to use for your research. Use only websites likely to be regarded as authoritative by your instructor.

You can use a few tricks to make your keyword search more precise. For example, you can place quotation marks around anything you want to search as a phrase. Because "models of the Church" is both the title of Dulles' book and a phrase likely to be found in discussions of it, repeating the search as follows—avery dulles "models of the Church" (you could also put quotes around "avery dulles") produces (on Google) a much smaller number of hits, 994. However, that is still a large number of results to look through in order to find something useful. Even if you find something worthwhile in the first few "hits," how do you know you are not missing something even better a little further on?

The important thing is to evaluate whatever you decide to look at. So, let's take a look at some of the results from this search to see the kinds of things you should be looking for in determining whether a particular Internet site is worthy of being cited in academic work.

The first hit has the following URL (universal resource locator, the standard designation of an Internet address):

http://dlibrary.acu.edu.au/staffhome/yukoszarycz/ecc/CHAP3.HTML

The URL informs us that this web page is hosted on the site of an educational institution (as indicated by the .edu extension) and that the institution is located somewhere in Australia (as indicated by the .au country extension). Other things being equal, material on an academic subject is more likely to be trustworthy coming from a ".edu" site than from a commercial (.com) or some other nondescript (.net) Internet site.

Besides reading the lengthy discussion of the various "models," what else can we learn about this site? Who is responsible for it? What are their qualifications? What authority does this person or organization have to make and post such statements on the Internet? (In some ways, these questions are like those in ecclesiology: Who has authority to speak for the Church?)

Several links appear at the bottom of the web page, including a link to a "Study Guide" (Who would put up a "study guide"? Why?) and links to an "Ecclesiology Home Page" and to a "Yuri Koszarycz Home Page." Who is Yuri Koszarycz? From his home page, we learn that he is a "Senior Lecturer" in the School of Theology at the Australian Catholic University in Brisbane, Australia. Another page gives information on his academic degrees. This academic appears to have placed a large amount of material developed for his courses on the Internet, including a series of essays under the rubric "History of the Christian Church & Ecclesiology" (including the essay on Dulles and his models). The site also lists a number of "Internet Awards," which might indicate something about the worth of the site, although you should put greater trust in a person's actual qualifications than awards. But these are the kinds of things you should be looking for as you evaluate whether (1) a particular site is worth your time (if there are no indications of qualifications, etc., even if the site otherwise looks good) and (2) the site can be used as a source in a paper or oral presentation.

Another site returned by the Google search is the "Wikipedia" entry on Avery Dulles. Wikipedia is an Internet encyclopedia project to which anyone can contribute. There have been stories of individuals uploading entirely false information in biographical articles, for example. Supposedly, steps are being taken to exercise a greater degree of quality control, but this is still a work in progress. At this stage in the development of the Internet, a printed encyclopedia in your library's reference collection is a more authoritative source than Wikipedia.

Tip #2

If you do cite Wikipedia or any other Internet site, a good rule of thumb for the purpose of academic research is never to accept as factual any information found on the Internet without verifying it from some other more traditional source.

One useful thing that Wikipedia does often do is include links to other sites that may actually be more useful than the Wikipedia entry itself. The entry for Dulles contains links to Dulles's faculty page at Fordham University (naturally with an ".edu" extension in the URL) and to another online archive of lectures by Dulles on video, interviews, articles by and about Dulles, and so on. The URL for this latter site has a ".com" extension, but what we otherwise know about Dulles leads us to view this site as potentially useful for research.

Another site offering a discussion of Dulles's models appears to be the "blog" of a self-described "amateur pastor, hack theologian, and wannabe mystic." This site may be useful for the perspective of a clergyman engaged in active ministry but is not appropriate for purposes of academic research.

You should indicate in some way what you know about the nature of your Internet source and the person(s) behind it if you intend to make formal use of it in your research. After all, you want your professor to regard what you have to say as authoritative, and this is only likely to be true if your sources can be regarded as authoritative. This is especially important if you are using a somewhat more offbeat source, such as a self-identified "hack theologian."

Another way to try to eliminate some of the chaff you run into on the Internet is to use a more specialized search engine such as "Google Scholar." This service aims to provide a "simple way to broadly search for scholarly literature." "Scholarly literature," as defined by Google, includes "peer-reviewed papers, theses, books, abstracts and articles, from academic publishers, professional societies, preprint repositories, universities and other scholarly organizations."

Searching Google Scholar using "Avery Dulles Models of the Church" produces fewer than one-hundred "hits." Some of these are potentially useful references to books and articles. Others are less helpful, such as course syllabi simply listing Dulles's book. (Is a course syllabus an example of "scholarly literature"?) Several other factors limit the usefulness of this service, including the following:

1. Searching is by keyword only. There are no subject headings to ensure that you actually retrieve the content you want, as opposed to retrieving merely the words you type.

2. The order in which "hits" are listed is based, in part, on popularity defined as the number of times a web page has been accessed and not on relevance to your subject.

3. The "scholarly literature" indexed by Google includes all possible subjects. By contrast, most libraries offer access to subject-specific databases, including, for theology, the *ATLA Religion Database, Religious & Theological Abstracts*, or the *Catholic Periodical & Literature Index*. Even databases covering a broad range of subjects, such as *Academic Search* Premier, offer far more refined search capabilities (and will not retrieve any course syllabi).

[Note: As explained in the introductory chapter on library research, this textbook does not discuss the use of periodical indexes and databases. Ask your librarian what databases are available for your subject and for assistance in using them.]

In short, while Google Scholar and similar services may be good for a quick search for resources, the best way to ensure you actually get what you need and want is to use the resources of your library.

Student: What printed reference sources should I use for ecclesiology?

Dr. Finucane's chapter introduces you to a huge topic—the Church and its history. The range of possible topics for research is vast. Once again, the key is getting started with the right reference tool. Are you interested in researching a person or an event? If so, you need to use a reference tool that includes biographical and/or historical coverage within its scope. Are you interested in researching present-day theological understanding of the Church or contemporary issues pertaining to the Church? If this is the case, you need to use a reference tool that includes coverage of this kind of material, that is, one that provides a more systematic treatment. Some reference works will include both types of coverage, but many will focus on either one or the other.

The New Catholic Encyclopedia (either the first or second edition), mentioned previously, is the most comprehensive reference tool providing coverage for all topics, historical and systematic. Several of the one-volume reference tools mentioned in previous chapters also provide all-encompassing but less detailed coverage.

For historical research, there are reference tools available for specific periods of Church history. You have already encountered the *Encyclopedia of the Early Church* in the last chapter. For the middle ages, many libraries will own the thirteen-volume *Dictionary of the Middle Ages* (1982–1989, supplemental volume published in 2004) or the more recent two-volume *Encyclopedia of the Middle Ages* (2000). For the Reformation and post-Reformation developments within Protestantism, there is the four-volume *Oxford Encyclopedia of the Reformation* (1996), the six-volume *Encyclopedia of the Renaissance* (1999), or the four-volume *Encyclopedia of Protestantism* (2004).

For research focusing on the Church in the United States, consult either the *Encyclopedia of American Catholic History* (1997) or the *Dictionary of Christianity in America* (1990); this latter reference work covers both Protestant and Catholic developments.

For research oriented toward contemporary or systematic issues, several reference tools focus specifically on these kinds of issues. Three titles mentioned in the preceding chapter—the *New Dictionary of Theology*, the *Dictionary of Fundamental Theology*, and the *Handbook of Catholic Theology*—all provide such coverage. There is even a one-volume reference work focusing entirely on ecclesiology:

> Christopher O'Donnell, O.Carm. *Ecclesia: A Theological Encyclopedia of the Church*. Collegeville, MN: Liturgical Press, 1996.

As always, if your library does not own one of these titles, ask the librarian to show you an alternative.

Student Tasks

1. Choose a topic in ecclesiology and go to a web browser, type it in, and see how many hits you receive. Check a few to see what types of hits show up. Can you think of different search terms to use for your topic? What difference does it make in your results? What difference does the use of quotation marks around phrases make? Identify a website that you would be able to cite in an academic paper. On what do you base your judgment of the website's worthiness?

2. Find an encyclopedia article on a topic on the Church or its history that interests you. How specific is the encyclopedia for your topic? Use the bibliography to identify subject heading(s) for that topic. Using the subject headings, identify, if possible, a book on your topic that is not listed in the encyclopedia bibliography. If you were to pursue the topic further, what would be your next step?

5

Grace and Sacraments: The Mystery of the Divine—Human Encounter

From the Editor

In the previous chapter on ecclesiology, we looked at the structure of the community, what it means to belong, its macro-structures, identity concerns, and its purpose in the world. In this chapter, the focus will be on the interior, or micro, theological understanding of sacraments and grace— the way we celebrate, communicate, initiate, solemnize, and live in God's love. In a theological nutshell, it is all about communication between God and us, and us together.

We all know what it is to communicate to another person what is deepest in our hearts, to be heard, to be ourselves, to be understood, and to be loved as we are. It is no less with the Christian community, where God is the source, support, and end. While communicating privately with God in individual prayer is necessary, the community also must engage God. This communication comes in many forms, but what we will theologically investigate in this chapter is the role of universal signs belonging to the heart of Christianity.

This chapter should be read in conjunction with the previous chapter. In this chapter, we investigate theology's understanding of grace (God's self communicated) by investigating the role of communication and symbol. Grace is foundational to Christian theology because it is the key term used in the tradition to describe the interaction of God with us. Grace describes the binding of the community called Church and its communal symbols— such as baptism and Eucharist—called sacraments. Both mediate God to us in symbols (invisible and visible together) that are grace filled and that teach us how to live our daily lives. Sacramental Christianity is at the heart of Christian spirituality as a paradigm of how to live a life of love in discipleship. What we will read is about the meaning and purpose of life itself, in symbol, in communication, in holy encounter with God.

Grace and Sacraments: The Mystery of the Divine–Human Encounter

Jay M. Hammond, PhD

Overview

The two preceding chapters on Christology and ecclesiology provide the framework for understanding the sacramental theology that emerged from Vatican Council II. On the one hand, Jesus is the primordial sacrament of God's presence and action, which means that Jesus' life, death, and resurrection reveal the mystery of God's love for creation because, for Christians, the incarnation is the mystery of the Divine–human encounter. On the other hand, the Church is the fundamental sacrament of Jesus' presence and action, which means that the Church is a sacrament because it makes Christ present in the world. Thus, the Church, symbolically called Christ's body (Rom 12:4–6), vicariously participates in the Divine–human encounter because when two or more are gathered in Jesus' name, he is among them (Mt 18:20).

To understand how Jesus Christ (Christology) and the Church (ecclesiology) inform Catholic sacramental theology, this chapter will (1) explain the importance of signs and symbols, (2) describe and define at greater length the word *sacrament*, (3) consider the two basic sacraments of Jesus and the Church in more detail, (4) survey the symbolic rituals of the seven formal sacraments celebrated by Roman Catholics, and (5) end by considering how active Christians themselves are living sacraments that point to and manifest God's presence and actions in the world.

Signs and Symbols: Creating Meaning in Human Communication

Humans are awash in symbols. They are ubiquitous in all our activities, thoughts, and dreams. We can neither construct meaning nor communicate with each other without them. However, we often take signs and symbols for granted. For example, you could not even read this text, or any text for that matter, unless you have learned the complex sign system of the English language. Likewise, discussion of this book, or any conversation, would be impossible without the symbols that both contain and communicate the meanings expressed by the sign system. The very act of your reflection about these meanings involves several levels of complex symbolic thinking through, in, and by which you just had a thought, whatever it was.

Accordingly, all communication and the meaning created therein assumes a common use of signs and symbols. On the other hand, communication breaks down when we interpret signs and symbols inaccurately, use them incorrectly, and/or are dishonest about them, that is, when we intentionally misconstrue our signs and symbols to others. In effect, signs and symbols are the basic building blocks of all human language, according to which we create meaning from our experiences and communicate it with others. They are the retainers, transmitters, and translators of all we know and love. Thus, we do not know or love reality immediately but can only experience reality mediated through the various symbolic systems that we call language. This principle of mediation is foundational to the meaning of sacramentality.

A sign and symbol are not the same. A sign is something that points to another reality and means what it signifies; the meaning is mostly fixed. In contrast, a symbol is a multidimensional sign that points to another reality and manifests the reality to which it points. For example, most readers would interpret and understand a stop sign in the same way: the sign signals them to stop at the intersection, but the sign is not the intersection. Likewise, they would know that a sign reading "St. Louis 10 miles" will lead them to the city but is not itself the destination. But the same cannot be said of a symbol as simple as a kiss, which can manifest many things to different people: love and affection (e.g., parent to child, between spouses, or between acquaintances), romance and seduction (e.g., husband to wife, boyfriend to girlfriend, or those on a date), greeting and farewell (e.g., a kiss hello, a kiss goodbye), respect and reverence (e.g., to kiss a ring, flag, or cross), forbidden and forced (e.g., used in incest, adultery, pedophilia, rape), betrayal and death (Judas kissing Jesus, and Michael Corleone kissing his brother Fredo in the movie *The Godfather, Part II*), and anger or frustration (e.g., "kiss my butt," "kiss off"). Other examples further illustrate the point: The sculptor Rodin was disappointed with people's reactions to his statue *The Kiss* (1886) because he thought most misunderstood his intention. And we would be remiss if we excluded the 1970s glam-rock music phenomenon KISS. While many other examples could be given, the point is this: Is a kiss ever really just a kiss?

Likewise, a symbol manifests the reality to which it points. For many, the activity of kissing manifests love, yet love is more than kissing. Saying, "I love you," also expresses love, but love is more than words. Love is a mom or dad hugging a child tight, but love is more than a hug. Paul says that love is both patient and kind (1 Cor 13:4), yet love is still more. Jesus taught that one should love God above all and neighbor as oneself (Mk 12:29–31, Mt 22:37–39, Lk 10:27), but even the golden rule does not exhaust the depths of love because there are many more dimensions to the mystery of love. Thus, while symbols manifest the reality to which they point, they always allude to more:

> A symbol is charged with many meanings, and once it has caused an interpreter to take account of its many meanings, its work still continues. There is always more depth of meaning to be uncovered in it, more questions to be asked of it, because the abundance and richness of its meaning are inexhaustible. The human mind can never get to the bottom of a symbol and be done with it. (Lawler, 1995, 21)

The inexhaustibility is the tricky thing about symbols because it moves away from "objective" knowledge that is quantifiable and observable to more "subjective" knowledge that is qualitative and personal. For some, this causes a problem because they prefer "objective" knowledge to symbolic ways of understanding. The empirical prejudice echoed in dismissive comments like "it's only a symbol" restricts human knowing to a narrow category of experience. While symbols may struggle to describe the human phenomenon of love, few doubt the reality of love. Experience dictates the existence of love, and humans use symbols to understand love's meanings and to communicate them with others. Thus, a better way to understand symbols is to interpret them as being fully real because they concretely and effectively communicate personal meanings that escape easy description. Otherwise, to say a symbol is not real prevents the communication of meaning, which is so integral to our human experience.

Of course, there are many variations in between a sign and symbol. Smoke can be interpreted as a sign, "where there is smoke there is fire," but also as a symbol; for example, we say a person who is performing at a high level is "smoking," which does not mean that person is physically aflame with fire. Nevertheless, while all symbols are signs, not all signs are symbols. The difference between the two often depends on the function of the sign according to the context within which it is used. A simple sign normally points to a physical activity or object, but a symbol opens to the human activity of creating meaning that moves beyond the physical world into the "spiritual" dimensions of human experience. The key is the activity of interpretation because signs and symbols require a personal response before their meanings can be understood. How we interpret a sign or symbol greatly influences what that sign or symbol means, but our interpretations are significantly shaped by the communities to which we belong, because while all of us were born naked into the world, none of us was born into a naked world. Accordingly, signs and symbols have socialized all of us, and we must personally interpret them if we want to participate in the human process of communicating meaning. In short, sacraments depend on signs and symbols.

Describing and Defining the Sacraments

Describing a Sacrament

Like signs and symbols, the sacraments are about the mystery of a threefold communication: from God to humans, from humans to God, and among humans in community. The very idea of communication implies relationship and interpretation. Thus, when you read or hear the word *sacrament*, for example, at the liturgy of the Eucharist during the mass when the bread and wine are elevated, broken, distributed, and so on, you should ask: "To what do the signs/symbols point? What do the signs/symbols communicate? How do the signs/symbols cultivate relationships?" These may seem like simple questions, but if they are overlooked and left unanswered, then the meaning of the sacraments will remain individually and communally obscure, confusing, and boring.

Moreover, signs and symbols provide the "content" for sacramental rituals, and those ritual actions, communally celebrated, supply the "context" for interpreting and understanding the significance of the sacraments. Such an understanding of the sacraments parallels the idea that the signs and symbols we use involve both our individual interpretations and the communal contexts that shape our perceptions. Thus, fuller participation in the sacraments requires that we understand both because to miss either the "content" of the sacraments' symbolism or the "context" of their communal celebration is to decrease their ability to convey meaningful communication.

Roman Catholics call their symbolic rituals "rites" (content), which they celebrate during the liturgy (context). While a rite describes the prescribed actions and words needed for administering a sacrament, the liturgy is the actual celebration of a sacrament by the community. *Liturgy* comes from the Greek word meaning "the work of the people." Since all relationships require the work of the participating members, the liturgy, communicated through and in its symbolic rituals, is a special and significant locus for the reciprocal "work" that unveils the mystery of the Divine–human encounter. In this relationship, the work is primarily God's action, but it also involves the participatory work of the community to love and serve God and neighbor. A better understanding of how "sacramental language" describes and expresses these relationships can open us to a greater appreciation of and participation in the sacramentality of all created reality.

Defining Sacraments

All world religions have sacraments, but only Christians call them sacraments (Martos, 2001, 3–16). Most Christian churches celebrate sacraments, but there is a wide spectrum of understandings on the number and meaning of the sacraments. Historically, the term *sacrament* comes from the Greek word *mysterion* and the Latin word *sacramentum*. *Mysterion* means "something hidden or secret," which has been retained today with the word *mystery*. Thus, even before Christianity began, the term *mysterion* described an experience of the divine and/or God's activity in human affairs. Thus, *mysterion* was also closely linked with the idea of revelation; that is, God's revelation is a mystery. These two meanings of mystery and revelation are common in both the Hebrew and Christian scriptures, especially Ephesians and Colossians. However, it was not until the third century that theologians Clement and Origin explicitly applied the meaning of *mysterion* to Christian ritual practices. Today, *mysterion* reminds us that the core meaning of the symbolic rituals we now call sacraments involves mystery and revelation of God's self-communication.

Tertullian (d. 230) was a native of Carthage in North Africa. He had a pagan education, became a lawyer, lived in Rome, converted to Christianity about 195 CE, and then became a priest. He was one of the first Christian theologians to write in Latin and became one of the great early theologians, especially in Christology and the Trinity.

An important development in this discussion happened in the third century when the theologian Tertullian sought to translate *mysterion* into Latin. He chose the word *sacramentum*, which meant a "sacred oath" taken by a recruit joining the Roman army. In the same way the soldier uttered a *sacramentum* to the emperor, who was considered a deity, the Christian pledges a sacred oath to Christ. Thus, Tertullian used *sacramentum* to mean a religious initiation into the Christian community via baptism and Eucharist, which were both a sign of initiation and the means of sanctification. Today, *sacramentum* reminds us that the core meaning of the symbolic rituals we now call sacraments involves an initiation into a community of believers that seek experience of God's mystery.

Following Tertullian was the fifth-century Augustine of Hippo. He developed the notion that a *sacramentum* is a sign that sanctifies because it is efficacious, meaning that the sign produces an intended effect or that it is effective. For example, Christ and the Spirit make effective, through grace, the cleansing that water signifies. Thus, for those with faith, baptism purifies by grace. Augustine did not only consider religious rituals to be *sacramenti* but he listed over three-hundred sacraments. The Church would gradually pare back the number of sacraments by distinguishing between those celebrated as symbolic rituals by the community, which were retained as sacraments, and those that came to be identified as sacramentals, that is, signs and practices that assist persons in their devotion and prayer (e.g., genuflection, crossing oneself, and a rosary). Nevertheless, Augustine's towering influence on Western Christianity framed the understanding of the sacraments as sacred signs. Thus, when the twelfth-century theologian Peter Lombard (France, d. 1160) devised the technical definition that states, "A sacrament is a sign of a sacred thing that is capable of conveying the grace of which it is the sign" (*Liber Sententiarum* IV, d. 1, c. 4), he was largely following in the footsteps of Augustine. Today, the medieval technical definition of a sacrament reminds us that only those symbolic rituals that confer the grace they signify are called sacraments.

The history of the terms *mysterion* and *sacramentum* teaches us that sacraments involve (1) the mystery of the Divine–human encounter wherein God reveals the divine presence, (2) the initiation of a believer into a communal participation of that Divine–human encounter, and (3) the faith community's active celebration of those symbolic rituals that confer the grace they signify.

With these three points in mind, a sacrament can be theologically defined as a symbolic ritual comprised of words, gestures, and material signs (bread, wine, water, oil, etc.) that points to and manifests Jesus' own actions, for the purpose of communicating God's grace to those who, by faith, perform and participate in their action. These three aspects are traditionally defined as (1) a sign (2) instituted by Christ (3) to give grace. Let us look at each aspect more closely.

Augustine (d. 430) was also from Carthage. He studied philosophy and rhetoric and became professor of rhetoric for the imperial court at Milan. After his conversion to Christianity in 386, he became bishop of Hippo (North Africa) in 396. He is one of the most influential Christian theologians, and the Catholic Church recognizes him as a "Doctor (teacher) of the Church."

A Sign

Previously, we made an important distinction between a sign and a symbol. While a sacrament is definitely a sign in that it points to another reality, it is also properly understood as a symbol because it manifests the reality to which it points. A good example is the Eucharist, which points both to the multifaceted mystery of Jesus' paschal meal, and to the manifestation of Christ's real presence in the Eucharist and among believing communities. Sacramental theology translates the symbol's two notions of pointing and manifesting into the understanding that the sacraments "effect what they signify" or "cause by signifying" (Lawler, 1995, 34). Thus, sacraments, like symbols, both point to or signify God's action and manifest, effect, or cause the grace of Christ that sanctifies the recipient.

> **Pasch** is Greek for "Passover." Thus, *Paschal Meal* is a term that refers to the Jewish Passover meal that Jesus shared with the Apostles the night before he died. By participating in the Paschal Meal, Christians share in the "Paschal Mystery," the redemption effected by Christ in his life, death, and resurrection.

The key is the signification because sacraments cause by signifying, so if they do not signify, then they do not cause. Simply stated, a sacrament is that which effects something by its significance, but sacraments do not always effectively signify for every person because the signification or meaning of the sacramental signs and symbols may be misunderstood and/or the participant may lack faith. For example, if my wife and I have been in an argument and she offers reconciliation with a kiss, if I do not understand the significance of the kiss and/or I do not trust her intentions, then the kiss will fail to effect or manifest what it signifies: forgiveness and reconciliation.

The point is that we need sacraments to communicate in the same way that we need symbols. Sacraments provide a language for relationship with God.

> In human life, signs and symbols occupy an important place. As a being at once body and spirit, man expresses and perceives spiritual realities through physical signs and symbols. As a social being, man needs signs and symbols to communicate with others, through language, gestures, and actions. The same holds true for his relationship with God. (*Catechism of the Catholic Church* [*Catechism*], n. 1146)

Sacraments, like symbols, strive to accomplish the difficult task of communicating spiritual reality. Just as symbols are necessary for human communication, sacraments are necessary for the communication of the Divine–human encounter. However, we should not assume that the sacraments restrict God's activity;

God does not need the sacraments to communicate with those he loves, but they are principle instruments that ritually manifest God's presence and actions to the community that celebrates their mystery.

Instituted by Christ

The Fourth Lateran Council (1215) held at Rome was the first council that officially numbered the sacraments at seven. The Church later confirmed this number at the Councils of Lyon II (1274), Florence (1439), and Trent (1547). During the Reformation (beginning in 1517), a thorny debate arose concerning the number of sacraments explicitly instituted by Christ. Many Protestants argued for the two dominical (*dominus* = "lord") sacraments of baptism and Eucharist because scripture records Jesus as directly instituting them. In contrast, the Council of Trent argued that Christ instituted all seven sacraments, and the council was left with the rather difficult task of demonstrating how Jesus historically instituted the specific rituals or general formula for each of the seven sacraments.

So who was right? As with most things, it depends on how you frame the question. If you look for specific scriptural instances where Jesus directly institutes the sacraments via word and action, then you will likely arrive at the two sacraments of baptism and Eucharist. However, if you look at Jesus as explicitly instituting the Church in a sacramental way, that is, the Church is Christ's body that locates Christ in the world, then Christ's explicit institution of the Church is the implicit institution of the Church's seven sacramental actions that reenact Jesus' own actions. In this view, Christ instituted the sacraments in a derivative sense because by "instituting the Church, Christ instituted the sacraments" (Rahner, 1963, 62).

Accordingly, the question of Christ's direct institution of the sacraments becomes subordinate to the question of Christ's direct institution of the Church as a sacrament of himself. Such an understanding of Christ's institution of the sacraments hinges on two notions: (1) Jesus as sacrament of God and (2) the Church as sacrament of Jesus. We will investigate these two important ideas in the third section of this chapter, but here it is important to mention that "the Christian sacraments are an attempt on the part of the Church to extend into the world the actions of Jesus in his humanity" (Noll, 1999, 30). Christ's institution of the sacraments requires nothing less than an imitation of Christ's own actions by Christians who celebrate the sacraments: (1) Jesus was baptized and commissioned the apostles to baptize (Mt 28:19), so the Church celebrates baptism as the initiation into discipleship with Christ; (2) Jesus' actions and teachings confirmed his Father's reign, so the Church celebrates Christians' confirmation to do the same;

(3) Jesus shared many meals with others and, at the last supper with his disciples, said, "Do this in remembrance of me," so the Church today celebrates a communal meal called Eucharist, where Christ continues to give himself, body and blood, to those he loves; (4 and 5) Jesus healed sickness and forgave sins, so the Church continues Christ's healing and forgiving actions in the anointing of the sick and reconciliation; (6) Jesus chose disciples and sent them as apostles into the world to serve others (Jn 20:21), so the Church continues the activity of Jesus' ministry in ordination; and (7) as Jesus lived in intimate friendship with the Father, thereby fulfilling the covenant relationship, so the Church today celebrates the covenant of marriage as a relationship centered in intimacy with God in Christ. In sum, Jesus did not institute the specific rituals of the sacraments; rather, he instituted the Church as a sacrament of himself to extend, in a tangible manner, his actions into the world.

To Give Grace

To understand the third aspect of a sacrament's traditional definition, we need to understand what "grace" means and how the sacraments "give grace."

First, grace (χάρις, *gratia*) is the free, unmerited assistance that God gives to humans for their salvation, which is nothing less than participation in God's life and love. In effect, grace makes a person a friend of God. Grace is both the cause and the effect of this friendship. Grace is the cause because grace is God's self-gift to humans that transforms, heals, and nurtures human existence. In theological terms, this is called either "uncreated grace" or "supernatural grace" because God's own presence personally dwells within those whom God draws into friendship, just as a lover experiences the personal presence of the beloved. Grace is also the effect because grace is the transformation of human nature, which brings forth depths of human growth that would otherwise remain dormant. In theological terms, this is called either "created grace" or "actual grace" because all the gifts God gives to humans, including their very existence, potentially deepen their friendship with God. In short, uncreated and created grace are two sides of the Creator–creature relationship that necessarily leads to the transformation of human experience. Thus, the mystery of grace lies at the heart of the mystery of the Divine–human encounter.

In practical terms, *grace* means "gift." Thus, all good things are gifts from God, which can rightfully be called grace. For example, my wife, children, and friends are all grace because they are gifts that manifest the gift of God's presence. A deeper examination of grace leads to the insight that "grace touches everything in our lives; it pervades everything we are and do" (Cooke, 1994, 79). What we should remember is that grace is a gift from God offered through the Son and in the Spirit. Thus, grace is not a thing; rather, it is always relational and comes to build authentic relationships between the Divine and human communities. Grace is always the root of this relationship, and friendship is its intended fruit.

Second, sacraments are not magic, nor are they grace machines. Rather, the grace that the sacraments "give" involves a relationship that emerges from, affirms, and returns to the mystery of the Divine–human encounter. On one side of the relationship, God always offers the grace communicated by a sacrament. Thus, a sacrament is a means of grace simply because God offers it. The terminology of the Council of Trent (1545–1563) called this "from the work worked" (Lat., *ex opere operato*), that is, properly performed sacraments, because they involve the agency of the risen Christ and the Spirit, contain and confer the grace they signify. This claim stresses that God, in Christ, is the primary agent of the grace offered in a sacrament. On the other side of the relationship, the participant must also accept the gift of grace that God offers for the sacrament to be an effective sign. Thus, the actual mediation of grace requires the recipient's participation. This dimension of the sacrament is called "from the work working" (*ex opere operantis*), that is, a freely participating subject who, through the Spirit, celebrates the sacraments by placing no obstacle to receiving them faithfully.

Simply stated, sacraments presuppose a personal faith where God offers and humans receive the grace of Christ. Such personal encounter rejects any passive, mechanistic, or magical understanding of the sacraments. Rather, sacraments are gifts of personal encounter between Christ and the Church.

The Two Basic Sacraments of Christ and Church

The years before Vatican Council II (1962–1965) saw a renewal of sacramental theology as theologians sought to return to the historical roots of the sacraments by recovering their original and primary meaning. In particular, the ideas of two theologians spearheaded the renewal: the German Jesuit Karl Rahner (1904–1984) and the Belgian Dominican Edward Schillebeeckx (1914; pronounced Skĭl-ah-bākes).

These two theologians explained the sacraments in ways that were both new and traditional because the same basic sacramental principles of Jesus and Church were operative at the inception of Christianity and are still operative today. Both of their groundbreaking works appeared in 1960. On the one hand, Rahner's *The*

Karl Rahner was one of the most influential Roman Catholic theologians of the twentieth century. He was born in Freiburg, Germany, and died in Innsbruck, Austria. His theology influenced Vatican Council II. Central to all his theology is the belief that God is self-gift. Thus, the fulfillment of human existence occurs in receiving God's gift of Himself, which is only fully experienced at the end of time but is present now as grace.

Edward Schillebeeckx is a Belgian theologian born in Antwerp. His books on Christology have made him one of the most well-known modern Roman Catholic theologians. Moreover, the influence of his thought at Vatican Council II contributed greatly to the reformist theology that emerged after the council.

Church and the Sacraments envisions the Church itself as the basic or "fundamental" sacrament. The seven sacraments are sacraments because they are the ritual actions of that sacrament that is the Church. On the other hand, Schillebeeckx considers Jesus Christ the basic or "primordial" sacrament of God. As such, Jesus is the preeminent outward sign of God's love and favor, so the Church and the seven sacraments are themselves sacraments because of God's self-communication in Jesus Christ.

Jesus, the Primordial Sacrament of God's Presence

The person of Jesus Christ pinpoints the mystery of the Divine–human encounter. Specifically, Jesus' actions, as the gospels record, provide us with the primordial meaning of the sacraments: "If you want to know what a sacrament is and what a sacrament does you can do no better than look at Jesus as we find him in the New Testament" (Noll, 1999, 20). In effect, the sacraments are the acts of Jesus Christ, and all other sacraments derive from him. But what does this mean? How is this possible? Schillebeeckx provides us an answer for the first question: "Even in his humanity Christ is the Son of God. The second person of the most holy Trinity is personally man; and this man is personally God. Therefore Christ is God in a human way, and [human] in a divine way" (Schillebeeckx, 1963, 13–14). The foundation for such thinking goes back to Jesus' words: "Whoever has seen me has seen the Father" (Jn 14:9; also see 1:18). Christ reveals the personal encounter with God, and celebration of the sacraments draws the Christian believer into personal relationship with Christ in his human actions that point to and manifest God's presence. Thus, to answer the second question (How is this possible?), we need to understand how the sacraments participate in Jesus' own ministry as performed and enacted in his life, death, and resurrection. Otherwise, the sacraments may become passive observation instead of active participation, service to rituals rather than service to neighbor, impersonal obligations instead of personal encounters, and abstract theory rather than embodied praxis.

Jesus' actions remind us that sacraments are not things but religious actions that express particular relationships that manifest presence. On one level, Jesus is God's mystery personified by revealing the relationships that both form and transform our human experience. On another level, Jesus is God's meaning personified by revealing who God is and who we are and should become through and in our human relationships. Together, the mystery and meaning of Jesus' life, death, and resurrection transform our human reality because the significance of Christ's actions forms our understanding of human experience and existence. Jesus embodies a new way of human existing, and he gives ultimate meaning to everything that was and is human. To perceive this significance is to open the door to a fresh understanding of the sacraments and sacramentality. For example, baptism celebrates the mystery of birth and transforms its meaning by recognizing that Christ himself invites the believer to participate in the mystery of his death and resurrection. Thus, the relationship expressed in baptism gives new meaning to the archetypical mystery of birth/death/rebirth because the significance of Jesus' past and present actions transforms how Christians experience God's presence in their lives.

Church, the Fundamental Sacrament of Jesus' Presence

With the birth of the Church in the gift of the Holy Spirit, Jesus gave the world a sacrament of himself: "Rising from the dead, [Christ] sent his life-giving Spirit upon his disciples and through this Spirit has established his body, the Church, as the universal sacrament of salvation" (*Lumen Gentium* 48). Through and in the activity of the Holy Spirit, the Church prepares for the reception of Christ by recalling the mystery of Christ and by working to make that mystery present in the world today. Thus, the Church is authentic to the degree it manifests Christ's humanity, actions, and ministry in the world. Just as Jesus only taught the words of the Father (Jn 8:28, 14:24), the Church should only teach the example of Christ, but because sinful humans comprise the Church, it often falls short of this realization. This fact should remind us that the Church is a sign of salvation but that it is Christ through the Spirit's activity that makes the sign effective.

Specifically, it is the Spirit that animates Christ's body, the Church. This imagery teaches us that the "Spirit is the very soul of the Church" (Noll, 1999, 36) because the Spirit brings our human community into relationship with the divine community: "The universal Church is seen to be 'a people brought into unity from the unity of the Father, the Son and the Holy Spirit'" (*Lumen Gentium* 4). Thus, just as the Father sent Jesus, Jesus sends forth the apostles by sending forth the gift of the Spirit (Jn 20:21–22). In short, the actions of Christ become the actions of his Church through and in the Spirit's power.

As a fundamental sacrament of Christ's presence and actions, the Church's vitality springs from the Spirit-filled celebration of the seven formal sacraments in a twofold sense.

> They are "by the Church," for she is the sacrament of Christ's action at work in her through the mission of the Holy Spirit. They are "for the Church" in the sense that *the sacraments make the Church*, since they manifest and communicate to [humans], above all in the Eucharist, the mystery of communion with the God who is love, One in three persons. (*Catechism*, n. 1118, emphasis added)

These two dimensions of Christ and Church express the Divine–human encounter. On one level, the sacraments are the acts of Christ in the Church, which means that the Church can only be a sacrament because it is in proper relationship with Christ. On another level, as sacrament, the acts of the Church sacramentally "incarnate" Christ's presence and actions in our world today through the communal concelebration of the sacraments by the human and Divine communities.

Diagram: The Sacramental Economy of Salvation

The following diagram operates on three levels: First, letters A–F remind us of the persons (Father–Son–Spirit, Christians) and personal actions (sacraments) involved in the mystery of the Divine–human encounter. Letters A–C indicate that the sacramental economy of salvation parallels the Trinitarian economy of the Father sending the Son and Spirit into the world, and letters D–F depict how the seven Sacraments respond to God's activity by drawing active Christians into the mystery of the Divine–human encounter.

Second, numbers I–VI remind us of the relationships that comprise the reality of the sacramental mystery. The Father sends Jesus Christ as the personal sacrament of God's love for all humankind. After his death and resurrection, Christ sends the Spirit to guide his Church, which is a personal sacrament of Christ. The Spirit animates the Church as it reenacts Jesus' own actions in the celebration of the seven sacraments. The graces of the seven sacraments transform active Christians into living sacraments who live in the basic attitudes and values of Jesus Christ. Finally, active Christians participate in the mystery of God's ongoing revelation by existing as living sacraments that point to and manifest God's love, forgiveness, healing,

The Sacramental Economy of Salvation

I → ⟶ B. ⟶ II ⟶ C.

A.
God the Father

B.
God the Son

C.
God the Spirit

1. Transcendent Mystery who desires relationship with creation through and in the Son and Spirit
2. The Giver of all Gifts or Graces
3. The mystery of the Trinity reveals distinction of persons (*individual*) and unity of nature (*community*)

1. Jesus Christ: Primordial Sacrament of God the Father's presence and actions
2. Jesus is the Gift or Grace of the Father
3. Jesus Christ is the *individual* and personal revelation of the Father

1. Church: Fundamental Sacrament of Jesus Christ's presence and actions
2. The Gift or Grace of the Father and Christ
3. The Church is a personal *community* that continues Christ's actions in the world

VI   V ⟵   E. ⟵ IV ⟶   D.   III

E.
Christians

D.
Seven Sacraments

F.
Divine-Human Encounter

1. The Mystery of the Divine-human encounter analogously manifests itself throughout I–V, whereby all relationships begin from and return to the Father (A, F)
2. The self-giving that is grace configures the mystery of interpersonal relationships, both Divine and human
3. Human relationships are individual and communal simply because they are personal

1. Active Christians are Living Sacraments who manifest Christ's presence and activity in the world. Since they live their lives in Christ, Christian individuality is always an imitation
2. Grace enables Christians to live into becoming more fully Christian
3. Individual and Personal imitation of Jesus' actions by active Christians

1. Initiation
    Baptism: Acceptance
    Confirmation: Commitment
    Eucharist: Thanksgiving
   Healing
    Reconciliation: Forgiveness
    Anointing: Strengthening
   Vocation
    Marriage: Service
    Orders: Service
2. Sacraments confer the grace they signify, i.e., they reenact Christ's actions by the power of the Spirit
3. Communal and personal celebration of Jesus' presence and actions by a Spirit-filled community of faith

and acceptance in their everyday encounters with others. Thus, all authentic human relationships and activities sacramentalize the Divine–human encounter.

Third, the six sets of numbers 1–3 remind us that grace is not a thing but a personal gift with individual and communal dimensions. Jesus Christ is the individual and personal gift of the Father. The Church is the communal gift of the Son and Spirit personally shared within the human community. The gifts of the sacraments enable the Church to celebrate communally Jesus' presence and actions. The gift of community enables individual Christians to imitate Jesus' attitude and actions in everyday life. Finally, the gift of self-giving itself indicates that the mystery of interpersonal relationships requires a communal and individual sharing, which the Divine life reveals (one God = community; three persons = Individuality) and human experience confirms (humans are psycho/individual social/communal beings). In short, Jesus as the primordial sacrament of God's presence and action reminds us that an authentic celebration of the sacraments should be a personal and individual encounter, while the Church as the fundamental sacrament of Jesus' presence and actions reminds us that an authentic celebration of the sacraments should also be a personal and communal encounter. Such individual and communal encounters transform active Christians into living sacraments that are always personal.

The Seven Sacraments

The Roman Catholic Church recognizes seven formal sacraments: baptism, confirmation, Eucharist, reconciliation, anointing, holy orders, and marriage. These seven sacraments can be classified in three groups: sacraments of initiation (baptism, confirmation, Eucharist), sacraments of healing (reconciliation and anointing), and sacraments of vocation (holy orders and marriage).

Sacraments of Initiation: Baptism, Confirmation, Eucharist

Baptism

The first sacrament of initiation, baptism, is a symbolic plunging/washing of a person in water that incorporates the person into the mystery of Jesus Christ and his Church and signifies the forgiveness of sin. These two effects are linked. The initiation into the Christian community is the forgiveness of sins because by forgiveness, Christ and his Church accept a person through a ritual whereby sin loses its power. The focus is on acceptance via forgiveness, not on the sin that causes alienation. This is pointedly expressed by the fact that Jesus, who was without sin, still desired to be baptized so as to be accepted by his Father, "You are my Son, the Beloved; with you I am well pleased" (Mk 1:11; also see Mt 3:17, Lk 3:22). In short, the example of Jesus teaches us that "baptism is the basis of the whole Christian life, the gateway to life in the Spirit, and the door which gives access to the other sacraments" (*Catechism*, n. 1212). Thus, baptism is the first of the three sacraments of initiation.

Water is the main sacramental sign and accomplishes what it signifies—new birth, new life, and new creation—by incorporating the initiate into Jesus' life, death, and resurrection. Baptism's womb–tomb symbolism conveys this mystery. Immersion in the water symbolizes dying with Christ, while the extraction from the water symbolizes being reborn with Christ (Rom 6:3–4; Col 2:12, 3:3). Both the pouring of water over an infant's head and the plunging of an adult under the water symbolize the passing from the death of the community of sin into the life of the Christian community (granted, adult baptism conveys this meaning more explicitly). Likewise, the symbolic act of the laying on of hands by the priest, parents, and godparents during the anointing of the initiate with chrism emphasizes the sacrament's communal character. It stresses that the sacrament is an initiation into a community (1 Cor 12:13; Gal 3:27) that will be a lifelong process. The laying on of hands signifies that the initiate will not have to undergo this journey alone because she will have the support of the Christian community. Other symbols include the baptismal candle, which signifies that Christ will light the person's journey; and the white baptismal gown, which symbolizes that the initiate has "put on Christ." Thus, while on the journey of this life, the initiate should be recognized as following Christ by her attitude and actions toward God, self, and neighbor.

The central mystery of baptism's symbolic ritual communicates a rebirth into new life in Christ, whereby the initiate becomes a child of God in joining the Church as a member of Christ's body through receiving the gift of the Spirit. In short, baptism is an initiation into the Divine–human encounter between the divine community of persons, Father, Son, Spirit, and the human community of the Church that celebrates the Trinitarian mystery. This mystery echoes in the Rite of Baptism:

> Father, look now with love upon your Church and unseal for her the fountain of baptism. By the power of the Spirit give to this water the grace of your Son, so that in the sacrament of baptism all those whom you have created in your likeness may be cleansed from sin and rise to a new birth to innocence by water and the Holy Spirit. We ask you, Father, with your

Son to send the Holy Spirit upon the waters of this font. May all who are buried with Christ in the death of baptism rise also with him in newness of life. We ask this through Christ our Lord. (*The Rites of the Catholic Church I [The Rites I]*, n. 91, p. 400)

Confirmation

Confirmation, the second sacrament of initiation, is a symbolic anointing with oil on the forehead that signifies (1) the public renewal of baptismal promises that (2) strengthens participation in the Church by (3) sealing the initiate with the gifts of the Spirit. These three aspects are interconnected. Due to the fact that confirmation complements, that is, completes, baptism, it should not be separated from baptism. So, if baptism is when Christ offers the Spirit's gifts to the initiate (either infant or adult), confirmation is when the person publicly accepts those same gifts of the Spirit. However, the confirmation of the gifts is twofold. On the one hand, the initiate confirms his or her baptismal promises, and on the other, the bishop confirms the person's desire to become an adult member of the ecclesial community by bearing and sharing the Spirit's gifts with the Church and wider community. In short, "the reception of the sacrament of Confirmation is necessary for the completion of baptismal grace" (*Catechism*, n. 1285) because the person must accept what has been given. This is true whether the initiate was baptized as an infant or adult.

Originally, confirmation was the third, postbaptismal anointing, administered by the bishop, which finalized the person's initiation into the Church. However, during the legalization of Christianity in the fourth century, there was a massive influx of people wanting to become Christian. The influx meant that the bishop could not be present at all the baptisms, which were therefore delegated to priests and deacons. Yet, the bishop retained the third anointing by later "confirming" the initiates' baptism, which reminded the local Church of their unity with the universal Church. Thus, over time and for practical reasons, confirmation became separate from baptism, and two distinct rites developed. Subsequently, the French councils of Riez (439) and Orange (441) identified confirmation as an independent sacrament. Although the separation of confirmation from baptism has led to some confusion regarding its theology, confirmation is best understood as the conclusion to baptism, which invites the initiate to share in the community's Eucharistic celebration.

Oil is the main sacramental sign that accomplishes what it signifies, a spiritual seal that identifies the initiate as belonging to Christ: "It is God who establishes us with you in Christ and has anointed us, by putting his seal on us and giving us his Spirit in our hearts as a first installment" (2 Cor 1:21–22). Anointing symbolizes that the initiate confirms Jesus' call to join him as both disciple and apostle. As disciple, literally "to follow," the anointing signifies that the initiate personally decides to follow the example and teachings of Jesus Christ, that is, to be personally named Christian. As apostle, literally "to send out," the anointing signifies that a Christian is sent to serve the wider communities of Church and world. The symbolic act of laying on of hands by the sponsor and bishop during the anointing highlights the sacrament's communal character. On the one hand, the bishop, as a symbol of the universal Church, confers the sacrament by anointing the initiate's forehead with the sign of the cross while saying the words, "Be sealed with the Gift of the Holy Spirit." On the other, the sponsor, as a symbol of the local Church, presents the initiate to the bishop and supports him or her as they together say "Amen" or "Yes" to the decision to accept the Spirit's gift of faith in Christ. The dual symbolic act of laying on of hands stresses that the sacrament is an initiation into relationships of mutual support; the community supports the initiate, who in turn builds the community.

The central mystery of confirmation's symbolic ritual communicates acceptance or confirmation of the gift of the Spirit, whereby initiates pledge their lives to God by accepting a share in the mission of Jesus Christ according to the Spirit's fullness of life. Again, confirmation invites the initiates into the mystery of the Divine–human encounter, where the Trinitarian community draws the Church community into relationship. This mystery echoes in the Rite of Confirmation:

> My dear friends, in baptism God our Father gave the new birth of eternal life to his chosen sons and daughters. Let us pray to our Father that he will pour out the Holy Spirit to strengthen his sons and daughters with his gifts and anoint them to be more like Christ the Son of God. (*The Rites I*, n. 24, p. 490)

Eucharist

The third initiation sacrament, *Eucharist*, is the Greek word for "thanksgiving" and signifies the new covenant of Jesus' body and blood, which (1) is "the source and summit of the Christian life" (*Lumen Gentium* 11; *Catechism*, n. 1324) that (2) completes the initiation sacraments, unites the seven sacraments, and sustains all ministerial activity by (3) drawing the Christian most fully into Christ's Paschal (Easter) mystery. These three aspects build upon one another. Since Eucharist completes baptism and confirmation, it signifies that God's offer of friendship in baptism, and the initiate's acceptance of that friendship in confirmation, fully becomes an enduring friendship through and in the activity of sharing a sacred meal together. During the last supper, Jesus said to his disciples:

> This is my commandment, that you love one another as have I loved you. No one has greater love than this, to lay down one's life for one's friends. You are my friends if you do what I command you. I do not call you servants any longer, because the servant does not know what the master is doing; but I have called you friends, because I have made known to you everything that I have heard from my Father. You did not choose me but I chose you. And I appointed you to go and bear fruit, fruit that will last, so the Father will give you whatever you ask him in my name. I am giving you these commands so that you may love one another. (Jn 15:12–15)

Jesus' table fellowship is marked by love and friendship, a friendship enacted by following Jesus' invitation that "as I have loved you, you also should love one another" (Jn 13:34). One way Christians love as Jesus loves is by celebrating the sacraments. Specifically, just as all of Jesus' own actions led to and were fulfilled in the loving act of his passion, the six other sacraments either involve the celebration of the Eucharist or lead the participant to the Eucharist. Thus, all Christian ministries should extend the Paschal mystery, which Jesus was offering to his disciples at the last supper.

Bread and wine are the main sacramental signs of the Eucharist, and they accomplish what they signify: Christ's real presence, which "by the words of Christ and the invocation of the Holy Spirit, become Christ's Body and Blood" (*Catechism*, n. 1333). Since the thirteenth century, transubstantiation has been the technical term for describing Christ's real presence in the Eucharist. Later in the sixteenth century, when the meaning of real presence was theologically argued by many of the new Reformation groups, the Council of Trent declared: "By the consecration of the bread and wine there takes place a change of the whole substance of the bread into the substance of the body of Christ our Lord and of the whole substance of the wine into the substance of his blood. This change the holy Catholic Church has fittingly and properly called *transubstantiation*" (*Catechism*, n. 1376). Although transubstantiation attempts to explain how Christ is essentially or ontologically (the nature of being; ontology is the branch of metaphysics concerned with the nature or essence of being or existence) present in the Eucharist as a result of a metaphysical change in the bread and wine, today this often leads to serious misunderstandings. Whereas medieval peoples understood substance as a metaphysical reality, we today understand substance as a physical reality. Michael Lawler explains this point well:

> In contemporary mentality substance no longer means what the medievals meant by it. Worse, it means something quite contrary. By taking substance in an essentially physical sense, moderns are tempted to understand transubstantiation in an essentially physical sense, which is not only contradicted by the unmistakable evidence of their senses, but is also the very interpretation that Scholastic theology wished, in the first instance, to exclude by the use of the term. By the use of the term *transubstantiation* the Scholastics, and the Church, wished to assert, on the one hand, the reality of Christ's presence in the eucharist and, on the other, the metaphysical nature of the wondrous change which takes place, leaving unchanged the physical properties of bread and wine. (Lawler, 1995, 124)

Transubstantiation tries to explain how the bread and wine are physical signs that point to and manifest the metaphysical reality of Christ's real presence. However, without proper understanding of medieval philosophy (substance/accident, form/matter), the "how" of transubstantiation will largely remain misunderstood by modern interpreters who mistake substance to mean a physical or "accidental" change rather than a metaphysical or "substantial" change of the sacramental elements. The Council of Trent was clear on this point when it declared that "the species of bread and wine alone remain" while their substance converts into Christ's body and blood (Session 13, Canon 2). In other words, while the substance (the metaphysical inner reality of a thing) changes, the accidents (the external, physical qualities of a thing, e.g., color, weight, taste) of the bread and wine, which are known by our senses, remain unchanged. Unfortunately, the new *Catechism of the Catholic Church* does not explain this important point nor does it explain the philosophy upon which transubstantiation depends. Thus, in today's scientific framework, many are confused by transubstantiation because if they do not understand and accept the philosophical framework transubstantiation presupposes, then it is likely that they will misunderstand, or even deny, the explanation of the real presence.

Scholastic theology refers to a method of learning taught by academic theologians at the first European universities, ca. 1100–1500. The primary purpose of scholasticism was to use the method of dialectical analysis to find answers to particular questions or to resolve a contradiction.

Instead of having to accept medieval philosophy to explain the real presence, the three words *consecration, conversion,* and *communion* can help us understand the mystery of the real presence in a way more suitable to our modern thinking.

First, the *consecration* is when the priest extends his hands over the bread and wine and says, "Lord you are holy indeed, the fountain of all holiness. Let your Spirit come upon these gifts to make them holy, so that they may become for us the body and blood of our Lord, Jesus Christ" (*The Sacramentary*, Eucharistic Prayer II, p. 549). The symbolic act of laying on of hands that transforms the Eucharistic elements into Christ's real presence again signifies the communal character of the sacraments. God's Spirit makes Christ present in the Eucharist so that it can be shared. Just as Jesus shared himself with his disciples at the last supper, the laying on of hands today points to and manifests the mystery of Christ's self-gift to his friends so that the Church can become the Body of Christ by sharing the Body of Christ.

Next, the consecration signifies a real *conversion* of the elements. The *Catechism* employs the term in this way: "It is by the conversion of the bread and wine into Christ's body and blood that Christ becomes present in this sacrament" (n. 1375). The effect of this conversion is the new reality of Christ under the visible signs of the bread and wine. In what sense, moreover, does the "inner or deepest reality" of Jesus become present in the transformed elements? An example from popular anthropology, which has its own limitations, may help explain the conversion. Like the medieval peoples, most today imagine a person to be comprised of body and soul, and most would consider the conversion of a person's "deepest reality" to involve the soul and only secondarily the body. In a similar way, the conversion of the elements means that the "deepest reality" of Christ is personally present in the Eucharist while the physicality of the species remains unchanged. In this sense, Christ's presence is not a thing but a personal presence that the signs of bread and wine point to and manifest. The symbolism realizes Christ's presence in his act of breaking and sharing the bread and wine because in that act, Christ reveals his "deepest reality" of sacrificially existing for others so as to fulfill his Father's will through the forgiveness of sins. This interpretation squares with the Jewish mentality of Jesus' time that focused on what a person did, rather than a person's abstract essence or being. In short, Christ is present in the Eucharist because it is Christ who acts in the Eucharist.

Finally, the conversion effects what it signifies in *communion*, which is the communal sharing of the body of Christ. On one level, communion signifies that Christ offers his very self to the Eucharistic community. Here, Christ acts by offering his body and blood to his friends. On another level, communion signifies the social dimension of Christians communing with each other through and in the presence of their Lord. Christians act by accepting Christ, whereby they become his body, the Church. The fact that the Eucharist is an initiation sacrament should remind us that the Eucharist calls us into deeper relationship with Christ and neighbor, and this is why it is called the source and summit of the ecclesial life (*Catechism*, nn. 1324–1327).

The Eucharist is the primary act by which Christ offers his sacramental presence to the Church and the primary act by which the Church worships God. Yet, such lofty language about the Eucharist should not lead us from the startling mystery that the grandeur of Divine–human encounter transpires with the down-to-earth act of sharing a meal in which the Divine community celebrates with the human community. This mystery echoes in the Eucharistic Rite:

> Before he was given up to death, a death he freely accepted, he took bread and gave you thanks. He broke the bread, gave it to his disciples, and said: Take this, all of you, and eat it: this is my body which will be given up for you. When the supper was ended, he took the cup. Again he gave you thanks and praise, gave the cup to his disciples, and said: Take this, all of you, and drink from it: this is the cup of my blood, the blood of the new and everlasting covenant. It will be shed for you and for all so that sins may be forgiven. Do this in memory of me. (*Sacramentary*, Eucharistic Prayer II, p. 549)

The Eucharist concludes the three initiation sacraments. Their ancient order was baptism, confirmation, Eucharist, but for historical reasons, they were separated, and more recently, Pius X inverted their order to baptism, Eucharist, confirmation by declaring in 1910 that the proper age for first communion is 7 (Martos, 2001, 254), while confirmation was delayed until a later date. However, their original and proper order, retrieved by the 1972 *Rite of Christian Initiation of Adults*, allows for a better understanding of the process of initiation. In baptism, God offers the gift of relationship; in confirmation, the initiate, sponsor, and bishop communally accept God's gift of relationship; and in Eucharist, God shares relationship with the Church community via a ritual meal. Gift offered, gift received, gift shared—these are the simple yet profound dimensions to the process of Christian initiation.

Building on this process, we can also look at the mystery of Christian initiation through the ancient tradition of hospitality. The story of Luke records the essentials of hospitality: washing, anointing, and the sharing of food with someone invited into your house:

> One of the Pharisees asked Jesus to eat with him, and he went into the Pharisee's house and took his place at the table. And a woman in the city who was a sinner, having learned that he was eating in the Pharisee's house, brought an alabaster jar of ointment. She stood behind him at his feet, weeping, and began to bathe his feet with her tears and to dry them with her hair. Then she continued kissing his feet and anointing them with the ointment. (Lk 7:36–38)

The Pharisee did not fully offer hospitality to Jesus because he only offered food without offering the usual washing and anointing. Luke 7:44–46 makes this point clear: Lapses in hospitality imply a lack of love. In contrast, the earliest origins of Christian initiation were synonymous with the gracious offer of hospitality. The initiate was washed (baptism), anointed (confirmation), and fed (Eucharist), which signifies loving acceptance. By recovering the richness of the symbolic acts of hospitality, we can envision God as offering hospitality in the initiation rites. When initiates come into God's house, that is, a Church, God washes, anoints, and feeds his guests. When taken together, the symbolism of baptism, confirmation, and Eucharist signify that God offers hospitality to the wayfarers in this world. Thus, God's hospitality is the foundation for the interpersonal relationships that the initiation sacraments symbolize and is why "the sacraments of Christian initiation—Baptism, Confirmation, and the Eucharist—lay the foundations of every Christian life" (*Catechism*, n. 1212), simply because God's hospitable love is that foundation.

Sacraments of Healing: Reconciliation and Anointing

Reconciliation

Reconciliation is heard in the words of forgiveness by the Church through the priest. The priest's words of absolution and gesture of extending the right hand over the penitent's head signify both (1) the forgiveness of sins and (2) the reacceptance into the ecclesial community. These two aspects are always connected because sin alienates us from God and damages the relationships within the Church community. If Jesus teaches us to love God, neighbor, and self, then sin is a rupture of those same three relationships that must be reconciled in the act of forgiveness. The gospels clearly record that Jesus' ministry was one of reconciliation. His announcement of the coming of his Father's reign was practically synonymous with the forgiveness of sins (Mt 1:21, Mk 2:5, Lk 1:77, Jn 1:29). Thus, just as the forgiveness of sin lies at the very heart of Jesus' public ministry and passion, reconciliation should comprise the very heart of Christianity. Because forgiveness is for giving, the Christian community, in imitation of Jesus' own actions, must reconcile with its members who become alienated by either personal or social wrongdoings. In short, God's forgiveness always works toward communal reconciliation: "And forgive us our debts, as we also have forgiven our debtors" (Mt 6:12; also see Jn 20:22–23).

The words of forgiveness and the laying on of hands express the main sacramental sign of penance, which confers what it signifies on two levels. On one level, it sacramentally manifests God's healing forgiveness, for "only God forgives sins" (*Catechism*, n. 1441). On another level, because private confession makes the role of the community less obvious, the priest simultaneously represents the community's reconciliation with the penitent. Since sin is relational, forgiveness too must be relational, and this requires real reconciliation that points to the mystery of the Divine–human encounter by manifesting the actual reconciliation within the human community. Such a relational understanding counters the common sentiment that "God has already forgiven me, so I don't have to go to confession" for two reasons. By speaking our sins, we stop denying the reality of our sinfulness and its destructive power, which in turn actually signals our acceptance of forgiveness because we no longer feel compelled to hide our sins from others. Thus, the power of forgiveness transforms the dynamics of our human relationships because without forgiveness, none of our interpersonal relationships would survive.

The 1973 revised *Rite of Penance* offers four different liturgical rites: (1) the rite for reconciliation of individual penitents, which transpires between the person and the priest in a private setting; (2) the rite for communal liturgy and examination of conscience followed by individual confession/absolution in a private setting; (3) the rite for communal examination of conscience, silent confession, and general absolution, which canon law restricts to the discretion of the local bishop; and (4) the abbreviated rite for emergency situations where death is imminent. While there are four forms, the guidelines for the revised rites stress that the liturgical celebration of the sacrament, in normal circumstances, should empha-

> Although the modern ritual of **penance** only calls for the priest to extend his right hand above the head of the penitent while giving absolution, it is important to realize that the gesture of "extending the right hand" echoes back to an earlier tradition where there was an actual laying on of the priest's hands upon the penitent's head. Such a symbolic act fitly signifies the forgiveness and healing offered in the sacrament.

size God's offer of forgiveness by the reading of appropriate scripture and highlight the role of ecclesial reconciliation by preferring public forms of penance to private forms.

Reconciliation ritually extends Christ's forgiving actions, which reconcile humans with God and one another. Just like all relationships, the mystery of Divine–human encounter would be impossible without the transformative and uniting grace of forgiveness. This mystery reverberates in the words of absolution during the Rite of Reconciliation:

> God, the Father of mercies, through the death and resurrection of his Son has reconciled the world to himself and sent the Holy Spirit among us for the forgiveness of sins; through the ministry of the Church may God give you pardon and peace, and I absolve you from your sins in the name of the Father, and of the Son, and of the Holy Spirit. (*The Rites I*, n. 46, pp. 546–547)

Anointing

Anointing is a symbolic laying on of hands with oil upon the forehead and hands of the sick person that (1) signals Jesus' compassion toward the sick and suffering by (2) his healing and forgiveness of sins, which (3) involves the faith of the one being healed. Suffering and sickness are universal aspects of human life and poignantly remind us of our human powerlessness and finitude unto death. While not necessarily causally linked (i.e., sin causes illness or illness causes sin), the threat of death, whether physical or spiritual, is one of the gravest problems of life, and both can have the same effect: the destruction of human dignity, life, and spirit. Thus, Jesus himself makes the link between healing and forgiveness (Mk 2:5–12) because illness can be a symptom of sin and sin a symptom of illness. So, as the good physician, Jesus came to cure both: "'Those who are well have no need of a physician, but those who are sick; I have come to call not the righteous but sinners'" (Mk 2:17).

Oil is the primary sign of anointing and accomplishes what it signifies: a person's participation in Christ's redemptive suffering and death, and faith in the promise of the resurrection, which grants the gift of peace. Just as in baptism and confirmation, where the community applies oil to signify their support of the initiate's new life, the oil in anointing signifies the community's solidarity with the suffering person who draws into deeper participation in Christ's Paschal mystery. The communal laying on of hands and prayer support the person as he or she undergoes the trials of sickness and suffering, which not only harm the body but also can ruthlessly ravage the human spirit. The communal support can help a person approach sickness and death as an opportunity to deepen his or her faith relationship with God. For example, the gospels repeatedly link Jesus' acts of healing with the recipients' faith (Mt 9:22, 15:28; Mk 5:34, 10:52; Lk 8:48, 18:42; cf. Mt 13:58). Thus, sickness can occasion faith if a person is open to the Spirit's power. Nevertheless, psychological and physical illness still glimpse the darkness of death and can destroy a person by overcoming faith with fear, hope with despair, and love with depression and bitterness. Anyone who has had much experience with illness and death knows just how horrible and powerful these realities can be. Yet, from this darkness, "Christ continues to 'touch' us in order to heal us" (*Catechism*, n. 1504).

The anointing of the sick ritually extends Christ's healing ministry to those who suffer physical and/or mental illness. Anointing transforms sickness and suffering into an occasion that manifests the mystery of the Divine–human encounter where the Trinitarian God of life overcomes the human fear of suffering and threat of death. This mystery echoes in the Rite of Anointing of the Sick:

> God of all consolation, you chose and sent your Son to heal the world. Graciously listen to our prayer of faith: send the power of your Holy Spirit, the Consoler, into this precious oil, this soothing ointment, this rich gift, this fruit of the earth. Bless this oil and sanctify it for our use. Make this oil a remedy for all who are anointed with it; heal them in body, in soul, and in spirit, and deliver them from every affliction. (*The Rites I*, n. 123, p. 824)

The sacraments of penance and anointing point to and manifest Jesus' acts of forgiveness and healing, which the Church now extends and celebrates as it continues to reconcile and restore the human community. On the one hand, the grace of God's forgiveness and the penitent's repentance and conversion are the basic ingredients of reconciliation, which build healthy relationships by transforming the alienating power of sin. On the other hand, the grace of God's healing and the sick person's faith in God's providential care are the basic ingredients of anointing, which alleviate the mental and physical sufferings of illness or old age by transforming the alienating power of death. In short, these two sacraments "continue, in the power of the Holy Spirit, [Jesus'] work of healing and salvation" (*Catechism*, n. 1421).

Sacraments of Vocation: Holy Orders and Marriage

Holy Orders

The holy orders is a symbolic laying on of hands upon an ordination candidate by a bishop, which signifies that (1) bishops, priests, and deacons continue the apostolic ministry enacted by Christ to (2) "nourish the Church with the word and grace of God" (*Lumen Gentium* 11) by (3) serving the local and global ecclesial community in the name and person of Jesus Christ. Although we can distinguish these three aspects, they all derive from Christ's own commission to his apostles: "Peace be with you. As the Father has sent me, so I send you. . . . Receive the Holy Spirit" (Jn 20:21–22). *Apostle* simply means "one sent out," and so, by the gift and power of the Spirit, Jesus sent his apostles to extend his mission of serving the people of God. Ordained ministers continue that service.

While the New Testament evidences that Jesus called the apostles to continue his ministry, it also demonstrates that the organization of ministerial order was a process in development. The earliest evidence comes from Paul, who teaches the tripartite division of apostles, prophets, and teachers (1 Cor 12:28; c. 54–55 CE). The Acts of the Apostles make it clear that such ministerial order emerged because the apostles needed pastoral assistance (Acts 6:2–7; c. 80–85 CE), and so the twelve appoint, by prayer and laying on of hands, seven candidates whom the Church community elected. Still later, the pastoral epistles of Titus and 1–2 Timothy (c. 100–110 CE) mention a new tripartite division of overseers (*episkopoi*), elders (*presbyteroi*), and servants (*diakonoi*), which seems to be normative by the early second century. Thus, within a century of Paul's initial and rather loose tripartite structure of apostles, prophets, and teachers, the Church adopted the new hierarchy ("sacred order," *hieros + arche*; hence, the term *holy order*) of episcopate (bishops), presbyterate (who were increasingly functioning as priests, which parallels the rising understanding of the Eucharist as sacrifice), and diaconate (deacons).

One explanation for this development could be the synthesis of Jewish Christian and Gentile Christian structures of leadership. On the one hand, the Jewish Christian leadership consisted of a council of elders or presbyters, while the Gentile Christian leadership consisted of a single overseer or bishop who was assisted by several assistants/servants or deacons, which followed the Roman model of governance. During this earliest development (50–100 CE), women may have served as deacons (Rom 16:1; 1 Tim 3:12), but scholars argue over whether the term *deacon* in the relevant passages technically refers to ordained deacons or is being used in the generic sense of "servant."

The laying on of hands upon the ordination candidate's head and solemn prayer of consecration (distinct prayers and ritual actions for each order) by the bishop is the main sacramental sign of holy order, which confers what it signifies on three levels. First, episcopal ordination is the fullness of the sacrament of holy order (*Catechism*, nn. 1555–1561) whereby the bishop, as a successor of the apostles, serves, by the Spirit's power, as "teacher, shepherd, and priest" in the name and place of Christ. Accordingly, the bishop simultaneously governs the local Church entrusted to him and shares in the apostolic leadership of the universal Church. As signs of his responsibility to teach and govern, at least three bishops usually lay their hands upon the bishop's head; his head is anointed with oil; the book of the gospels is presented; and the new bishop is vested with a miter, ring, and crosier (pastoral staff) and is seated on the bishop's chair.

Second, priestly ordination calls priests, by the Spirit's power, to be the bishop's coworkers within the ecclesial community by preaching the gospel and administering the sacraments, especially the Eucharist, which exercises "in a supreme degree their sacred office" (*Catechism*, n. 1566). As signs of his responsibility as "co-worker of the episcopal order," the bishop lays his hands upon the priest's head; then, the priest is anointed on the hands with chrism, is vested in his proper vestments by fellow priests, and is given the bread on a paten and the wine and water in a chalice for the celebration of Mass. Third, deacons are ministers ordained for service in the Church by assisting "the bishop and priests in the celebration of the divine mysteries, above all the Eucharist" (*Catechism*, n. 1570). As signs of his responsibility as "servant" in liturgy, word, and charity, a bishop lays hands upon the deacon's head, and then the deacon is vested in appropriate vestments by fellow deacons and is given the book of the gospels. In the Anglican Church, and among some other Christian denominations, this same process is followed when ordaining a woman to the office of priesthood.

Although the ordained hierarchy is threefold, the uniform laying on of the hands during the three ordination rites contains a uniform symbolism that is threefold. On one level, it signifies that bishops, priests, and deacons, each in their own way, have accepted the Spirit's power to fulfill the apostolic task of preaching the gospel, teaching the faithful, and caring for those with physical and spiritual needs. In return, while in the Catholic tradition the laity no longer exercise the early Church practice of electing their ecclesial leaders, each of the ordination rites calls for the people's consent for those who will lead, teach, and serve them. Here, the laying on of hands emphasizes the Church's sacramental character, which exists by the Spirit's power. On another level, the laying on of the hands signifies that the local bishop is part of the universal Church and that the ecclesial ministries of priests and deacons participate in this apostolic service, which originates from Christ himself, the "High Priest" (Heb 4:13–15), who came "not to be served but to serve, and to give his life [as] a ransom for many" (Mk 10:45). Here, the laying on of hands emphasizes ordination as manifesting the sacramental character of Christ's own ministry.

The central mystery of holy orders involves Jesus sending his apostles forth to love and serve God and neighbor. Apostolic ministry continues Christ's own mission that manifests the mystery of the Divine–human encounter in obedience to the Father's will and through service to neighbor by the Spirit's power. This Trinitarian mystery echoes in the Rite of Priestly Ordination:

> Almighty Father, grant to this servant of yours the dignity of the priesthood. Renew within him the Spirit of holiness. As a co-worker with the order of bishops may he be faithful to the ministry that he receives from you, Lord God, and be to others a model of right conduct. May he be faithful in working with the order of bishops, so that the words of the Gospel may reach the ends of the earth, and the family of nations, made one in Christ, may become God's one, holy people. (*The Rites II*, n. 22, pp. 44–45)

Marriage

The final sacrament, marriage, is a covenantal union between spouses that signifies (1) "the mystery of that unity and fruitful love which exists between Christ and his Church" (*Lumen Gentium* 11) manifested in (2) "an intimate community of conjugal love" (*Gaudium et Spes*, n. 48) where (3) husband and wife freely and totally commit themselves to each other in Christ as a celebration of God's love. These three aspects are closely linked. Ephesians 5:21–33 portrays marriage as a symbol of Christ's union with his Church, which signifies that marriage is directly rooted in the two basic sacraments of Christ and Church. In one way, marriage challenges spouses to selflessly love as Christ loved (Jn 13:34, 15:12). In another way, the community of love fostered by the Spirit creates

The sacrament of **marriage** (an English word) is sometimes referred to through its Latin language root as "matrimony" (*matrimonium*), which means "the union of man and woman as husband and wife." Hence, we often see the phrasing "the sacrament of matrimony" as well.

"the domestic Church" (*Lumen Gentium* 11), which bears witness to and builds up the wider ecclesial community.

The spouses themselves are the main sacramental sign of marriage who cause what they signify: Christ's free and self-giving love to another. The couple's holding of hands during their exchange of vows acts as a laying on of hands whereby the two confer the sacrament on each other, which is a communal event on two levels. First, the couple forms a community in Christ by the gift and power of the Spirit, and second, the ecclesial community that witnesses the vows supports the spouses in their decision. The exchange of vows while holding hands manifests human love as a symbol of and participation in God's covenantal love. While the post-Vatican II Church still defines marriage as a contract, it also expands its understanding by explicitly naming it a covenant:

> The matrimonial covenant, by which a man and a woman establish between themselves a partnership of the whole of life, is by its nature ordered toward the good of the spouses and the procreation and education of offspring; this covenant between baptized persons has been raised by Christ the Lord to the dignity of a sacrament. For this reason a matrimonial contract cannot validly exist between baptized persons unless it is also a sacrament by that fact. (Canon 1055, nn. 1–2)

Notice that the "the good of the spouses" precedes procreation and care of children. Thus, the Church recognizes that mental, emotional, spiritual, and sexual intimacy are necessary for a mature sacramental marriage. All these aspects coalesce into the mystery of intimate friendship: "Perhaps the most basic sacrament of God's saving presence to human life is the sacrament of human love and friendship" (Cooke, 1994, 80). Marriage invites couples into Jesus' friendship (Jn 15:14–16), where they learn daily how to love their spouse as themselves.

The central mystery of the self-giving and self-communication of marriage is a sign, symbol, and sacrament of God's own loving self-giving and self-communication. In short, the joys and sorrows of marriage act as a special locus of the Divine–human encounter because "authentic married love is caught up into divine love" (*Gaudium et Spes* 48). The Rite of Marriage conveys this mystery:

> Father, you have made the union of man and wife so holy a mystery that it symbolizes the marriage of Christ and his Church. . . . Father, keep them always true to your commandments. Keep them faithful in marriage and let them be living examples of Christian life. Give them the strength which comes from the gospel so that they may be witnesses of Christ to

others. Bless them with children and help them to be good parents. May they live to see their children's children. And, after a happy old age, grant them fullness of life with the saints in the kingdom of heaven. (*The Rites I*, n. 33, pp. 730–731)

The sacraments of holy orders and marriage point to and manifest Jesus' ministry of loving service, which brings communion with God and peace through justice to the human community. On the one hand, the grace of holy orders expresses the Church's sacramental reality, and through it, Jesus Christ continues his ministry of salvation by the Spirit's power. On the other hand, the grace of marriage reveals God's love for us in Christ, which is a community of love animated by the Spirit's power. In short, both sacraments "are directed towards the salvation of others; if they contribute as well to personal salvation, it is through service to others that they do so. They confer a particular mission in the Church and serve to build up the People of God" (*Catechism*, n. 1535).

Conclusion: Christians as Living Sacraments

Christians do not celebrate the sacraments simply because they are Christian; rather, they celebrate the sacraments because they are human, and humans communicate through and in symbolic ritual. Christians call these symbolic rituals "sacraments," which help them identify, interpret, enact, and manifest the mystery of the Divine–human encounter. Thus, sacraments are "masterpieces of God" (*Catechism*, n. 1116) that call humans into relationship. There is an ancient truism, "sacraments are for people," and they are for us so that we can become living sacraments. In a very real sense, when Christians choose to imitate Jesus, to act as he acted and to love as he loved, they become living sacraments that point to, participate in, and manifest for the world Jesus' own teachings and actions. When you truly love, serve, and honor someone, you become a sacrament of Jesus' own love, service, and honor, which sacramentally realizes, reveals, and enacts his Father's parental care for creation. The sacraments are the Father's gifts offered through Christ's actions in the Spirit's power, which each of the sacraments confers by the laying on of hands. Repeatedly, the simple gesture of the laying on of hands points to and manifests the mystery of the Divine–human encounter, where the Divine community of persons communes with the human community of persons and vice versa. The symbolic "language" of sacramentality mediates such interpersonal communication.

Questions about the Text

1. What is the difference between a sign and a symbol? Give your own example.

2. What is the meaning of *mysterion*, the Greek word for sacrament?

3. What is the meaning of *sacramentum*, the Latin word for sacrament?

4. What is the theological definition of *sacrament*?

5. What is the etymology of *grace*, and what does *grace* mean?

6. Why does Schillebeeckx call Jesus the "primordial" sacrament?

7. Who or what is the fundamental sacrament of Jesus' presence?

8. What are the sacraments of initiation? Identify their main signs. Why are they called this?

9. What are the sacraments of healing? What are their signs?

10. What are the sacraments of vocation? What are their signs?

Questions for Discussion

1. In your interactions with others, can you give any examples of differences among a sign, symbol, and sacrament?

2. Why might the physical signs of each sacrament be important? What communicative role might they play, and how would they function?

3. The Church has defined only seven sacraments. From your knowledge of the article, do you think other experiences described in the chapter might share in some ways with a sacrament?

4. In what ways do the seven sacraments as a whole reflect what the Church is about?

5. What do the sacraments indicate about believers' lives in God?

6. If a person from another religious tradition, such as Hinduism or Islam, came with you to a Sunday service and asked you to explain what it was all about, how would you respond?

7. The conclusion speaks about Christians as living sacraments. What might this mean and imply for being Christian?

For Further Study

Catechism of the Catholic Church (Part II, Sections 1–2). Liguori, MO: Liguori/Triumph, 1994.

Cooke, Bernard. *Sacraments and Sacramentality*. Mystic, CT: Twenty-Third Publications, 1994.

Lawler, Michael. *Symbol and Sacrament: A Contemporary Sacramental Theology*. Omaha, NE: Creighton University Press, 1995.

Martos, Joseph. *Doors to the Sacred: A Historical Introduction to Sacraments in the Catholic Church*. Revised and updated ed. Liguori, MO: Liguori/Triumph, 2001.

New Dictionary of Sacramental Worship. Edited by Peter Fink. Collegeville, MN: Liturgical Press, 1990.

Noll, Ray. *Sacraments: A New Understanding for a New Generation*. Mystic, CT: Twenty-Third Publications, 1999.

Rahner, Karl. *The Church and the Sacraments*. New York: Herder & Herder, 1963.

The Rites of the Catholic Church. Vols. I–II. Collegeville, MN: Liturgical Press, 1990.

The Sacramentary. New York: Catholic Book Publishing Co., 1985.

Schillebeeckx, Edward. *Christ the Sacrament of the Encounter with God*. New York: Sheed & Ward, 1963.

Smolarski, Dennis. *Sacred Mysteries: Sacramental Principles and Liturgical Practice*. New York: Paulist Press, 1994.

Vatican Council II. Edited by Austin Flannery. New York: Costello Publishing, 1998.

From the Reference Librarian
Combining Subject Headings—Sacraments

Skill Key #1

Use the library's reference collection to begin your research.

a) Use a subject-specific encyclopedia to acquire specialized knowledge about a subject.

b) Use a subject-specific encyclopedia whose scope is appropriate for both your topic and the approach you want to take to that topic.

Once again, the kinds of topics available for researching the sacraments fall into the basic categories of history, on the one hand, and systematics (concepts, issues), on the other. If you are researching a historical topic, make sure the reference tool you use includes historical coverage. If you are researching a systematic topic, you will want a tool that includes this type of topic. The first three titles listed focus specifically on the sacraments and vary in their historical and systematic emphases.

Paul Bradshaw, ed. *The New Westminster Dictionary of Liturgy and Worship*. Louisville, KY: Westminster John Knox Press, 2002.

> This text incorporates ecumenical scholarship from both Protestants and Catholics, so the views of both Catholic and non-Catholic Christians are included. For example, the article on marriage includes sections for "Baptist," "Lutheran," "Methodist," and so on, as well as for Catholics. The focus is on coverage of systematic topics with some historical coverage.

Peter E. Fink, S.J., ed. *The New Dictionary of Sacramental Worship*. Collegeville, MN: Liturgical Press, 1990.

> This title was written by and for Catholics as indicated, for example, by the fact that several articles on marriage would be of interest mainly to a Catholic audience ("Marriage, Canonical

Issues Concerning," "Marriage, Liturgy of," "Marriage, Sacrament of "). The focus is on systematic topics.

Michael O'Carroll, C.S.Sp. *Corpus Christi: An Encyclopedia of the Eucharist*. Wilmington, DE: Michael Glazier, Inc., 1988.

As the title indicates, this encyclopedia focuses entirely on the sacrament of the Lord's Supper and offers a somewhat haphazard mix of systematic and historical coverage.

Titles mentioned in previous chapters, such as *The Oxford Dictionary of the Christian Church* or the *Dictionary of Historical Theology*, will primarily be of use for historically focused research (see also other titles among those mentioned in the chapters on Christology and ecclesiology whose scope includes historical coverage).

For coverage of systematic topics, the *Handbook of Catholic Theology* (which includes both historical and systematic coverage but with emphasis on the latter) is a good resource and even has an article entitled "Sacraments: Contemporary Issues."

Two additional titles that, like the *Handbook of Catholic Theology*, place the emphasis on coverage of systematic issues while including historical elements are the following:

Karl Rahner, ed. *Sacramentum Mundi: An Encyclopedia of Theology*. Six vols. New York: Herder & Herder, 1968–1970.

Karl Rahner, ed. *Encyclopedia of Theology: The Concise Sacramentum Mundi*. New York: Seabury Press, 1975.

(This is an abridgement and partial updating of *Sacramentum Mundi*.)

Don't let the word *sacramentum* throw you off—both of these works are comprehensive in covering the field of theology, not just sacraments.

Expanding Skill Key #2: Combining Subject Headings

In the introductory chapter on research, we explained how to use the bibliographic information from encyclopedia articles to determine subject headings to use to find books on a topic.

Unfortunately, no subject classification scheme is perfect, including Library of Congress subject headings. The main reason is that authors can choose to write a book about any subject or range of subject matter they please. Authors do not write a book thinking that it has to correspond to a particular subject heading, so there may not be a single subject heading that applies to the subject (and therefore the book) you want to find. In a case like this, you will need to combine two or more subject headings in a single search to find a book on your subject. We can now add another refinement of the technique for searching the library catalog.

Skill Key #2

Use the library's catalog to locate sources of information.

a) Use subject headings to locate precisely books on your topic.

b) Use subject headings whose scope fits your topic as closely as possible, then adjust your search with a broader or narrower subject heading as necessary.

c) As an alternative to using encyclopedia bibliographies, use keyword searching to identify subject headings for your topic.

d) Combine one or more subject headings in a search to retrieve books on a topic for which no single subject heading exists.

There are two basic ways of using subject headings: The first applies if there is a single subject heading (sometimes including a subdivision) that covers your topic. Taking up the subject matter of this chapter, let's say you are interested in the views of Saint Augustine on the Eucharist. We have already seen that one subdivision often found with theologians' names in library catalogs begins with the words "Contributions in . . ." To search for books on Augustine and the Eucharist in the library catalog, you could use the following subject heading.

Search Format:

Last name	Descriptive phrase(s)	Subdivision
Augustine	Saint, Bishop of Hippo	Contributions in Doctrine of the Lord's Supper

Such specific subject headings are more likely to be found in large research libraries, especially those with large theology collections; smaller library collections (or even large libraries with nothing under this subject heading) may require the use of a broader subject heading, such as the following (see Skill Key #2b):

Search Format:

Last name	Descriptive phrase(s)	Subdivision
Augustine	Saint, Bishop of Hippo	Contributions in theology

"Theology" is a broader subject than the "Lord's Supper," so books with this subject heading may (or may not) include material specifically on the Lord's Supper. The only way to tell if a book does include such material is by looking at book titles, tables of contents, and/or indexes to see whether and where the subject is covered.

The second way of using subject headings applies when there is no single appropriate subject heading (as would be the case, for example, in libraries following the Library of Congress practice of doing away with the "Contributions in . . ." subdivision; see the previous discussion on this in chapter 3). For example, if I were interested in the views of Saint Thomas Aquinas on the sacraments, as it happens, there is no "Contributions in . . ." subdivision with the heading "Thomas Aquinas Saint" that relates specifically to sacraments (although there is a subdivision "Contributions in Theology"). In this case, I can combine the subject heading "Thomas Aquinas Saint" with the subject heading for sacraments, which is "Sacraments" (not all subject headings are difficult). The important thing is that instead of entering a single subject-heading "string," as you have been doing so far, you are combining two separate subject headings. The precise way you combine subject headings varies from one library catalog to another. Some library catalogs allow the use of "Boolean operators" (AND, OR, NOT) to combine subject headings. [Note: The use of "AND" in a search statement means that all of the terms must be present in any record retrieved. The use of "OR" means that any of the terms (always at least one) may be present in any record retrieved. The use of "NOT" with a search term means that none of the records retrieved will include that term.]

Different library catalogs will provide different ways of accomplishing this. For example, some library catalogs may not allow you to combine subject headings but will allow you to combine keywords. In that case, you can simply treat your subject headings as if they were keywords. What you should understand now is that you can do this; you can always ask the reference librarian to show you how.

Search Format:

Subject heading #1	Boolean operator	Subject heading #2
Thomas Aquinas Saint	AND	Sacraments

Combining these two subject headings produced the following catalog record, which is exactly what we are looking for. (Note that you do not have to know the subdivisions after "Sacraments" to be able to combine it with another subject heading in a search.)

Author	Garland, Peter B.
Title	The definition of sacrament according to Saint Thomas.
Published	Ottawa : University of Ottawa Press, 1959.
Location	**Call #** **Status**
Pius Stacks	BX2200 .G37 NOT CHECKD OUT
Description	x, 115 p. ; 25 cm
Series	Publications sériées de l'Université d'Ottawa, 60.
Thesis	Diss.—Pontificium Athenaeum Angelicum, Rome.
Bibliography	Bibliography: p. [105]–108.
Subjects	Thomas, Aquinas, Saint, 1225?–1274.
	Sacraments—History of doctrines—Middle Ages, 600–1500.

In my library, there are currently 999 titles listed with the subject heading "Thomas Aquinas, Saint, 1225?–1274." Combining that search with a search on "Sacraments" is much faster than plowing through 999 titles to find what you want.

Student Tasks

1. Using a dictionary, encyclopedia, or handbook, find one resource that treats the topic of sacraments from a historical approach and one that takes a systematic approach (concepts, issues).

2. Choose the name of a theologian. Search for books about that person in your library catalog, using the person's name as the subject heading. Do any "Contributions in . . ." subdivisions appear with the name?

3. Combine subject headings in a search using the name of a theologian as one subject heading and the subject heading for one of the sacraments as the other. (If you feel adventurous, expand your skills and try this kind of search on one of the topics from

the earlier chapters on the Old or New Testament, Christology, or ecclesiology. You will need to use a valid subject heading you have come across in the earlier chapters to do this.)

III

THE CHURCH'S MISSION
IN THE WORLD

6

Christian Morality: Choosing God in This World

From the Editor

There is a provocative question that goes like this: "If you were arrested for being a Christian, would there be enough evidence to convict you?" The evidence presented would need to include events or actions witnessed by others, not simply your privately held beliefs. If I say "I love you," then I must mean it and prove it in action; if I say "I trust you," then I must mean it and prove it in action; if I say, "I will be there when you need me—I am your friend," then I must mean it and actually do it. It is a matter of religious integrity, of actions matching beliefs and intentions. We are not talking about disposable commitments; we are talking about our cherished beliefs and hopes. For this, Christians rely on the grace of God to sustain us.

Theology reflects on these daily experiences of trust and mistrust, fidelity and infidelity, truth and lies. The discipline in theology is called "Christian morality," or sometimes "Christian ethics." It is Christian because it flows from a religious belief in God's encounter with us, a love relationship; consequences result where "my actions speak louder than words." Whether an action is moral or ethical is in the response to two interrelated questions: (1) Is it truly human, or not? and (2) Does it express love of God and neighbor, or not?

The following explanation of Christian morality will address these various areas of our decisions and the formation of our conscience toward what is good. It takes on the question of our freedom and limitations, the twin wisdom sources of tradition and authority, and how to think morally. An important condition for moral decisions is the changing situations and circumstances of life. The challenge of living a moral life requires Christians to reflect on, examine, and clarify their motives; consult others; and pray to God for guidance to respond as loving followers of Jesus. If we are living a moral life, then there will be an abundance of evidence to answer the question regarding our conviction.

Christian Morality: Choosing God in This World

Barbara W. Blackburn, PhD

Decisions, Decisions, Decisions

Life is full of decisions—which school to attend, which course of studies to pursue, which organizations to join, careers, friends, parties. Every morning, we face a decision to get up or hit the snooze button, eat breakfast or just grab some juice, dress in jeans or shorts. Should I go to my first class or study for my second class? Sometimes, our decisions involve choosing between good things (tacos or pizza), and other times they involve choosing between things that are difficult but unavoidable (8:00 a.m. chemistry lab or Spanish lab). Even when we are not totally aware, we are making choices of what to look at, what direction to walk or drive, what to say to people we meet.

While these types of choices and decisions are a part of our daily life, other types of choices can be a greater challenge. What would you do if you found a $20 bill on the floor in the cafeteria? Would you ask if someone dropped it? Hand it to the cashier in case the one who lost it asks about it? Would you pocket it on the principle of "finders, keepers"? How would you decide? Would it make a difference if it were a $100 bill? In another scenario, what would you do if your best friend asked you to help her find an abortion provider? Would you help her find counseling and support? Would you get out the Yellow Pages and call the first abortion clinic listed? Would you dump her as a friend? How would you decide? What would be the basis for your decision? Would you seek advice? Where? From whom? These kinds of decisions are called "moral decisions" because they involve choices between what is right and wrong, between good and evil.

This chapter examines the nature, sources, and methods of moral theology—that is, what moral theology is, what the sources and the tools for forming our conscience and making moral decisions are, and how we use the sources and tools to make our decisions in a morally appropriate way.

What Moral Theology Is

Christianity, like other major religious traditions of the world, is a way of life expressed in creed, cult, and code.

Creed

A *creed* is a profession of common beliefs that a community maintains as the essential truths forming the identity of the community. To be a member of a faith community means to believe, as a community and as an individual, those certain basic tenants of truth that unite individuals into a believing community (Greek: *koinonia*). In the moral life, this means we live out what we say we believe.

Cult

In a *cult*, believers come together to express those beliefs in rituals and customs of worship. The ancient Latin saying "*Lex credendi sequetor lex orandi*" suggests that the "Church praying gives rise to the Church believing." Ritual is, therefore, both normative and formative to a religious tradition. In the moral life, this means that as we pray, we live.

Code

There are implications of faith for the way people live. Professing a set of common beliefs and publicly ritualizing those beliefs leads to an all-encompassing way of life. What we believe and how we express it becomes who we are, how we act, and what choices we make. Christianity is, therefore, situated within the context of a faith tradition. It is a response to what we believe God has done for us in and through Jesus Christ.

Moral Theology

How do we define *moral theology*? During the age of Scholasticism, Saint Anselm of Canterbury (d. 1109) defined the entire discipline of theology as "faith seeking understanding." His theological successor, Peter Abelard (d. 1142), added: "I believe in order that I might understand." Pope John Paul II also examined the relationship of faith and reason for our time in his document titled *Faith and Reason* (1998). As a formal theological discipline, moral theology is the study of how we live in response to what God has done for us.

Moral Theology	Morality
Study of the implications of faith for the way we live	From the Latin *mores*, group customs or rules

As we continue to explore the definition of moral theology, we consider another term often used in the study of human conduct: ethics. What is the relationship between the terms *morality* and *ethics*?

Morality/Ethics?

It feels right (?)   Obedience (?)   Happiness (?)

What is legal (?)   What everyone is doing (?)

Ethics can be defined as a discussion of the formation of human conduct—how responsible human beings capable of critical judgment should live using reflection on fundamental issues and description of concrete cases.

Morality is all that and more. Morality is concerned with human conduct but goes to a deeper level of personhood, such that our conduct is a reflection of who we are, a reflection of our character.

Any discussion of morality involves a discussion of character and how it is formed, because being a Christian carries a particular commitment to becoming a certain sort of person, living a way of life that entails certain reasons for being moral, and making certain choices that follow from Christian beliefs. Human conduct is integral to morality, but since the Second Vatican Council, there has been a shift in focus from the act to the person. Faced with a moral dilemma, we often ask, "What should I do?" A more basic question would be "Who am I?" or "What sort of person acts this way?" So, for example, what sort of person does not turn in a $20 bill or a $100 bill? Why would I or would I not turn it in? Character counts; it will influence how we act and the decisions we make. In turn, the choices we make shape the sort of person we become.

It might go something like this: The first time you tell a lie, it might be difficult. You might feel as if you are acting out of character. The fifth time you tell a lie, it is easier. By the time lying becomes a habit, you are a "liar." The first time you are challenged to tell the truth, it might be difficult. The fifth time, it becomes easier as you become a "truthful person." Aristotle taught that people do not naturally become morally excellent or practically wise. They become so only as a result of lifelong effort to build character.

Character	Values
A settled disposition to behave in a morally good way	Basic truths that undergird human excellence; include attitudes and affections chosen as pivotal realities and source of meaning

Character is developed by monitoring behavior along with motivations, intentions, relationships, and values, which have often been referred to as "pillars of character." Employers know that character tells them how and why a person will act in a big decision. Voters know that character tells how and why a political candidate will most likely act in a big decision or crisis. Appreciation of human values forms a person's character.

Decisions   **Decisions**   **Decisions**

AIDS

Stem Cell Research   Poverty

Global Economics

Human Cloning   War and Peace

We need not wander aimlessly in a life full of moral dilemmas without guidelines. As humans and as Christians, we have been gifted with sources of conscience formation that serve to direct us through a lifetime of choices. Moral theology provides us with sources and systems to examine fundamental issues and concrete cases.

To be persons of reason informed by faith, we must seek information and wisdom from a variety of sources that will be defined and explained in this chapter:

Scripture

Natural law philosophy

Magisterium

Theology

Sensus fidelium

Empirical sciences

Both faith and human resources are dimensions of discovering the moral demands of being human. Some of these sources come to us as revelation (the Bible), and some are based on our faith tradition (*magisterium* and theology). Some, which give us the facts, data, figures, and definitions of the moral issue, are based on human reason (empirical sciences). Some sources are based on what it means to be a human being (natural law) of reason informed by faith (*sensus fidelium*). These sources, which will each be explained, are basic tools we need to form our conscience and help us make good moral decisions.

The reason we use such a variety of sources is important. We must avoid separating morality into an exclusively "rational morality" while we avoid an exclusively "revealed faith morality." The former yields humanism and the later sectarianism, such that only Christians can be truly moral. What is needed is a creative tension of faith in divine revelation and human reason. This understanding of human conscience formation understands that (1) Divine grace builds on human nature and is not opposed to it, (2) human beings bear the image of the Creator, and (3) God has gifted humanity with God's self-revelation through the scriptures and the tradition of the Church.

Before we begin a study of the basic sources, we must examine how conscience enters into its important role in morality. Let me propose it in a slightly different and more pointed way: Without conscience, would there be any morality?

What is conscience? Does everyone have a conscience? What if a conscience is misinformed? Is conscience individual or communal?

Conscience is a difficult term to pin down because it involves several aspects of human reasoning. The Second Vatican Council explained that conscience is the voice of God written in our hearts: "On his part, man perceives and acknowledges the imperatives of the divine law through the mediation of conscience. In all his activity a man is bound to follow his conscience faithfully, in order that he may come to God for who he was created" (*Declaration on Religious Freedom* 3). Look also at the following and notice what it says is characteristic of conscience:

> In the depths of his conscience man detects a law which he does not impose upon himself, but which holds him to obedience. Always summoning him to love the good and avoid evil, the voice of conscience can when necessary speak to his heart more specifically; do this, shun that. For man has in his heart a law written by God. To obey it is the very dignity of man; according to it he will be judged. Conscience is the most secret core and sanctuary of a man. There he is alone with God whose voice echoes in his depths. (*Pastoral Constitution on the Church in the Modern World* 16)

We can say, then, the following about conscience:

1. Conscience is the fundamental characteristic of being human that makes it possible to know and do good. It involves an awareness of personal responsibility, a general sense of value, and an inner vision of reality.

2. The aim of conscience formation is not simply to increase facts and skills for solving moral dilemmas but, rather, to help determine what sort of person I ought to become. An act of conscience is expressive of who I am. Conscience is an exercise of moral reasoning involving discussion and analysis of sources or moral wisdom. It is the ability to make up one's mind *for* oneself but not *by* oneself.

3. Conscience is a judgment, a determination of good versus evil in a specific case. Conscience is, therefore, a human characteristic, a human process, and a concrete judgment of good versus evil.

4. Conscience is also both individual and communal. Human persons with conscience construct and maintain many societies, both in numbers and in types. Society does not have a conscience; people do. Hence, society needs a critical conscience formed by the reciprocity of many consciences. The morality into which we are socialized is not so much a set of rules but rather a collection of stories and images of what makes life worth living. Being a part of a community—its history, its language, its rituals and celebrations—forms our "moral imagination."

At times, society is challenged by people who have the vision and courage to shake us up and unmask our errors. This "prophetic voice" is as ancient as the prophets of the Hebrew scriptures—Isaiah, Jeremiah, Ezekiel, Hosea, Amos, and so on—and as contemporary as social justice advocates of our own times—Martin

Luther King, Mother Theresa, Ghandi, Oscar Romero, and Dorothy Day, who remind us that "the way things are" might not be "what should be."

The development of conscience is a lifelong task. The decisions we make today might need to be revised as we gain additional wisdom and insight. Moral certitude seldom equals absolute certainty. We make the best decision we can given the information we have at our disposal, knowing that, if new information emerges, we might need to rethink our decision. It is a lifelong process of loving God and neighbor.

Does that mean our original decision was immoral? The *Catechism of the Catholic Church* explains, "A human being must always obey the certain judgment of his conscience. If he were deliberately to act against it, he would condemn himself. Yet it can happen that moral conscience remains in ignorance and makes erroneous judgments" (*Catechism*, 1797).

The *Catechism* goes on to explain that ignorance can sometimes be imputed to personal responsibility. We are responsible for informing our decision making. If, however, we have truly consulted the moral sources and then later discover that our choice or decision needs to be changed because it is now considered wrong or evil, then we are not responsible for the evil that resulted from our original decision.

Conscience is not an imaginary friend on our shoulder or an occasional pang of guilt, fear, or anxiety located in some part of our body. These feelings, however, are powerful and, in many cases, monitor our behavior. People might say, "My conscience is bothering me." They might lose sleep, lose their appetite, experience nightmares, or become physically or emotionally ill because of a decision they question or regret. While guilt is a powerful tool that can regulate our conduct, it cannot always be trusted as a completely objective indicator of what is a good or bad decision. That is because people have varying degrees of the capacity for guilt. Some people feel guilty about almost everything—mistakes, minor faults, or imperfections. These people are called "scrupulous." Other people might not feel guilt at all, even when they are aware that they have made an evil decision.

We also make a careful distinction between conscience and superego, which is the conscience of another person superimposed on our own to serve as an internal sensor to regulate our conduct by using guilt as its powerful weapon. Superego is related to our need to be loved and maintain approval of authority figures. It can be a step in the early development of conscience as we store advice from authority figures in the process of growing up: "Brush your teeth." "Walk in from recess in a straight line." "Keep your room neat." "Do your homework." "Respect authority." As we mature, however, superego cannot be a substitute for using our own conscience.

What is missing in superego is the personal involvement of two critical aspects of moral decision making—freedom and knowledge.

Freedom

The *Catechism* states:

Freedom is so central to the moral life that without it we cannot properly speak of being moral persons at all. Responsibility for an action can be diminished or even nullified by ignorance, duress, fear, habit, inordinate attachments, and other psychological or social factors. . . . If we are beyond freedom, we are beyond morality. Freedom properly defined is not unbridled liberty. Theologically speaking, freedom is the ability to choose the good. The choice to do what is evil is an abuse of freedom and leads to the slavery of sin. (*Catechism*, 1735, 1739)

Knowledge

Knowledge is critical for all decision making. We must be aware that what we have chosen is good or evil. Two types of knowledge are necessary for moral decisions—cognitive knowledge and evaluative knowledge. *Cognitive knowledge* is gained through information and facts ("head" knowledge). For example, I can memorize the Ten Commandments and be aware that the Third Commandment states, "Keep holy the Lord's Day." *Evaluative knowledge* is gained through relationships and experience and involves a personal, heartfelt grasp of value (heartfelt knowledge). With evaluative knowledge, the Third Commandment is not so much an obligation as an opportunity to celebrate my relationship with the risen Savior along with a community of believers. Cognitive knowledge and evaluative knowledge represent acceptance of both the "letter of the law" and "the spirit of

Sin

Relational · Personal · Social · An Evil Choice · An Action · Scandal · Crime the law." Both are critical in moral choices. If, therefore, we freely choose to do what we know is wrong, we "sin."

The book *What Ever Became of Sin?* by Karl Menninger reminds us that while fewer sermons are given on sin these days and the lines for making Confession are shorter, sin looms as large as ever in our lives. There are several reasons why we do not hear much about sin. One of the reasons is that the definitions of sin and our understanding of sin have changed in some ways since the Second Vatican Council. Moral theology prior to Vatican II (the Council of 1962–1965) emphasized sin as an action or an omission in violation of God's law. Since Vatican II, there has been more of an emphasis on the person who acts. The emphasis switched to the person as a disciple, a person of virtue, a person of character and moral maturity on a journey of faith. Morality became equated with a person's spirituality in a much more holistic manner.

Sin is a human reality involving the whole person, including his or her intellect and will. Sin is never an accident. No one makes us sin or become sinful people. The human condition is, however, prone to sin. This human inclination to sin, theologically referred to as "concupiscence," is described by Saint Paul in his Letter to the Romans: "For I know that nothing good dwells within me, that is, in my flesh. I can will what is right, but I cannot do it. For I do not do the good I

Why is it sometimes difficult to know and choose what is good?

Where did this human condition originate?

Didn't God make us good?

---

want, but the evil I do not want is what I do. . . . Wretched man that I am!" (Rom 7:18–19, 24).

The creation accounts in Genesis 1 and 2 describe the goodness of God's creation in which humanity is the epitome of God's creative work. Genesis 1:27 describes man and woman as the "*Imago Dei*": "So God created humankind in his image, in the image of God he created them; male and female he created them." Unique in all creation, Adam and Eve were gifted with intellect and will, so they would be able to know and choose what was good. Instead, they chose to go against the goodness for which they were created. Genesis 3 describes humanity's fall from a perfect relationship with the Creator. When the relationship was broken through pride and disobedience, all relationships suffered. Adam and Eve experienced guilt and shame for the first time and covered their nakedness with fig leaves (Gen 3:7). The peace and harmony these humans experienced in paradise was shattered as they felt new and horrible feelings of regret. Adam and Eve's relationship with themselves was damaged. The word *sin* in Hebrew, *hatta*, means "to miss the mark, the target" and, in this case, to miss being human, which is to be related to God and act accordingly.

Whatever the transgression, it had the effect of destroying the intimate trust and friendship between God and humanity. After the sin, Adam and Eve hid from God (Gen 3:8). The relationship between husband and wife was damaged as they blamed each other for what they had done—the first family argument. Harmony within creation was broken, and death made its entrance into human history. The disharmony and alienation of sin affects all relationships.

1. Relationship with self is one of shame and regret.
2. Relationship with others is damaged with blame and argument.
3. Relationship with God is changed from intimacy to alienation.

In spite of this dismal situation experienced by all persons since the fall of humanity, the Church teaches that the human condition, while wounded, flawed, and weakened, is not totally corrupted or destroyed. Grace, the capacity to overcome this state of affairs, comes to us as the gift of an inner elevating and transforming power. Grace restores relationship and kinship with God, self, and others. As Saint Paul explained to the Romans: "[W]here sin increased, grace abounded all the more . . . through Jesus Christ our Lord" (Rom 5:20–21). As horrible as sin is, the grace of God is even more powerful if we are open to radical transformation.

While Original Sin marked humanity as a whole, we as individuals or as a society today are also capable of choosing to go against the goodness for which we were created. This is called "actual sin." In describing and understanding actual sin, three aspects must be considered:

1. The intention—the purpose, the end in view. This formal element gives meaning to the action.
2. The means used—the kind of action this is. This is the external, observable material element of the action.
3. The circumstances—Who? What? Where? When? How much? How little? What if? What else? These are all reality-revealing questions.

We do not have a true moral evaluation until the intention, act, and circumstances are considered together. The act in itself cannot be accurately evaluated as moral or immoral apart from considering the intention, means, and circumstances as one reality. While we examine each of the three elements, each is dependent on the others. For example, we must consider the intention of the person acting. A good intention, however, cannot justify simply any means used. Only an action congruent with the intention adequately and morally expresses the intention. For example, a person who is passionately against abortion kills an abortion provider in order to save hundreds of babies' lives. The means used, murder, is incongruent or inconsistent with the intent of saving lives. Another example illustrates the role of circumstances in moral evaluation. Suppose you are walking alone when you see a stranger walking toward you. You take a gun from your pocket and shoot the person approaching you. Is this self-defense or murder? Is this a moral or an immoral act? We cannot evaluate this situation without asking questions about the circumstances, as well as about your intention. What circumstances would render you guilty of murder? Of self-defense? The intention, means, and circumstances comprise one act. If any one aspect is incongruous with the others, the act or decision is immoral. If any one aspect (the intent, means, or circumstances) is evil in itself, intrinsically evil, then the entire action or decision is morally evil. Let's take a controversial example today:

Intent:	Discover a cure for Parkinson's disease
Means:	Destroy human embryos to extract stem cells for research
Circumstances:	Carefully monitored, legal lab procedures

If respect for life is a primary value, intentional destruction of human life, even at its earliest stage, is an intrinsic evil. Even if the research results in the discovery of a cure, the entire process is immoral because the end cannot justify the means used. If, on the other hand, stem cells were obtained from adult donors or from donated umbilical cord blood, the entire research effort could be considered moral. The intent, the means used, and the circumstances would be proportionate or congruous with each other.

This method of moral evaluation is called "casuistry" or "case study." It is based on logic and the human ability to use reason informed by faith.

Natural Law

Natural law is considered one of the major sources of moral theology and answers the question: How do I know what is good or evil?

Throughout the history of humanity, natural law has been a factor in our decisions of what is morally right and wrong, good and evil. God fashioned the world such that the laws guiding all activities of created beings are somehow built into the nature of these beings. For humans, this means moral knowledge is accessible to anyone willing to reflect on human experience. Natural law is not dependent, therefore, on a particular religion or belief system but on insight into human experiences. The Book of Deuteronomy in the Hebrew scriptures explains:

> Surely, this commandment that I am commanding you today is not too hard for you, nor is it too far away. It is not in heaven, that you should say, 'Who will go up to heaven for us so that we may hear it and observe it?' Neither is it beyond the sea, that you should say, 'Who will cross to the other side of the sea for us, and get it for us so that we may hear it and observe it?' No, the word is very near to you; it is in your mouth and in your heart for you to observe. (Deut 30:11–14)

In the Christian scriptures, Saint Paul's Letter to the Romans says that those who have not heard of the Law of Moses, the Ten Commandments, still know what is right and wrong because "what the law requires is written on their hearts" (Rom 2:15).

This knowledge of what is right and wrong, somehow written on our hearts, has traditionally been referred to as the natural moral law. We discover these basic laws by observing human behavior and by using common sense. No government, bishop, or ruler made up the natural law. Rather, natural law claims the existence of an objective moral order imprinted on humanity that directs humanity to God, the creator whose image we bear. The *Catechism* tells us that "natural law is a participation in God's wisdom and goodness . . . expressing the dignity of the human person and forming the basis of his fundamental rights and duties" (*Catechism*,

Questions for Discussion

1. How would you define *sin*?

2. Could a sin ever be considered a "mistake"? Why or why not?

3. What are some psychological factors that could diminish a person's ability to make a moral decision?

4. Give examples of how duress or fear could keep a person from making a moral decision.

5. What are some social factors that could diminish a person's ability to make a moral decision?

6. What is the difference between killing in self-defense, manslaughter, or murder, considering that in each case a person is dead?

1978). To violate the norms of natural law, therefore, is to violate our own humanity. Since the natural law is universal, it is very general: Do good and avoid evil.

Its premise is basic: Be respectful, honest, keep promises, play fair, care for children, and so on. The natural law is not a written code of conduct. It is not static because it changes as we continue to discover what it means to be human and what the moral community discovers in its experiences to contribute to human wholeness. We are always discovering more about nature and the natural law. New moral issues surface as we continue to reflect on human experiences: child labor, organ transplants, endangered species. Some of these issues might previously have been considered immoral according to natural law but are now considered the moral norm. The idea of organ donations was once considered abhorrent and immoral. Now, it is considered to be a heroic act to donate organs and morally commendable to transplant them. Other issues might have previously been considered moral but are now considered "inhumane" or immoral—for example, sweatshops, slave and child labor, withholding medical treatment. Issues emerge as society and technology continue to develop. The natural law will always compel humanity to seek the good and avoid evil. This is God's eternal law written upon us.

> **Questions for Discussion**
>
> 1. Give some examples of how we expect people to act in a "humane" manner.
>
> 2. Give further examples of situations that had previously been considered natural to humanity but are now considered inhumane.

Scripture

Examining the sacred scripture of the Christian faith tradition helps us answer such questions as whether the Bible can help us make moral decisions, how it can do so, and whether it can be misused. In this regard, the Second Vatican Council made some important statements about the relationship of sacred scripture and moral theology. The bishops of the council affirmed scripture as the "soul of theology" (*Constitution on Divine Revelation* 24), stating: "Special attention needs to be given to the development of moral theology. Its scientific exposition should be thoroughly nourished by scriptural teaching" (*Decree on Priestly Formation* 16). In addressing the challenge of how to use scripture in moral theology, the bishops wrote:

> The Church guards the heritage of God's Word and draws from it religious and moral principles, without always having at hand the solutions to particular problems. She desires thereby to add the light of revealed truth

to mankind's store of experience, so that the path which humanity has taken in recent times will not be a dark one. (*Pastoral Constitution on the Church in the Modern World* 33)

What the council confirmed was that, even though the Bible nowhere mentions such contemporary issues as genetic engineering, cloning, nuclear weapons, AIDS, or global economics, the Church can use the principles found in the Bible to help make moral decisions on specific issues, for it is the Bible that grounds Christians' basic convictions. The Bible is both the normative and the formative articulation of the Judeo-Christian belief system. It is the place where God's intentions for humanity are revealed. The question of how to use the Bible has sometimes resulted in two extremes:

Irrelevance

The Bible is literature

Concerned with specific cultural interests

Deals with ancient history

Not relevant to contemporary moral issues

Biblicism

Literal interpretation

Prooftexting or quoting out of context to prove a pre-established point

In order to use the Bible effectively in moral theology, both extremes must be avoided. Historical criticism recognizes that the biblical text is a result of human expressions of faith and that this truly inspired Word of God cannot come to us apart from time-bound cultural categories. God has spoken to us through history, events, people, and experiences that are only interpreted after the fact. Finding the original meaning of the original text using the tools of historical criticism allows us to apply the meaning of that message to us today. This interpretation, called "hermeneutical criticism," is the application of the message of the ancient text to a contemporary audience. For example, the story of Exodus relates the events of the Israelite's escape from slavery in Egypt through Yahweh's saving intervention. Moses, who serves as a messenger and a mouthpiece of Yahweh to the pharaoh and to the people, is the human instrument of God's plan to deliver the Israelites into a new land and a new way of life. Hermeneutical criticism of the text would require us to apply the lessons of this story to issues we face today. Use the following questions to interpret the meaning (the hermeneutic) of Exodus for today.

1. Can you think of situations today in which certain groups of people are intimidated, persecuted, or held captive, because of their ethnic or religious beliefs?

2. Give examples where people in different parts of the world are denied the opportunity to own the land on which they work.

3. Applying the lessons of the story of Exodus, what do you think God would want for these people?

4. What are some situations, habits, or human circumstances that "tie you down" or keep you from being who you really want to be?

The Bible can and must be used as a tool for making moral decisions but never as a weapon to prove a pre-established point by choosing and lifting an isolated quotation, which is prooftexting, or by referring only to an isolated book of the Bible to the exclusion of others, which is genre reductionism. To use the Bible correctly, the entire collection of its books must serve as reference, even as each book has its individual contribution within the context of the whole. For example, while referring to the story of Exodus, we must keep its story in the context of what the other books of the Bible reveal about the themes of covenant, freedom, promise, and so on.

The Bible was not written as a detailed rulebook for morality. In fact, the Bible nowhere establishes a singular or systematic method for moral decision making. Instead, it serves as a context for the attitudes and dispositions of the human heart. The Bible is the drama of a relationship between God and humanity. This relationship called "covenant" was initiated by God with the great patriarchs and matriarchs of the Hebrew scriptures—Noah, Abraham and Sarah, Moses, and all of Israel. The covenant is based on a promise made by God to establish a relationship with a specific group of people, the Israelites. The relationship is simply stated, "I will be your God and you will be my people." The history of this promise spans the Hebrew and the Christian scriptures as humans continue to discover what it means to respond to God's call to relationship.

Moral theology continues to study how we, as a people who have been called to covenant, should appropriately respond to that call. We continue to ask the questions: What does it mean to be a people of God? How do God's people behave? How do they live? What do they stand for? The answers to these questions are guided by the principles and themes found in the stories, poetry, parables, letters, and events in the Bible. Many major themes thread through the Bible, holding its message in a tapestry depicting the history of the relationship between God and humanity. Three of the most important moral themes are covenant law, the voice of the prophet, and discipleship.

Covenant Law

What is the place or the purpose of "law" in making moral decisions? No society can survive without some organization; laws identify certain basic values. Laws safeguard public order. Laws protect rights and freedoms. Laws serve as a basic roadmap through conflicting situations in life. Laws free us to go about the business of living. Laws interconnect and rank more- or less-important values. They establish a hierarchy of values, ranking the significance of values from most important to least important.

The Hebrew scriptures consider the Ten Commandments to be the basis of all the laws that united them in covenant to God and each other. The Decalogue, the ten Words of God, was a gift from Yahweh providing the people of Israel with the means, the know-how, to live in covenant relationship. The Law given to Moses on Mount Sinai provided the Israelites with an identity. They became known as "The People of the Law." The Law bound them together in fidelity to Yahweh and each other, safeguarded the public order, and provided a basic guide by which to live the covenant relationship. The Law became a point of pride, a symbol of the divine gift of election. Obedience to the Law was considered a privilege. Happiness was impossible apart from obedience to the Law. Psalm 119 is an example of Israel's praise of and sentiment for God's Law:

> Happy are those whose way is blameless, who walk in the law of the Lord. (Ps 119:1)

Eventually, the 613 dietary and disciplinary laws of the Torah ordered every aspect of life, but the first and the greatest law was always the *Shemas*, the creed every Jew knew by heart: "Hear, O Israel: The Lord is our God, the Lord alone. You shall love the Lord your God with all your heart, and with all your soul, and with all your might" (Deut 6:4–5).

In the New Testament (NT), the gospels of Matthew, Mark, and Luke recount that Jesus referred to this passage when questioned by the Pharisees as to what was

Questions for Discussion

1. What is your opinion of law?
2. Do you see law as keeping you from what you want to do? Explain.
3. How is law beneficial at your school or in your society?
4. How can law be a source of pride?
5. Who has authority to give laws? Why?
6. How do you decide if you will obey a law?

the greatest law or commandment. Jesus' answer was the *Shemas*, the command to love God and neighbor. Jesus brought the law of love to its ultimate climax on the cross, when he died as a total gift of self. This is the kind of love we are challenged to have for God and each other in imitation of Jesus. The "New Testament" is, therefore, the "new covenant" established by Jesus Christ, bringing humanity into an intimate and eternal relationship with God. To be a Christian is to be a person of the new covenant, this new relationship with God and each other based on the example of Jesus.

The Voice of the Prophet

The second major theme of scripture that we will examine is referred to as "the voice of the prophet." A prophet is a messenger and a mouthpiece for God. The prophets' job was to remind Israel of the covenant commitment and its implications for the way people should live. The message of the prophet was often a challenge against the complacency toward oppression of the poor, corruption in courts and in the marketplace, infidelity to relationships, or abandonment of the marginalized in society. For the prophet, the greatest sin is the ability to stand dry-eyed in the face of injustice. Prophets unmask our prejudices and challenge our set ways of looking at realities. They remind us that the way things are might not be the way things should be. We become so used to the status quo that we are sometimes unaware of a better and more just way of behaving. The prophet opens our eyes to reality and challenges us to do better in a world often marked with racism, materialism, sexism, homophobia, militarism, genocide, economic colonialism, consumerism, and greed.

One of the major messages of the prophets is that God wants our hearts to be pure, full of compassion and mercy. The opposite of this is to be "hard-hearted." Repeatedly, the prophets challenged Israel to change her heart, considered the very core of her being. Rituals, sacrifices, and holocausts (burnt offerings) are all important in observance of the Law. The prophets reminded the people, however, that sincerity was pivotal to all of these undertakings. The prophet Amos, as a mouthpiece for

Questions for Discussion

1. What would be the difficulties or challenges of being a prophet?

2. Who might be some prophets of our own time? What is their message?

3. What prejudices or "old notions" do they unmask?

4. What might the term *hard-heartedness* mean today?

5. What injustices remain part of our reality today?

6. How can art, media, poetry, or movies awaken our sensitivities?

God, insisted: "If you would offer me holocaust, then let justice surge like water, and goodness like an unfailing stream" (Am 5:23–24).[1]

The prophets also reminded Israel of her covenant relationship with Yahweh and her duty to fidelity. Israel was not to chase after false gods. The prophet Hosea compared his own marriage to the spiritual marriage of Yahweh and Israel. Hosea's wife, Gomer, was unfaithful to him just as Israel had been to Yahweh. Through his passionate story of betrayal, Hosea calls Israel to return to the way of life prescribed by the covenant relationship.

The prophet Micah offered a simple message of what God really expects of his people: "to do justice, and to love kindness, and to walk humbly with your god" (Mic 6:8). Though simple, it is also a challenging message.

Discipleship

As the covenant provided Israel with the motive for observing the Law, so Jesus' example of ultimate love became the motive for all his disciples to imitate him in all aspects of their lives. Jesus' disciples became known as "The People of the Way" because their way of life was centered on him. Imitation of the lifestyle of Jesus became normative for the Christian moral life. At the center of discipleship lies a relationship with the risen Christ, and this relationship influences how a person lives, the decisions she makes, her attitude toward life, and her very character. It is as if Christ supports us from our past and draws us to a new future in God.

Conversion to discipleship can be sudden and abrupt, such as Saint Paul's conversion in chapter 9 of the Acts of the Apostles, or a slow and lifelong journey of faith. However and whenever this conversion happens, it involves the transformation of the whole person, affectively, intellectually, morally, and religiously. The term *metanoia* ("conversion") means "change of mind or regret," an about-face after discovering one is traveling in the wrong direction, and it is often used to describe this graced transformation with God.

The *Didache* ("teaching" or "instruction"), a short, first-century instructional manual on morals and Church practice for nonbelievers ("pagans") wanting to become Christians, describes this total conversion as a choice between "two ways: the way of Life and the way of Death." The Way of Life is described: "First love the God who made you; secondly, your neighbor as yourself. Do not do to another what you do not wish to be done to yourself" (*Didache* 1). This beautiful summation of Jesus' words to love God above all things and your neighbor as yourself puts it in the context of a choice to be made and a community of faith where

Questions for Discussion

1. Describe a time when you totally changed your mind about a decision or lifestyle with which you had been involved. Was it sudden or gradual?

2. What changes have you experienced in your personality or spiritual outlook on life since you started grade school? High school? College?

3. Who has had an important influence on your decisions or inspired you to do something special?

it is lived out. Twenty centuries later, we still make this choice through which every aspect of life is changed and directed toward relating with Jesus Christ in the community of believers.

What Resources Guide Us?

Magisterium, Sensus Fidelium, and Theology

This section will describe the teaching authority of the Church, known as the *magisterium*; the source of moral theology, known as the *sensus fidelium*; and the discipline of theology in order to answer the questions: What or who is the Church? How can the Church help us make moral decisions? How does the Holy Spirit guide the Church today?

The Catholic Church teaches that scripture and tradition form one source of revelation. The two are considered one source because tradition is understood as scripture in the ways it is lived, prayed, and proclaimed in the life of the faithful community. It was the followers of Jesus Christ, the early Church, who wrote the Bible, and it is the Church today that continues to keep the Word of Scripture vital in the contemporary community of God's people.

There are many models, or ways of describing what the Church is and how it functions. Through the centuries of Church history, the Church has been known as the following:

1. Institution with a hierarchical authority and administration
2. Prophet to the world
3. Servant of all God's people
4. Missionary
5. Mother
6. Body of Christ
7. Teacher
8. Community of disciples
9. Temple of the Holy Spirit

The Second Vatican Council described the Church as "The People of God who share in Christ's priestly, prophetic, and kingly offices" (*Dogmatic Constitution on the Church* 9). In each of these models, the Church serves as a source and a guide for moral decisions and for developing moral character. It is in the role of teacher that the Church exercises its authority as a source for the formation of Christian conscience. This teaching authority is called the *magisterium* (Lat., *magister* = "teacher").

The Catholic Church is responsible for proclaiming and living the "Good News" of Jesus, the final command or sending forth: "Go and preach the Good News to all people, even to the ends of the earth" (Mt 28:19; Mk 16:15). The Catholic Church maintains that the Pope, and the bishops in union with the Pope, are responsible to teach authoritatively on faith and morals with unique prerogatives. Aided by the Holy Spirit, the *magisterium* helps protect the Church from errors. Either a worldwide gathering of bishops, called an ecumenical council, or the Pope, as head of the bishops, can exercise ultimate doctrinal or moral authority in rendering a definitive judgment on a particular question. When the Pope defines a dogma of faith, he is said to speak *ex cathedra*—"from the chair," meaning he is speaking in his authority as successor to Saint Peter, the first Pope. The most recent pronouncement of such an extraordinary statement is the teaching about the Assumption of the Blessed Virgin Mary, defined by Pope Pius IX in 1950. Other examples of ordinary teaching authority include the sixteen documents generated by the Second Vatican Council, pastoral letters of bishops' conferences, encyclical letters of the Pope, or bishops' pastoral letters to their own dioceses.

The presumption of truth in the Church's teachings is based on faith that it is the Holy Spirit who guides the Church and will not allow the Church to turn away from God or to self-destruct. Since the Second Vatican Council described the Church as "The People of God," we understand that the Holy Spirit guides popes, bishops, and lay people. The Church believes that the People of God have been gifted with an instinct or "sense" about moral truth called the *sensus fidelium*. Vatican II taught:

> The body of the faithful as a whole, anointed as they are by the Holy One, cannot err in matters of belief. Thanks to a supernatural sense of the faith which characterized the People as a whole, it manifests this unerring quality when from the bishops to the last member of the laity, it shows universal agreement in matters of faith and morals. (*Dogmatic Constitution on the Church* 12)

Because the Holy Spirit is present in the entire People of God, the *sensus fidelium* is a source for moral decision making that complements and includes the magisterial authority of the Church. The *sensus fidelium* is not a majority vote nor a public opinion poll but a charism of the Holy Spirit moving the Church toward truth. The authority of the Church, therefore, is found in scripture and tradition expressed in the *magisterium* and the *sensus fidelium*.

The question remains as to how to use these sources to make a moral decision. With regard to obedience to authority, one must avoid two extremes:

1. Unquestioning obedience where people are more comfortable under the guardianship of others; the motto here would be "Just tell me what to do." While assent of faith and respect for the wisdom of authority are true virtues, blind obedience is not the same as making a moral decision. Moral choice always involves a personal decision.

2. Rejection of authority—the opposite of unquestioning obedience. This is not a sign of maturity but rather a sign of adolescent behavior. For people of reason informed by faith, the acceptance of authority does not mean the abandonment of reason. As people of faith, there are situations when we assent to a mystery, even when understanding is not possible.

The balanced and mature way of using authority as a guide for making moral decisions is to respect the wisdom of the Church and combine Church teachings with the other sources: scripture, natural law, the *sensus fidelium*, empirical sciences, and theology. Church teachings are available to the public and can be found in such sources as the sixteen documents of Vatican II or the *Catechism of the Catholic Church* (1994). These magisterial sources form a foundation for making decisions on many issues.

The process of applying the universal values included in these sources to specific decisions that challenge us today is the work of moral theology. Theology is the science that studies and speaks the Good News to each new generation in terms and ways that are meaningful. A theologian is a degreed professional who writes or teaches about the faith, describing the foundations of faith for diverse audiences and investigating implications of the faith for the way we live. New moral situations and challenges emerge as medicine, technology, and global societies continue to develop. Issues not yet even dreamed of will confront us tomorrow. Today, we can clone animals; tomorrow, humans? Today we can map human genes; tomorrow, re-engineer them? What we will be able to do might not be what we should do. Moral theology will help us in those decisions.

Even though most of us are not official "moral theologians," we can use the same method to make moral choices. To do moral theology, even in everyday life, is to consult all the sources of reason and faith, including scripture, natural law, *magisterium*, *sensus fidelium*, empirical sciences, and theology, and then ask the questions: What if? What else? How? When? As a student of moral theology, you can gift others with your understanding, so they can come to the necessary freedom in God to make their decisions well. Your study at the college level is not only for you but also for others, a gift to the Church and to your society.

Recognizing Moral Issues

Recognizing moral issues can be a challenge. We are surrounded with realities that often numb us into complacency. In society, issues such as war, poverty, immigration, or child abuse seem so overwhelming that we might feel any individual effort we attempt would be insignificant and futile. In scientific and medical advances, many issues are morally controversial—stem cell research, fertility and reproductive technologies, and so on—and most of us lack the professional expertise to decide for ourselves the value and the goodness of such progress. Living in a fast-paced world of ever-changing politics, economics, social values, and scientific and medical breakthroughs can dizzy us. Ignoring the issues or even insulating ourselves from them may seem easier. Students often explain that they consider reading or watching the news to be a depressing waste of time. They feel that because they cannot solve the issues, they would rather not be confronted with them. Ignorance of contemporary issues seems to create a more manageable personal life. After all, why should we invest personal concern, time, or emotions in problems we cannot solve?

Remember what was said previously: Insulating myself from moral challenges that surround me is, in fact, a decision. It is actually a decision to live a life where the other person's problems are not my problem. We are all in it for ourselves. The attitude of "You work on your problem, I'll work on mine" is a characteristic of individualism so woven into the fabric of our contemporary society that it can be a stumbling block to true moral living.

A primary challenge to moral living, then, is to live with eyes and hearts wide open to the realities of the world of yesterday and today and to the possibilities of tomorrow.

Faith traditions, including Christianity, have rich histories of leading people to holiness in and through the challenges of daily life. Christians call this "Incarnational living." This means that the ordinary and the extraordinary events of our life can be made holy because Jesus Christ became part of our human reality, embraced it, and transformed it into God's reality. To become fully human, therefore, requires a moral decision by each of us to be aware of the needs, hopes, dreams, possibilities, fears, and pain of other humans and the world we share. Put into a Christian phrase, it is called "Christian intentionality." However, it goes beyond all faith traditions. Natural law theory, at the same time, would argue that it is a universal imperative placed on all humanity. This universal imperative—to be human—is integral to Incarnational living and to Christian intentionality. Admitting the interdependence of all humanity is a first step in moral living.

When I admit that I am a part of a living, breathing, human community, I have awakened my "moral imagination." The next step is to inform myself with what is happening in the world, for better or worse. Moral issues can be found as close as my classroom, dorm, family, sorority, fraternity, or campus or as far away as the Middle East, Africa, Latin America, Asia, and now, outer space, beyond the planet Earth. (For example, "Star Wars" missile defense systems; satellites of all kinds—where would television and cell phones be without them?; space junk; and proposed colonies on the moon are some of the everyday issues in the news that will not be going away; in fact, they will only increase.)

Moral issues, moreover, go further. Moral issues are also political, economic, medical, or sexual. Moral issues are present in the bedroom and the boardroom, the media and advertising, banks and food pantries, universities and preschools. What might I do? The daily newspaper might be a good place to begin a personal confrontation with the real world, but even here, some critics of journalism would remind us that the reporting of news involves moral decisions about what information to include or exclude, which nuances to add, and so on. Therefore, no news is pure information. With that caution in mind, I can continue with the news as a starting place: What are the headlines? What stories have been deemed by the editorial staff to be worthy of our intellectual and emotional energies? The wars in Afghanistan, Iraq, and the Middle East; conflict in Africa; acts of terrorism; child abductions; airplane crashes; wildfires; global warming; political disputes; economic trends; scientific breakthroughs; acts of heroism.

Turn then to the sports section. What stories have been included along with the statistics of winners and losers? Allegations of misconduct by players, coaches, officials; bribery or betting scandals; performance-enhancing drugs. Who is deemed worthy of admission into a hall of fame? Who are our true sports heroes?

Now turn to the entertainment section. Check the movies that are playing. What do they say about society's appetite for violence, sex, deceit, or decadence? Are there some movies that challenge us to explore new ways of viewing reality or that open our eyes to the needs and tragedies of people? What entertains us or makes us laugh? Slapstick has amused us for many generations, but is it at the expense of respect for a particular race, gender, or creed?

Turn to the business section. Money is never morally neutral because it involves the human being who needs it, earns it, spends it, shares it, invests it, saves it, and so on. Businesses are deemed moral or immoral depending on how they affect the lives of workers, stockholders, CEOs, managers, and consumers. Dishonesty, greed, or corruption can topple the smallest or the mightiest corporation, affecting the lives of countless people. Mergers, takeovers, and acquisitions might seem objective and carefully calculated but can involve the often-hidden human expense of loss of jobs; diminishment of income; destruction of pensions and insurance coverage; uprooting of families; and changed lives, sometimes for the better and sometimes for the worse. Economic and business decisions can improve the quality of life for many people or line the pockets of the exclusive few.

Turn to the comics section. Some of the wisest philosophers of our day share their profound insights in the form of a comic strip. Many have taken on the issues of honesty, fidelity, and friendship and the consequences of deceit, selfishness, laziness, pride, and so on. Their pithy wisdom and often-humorous look into our own humanity make this section of the paper the first section many people open each day. Here, we see our own moral dilemmas unmasked. We can relate to Garfield's sloth and gluttony or Lola's disregard for speed limits and traffic lights. A successful comic strip is one that helps us see ourselves. Comics are valuable moral material as we humorously examine what makes us "tick" and how we choose to become a certain sort of person.

The local or university newspaper is a valuable, but not exclusive, tool for broadening our moral imagination. Internet, television, radio, magazines, and periodicals add to our sources of moral issues. While we might not have the energy to address a study of every issue confronting humanity, there are times when we are personally challenged to deal with a specific moral dilemma. For example, honesty is a moral issue in politics, economics, business, entertainment, sports, and so on. There are ramifications of honesty or dishonesty at the international, national, or local levels of all human endeavors. Sometimes, honesty can be a personal issue in the classroom, in research, or in personal relationships.

What would I do if . . .?

This incomplete question can frame the scenario for many decisions a student might encounter. Try these examples. What would I do if someone offered me a copy of an exam I was scheduled to take tomorrow? What would I do if I needed an "A" to get into graduate school, and the only way I could be sure to get it was to take answers into the exam room by writing them on my hand or on hidden notes? What would I do if I saw someone else doing this? What if I could save money on cable access or Internet access by splicing wires and "sharing" with my next–door neighbors? Most of these scenarios involve personal integrity and might be guided by conscience, but what if the issue seemed more complex and required information and guidelines from sources other than a personal sense of right or wrong?

Let's take a high-visibility example on campus that affects the school and its reputation. What if I am an athlete on scholarship? There are many demands on my time and energy. My grades were good enough to get into college, but keeping up my GPA has been a challenge. I feel a sense of responsibility to my team and my school to stay eligible to play. Traveling to "away games" creates academic challenges. I miss Thursday and Friday classes almost every time we travel. I get notes and the instructor cooperates, but it is tough to grasp the information and the concepts. If I do not do well on midterms, my career on the team and my scholarship are in jeopardy. Teachers have accommodated my absence from midterms by sending the exam with a proctor who will let me take the test on the bus or in a hotel room. They all trust me to be honest, but the pressure is on. I have a responsibility to my team, my school, and my family. It would be so easy to use notes of some kind to help me get the grade I need. So much is riding on this that I am confused as to the right thing to do.

Certain questions and sources should inform my decision. What are the facts here? What is my GPA? What have I needed to do in order to maintain it? What are the team and school rules for administration of exams off campus? What is the likelihood of being discovered using unauthorized assistance? What would be the consequences of being discovered? How prevalent is such activity? What are the consequences if I do poorly on this exam? What are the consequences if I lose my scholarship? What would be the consequences for the team if I were discovered? Will the whole team be held suspect? These are all real questions and concerns for such a decision. When asking so many questions, I feel like a detective and a lawyer, but decisions have ramifications for myself and society. Detectives and lawyers try to raise questions that are important and significant, but how do they find answers?

The Bible offers stories about people who needed to make difficult decisions. The Bible also puts forth both honesty and responsibility as important virtues. Warriors and great leaders are praised for their cunning in securing favorable outcomes in difficult situations. The point seems that God helps those who help themselves. At the same time, other stories praise those who put their trust in the Lord during times of insecurity and self-doubt. Some stories seem to say that honesty is its own reward, even if the results are undesirable. Is the Bible telling me to do whatever it takes to meet my responsibilities, or is it saying that my greatest responsibility is to be honest at all costs? These values seem to be in conflict in my life. How can I choose both when they seem mutually exclusive? Even the Ten Commandments include a prohibition against deceit but also a command to honor my mother and father. The moral dilemma seems to be whether living up to so many expectations justifies cheating on an exam.

Seeking wisdom in this difficult decision, I could turn to the natural law, which I believe to be inherent to human behavior. What is the essential human obligation in this situation? What do reason and my conscience tell me? My conscience would bother me if I referred to unauthorized notes in order to do well on my exam. Maybe I could rationalize my way out of guilt feelings. Maybe those feelings of guilt would haunt me even though I would be glad to stay on the team and keep my scholarship. Would I be able to live with myself?

Does my faith tradition, my church, offer any advice that might help me here? I remember my pastor once noting how difficult it is to maintain integrity in today's complex world. I remember a religion teacher who once said that how we reach our intended goal does matter. From what I remember, it seems that the decision is either moral or immoral depending on the integrity of the intention, the means, and the circumstances. The result might be desirable but wrong because of the means used. This all seemed so useless and academic when we discussed it, but it makes sense now. If I use notes on a closed-book exam, even if I intend to accomplish something important to me and other people, I will go against my integrity. I cannot use dishonest means to meet my responsibilities in this situation. Cheating is not the answer to my moral dilemma. The situation worries and frightens me, but I know this is my decision for now—to try my honest best and face the consequences with whatever courage and hope I can muster.

Some decisions are difficult and complicated. We might even question a decision and wonder if we made the right choice, the "good" choice. How do we know if we have made the best decision? That is difficult. Sometimes, only time will tell. Sometimes, if new information becomes available, we might need to change our mind about a decision. If a person has truly sought the sources of moral wisdom, has reflected and prayed about a decision, chooses what to do, and then discovers it was the wrong choice, he is free to change his mind and make a new choice, but he needs not be troubled with guilt for his original decision. As people of reason, we can only stand where we are and make decisions with the resources available to us. As people of faith, we believe in a God who understands our human limitations and forgives our failings. Integrity before God is to live life as best we can. Morality is a lifelong journey of discovering and choosing the good. Subtract an "o" from "good" to discover the real purpose of our journey—God.

Suggested Activities

1. Research Rosa Parks and her courageous refusal to cooperate with racial segregation on public transportation in the 1950s.

2. Watch the movie *Romero*, the story of Bishop Oscar Romero of San Salvador, who was martyred for his refusal to cooperate with military oppression of the poor and landless natives.

3. Volunteer at a soup kitchen or shelter. Take time to listen to the stories of the people there.

4. Read the Acts of the Apostles, chapter 9, to discover what it means to be "knocked off your high horse." What does that expression mean today? Describe a time when you might have been "knocked off your high horse."

Questions about the Text

1. Explain how Christianity is a way of life.

2. What does it mean to be a person of reason informed by faith?

3. Describe the role of character development in making moral decisions.

4. What is natural law, and how does it inform our conscience?

5. What are the two extremes to be avoided in using scripture as a source for moral theology?

6. Explain the role of the "voice of the prophet" in forming our individual and communal conscience.

7. Distinguish between "conscience" and "superego."

8. Explain two kinds of knowledge necessary for moral decisions.

9. What are the three aspects of any act or decision that must be considered as one is evaluating the act as moral or immoral?

10. What is the *magisterium*, and how does it serve as a source for moral theology?

Questions for Discussion

1. How do you know when you have made a good decision?

2. Whose opinion do you seek when you make an important decision?

3. What role do you think obedience to authority serves in making moral decisions?

For Further Study

Ashley, Benedict M., and Kevin D. O'Rourke. *Ethics of Health Care: An Introductory Textbook*. Second ed. Washington, DC: Georgetown University Press, 1994.

This text on medical ethics from a Christian perspective includes case studies and reflection on the meaning of health care.

Bohr, David. *In Christ a New Creation: Revised Catholic Moral Tradition*. Huntington, IN: Our Sunday Visitor, Inc., 1999.

This introductory summary of contemporary Catholic moral teaching offers good sections on the history of moral theology and good use of encyclicals and the *Catechism of the Catholic Church*.

Callahan, Sidney. *In Good Conscience: Reason and Emotion in Moral Decision Making*. San Francisco: Harper Collins, 1991.

This text deals with aspects of conscience, including the place of personal emotions in making moral decisions.

Catechism of the Catholic Church. Part III: Life in Christ. Washington, DC: U.S. Catholic Conference, 1994.

This section of the official Catholic catechism summarizes Catholic ethics, from its foundations to its many specific teachings.

Crossin, John W. *What Are They Saying about Virtue?* Mahwah, NJ: Paulist Press, 1985.

This text is a good summary of the meaning, interpretation, and place of virtue in ethics.

Gomes, Peter. *The Good Book: Reading the Bible with Mind and Heart.* New York: William Morrow & Co., 1996.

Gomes's book provides an overview of historical critical methodology for biblical interpretation on issues of race, women, homosexuality, and anti-Semitism and deals with the use and abuse of scripture in these and other moral issues.

Gula, Richard M. *What Are They Saying about Moral Norms?* Ramsey, NJ: Paulist Press, 1982.

This is a comprehensive introduction to fundamental aspects of moral theology.

Hamel, Ronald P., and Kenneth R. Himes, eds. *An Introduction to Christian Ethics: A Reader.* Mahwah, NJ: Paulist Press, 1989.

This is a collection of articles on many aspects of moral reasoning from a Christian perspective with good contributions on the use of scripture as a source of conscience formation.

O'Connell, Timothy E. *Principles for a Catholic Morality.* Revised ed. San Francisco: Harper & Row, 1990.

This thorough examination of a systematic moral theology includes conscience, natural law, scripture, sin, and virtue, with good pastoral and spiritual implications.

O'Keefe, Mark. *What Are They Saying about Social Sin?* Mahwah, NJ: Paulist Press, 1990.

This text is a discussion of what is meant by social sin and a discussion of the challenges it poses for ethics.

Spohn, William C. *What Are They Saying about Scripture and Ethics?* New York: Paulist Press, 1984.

This short, easy-to-read summary of contemporary theologians' views of scripture serves not as a rulebook for Christian morality but rather as a context for attitudes and dispositions of the Christian heart such as, for example, response and discipleship.

From the Reference Librarian
The Synoptic Outline—Moral Issues

Student: What kinds of topics can I research in moral theology?

In addition to research on specific ethical issues (e.g., abortion, employer hiring practices, plagiarism), you could also research individuals or groups who, for whatever reason, are of historical or contemporary significance in the realm of ethical thought (Mahatma Gandhi, Martin Luther King Jr., Greenpeace) or specific ethical concepts or various approaches to ethics (virtue, deontological ethics, feminist ethics).

Student: What if I don't even know what topic I want to research?

We could, of course, give many other examples of possible topics in moral theology, but the goal of this textbook is to help you become an independent learner, to seek out and find what interests you as you learn, and to give you the skills to learn how to continue to learn all your life.

An encyclopedia might help you in your quest for a topic. Encyclopedias often provide a feature that, at a glance, will give you an idea of the specific subjects covered (within the subject scope of the encyclopedia) while at the same time providing a list of possible topics for research. This feature goes by various names, such as "synoptic outline of contents," "list of entries by category," "topical list of entries," and so on. Whatever the name, this feature always provides a list of broad subject categories under which the various individual articles relating to that broad subject are listed. Such a simple step lets you begin to dialogue with the entire tradition in this field.

Let's see how a synoptic outline can be used. To demonstrate, I will use a portion of the "List of Entries by Category" in volume three of *Ethics* (three vols., ed. John Roth, listed in the reference bibliography). This list organizes the encyclopedia's 1007 entries into 31 categories.

LIST OF ENTRIES BY CATEGORY

ANIMAL RIGHTS III
ARTS AND CENSORSHIP III
BELIEFS AND PRACTICES III
BIOETHICS IV
BUSINESS AND LABOR ETHICS V

[...]

ANIMAL RIGHTS

Animal consciousness, 59
Animal research, 60
Animal rights, 62
Cruelty to animals, 342
Humane Society of the United
States, 689
Moral status of animals, 965
National Anti-Vivisection Society, 998
People for the Ethical Treatment of Animals, 1107
Sentience, 1343
Singer, Peter, 1371
Society for the Prevention of Cruelty to Animals, 1393
Vegetarianism, 1543
Vivisection, 1564
World Society for the Protection of Animals, 1607

(From *Ethics*, Revised ed., vol. 3, ed. John Roth, Pasadena, CA: Salem Press, 2005.)

Let's take the very first category listed—"Animal Rights." Note that all of the types of topics mentioned earlier are included among the fourteen articles listed, for example, specific ethical issues ("cruelty to animals," "vivisection"), individuals and groups ("Peter Singer," "People for the Ethical Treatment of Animals"), and ethical concepts and approaches ("Animal rights," "Moral status of animals"). You can observe not only what topics might be available but also cases where you might want to examine more than one article for the same topic (e.g., animal rights, moral status of animals).

Student: What if the encyclopedia does not have a synoptic outline of contents?

In that case, try using the encyclopedia's index to explore possible research topics (although this works best if you have some idea of what you are interested in, unless you want to browse through the entire index). It would be helpful to know already that you are interested in, for example, animal rights (or whatever else interests you). In this case, the index of *Ethics* has not only several entries under "Animal rights" but also several other entries containing the word *animal* that might suggest an idea for a topic ("Animal research," "World Society for the Protection of Animals").

Tip

If the encyclopedia you are using has neither a synoptic outline nor an index, try a different encyclopedia.

Another feature of encyclopedias that is often ignored is the cross-references to other relevant articles that appear in addition to the bibliography at the end of the article. Notice the cross-references appearing at the end of the article on the "Moral Status of Animals" in *Ethics*:

FURTHER READING
Fox, Michael A. *The Case for Animal Experimentation: An Evolutionary and Ethical Perspective.* Berkeley: University of California Press, 1986.
Midgley, Mary. *Animals and Why They Matter.* Harmondsworth, England: Penguin Books, 1983.
Regan, Tom. *The Case for Animal Rights.* Berkeley: University of California Press, 1983.
Rodd, Rosemary. *Biology, Ethics, and Animals.* Oxford, England: Clarendon Press, 1990.
Scully, Matthew. *Dominion: The Power of Man, the Suffering of Animals, and the Call to Mercy.* New York: St. Martin's Press, 2002.
Singer, Peter. *Animal Liberation.* New York: Ecco, 2002.
SEE ALSO: Animal consciousness; Animal research; Animal rights; Endangered species; Environmental ethics; Nature, rights of.
(From *Ethics*, Revised ed., vol. 2, ed. John Roth, Pasadena, CA: Salem Press, 2005.)

Note that some of the cross-references to other articles in the encyclopedia may not have appeared anywhere we have looked previously (e.g., "Endangered species" is not listed under "ANIMAL RIGHTS" in the "List of Entries by Category," although it does appear in the index under "ANIMAL RIGHTS").

The titles from the bibliography will, of course, help you identify subject headings to enable you to locate other relevant titles in your own library's collection, as described in the introduction of this text.

Tip

Use cross-references to identify additional encyclopedia articles relevant to your topic.

Expanding Skill Key #1 by Using Skill Key #2

So far in each chapter of this textbook, in accordance with Skill Key #1, you have been given the titles of encyclopedias whose scope is appropriate for the subject of each chapter. At this point, you are ready to start identifying relevant encyclopedias on your own (if you choose to do so; remember, you can always ask the librarian to help you identify relevant encyclopedias). The way to identify encyclopedias exploits what we have learned about subject headings and keyword searching. If you look at the catalog record of any of the encyclopedias mentioned thus far, you will notice that "Encyclopedias" usually appears as a subheading following some subject heading. For example, the *Encyclopedia of Early Christianity* has the subject heading "Church history, Primitive and early church, ca. 30–600 Encyclopedias." (Sometimes, "Dictionaries" is also used, especially in the case of reference works more like what we have been describing as "concise dictionaries.") Knowing this, we can do a keyword search with some broad term related to a topic we are interested in (unless you just happen to know the correct subject heading) combined with "Encyclopedias," which we now know is used in subject headings as a designation for this kind of reference work. For example, to see what encyclopedias that include coverage of ethical issues your library owns, try entering the phrase "ethics AND encyclopedias" as a keyword search in your library's catalog. (Remember that the use of "AND" in a search statement means that all of the search terms must be present in items retrieved.)

The following titles might be among those retrieved.

Title	Ethics / edited by John Roth.
Published	Pasadena, Calif. : Salem Press, 2005.
Description	3 v. : ill. ; 26 cm.
Bibliography	Includes bibliographical references and index.
Subjects	Ethics—Encyclopedias.

Title	Encyclopedia of science, technology, and ethics / edited by Carl Mitcham.
Published	Detroit, MI : Macmillan Reference USA, c2005.
Description	4 v. (cxiv, 2378 p.) : ill., maps ; 29 cm.
Bibliography	Includes bibliographical references and index.
Subjects	Science—Moral and ethical aspects—Encyclopedias. Technology—Moral and ethical aspects—Encyclopedias.

Author	Roberts, Robert North.
Title	Ethics in U.S. Government : an encyclopedia of investigations, scandals, reforms, and legislation / Robert North Roberts.
Published	Westport, Conn. : Greenwood Press, 2001.
Description	xix, 367 p. : ill. ; 25 cm.
Bibliography	Includes bibliographical references and index.
Subjects	Political ethics—United States—Encyclopedias. Political corruption—United States—Encyclopedias.

Title	An encyclopedia of war and ethics / edited by Donald A. Wells.
Published	Westport, Conn. : Greenwood Press, 1996.
Description	ix, 539 p. ; 25 cm.
Bibliography	Includes bibliographical references and index.
Subjects	War—Moral and ethical aspects—Encyclopedias. Just war doctrine—Encyclopedias.

Notice that while "ethics" may appear anywhere—in these examples, either in the title or the subject heading— "Encyclopedias" consistently appears in the subject heading and indicates an encyclopedic reference work.

[Note: You can try this for subjects we have already encountered (Bible and encyclopedias, theology and encyclopedias; what would you search for in relation to Christology? Ecclesiology?).]

Student: I'm supposed to find sources presenting arguments both pro and con regarding a particular issue. How do I find that kind of thing?

This kind of question often comes up when students research ethical issues because professors want their students to become familiar with the arguments made by those on all sides of an issue. Unfortunately, there is no way of searching by subject, and no efficient way of keyword searching, to find specifically "pro" or "con" books in the library catalog. Let's see why that is.

If you look at records for the titles in the bibliography from the article on "Moral status of animals," you will discover a number of useful subject headings, including the following:

Subject heading	Subdivision ("moral and ethical aspects")
Animal experimentation	Moral and ethical aspects
Animal rights	Moral and ethical aspects
Animal welfare	Moral and ethical aspects
Vivisection	Moral and ethical aspects

The subdivision "Moral and ethical aspects" also occurred in several of the "ethics and encyclopedias" catalog records. Librarians call this type of subdivision a "floating" subdivision; that is, it can be used with various subject headings. This means that you can often find this phrase used in a subject heading for a book on the moral or ethical aspect of many topics—politics, public policy, economics, science, business; in short, it can be found in any subject with a moral and ethical component. Are you interested in the moral aspects of abortion? Try "Abortion—Moral and ethical aspects." Genetic engineering? Try "Genetic engineering—Moral and ethical aspects." What about the ethics of writing books? Try "Authorship—Moral and ethical aspects."

[Note: "Religious aspects" is another floating subdivision that may be useful when researching the ethical aspects of an issue. When the "religious aspects" covered in the book are those of a specific religion, there will be an additional subdivision for that religion, for example, "Abortion—Religious aspects—Christianity," "War—Religious aspects—Judaism," and so on.]

Now, look at the following library—catalog records, both of which share the same subject heading: Animal welfare moral and ethical aspects.

Author	Rodd, Rosemary.
Title	Biology, ethics, and animals / Rosemary Rodd.
Published	Oxford [England] : Clarendon Press ; New York : Oxford University Press, 1990.
Description	272 p. ; 22 cm.
Note	"First issued in paperback 1992"—T.p. verso.
Bibliography	Includes bibliographical references and index.
Subjects	Animal welfare—Moral and ethical aspects. Animal rights. Bioethics.

Author	Scully, Matthew.
Title	Dominion : the power of man, the suffering of animals, and the call to mercy / Matthew Scully.
Published	New York, N.Y. : St. Martin's Press, 2002.
Description	xiii, 434 p. ; 24 cm.
Bibliography	Includes bibliographical references (p. [399]–421) and index.
Subjects	Animal rights—Moral and ethical aspects. Animal welfare—Moral and ethical aspects.

What do you think Matthew Scully's position might be on the question of animal rights? Rosemary Rodd's? How do you know? The only hints come from the words used in the respective titles, words like *suffering* and *mercy*.

Now look at the following record:

Author	Leahy, Michael P. T., 1934–
Title	Against liberation : putting animals in perspective / Michael P.T. Leahy.
Published	London ; New York : Routledge, 1991.
Description	xi, 273 p. ; 23 cm.
Bibliography	Includes bibliographical references (p. 260–265) and index.
Subjects	Animal rights. Animal welfare—Moral and ethical aspects.

The same subject heading appears—"Animal welfare Moral and ethical aspects"—but this time, the title seems to express a point of view opposed to that of Matthew Scully's book. If you had used a keyword search combining the terms *animals* and *liberation* to retrieve this record—thinking that *liberation* might be a good word to use to find a "pro" animal rights perspective—you would be disappointed in this case because "liberation" appears after "against"; the entire phrase thus denotes precisely the opposite of what you are looking for. This is one reason why keyword searching is often inexact. This is a problem we took up in searching on the Internet with only a keyword search in chapter 4. You would still have identified a "con" author, but that's not what you were looking for.

Tip

The important thing to remember is that *the subject heading will be the same regardless of an author's point of view*. Nevertheless, the advantage of using the subject heading is that you know exactly what the book is about (i.e., pro or con—it is about animal welfare as an ethical issue). You must examine the information about the book in the library catalog or the book itself to determine whether the author is "pro" or "con."

As you continue to read and explore the further sources the research techniques described reveal to you, you will begin to learn who is "pro" and who is "con." More importantly, you will begin to absorb the overall contours of the debate, develop an understanding of what the debate is about, and learn what the substantive issues are, not just who is on which side of an issue. In a word, you will start to become an educated person.

To sum up, subject headings are helpful, but they do not do everything. The use of subject headings helps to ensure that a book is actually about the topic you are researching, but subject headings cannot inform you in advance of an author's point of view.

In this chapter, we have expanded our library skills in a number of ways:

Skill Key #1

Use the library's reference collection to begin your research.

a) Use a subject-specific encyclopedia to acquire specialized knowledge about a subject.

b) Use a subject-specific encyclopedia whose scope is appropriate for both your topic and the approach you want to take to that topic.

c) Use encyclopedia bibliographies to identify subject headings for your topic.

d) Use a concise subject-specific dictionary to look up the specialized vocabulary of a particular field.

e) Use an encyclopedia's index to locate information on subjects (including persons) for which there is no separate article.

f) **Examine the synoptic outline of contents (or however it is designated) in an encyclopedia (1) to get a quick overview of the contents and (2) to get topic ideas for research.**

g) **Use an encyclopedia's index to get ideas for research topics.**

h) **Use cross-references to locate additional relevant materal in an encyclopedia.**

[Subject heading] Moral and ethical aspects

Use the same subject heading with the subdivision "Religious aspects." Are there further subdivisions indicating particular religions? Judging by the titles, how do the books you retrieve with the "moral and ethical aspects" subdivision seem to compare with the books retrieved with the "religious aspects" subdivision? Do any titles appear with both subdivisions in the catalog record?

Skill Key #2

Use the library's catalog to locate sources of information.

    a) Use subject headings to locate precisely books on your topic.

    b) Use subject headings whose scope fits your topic as closely as possible, then adjust your search with a broader or narrower subject heading as necessary.

    c) As an alternative to using encyclopedia bibliographies, use keyword searching to identify subject headings for your topic.

    d) Combine one or more subject headings in a search to retrieve books on a topic for which no single subject heading exists.

    e) Use the floating subdivision "encyclopedias" in combination with a keyword to identify encyclopedias on a subject.

    f) Use the floating subdivision "moral and ethical aspects" to identify material, whether "pro" or "con," related to the ethical aspects of an issue.

Student Tasks

1. To see what encyclopedias that include coverage of ethical issues your library owns, try entering the phrase "ethics AND encyclopedias" as a keyword search in your library's catalog. How many encyclopedias relevant to ethics can you locate in your library catalog?

2. Try the same technique to find encyclopedias on subjects we have already encountered ("Bible AND encyclopedias," "theology AND encyclopedias"; how would you search for an encyclopedia where you might find material on Christology? Ecclesiology?).

3. Locate a synoptic outline of contents in any encyclopedia. Look up the article on a topic suggested to you by the outline.

4. Find an encyclopedia article on a topic in moral theology. After you have identified subject heading(s) for that topic, use those subject headings in combination with the subheading "Moral and ethical aspects" and see what results you get. Here is the search format you should use:

Endnotes

[1]This scriptural quotation is from the *New American Bible with Revised New Testament and Revised Psalms (NAB)*. Copyright © 1991, 1986, and 1970 by the Confraternity of Christian Doctrine, Washington, DC.

Social Justice: Gospel Witness and Mission of the Church

From the Editor

Jesus revealed God's love for us in a tiny area of the world about seventy miles long, stretching from the Sea of Galilee to the Dead Sea. It is a trip most bicyclists can make in one day, yet Jesus preached in word and deeds the Reign of God that encompassed all of human experience. In Jesus' time, when "neighbor" meant someone from one's own religious, tribal, or ethnic group, Jesus told the simple and astonishing parable of the Good Samaritan, a shunned outsider who stopped and cared for the beaten man lying on the lonely, winding road and even paid for the Samaritan's lodging and medical bills. With that parable, Jesus exploded all borders, limits, and excuses because our neighbor is everyone we encounter.

Nowadays, those who are our neighbors can be far removed from the house next door. We encounter people not only by physical presence but also through information resources, such as communication via satellite transmission over television, cell phone, digital news, the Internet, and newspapers. We are challenged to expand our hearts to include all the neighbors whom we encounter—the rich and poor; those who work seven days a week (including children) and still cannot feed their family; those who take jobs in hazardous conditions, whether toxic poisons or working conditions without safety features; those ravaged by slave trade, war, famine, tsunamis, hurricanes, the AIDS pandemic, global warming—and the list goes on and will only increase in our lifetime.

For Jesus, the call to love as God does means we are inextricably involved in every life. Our hearts, according to God, can expand to encompass all. Furthermore, if we love so that we can even include the unthinkable, our "enemies," then there are no limits to love. That is what Jesus did and showed us.

We will not find the phrase *social justice* in the gospels, but we know Jesus preached it in the terms of his times. Social justice addresses the reality of love in the marketplace, the banks, trade, the public arena, and the working of societal governance; in short, it is Christlike love in action. Some people call this "orthopraxis" (*ortho* = "straight or correct," and *praxis* = "action stemming from reflection on experience"). Perhaps more familiar to us is the related word *orthodoxy* ("correct"+ "teaching").

Social justice is related to Christian spirituality, which means the way in which Christians live out their particular relationship with God. We must take responsibility to direct our resources in a Christ-like way while also being aware of and responsible for our global connectedness to others. This is love in action and is what the community called Church is all about. As Church, and as individuals who comprise the Church, we need to probe this concept of social justice. The stakes are higher today and more involved than ever before. By his example, Jesus gives us hope that we can love the world, no matter how far our regions extend.

The following article examines (1) what social justice means in today's world for a Christian, (2) the new consciousness of "mission" that Jesus tells the Church to do at the end of Matthew's gospel, and (3) some theological reflection on what this might mean for the spiritual life of the followers of Jesus.

Social Justice: Gospel Witness and Mission of the Church

J. A. Wayne Hellmann, OFM Conv, ThD

Overview

Let's look at a historical snapshot of why social justice is so important to Christians today. Since the advent of the nineteenth-century industrial revolution in Europe, there has emerged within the Church an increasing consciousness of the plight of the poor, initially of the workers who were deliberately abused by an economic system that did not provide them with an adequate salary. The twentieth century witnessed the masses of poor in new and underdeveloped nations who had suffered the tragic consequences of recent colonialism. Foreigners had come into their land, stolen their natural resources, and crushed their culture and way of life. Two world wars in the twentieth century caused the most massive destruction of human life ever known. Also, in the latter part of the twentieth century in the United States, evils of racism that deprived black people of civil rights became even more apparent. At the beginning of the twenty-first century, simply in order to survive, masses of humanity, especially from the southern hemisphere, are forced to migrate to strange and cold places in the North where they are often not welcome.

The majority of these millions suffer not because of natural disasters of floods and earthquakes but because of economic, political, and military decisions made by their fellow human beings. The decisions of a minority in positions of power and excessive influence exclude a great majority of human beings from the economic and social benefits of life in the human family. As a consequence, they have no recourse to meet their basic human needs. Tragically, this reality separates human beings from each other more and more.

In response to the gospel in these new situations, the popes, bishops, teachers of social sciences, and theologians have attempted to move the Catholic community and all men and women of good will to acknowledge and then to address these appalling social evils. They have provided the necessary leadership to step back and reflect on these new social realities in the light of the gospel teachings of Jesus. Their purpose was to draw attention to the needs of our next-door neighbors and the millions who suffer through no fault of their own and to articulate gospel principles as a basis for responding to their agonizing cry. The result is that a new body of Catholic social teaching has grown and developed over the last 125 years.

This new and ever-developing teaching of the Catholic Church has shifted from emphasis on charity for those in need to an intentional focus on ways to correct unjust social situations. As a result, the Church has moved away from its traditional support for the established social order and has become an active agent for social change. It no longer simply makes moral appeals to the rich and powerful to be more generous, but it encourages all members of society, including the poor themselves, to work for the reform of social and economic structures that oppress and deprive people of their basic human dignity. Catholic social teaching is a new development in the 2000-year tradition of Catholic teaching, and it forms the basis for social action now known as social justice.

The foundation for this new social teaching remains rooted in the ancient biblical teaching of the Jewish and Christian scriptures, especially in the teaching and example of Jesus as found in the four gospels, for example, the Beatitudes (so named because of the first word, *blessed*, in Mt 5:3–12 and Lk 6:20–26). Catholic social teaching interprets and applies the teaching of Jesus to today's complex world, including encouragement for needed actions and decisions for change. Unless the followers of Jesus take responsibility for the structures of society that oppress others, how do they love their neighbor? The great commandment Jesus gave to his followers remains unfulfilled. Catholic social teaching simply attempts to help the followers of Jesus implement that great commandment. The Church's mission to serve the human family now explicitly and consciously includes commitment to overcome unjust social and economic structures that cause the suffering of so many.

The following discussion is theological and concerned primarily with the Catholic social justice tradition. However, the discussion presupposes that doing justice is always in cooperation with other religious communities, groups, and organizations.

The essay has two parts and a theological reflection. The first part asks and examines what it means in today's world to be a witness of the gospels and a follower of Jesus. Pursuit of this question moves toward a reflection on the Beatitudes as found in the gospel of Matthew, as well as a review of how Christians throughout the centuries have responded to Jesus' teaching in the Beatitudes. The second part of this essay reflects on the new consciousness of the mission of the Church, which is to search for new and effective approaches to social justice and to confront directly the reality of social sin. The essay then moves toward an overview of contemporary Catholic social teaching and to an enumeration of eight principles for social justice that emerge from this overview. Finally, the essay concludes with a short theological reflection on what all of this might mean for the spiritual life of a follower of Jesus.

Gospel Witness

Following Jesus

What does it mean to follow Jesus in the world today?

The Christian vocation is simple: It is to follow the example and the teaching of Jesus. Following him leads to the way of his cross, where his followers are invited to share in the pouring out of his life for others, that is, in his suffering, death, and ultimately his resurrection. A life of gospel witness proclaims the "Good News" that all are loved. A disciple or follower of Jesus is first called to know him, to follow him, and to experience a profound mystery of God's love. Christian discipleship is based on the new law of love that embraces the whole human family and knows no limits. Why? Because in the gospels, Jesus proclaims a salvation that extends "to the ends of the earth" (Acts 1:8).

In the acceptance of the new law of love, every Christian is called in the name of Jesus to witness to the dignity of every human person, to foster the vocation of every human person, and to live in respectful relationship to and within the whole human community. To follow Jesus as a disciple demands a faith that trusts totally in God's plan for the salvation of all, a hope that empowers difficult practical decisions and sustains a perseverance that moves society toward a more just world, and ultimately a love that makes all members of humankind truly brothers and sisters (see the *Compendium of the Social Doctrine of the Church* 3).

In 1971, the College of Catholic Bishops articulated a strong statement that the pursuit of social justice on earth is at the heart of the gospel message and the mission of the Church: "Action on behalf of justice and participation in the transformation of the world fully appears to us as a constitutive dimension of preaching of the Gospel, or, in other words, of the Church's mission for the redemption of the human race and its liberation from every oppressive situation" (*Justice in the World* 6). The key word in their statement is *constitutive*. In their bold statement, the bishops argue that there can be no living or preaching of the gospel message that does not follow through with "action on behalf of justice." This clearly means we are not following the example and teaching of Jesus if we have no care or concern to liberate others "from every oppressive situation."

John Paul II not only reaffirmed this position of the 1971 Synod of Bishops but he also developed it. He emphasized that "action on behalf of justice" is essential to the mission of the Church. He proclaimed "concern for human beings, for their humanity, for the future of the human race on earth and therefore also for the direction of the totality of development and progress—to be inextricably linked to the Church's own mission and an essential element of it" (*Redemptor Hominis* 15). Both of these statements are important in the more recent development of Catholic social teaching, for they offer a new manner of interpreting the gospel and explain in a more profound way what it means to be a disciple of Jesus. In today's world, the gospel is not about preserving the current social order. Rather, for the sake of and out of love for one's neighbor, the gospel demands that the followers of Jesus work together for social change.

In the twenty-first century, the power of the gospel message and the mission of the Church marvelously merge in wholehearted commitment to the struggle for human dignity, that is, for greater human freedom and for liberation of those oppressed by poverty, exploitation, and abuse of any kind. This means those who follow Jesus must take responsibility for all aspects of human development and progress. Any scientific, economic, military, or social progress that oppresses human persons rather than liberates them must be critiqued, challenged, and changed. This implies, of course, that those who do so must be competent to address the ever-more complicated and technical issues that shape our world.

An important step toward further understanding of what it means to follow Jesus in today's world is the emergence of a new concept: "the preferential option for the poor." This phrase was first used by the Latin American bishops in 1979, and the U.S. bishops identified it as a central feature of their 1986 pastoral letter, *Economic Justice for All.* And again, in his 1987 encyclical *On Social Concerns,* Pope John Paul II developed this same concept of "a preferential option for the poor." This means the "rightness" of social structures, of economic policy, and of ever-increasing military investment must all be examined from the perspective of the poor, the marginalized, and the powerless. As members of society, we must always ask questions about the decisions made by those in positions of responsibility for society. How do specific policies or administrative structures affect children, the aged, the sick, single mothers, immigrants, refugees, minorities, the homeless, victims of natural disasters, victims of war, and the peoples of underdeveloped poor nations of the world, for example?

In order to answer this question, Pope John Paul II teaches it is first necessary to "stand with the poor"; that is, explicitly and experientially, he invites the followers of Jesus to cross the bridge that separates the wealthy few from the massive majority on suffering and forgotten margins. One must always listen to them and in some way share in their experience. John Paul II suggests that only in this way can one learn how the poor are affected by the decisions of political or economic powers. He boldly proclaims that the follower of Jesus must experience the suffering of the poor in order to know how "to organize socio-economic life . . . in such a way that it will tend to bring about equality between people, rather than putting a yawing gap between them" ("Address to Bishops of Brazil," 1980, 135).

For those in the United States, this first means the widespread cultural bias toward the rich must be overcome. In the United States, economic policy, politics, media, and ambition are built on worship of the "rich and famous." Action for social justice must be countercultural, giving priority and attention to the poor. This priority runs counter to the so-called "American Dream" that emphasizes wealth, power, and individualism, but it moves toward the heart of the gospel message of simplicity, humility, and solidarity.

It is not that poor people are better than rich people; it is rather that the world's poor live in misery, and their basic human needs are not met. John Paul II connects "preferential option for the poor" and "action for social justice" when he speaks of the "duty of solidarity." Solidarity is "the shared and multilateral commitment toward effective action" that will change the economic, social, cultural, and political "ways of doing things" that perpetuate the structures that oppress the poor and marginalize the weak. According to John Paul II, new inclusive structures and new forms of cooperation are necessary so that the poor may participate in decisions that affect them.

Solidarity with the poor, the pope writes, is not a "vague feeling of compassion or shallow distress at the misfortunes of so many people, both near and far. On the contrary," he writes, "it is a firm and persevering determination to commit oneself to the common good; that is to say, to the good of all and of each individual because we are all really responsible for all." This demands that the followers of Jesus oppose unrestrained "desire for profit" and "thirst for power." They are called for "commitment to the good of one's neighbor with the readiness, in the Gospel sense, to 'lose oneself' for the sake of the other instead of exploiting him, and to 'serve him' instead of oppressing him for one's own advantage." Only in fidelity to the gospel way of love for and service of one's neighbor can evil mechanisms and structures of sin that oppress and marginalize the poor at home and in the developing nations of the world be overcome (*Sollicitudo Rei Socialis*, 1987, #38).

The Beatitudes: "Blessed Are They . . ."

Why are the Beatitudes important?

In the previous citations on solidarity from *On Social Concern* (pp. 38–40), John Paul II draws from the gospel of Mark 10:43: "[W]hoever wishes to become great among you must be your servant, and whoever wishes to be first among you must be slave of all." Solidarity with the poor brings us back to the gospels. In the gospels, Jesus teaches his disciples how they are to live and work so that the Kingdom of God might be realized in this world. Many would agree that the Beatitudes are among the most important passages of the gospels. The Beatitudes capture the vision of Jesus and the new way he interprets and applies the earlier Jewish biblical tradition.

There are two accounts of the Beatitudes. One is in the gospel of Matthew, and the other is in the gospel of Luke (Mt 5: 3–12; Lk 6:20–26). In Matthew's gospel, Jesus is the new lawgiver, and he ascends the mountain just as Moses ascended Mount Sinai. There, he begins to teach. Matthew's account further emphasizes the solemnity of Jesus' instruction by the sitting posture he adopts, the same posture taken by the great teachers in the Torah schools. In Luke's gospel, the Beatitudes are situated in the context of prayer and the call of the twelve apostles. The Beatitudes are announced on the plain, a level playing field for all.

Both evangelists present the oldest summary of Jesus' teaching: Jesus fulfills Old Testament (OT) promises and inaugurates a new age. Notice Matthew's version:

When Jesus saw the crowds, he went up the mountain; and after he sat down, his disciples came to him. Then he began to speak, and taught them, saying:

"Blessed are the poor in spirit, for theirs is the kingdom of heaven.

"Blessed are those who mourn, for they will be comforted.

"Blessed are the meek, for they will inherit the earth.

"Blessed are those who hunger and thirst for righteousness, for they will be filled.

"Blessed are the merciful, for they will receive mercy.

"Blessed are the pure in heart, for they will see God.

"Blessed are the peacemakers, for they will be called children of God.

"Blessed are those who are persecuted for righteousness' sake, for theirs is the kingdom of heaven.

"Blessed are you when people revile you and persecute you and utter all kinds of evil against you falsely on my account. Rejoice and be glad, for your reward is great in heaven, for in the same way they persecuted the prophets who were before you." (Mt 5:1–12)

Luke's version follows:

Then he looked up at his disciples and said:

"Blessed are you who are poor, for yours is the kingdom of God.

"Blessed are you who are hungry now, for you will be filled.

"Blessed are you who weep now, for you will laugh.

"Blessed are you when people hate you, and when they exclude you, revile you, and defame you on account of the Son of Man. Rejoice in that day and leap for joy, for surely your reward is great in heaven; for that is what their ancestors did to the prophets.

"But woe to you who are rich, for you have received your consolation.

"Woe to you who are full now, for you will be hungry.

"Woe to you who are laughing now, for you will mourn and weep.

"Woe to you when all speak well of you, for that is what their ancestors did to the false prophets." (Lk 6:20–26)

Matthew's version is longer than Luke's; Luke's version has four beatitudes and Matthew's has nine. Some scripture scholars would argue that the first three beatitudes found in both Luke and Matthew are the earliest and most authentic. Matthew's additional beatitudes are a further development to situate the Beatitudes in the prophetic biblical tradition of the OT. His expansion of the first three beatitudes into an additional five reflects the spirit of many of the psalms and prophets, especially the prophet Isaiah:

The spirit of the Lord God is upon me, because the Lord has anointed me;

he has sent me to bring glad news to the oppressed,
to bind up the brokenhearted,
to proclaim liberty to the captives,
and release to the prisoners;

> to proclaim the year of the Lord's favor,
> and a day of vengeance of our God;
> to comfort all who mourn;
> to provide for those who mourn in Zion—
> to give them a garland instead of ashes,
> the oil of gladness instead of mourning,
> the mantle of praise instead of a faint spirit.
> They will be called oaks of righteousness, the planting of the Lord, to display his glory.
> They shall build up the ancient ruins,
> they shall raise up the former devastations;
> they shall repair the ruined cities,
> the devastations of many generations. (Isa 61:1–4)

Matthew's version of the Beatitudes can then best be read and understood in light of the prophet Isaiah. Both versions, however, draw explicit attention to the lowly, the wailing, the captives, and all who live in "the ruined cities, for the devastations of many generations." In both versions, we find the fundamental teaching Jesus gives his disciples. His mission is to those who are needy, both in the socioeconomic and in the personal and moral dimensions of life. This obviously makes demands on those who follow Jesus. To share in his mission to the poor and lowly, his disciples must be hungry for holiness. They are called to be merciful, single-hearted peacemakers and to be willing to suffer persecution. His disciples are the "oaks of righteousness" that "shall repair the ruined cities." They will be blessed because they have connected with the poor by crossing the social and economic divide to embrace them and all the alienated of society. This is discipleship. Disciples are those who share in the revolutionary stance of Jesus, who throughout his public ministry aligned himself with the poor and outcasts, and he calls his followers to do the same.

The Beatitudes through the Centuries: How have the Beatitudes been lived?

In the early centuries of the Christian experience, Matthew's version of the Beatitudes was used to instruct believers in basic requirements of the Christian life. Saint Augustine (d. 430) may have been the first one to name the Beatitudes in Matthew's "Sermon on the Mount" (Mt 5). He believed these passages applied to all Christians, and he taught that the Beatitudes are "the perfect measure of the Christian life." Saint Gregory the Great (d. 604), in his *Pastoral Care*, turned to the same Sermon on the Mount to explain it was the duty of all Christians to reach out to the poor. Martin Luther (d. 1546) moved this same perspective into the Reformation. These words of Jesus are ordered to challenge every aspect of one's life, that is, one's professional or official duties and one's personal or spiritual relationship to God and others.

Concern for the poor has marked the centuries of Christianity; the many lives of the saints idealized care of the poor as God's deliberate plan of salvation. Monasteries of the early Middle Ages not only were centers of prayer and study but also contributed to the economic development of the areas around them. Monastic hospitality, however, was specifically directed to the poor. The monk voluntarily chose to become poor, and through this voluntary asceticism, he opened his heart to those who were involuntarily poor. With the arrival of Saint Francis of Assisi (d. 1223), the poor were honored as the bearers of salvation. Saint Francis recognized that Christ was not only the Son of the living God but also "a poor man and a transient who lived on alms." Therefore, Saint Francis taught his brothers they "must rejoice when they live among people of little worth and who are looked down upon, among the poor and the powerless, the sick and the lepers, and the beggars by the wayside" (Armstrong and Brady, 1982). The disciple of Christ is to share the lot and the life of the poor. The poor are all brothers and sisters of Christ, and it is to them that Christ leads all his disciples.

Later in the seventeenth and eighteenth centuries, religious congregations provided hospitals, orphanages, shelters, and schools. Saint Vincent de Paul articulates this social aspect of discipleship. In his *Talks to the Daughters of Charity*, he encourages the sisters to interrupt their schedule of prayer when the poor call upon them: "If you hear the poor calling you, mortify yourselves and leave God for God. It is not leaving God to leave God for God, that is, one work of God for another." In other words, no facet of personal life or spiritual exercise can be a reason for separation from the poor.

In the twentieth-century United States, Dorothy Day (d. 1980) is an outstanding example of one who dramatically brought to life the gospel message. She saw it as imperative that the followers of Jesus participate in socioeconomic action on behalf of the deprived and the oppressed. Her life of advocacy for the poor was articulated in her newspaper, *The Catholic Worker*. Her Houses of Hospitality were open to all, and these became centers of conscious involvement in social politics on behalf of workers who were exploited as cheap labor. In her autobiography, *The Long Loneliness* (1981), she wrote that "to give what you have for relief

Sura 30:38–39 Qur'an

38. So give what is due to kindred, the needy and the wayfarer. That is best for those who seek the Countenance of God, and it is they who will prosper.

39. That which ye lay out for increase through the property of (other) people, will have no increase with God: but that which ye lay out for charity, seeking the Countenance of God, (will increase): it is these who will get a recompense multiplied.

. . . is not enough. One must live with them; share with them their suffering too" (214). Far ahead of her time, she understood what was meant by "the preferential option for the poor" and "solidarity." She was a living example of the Beatitudes. Throughout her life, therefore, she was puzzled how Catholics in the United States could in conscience tolerate the death-dealing social structures of a "filthy rotten system" that marginalizes and oppresses the poor.

Mission of the Church

Why is social justice inseparable from the mission of the Church?

The previous section noted that "action on the behalf of justice" is a "constitutive dimension of preaching the Gospel." It also stated that action on behalf of justice is "the mission of the church." John Paul II was very clear when, as cited previously, he stated, "Concern for human beings . . . the future of the human race . . . is linked to the Church's own mission and an essential element of it." *The Pastoral Constitution on the Church in the Modern World* (*Gaudium et Spes* ["Joy and Hope"]) from the Second Vatican Council also emphasized this same point. The Church's mission is to participate in defense of human rights, promote human dignity, and build up the unity of the human family. Just as gospel preaching is identified with action on behalf of justice, must not the mission of the Church, whose mission it is to preach the gospel, also be identified with that same "action for justice"? The mission of the Church is not just about salvation of souls or the holiness of its individual members. It is rather more about the salvation of the world. Jesus is not just a personal savior, but more importantly, his life, death, and resurrection are for the salvation of the whole world. He poured out his blood for all. Thus, following Jesus and sharing in the mission of the Church must include concern about the formation of public and social order. This now includes how we relate to the earth and its resources and how we care for the heavens of outer space. It is a commitment to construct a world more genuinely human. We do this not by political power or ideology but by constant reflection on the signs of the times, that is, on the actual realities of the world in which we live and on the teaching of Jesus in the gospels. This ongoing reflection gives birth to Catholic social teaching intended to help Catholics, other Christians, and all believers and nonbelievers work toward solutions for the many problems that tear apart human social relationships. It is out of this understanding of the mission of the Church to foster human solidarity that the modern concept of social justice has emerged.

Social Justice

What is social justice?

Social justice is a recent term, first used by Pius XI in 1931, though as a general concept it had already begun to emerge earlier in the late nineteenth century with the 1891 publication of Pope Leo XIII's encyclical, *Rerum Novarum*. (Official papal letters are usually identified by the opening words of the official Latin text. In this case, the title literally means "on new things.") The "new things" to which Pope Leo referred were the new social problems resulting from industrialization. After examining the situation of poor people and the workers in recently industrialized countries, he condemned employers who abused workers as "mere instruments for making money." He called for a "just wage." While upholding the right to private property, he insisted the worker receive sufficient means for meeting basic human needs, thereby rejecting radical socialism. He challenged laissez-faire capitalism, believing the economy should not function only according to the laws of the market, without oversight of the state. However, what was truly new about Pope Leo's encyclical is that he applied both the biblical tradition of works of mercy, such as feeding the hungry and clothing the poor, and traditional moral principles, beyond the simple duty of doing charitable works to the daunting task of constructing a just social order.

With this encyclical, according to theologian Richard McBrien and others, Leo XIII laid the foundation for a theology of social justice. The pope made it clear that social justice is not about rejection of wealthy people, but it is about bringing the spirit of the gospels and the Beatitudes to the manner in which all social structures operate. Fundamentally, the social task is to develop a society in which no human being is deprived of human dignity or of basic human needs that impede the necessary freedom to develop his or her full human potential. Concern for the poor is not about feelings of compassion. It is about concrete and persevering decisions to change the social, economic, and political structures that marginalize and oppress any human person.

Why "social"?

The Catechism of the Catholic Church defines social justice in the following manner: "The respect for the human person and the rights which flow from human dignity and guarantee it. Society must provide the conditions that allow people to obtain what is their due, according to their nature and vocation" (1930). In this definition, the emphasis is on the responsibility of all members of society to provide positive conditions in society that foster "respect for the human person." Especially after Pius XI's 1931 *Quadragesimo Anno* ("Forty Years Later," i.e., after *Rerum Novarum* [1891]), it became clearer that social justice is about the "common good" of all human persons who make up society, especially in the distribution of benefits and burdens.

All people are bound together as members of one human family and share one planet. Social life is therefore not something "added on" to human life, but it goes to the heart of what it means to live as a human being. Family and community provide the context for human growth, identity, and fulfillment. The family is "the first vital cell of society" and the place where the generations come together, and family has a social role in building up the broader human community. According to the Second Vatican Council, other "reciprocal ties and mutual dependencies increase day by day and give rise to a variety of associations and organizations, both public and private," and "this human interdependence grows more tightly drawn and spreads by degrees over the whole world" (*Gaudium et Spes* 25, 26). Multiple relationships are essential to the human experience, but they must be ordered in a way that fosters the growth and dignity of all persons.

Human life is thus embedded in a world of multiform relationships. A human life is a social life. The idea of a totally autonomous person misses the reality of what is human. From the beginning, God created all members of humanity to be with and for each other. God created human persons "in his image, in the image of God" (Gen 1:27). Just as the revelation of three divine persons, Father, Son, and Holy Spirit, are bound in a community of love, so human persons are called to mirror that community of divine persons bound in relationship to each other by love. This was the prayer of Jesus: "[T]hey may all be one. As you, Father, are in me and I am in you" (Jn 17:21).

However, social relationships do not develop automatically, out of their own doing. Social relationships require intentional choices and decisions. Actualization of mutual values and goals requires organization structured in such a way to support human interaction, foster collaboration, and provide a stable framework for humans who live and work together. A guiding principle for a just society is not simply the good of the majority. This can disenfranchise the minority of their rights and dignity. Rather, for a just society, it is the common good that must be the guiding light for all structural and organizational decisions. The Second Vatican Council addressed this principle of the common good and its complexity. One of the final documents of that council, *Gaudium et Spes*, proposed a comprehensive description of the common good:

> [T]he common good, that is the sum of those conditions of social life which allow social groups and their individual members relatively thorough and ready access to their own fulfillment, today takes on an increasingly universal complexion and consequently involves rights and duties with respect to the whole human race. Every social group must take account of the needs and legitimate aspirations of other groups, and even of the general welfare of the entire human family. (*Gaudium et Spes* 26)

It is precisely in these multiform dimensions of social life, that justice becomes vital in order to protect and foster the welfare of all members, communities, and groups within broader human society.

What does *justice* mean?

Justice (Hebrew: *sedq, sedaqa*) in the OT is identified with the nature of God and with the activity of God. The Ten Commandments establish justice in lives of God's people (Jer 23:6). To be "just" is to know Yahweh and to imitate the divine activity of Yahweh. Ultimately, justice will prevail in the messianic reign. In the New Testament (NT), *justice* (Gk., *dikaiosyne*) is used only once in Luke and in Mark, but in Matthew it is found seven times. One of these uses is in the Beatitudes, and the other six uses concern respectful relationships with the poor. In addition, John the Baptist sees Jesus as the fulfillment of all justice. The proclamation of the gospel is about justice. All in all, this means that in the Old and New Testaments, the experience of God's justice overflows into a harvest of justice in the world.

Later, in the Middle Ages, moving to the writings of Thomas Aquinas, which were based on Aristotle's *Nichomachean Ethics*, the general virtue of justice was defined as "the strong and firm will to give to each his due." According to Aquinas, justice subordinates individual human behavior to the common good. This means the good of the individual cannot be separated from the common good of the community. Three more distinctions traditionally characterize different aspects of the virtue of justice: commutative, distributive, and legal.

Commutative justice is about the relationships of society's members with one another, that is, about how they give and take with one another. *Distributive* justice governs the fair distribution of benefits and burdens between a government and its people. The community is to assure the basic rights of all members of the community, especially the needy. *Legal* justice governs the responsibilities of citizens toward the state. Social justice includes all of the aforementioned characteristics, but it goes beyond these three dimensions. Social justice moves beyond the individual person or the manner in which a social group operates. It looks deeper and more comprehensively into the multiple structures that shape human relationships, including the environment and all living creatures.

So then, what is justice? The U.S. bishops refer to it as doing "what is right." Martin Luther King went to the heart of the matter when he commented upon the difference between "just" and "unjust" laws. He said, "Any law that uplifts the human personality is just. Any law that degrades human personality is unjust" ("Letter from the Birmingham Jail," 1963). Finally, the Irish bishops were plainspoken about the matter:

Martin Luther King Jr., 1962 sermon

"Any religion that professed to be concerned about the souls of men and not concerned about the city government that damns the soul, the economic conditions that corrupt the soul, and the slum conditions, the social evils that cripple the soul, is a dry, dead do-nothing religion in need of new blood."

Justice is about my work, my business, my commercial dealings, my style of life. Justice is about paying a fare wage for a job, and doing a just and honest job for the wage. Justice is about buying and selling. It is about employing men and women or making them redundant. Justice is about meeting my contracts, promising and delivering what I promise at the promised time. Justice is about fare prices and just profits. It is about honesty and truthfulness and straight dealing in business, in public service, in political life.

How is sin social?

We have seen that since the time of Pope Leo XIII at the end of the nineteenth century, greater awareness of the need for justice in all social structures has developed. It is now more clearly understood that the reality of sin is therefore not only personal and private but it is also somehow much broader. Theologians have reflected on the injustices facing the millions of poor people in the developing world and in modern industrialized urban areas, and they realized that the common traditional notion of sin is too narrow and individualistic. Sin is more than personal acts of disobedience, dishonesty, laziness, lust, greed, or envy. Evil caused by social interactions or by social factors rooted in human institutions is also sinful, for example, sweatshops, child labor, toxic dumping, and unsafe working conditions, to mention only a few. This implicates sincere and good persons who, by their uncritical acceptance and support of such institutions, indirectly cause the suffering of others. Thus, people who may personally and individually be moral and good people and have no intention of inflicting harm on others often share in a collective guilt called "social sin."

Some theologians have linked this insight to the doctrine of original sin because social sin attests to solidarity in sin. In some sense, social sin is an inherited reality. All of us inherit the unjust social structures into which we are born. Sin goes beyond the acts of a simple individual to permeate the collective action of all the members of community. Saint Paul addresses this issue in the NT books of Corinthians and Romans. He speaks of the world and the reign of sin. He writes that sin "enslaves humanity because the rulers and spirit of the age are in opposition to God." Although Saint Paul does not use the specific term *social sin*, he understood that some kind of collective sin is found in groups and in communities.

Why? Some of us find advantages in social structures that at the same time cause disadvantage to others, for example, tax structures, salary structures, and access to health care. This biblical appreciation of social sin was revived shortly before and again after the Second Vatican Council. The Council itself alluded to sinful structures that make a society unjust. John Paul II again went even further. He said that social sins are the "collective behavior of certain social groups, big or small, or even of whole nations or blocks of nations" (*On Social Concern*, ftn. 65). However, he maintained that unjust collective behavior of social groups ultimately remains the responsibility of persons. Social sin becomes personal sin of individuals through either complicity, indifference, or reluctance of those in a position to exert influence for change who do not do so. John Paul admonished those who "take refuge in the supposed impossibility of changing the world" and who "sidestep the effort and sacrifice," make "social sin" their "personal sin" (*On Social Concern*, ftn. 65).

The development of even further understanding of social justice in society has led to greater awareness of the social sin that stands behind sinful structures. This calls for social conversion. The first step, and often most painful step, toward social conversion is the need to unmask unjust realities that hide behind legitimized structures or institutions. The followers of Jesus are to oppose sin in all forms and manifestations. To bring into light of day the dark and hidden unjust realities of commonly respected social institutions is what goes to the heart of what it means to work for social justice. This is why social justice is about both personal and social conversion. This demands a high price, but the followers of Jesus remember his teaching: "Blessed are those who are persecuted for righteousness' sake" (Mt 5:10). To be effective, however, drawing public awareness to hidden social sins of respectable institutions must be done in a manner that does not condemn but invites conversion and embrace of the gospel.

A clear example of social sin in the United States is the racism that has permeated the social fabric of U.S. life from its origin. Racism predated the founding of the United States. When initial social structures in the new republic were formed, racism in the form of slavery was accepted by the founding fathers as a given social reality. Thus, this social sin was already present in those who settled the United States, and they sealed this sin into the structure of U.S. life. The social structure of slavery provided profit for the economy and furthered the development of the nation. Many people enjoyed the economic benefits that flowed from a social system based on the oppression of those who had been abducted from their African homeland. So, it is easy to understand why the U.S. court system, in the Dred Scott decision of the court of St. Louis, declared that black people were property that could be bought and sold. Even after the abolition of slavery, the social sin of racism continued to marginalize black persons and deny them access to work, education, and housing.

In this horrible social sin, most generations of Americans have been uncritical active accomplices (*What Are They Saying about Social Sin?*, 58–75). It took Rosa Parks (d. 2005), a seamstress who in 1955 refused to give up her seat to a white person on a public bus, to unmask the sin of the accepted social and legal structure that relegated her to the back of the bus. When she sat down where it was not permitted for black persons to sit, she stood up to an unjust system. At that moment began a social conversion known as the civil rights movement, which can rightly be called work for social justice. Confession of this social sin of racism was an important step forward for Americans to begin to make their society more just and more accepting of others. When we begin to see in new ways, we also begin to see more. When we see the injustice of such an example, we often see more than we thought; for example, a follow-up question must be asked: Will Americans ever acknowledge and come to terms with that other social sin prevalent in the founding of their country—yet untold crimes against Native Americans? The list may go on and into other circumstances of social sin in our history.

Social Teaching

What is meant by "Catholic social teaching"?

Pope Leo XIII stands out as a giant. He is the one who provided the starting point for what is now more than a century of Catholic social teaching. He was the first to emphasize the radical primacy of human dignity and human solidarity and use this as basic moral criteria for evaluating the validity of political, social, or economic policies and structures. The pope proclaimed a firm "no" to those who attempted to privatize religion and to those who espoused an excessive individualism at the expense of the broader community. This was his "yes" to the gospel message and to the example of Jesus. His Magna Carta for justice was his encyclical letter *Rerum Novarum*, already mentioned. Over more than one-hundred years, subsequent popes up to and including John Paul II have continued to develop and apply the principles of human dignity and human solidarity to criticism of emerging social, political, and economic situations. There has thus developed within the Catholic tradition of the last hundred years a body of literature known collectively as "social teaching." The *Catechism of the Catholic Church* defines *social teaching*: "The teaching of the Church on the truth of revelation about human dignity, human solidarity, and the principles of justice and peace; the moral judgments about economic and social matters required by such truth and about the demands of justice and peace" (2419–2422). John Paul II reflected on this further when he described Catholic social teaching:

> Nor is it an ideology, but rather the accurate formulation of the results of a careful reflection on the complex realities of human existence, in society and in the international order, in the light of faith and of the Church's tradition. Its main aim is to interpret these realities, determining their conformity with or divergence from the

Calls to Justice in World Faiths

Christianity "In everything do to others as you would have them do to you; for this is the law and the prophets." (Mt 7:12)

Islam "None of you shall be true believers unless you wish for your brother the same that you wish for yourself." (Sunnatt)

Judaism "That which you do not wish for yourself you shall not wish for your neighbor. This is the whole law: the rest is only commentary." (Talmud Shabbat 31)

Taoism "The successes of your neighbor and their losses will be to you as if they were your own." (T'ai-Shang Kan-Ying P'ien)

Buddhism "Do not offend others as you would not want to be offended." (Udanavarga 5:18)

Hinduism "Everything you should do you will find in this: Do nothing to others that would hurt you if it were done to you." (Mahabharata 5:1517)

Confucianism "Is there any rule that one should follow all of one's life? Yes! The rule of the gentle goodness: That which we do not wish to be done to us, we do not do to others." (Analectas 15:23) lines of the Gospel teaching on man [sic] and his vocation, a vocation which is at once earthly and transcendent; its aim is thus to guide Christian behavior. It therefore belongs to the field, not of ideology, but of theology and particularly of moral theology. (*On Social Concern*, 44)

Thus, Catholic social teaching looks to gospel teaching to form the moral foundation for the Catholic approach to questions of social justice. It assists the disciple in the ongoing task of reflecting on the challenge of Jesus in the Sermon on the Mount and in discerning what it means in a consumer, technological, and globalized society to be poor in spirit and to embrace the sorrowing and the lowly. The whole body of social teaching moves forward from the conviction that every aspect of human endeavor, although having distinct and unique operative principles, is accountable to moral scrutiny. The call of the gospel is constant, and it demands continuous rethinking and reassessment of what the dignity of the human person means in the complex and ever-changing organizational structures of our society.

Although texts of papal encyclicals and of the Second Vatican Council are important for development of the body of literature now known as the social teaching of the Church, there are many other contributions to this broad and diverse body of literature. There are documents from bishops. In this regard, the Latin American bishops (called CELAM for *Conferencia del Episcopado Latinoamericano*) took the lead, beginning with their conferences at Medellin (1960) and Puebla (1979). There are two important documents from the North American National Conference of Catholic Bishops (NCCB, now called the United States Catholic Conference or USCC): *The Challenge of Peace* (1983) and *Economic Justice for All* (1986). These documents manifest an ongoing learning process. They are largely the result of a broad dialogue among bishops and specialists in social ethics and the social sciences, as well as other well-informed observers from among the people of God. There has been broad participation. This is in the spirit of the Second Vatican Council that all Christians are called to "the duty of scrutinizing the signs of the times and of interpreting them in the light of the Gospel" (*Gaudium et Spes* 4).

Broad participation in the social mission of the Church is imperative. Pope Paul VI (d. 1978) made concrete this directive to observe and examine the signs of the times:

It is up to the Christian communities to analyze with objectivity the situation which is proper to their own country, to shed on it the light of the gospel's unalterable words . . . and in dialogue with other Christian brethren and all men of good will, to discern options and commitments which are called for in order to bring about the social, political and economic changes seen in many cases to be urgently needed. (*Octogesimo Adveniens* 4)

Thus, the body of social teaching develops within broad Catholic experience in order to present an organic and ongoing discernment of Gospel teaching. This discernment has given rise to three basic steps: observe the situation, reflect on the gospel, and act out of love on behalf of the oppressed.

Eight Principles for Social Justice

In a 1998 document, *Sharing Catholic Social Teaching*, the U.S. Catholic bishops highlighted a number of principles that flow out of their understanding of Catholic social teaching. What follows is based on their insights but has been developed further to accentuate several current issues important in the Church's mission of concern for the human person and the future of the human race. These can be helpful for the discernment of today's follower of Jesus.

1. Life and dignity of the human person.   Human dignity means that all persons have worth and value. Why? God's likeness bears on every dimension of the human being. Created in the image of God, the human person has characteristics of God and is therefore a being intimately and essentially related to God. The human person is at the center and the summit of the created order. The origin of social life is the human person, and every expression of the social order must be directed toward the dignity and the welfare of the human person. Humans ultimately share in God's freedom, a freedom that enables recognition of what is good and the will to choose it. Human dignity is not something that humans decide. Its origin is the wisdom of God, whose love created and continues to sustain every person. Disrespect of a fellow human being is blasphemy or an attack against God. As the bishops stated: "Every human being is created in the image of God and redeemed by Jesus Christ, and therefore is invaluable and worthy of respect as a member of the human family" (*Sharing Catholic Social Teaching*, 1998).

Furthermore, because the dignity of the human person is rooted in the actual creation of the human person, dignity applies to every moment of human life, from beginning to end. Thus, the bishops are consistent when they point out that the human person enjoys an inherent dignity from the moment of conception to natural death. John Paul II, in his encyclical *On Human Life* (n. 101), likewise taught that "unconditional respect for the right to life of every innocent person . . . is one of the pillars on which every civil society stands." Any society or civil government that fails to do this thus fails in its duty. As a result, its decrees in this regard are wholly lacking in binding force. Human dignity comes before any social structure or political power. More and more, John Paul applied this principle to questions about the death penalty and about war. With regard to the death penalty, John Paul, in his 1999 St. Louis visit, stated: "The dignity of human life must never be taken away, even in the case of someone who has done great evil." According to John Paul II, capital punishment is no longer necessary to protect society, and thus, it should rarely, if ever, be used. Concerning war, saddened by the failure of his attempt to dissuade the United States from going to war against Iraq, he simply cried out: "War is always a failure for humanity" ("Address to the Diplomatic Corps," Vatican City, January 13, 2003).

2. **Call to family, community, and participation.**   Children are conceived in a relationship and have a natural right to be nurtured in the enduring and loving relationship of their parents. This helps children become capable of loving relationships. The human person is not only a "being intimately and essentially related to God" but also a being ordered to relationships with fellow human beings that extend beyond the immediate family. From the sphere of the family, one moves into participation with the broader society of the human race. Thus, the U.S. bishops teach that "the family is the central social institution that must be supported and strengthened, not undermined. Furthermore, people have a right to and duty to participate in society, seeking the common good and well being of all" (*Sharing Catholic Social Teaching*, 1998).

3. **Rights and responsibilities.**   The most fundamental rights are the right to life and the right to the means necessary and suitable for a full human life. This includes the right to a standard of living in keeping with human dignity. Everyone has a right to active participation in society, to share in the benefits of society, and to move between countries. The right to religious liberty and what flows from it (i.e., freedom of conscience, public exercise of faith, and the promotion of cultural tradition) is intimately connected to the right of a full human life. Religious freedom, according to John Paul II, is basic to understanding the dignity of the human person. As the human person exists prior to the state, any state that restricts religious freedom deforms itself because it restricts human persons from expressing concretely what is deepest within them and attempts to deny that dimension of

the human person that transcends the state. This is why denial of religious liberty often leads to a totalitarian state.

Rights, however, have corresponding responsibilities and duties. With the right to life comes the responsibility to foster the lives of others, especially those associations that support the family and foster human growth and economic development. This includes active support for national and international bodies that work for justice among nations and safeguard the natural environment. This duty extends far beyond the responsibility to vote; it means taking responsibility for the political landscape and for the shape of specific policies. The right to participate in society is the obligation to participate, not ideologically but critically. The right to freedom of religion is also a responsibility to respect and foster all faiths and religious traditions.

4. The common good.   As indicated, the common good involves creating social conditions that permit all people to participate and realize their human dignity. Today, in an increasingly interdependent and globalized world, the common good involves a universal common good that creates international structures to coordinate resources and projects for the good of the human race and the care of the planet.

5. The preferential option for the poor.   This principle has already been treated; however, it is worth noting how Peruvian theologian Gustavo Gutierrez underscored the reason for the option for the poor: "We must be committed to the poor because we believe in the God of the Kingdom. The preferential option for the poor is a theocentric option. We must be committed to the poor, not necessarily because they are good, but because God is good" (*Theology of Liberation*, 266). Thus, according to this principle, the important question to ask about policies and decisions of government and the manner of constructing society is this: How will this affect the poor? To answer this question properly, however, one must know the poor and have experienced in some way their misery and powerlessness. Today, this principle urgently forces the question about the "rightness" of developed consumer societies based on surplus of goods while the remaining underdeveloped societies suffer from hunger.

6. Dignity of work and rights of workers.   The economy must serve people, not the other way around. John Paul II said work is the key to the whole social question. Labor is not to serve capital as a tool in the productive process, but rather, capital is to serve labor. This implies not only a more equitable redistribution of income and wealth but also a more equitable redistribution of work itself in order to provide employment for all. John Paul II insisted on a just wage and other social allowances that "suffice for establishing and properly maintaining a family and for providing security for its future" (*Laborem Exercens* 3, 19). This right to work applies to the handicapped and to those forced to migrate from their homeland in order to find work elsewhere. All work has dignity because all work is done by human persons created by God, and as workers, they participate in the creative activity of God. Respecting the right of all persons to work "promotes an economy that protects human life, defends human rights, and advances the well being of all" (*Sharing Catholic Social Teaching*, 1998).

7. **Principle of solidarity.** The principle of solidarity became a key component of John Paul's approach to social issues. He wrote that we are all responsible for all. In *On Social Concern* (76–78), he emphasized that solidarity is the Christian virtue that "helps us to see the other—whether a person, a people, or a nation— . . . as our 'neighbor,' a 'helper' [cf. Gen 2:18–20], to be made a sharer, on a par with ourselves, in the banquet of life to which all are equally invited by God." He reflected on this principle in the light of reason and in the light of faith. In the light of reason, he taught that solidarity is the path to peace and to global human development. On the global scale, solidarity is interdependence "that in itself demands the abandonment of the politics of blocs, the sacrifice of all forms of economic, military or political imperialism, and the transformation of mutual distrust into collaboration" (*On Social Concerns*, 1987, 39). This advocates solidarity among individuals and nations. On the level of faith, the pope goes further. Solidarity takes seriously the gospel command of forgiveness and reconciliation. One's neighbor must be loved, even if an enemy, even to the ultimate sacrifice: "to lay down one's life for the brethren" (cf. Jn 3:16). This solidarity is the solidarity of the follower of Jesus that will bring him or her to share in the suffering of his cross.

8. **Principle of stewardship.** The principle of stewardship, that is, the careful and responsible management of something entrusted to you, is related to the principle of solidarity. We are called to relate respectfully not only to people as our neighbors and to our interdependent world of peoples and nations but also to the shared space of the earth, the air above, and the resources below. Interdependence applies also to the entire ecosystem. Each creature, every being of the planet, is profoundly implicated in the life and existence of every other being. This is be-

cause each creature and creation itself taken together as a harmonious whole was spoken by God. Human persons are created in the image of God, but every created being is a manifestation of the glory of God. The beauty of the earth invites awe, reverence, and wonder.

Saint Francis of Assisi understood this when he called all creatures his "brothers and sisters." Saint Francis realized he shared life with the earth and all that is of the earth. He, along with all creatures, whether worms, birds, or stones, came forth from the same origin, the same Father, who created heaven and earth. As the common inheritance of the human race, the earth provides for human needs. It nurtures the body with its nutrients and the soul with its awesome beauty. Thus, the earth and its environment must be honored, preserved, and shared.

Seven Deadly Social Sins (M. K. Gandhi)
Wealth without work
Pleasure without conscience
Science without humanity
Knowledge without character
Politics without principle
Commerce without morality
Worship without sacrifice

It is not to be dominated or exploited by one group against another, including the current generations now living against the future generations not yet born. Stewardship cares and protects the earth's resources. Stewardship contains, therefore, within it the principle of sustainability. On this point, Gandhi's observation about the sustainability of the resources of the earth bears repeating: "The earth is sufficient for everyone's needs but not for everyone's greed."

Conclusion: Social Justice and Christian Spirituality?

Faith That Acts to Promote Justice

"Follow me" (Jn 21:19) is the invitation Jesus extends to all. Those who respond to his call embrace the vision and program Jesus outlines for his followers in the Beatitudes. They take seriously the command to love God and to love neighbor and enter into dynamic relationship with Jesus. That is, they share his experience of obedience and worship of God, the Father, which is so beautifully expressed in the prayer he taught, the Lord's Prayer. In this manner, his followers receive the gift of the Spirit that transforms hearts of stone into hearts of flesh, connecting them with the human family. In this, the followers of Jesus manifest the heart of the Church's mission. They learn to share in the joy and hope, the suffering and anguish of the human family. This is what conversion and the baptismal promise of "renouncing sin" are all about: liberation from egoism, from self-seeking, and from focus only on one's own advantage. Conversion is a new and graced freedom that enables one humbly and courageously to challenge the spirit of the world that glorifies the minority of rich and powerful while dismissing the great masses of poor, suffering, and hungry. Commitment to social justice requires a faith that is not a simple conviction about a truth, the revelation of God in the Incarnation of Jesus, but rather a faith that is a personal act in which the follower of Jesus turns his or her whole life totally over to God. To do so is to respond to Jesus' invitation: "If any want to become my followers, let them deny themselves and take up their cross daily and follow me" (Lk 9:23). That is not a wooden cross but the cross of reality that we bear each day and that is the world we live in and in which we encounter God.

Faith trusts in the mystery of the unlimited love that God has for us and for all. Faith justifies, heals, and makes whole in God's love. This requires great openness of mind and heart and makes possible works of justice. Faith affirms that the mystery of God's love is for all. It proclaims a love that is readiness to give from the very substance of one's life so that others too may experience and live in that love. This is the social justice that is, at the same time, response to the gospel call of Jesus and powerful experience of the communion of saints. This is the kind of faith Christians experience in the mystery of the Church, which is ever called to be a sign of God's presence in the world and an instrument of unity among all.

Works of social justice that correct the economic and social structures that divide and oppress peoples are more than doing good and avoiding evil. They look evil directly in the eye and attempt to overcome it, or at least to lessen its effects that destroy human community, depriving our neighbors of their food, their health, their families, their education, and their cultural development. Social justice challenges ravenous market systems of economics and excessive militarization of nations. It negotiates with decision makers to protect workers, environments, local cultures, and the vulnerable. Social justice is not then just charitable aid, although that too is necessary, but it is also about policies and structures that make charitable aid necessary. However, although social justice is not just charity, it begins and ends in charity. Thus, action for justice begins with exclusion of any kind of violence because it begins with the conviction that love of God and of neighbor is undivided and excludes no one. Working for justice then ends with a profound and even mystical experience of being loved by God, a love that empowers us to love and be loved.

Injustice, in fact, is a denial of God. It denies the image of God in our brothers and sisters and in the rest of creation. Social justice always rests on the fundamental and opening lines of the Nicene Creed, accepted by all Christians: "We believe in God, the Father Almighty, Creator of heaven and earth." Every creature and every human person shares in the power, beauty, and awesome dignity of the Creator. Social justice based on the teaching of Jesus acknowledges, and thereby worships and honors, the Creator of all. The whole body of Catholic social teaching ultimately points toward the great mystery of a God who, in the Divine Being itself, is an immense dynamic communion of interpersonal love and equality among persons. Working for social justice thereby allows the followers of Jesus to be instruments of that triune love of Father, Son, and Holy Spirit overflowing into human interpersonal love and equality.

Social justice teaching is a profound insight into two realities: into the mystery of God and into the basic unity of the human race. Both of these speak of harmony, forgiveness, and reconciliation. Both are about relationship—relationship to God, to each other, and to the gifts of the earth. Both are shaped by the Word of God and graced with a message of hope for the future.

Social justice then sends the followers of Jesus on the road of a long pilgrimage to build the Kingdom of God here on earth. To remain faithful to the insight and vision taught by Jesus in the Beatitudes, the followers of Jesus must repeatedly reconstitute themselves in his own Body and Blood and renew themselves in the memory of his command to love God and neighbor. Thus, in the liturgy of the Eucharist or in the celebration of the Mass, by breaking bread and pouring wine, followers of Jesus rejoice in marvelous gifts of the earth shared by all; in the Eucharistic blessing, they themselves share in the Body and Blood of Christ, broken and poured out for all. In this radical openness, the followers of Jesus are made holy. They then bless all the elements of the earth and all their brothers and sisters, wherever they may be. In the celebration of the Eucharist, Christians extend themselves beyond their own secure worlds to the vastness and vulnerability of the human race. In 1981, Father Robert Hovda, in writing about the social experience of the Eucharist, expressed it this way:

> Where else in society are all of us called to be social critics, called to extricate ourselves from the powers and principalities that claim rule over our daily lives in order to submit ourselves to the sole dominion of God before whom all of us are equal? . . . Where else are food and drink blessed in a common prayer of thanksgiving, broken and poured out, so that everybody, everybody shares and shares alike? (Henderson, Quinn, and Larson, 1989, 79)

Questions about the Text

1. How did the industrial revolution impact the concept of social justice?

2. What does the word *solidarity* mean in this document?

3. What does "preferential option for the poor" mean and imply?

4. What does the "theocentric option" mean and imply?

5. Why are the Beatitudes important?

6. What is the meaning of commutative, distributive, and legal justice?

7. List the eight principles for social justice offered by the U.S. Catholic bishops.

8. What does the sentence "Injustice, in fact, is a denial of God" mean in the conclusion?

Questions for Discussion

1. Describe a firsthand experience of social injustice, done either to you or to someone else.

2. What are some new areas of social justice today?

3. What strategies might be considered for making one's voice for social justice heard in our world?

4. Who are the voiceless, invisible, and powerless in our world? In our city? In our households?

5. On what grounds should the Christian community be involved in public questions? How should they do this?

6. Does the separation of church and state in the United States mean that religion and religious people have nothing to say to the state? How should religion relate to the state? The state to religion?

7. What does one's spirituality have to do with social justice?

For Further Study

Introductions to the Topic

Armstrong, Regis J., and Ignatius C. Brady. *Francis and Clare: The Complete Works*. Mahwah, NJ: Paulist Press, 1982.

Burkhart, Walter, SJ. *Justice: A Global Adventure*. Maryknoll, NY: Orbis Books, 2004.

> This prophetic book draws heavily from the biblical tradition of the Old and New Testaments to illustrate that biblical justice is about relationships based on covenant. The author then applies this biblical vision as the basic social ethic, especially for the critical stance necessary for evaluation of ever-increasing globalization.

Day, Dorothy. *The Long Loneliness*. San Francisco: Harper & Row, 1981.

Henderson, J. Frank, Kathleen Quinn, and Stephen Larson. *Liturgy, Justice and the Reign of God: Integrating Vision and Practice*. New York: Paulist Press, 1989.

Krammer, Fred, SJ. *Doing Faith Justice: An Introduction to Catholic Social Thought*. New York: Paulist Press, 1991.

> In this manageable book, the student will find a clear, engaging, and dynamic theological reflection on basic elements of Catholic social teaching.

Church Documents

Compendium of the Social Doctrine of the Church. Pontifical Council for Justice and Peace: Liberia Editrice Vaticana, 2005.

> This compendium is a resource that presents in a systematic manner one-hundred years of official Catholic social teaching, mostly in the form of official texts, arranged according to various themes: principles, family, human work, economics, political life, international community, peace, and environment.

Calvez, Juan-Yves. *Faith and Justice: The Social Dimension of Evangelization*. Trans. John E. Blewett. St. Louis, MO: Institute of Jesuit Resources, 1991.

This book offers a summary of the discussion and resolution of the Jesuit General Congregation in 1975. At that time, the Jesuits rearticulated their common mission to be "in the service of faith of which the promotion of justice is an absolute requirement."

Sharing Catholic Social Teaching: Challenges and Directions. Washington, DC: USCCB, 1998.

Encyclicals

John Paul II. "Address to Bishops of Brazil," *Origins* 10, no. 9 (July 31, 1980): 135.

On Social Concern (Sollicitudo rei socialis). Washington, DC: United States Catholic Conference, 1988.

In this encyclical letter, Pope John Paul II develops further the earlier encyclical letter of Paul VI, *On the Development of Peoples* (1967). John Paul applies principles of economic and human development to address the widening gap between rich nations and the poor nations where the majority of human beings live.

From the Reference Librarian
"Floating" Subdivisions and Social Justice Issues

Student: How do I research social justice issues?

You can do research on some of the topics mentioned in Fr. Hellmann's chapter using the sources and techniques you have learned in the previous chapters. For example, you could explore the social significance of the Beatitudes by using the sources and techniques learned in chapter 2, or you could study important individuals, such as Augustine, Gregory the Great, and so on, with regard to their importance for Catholic social thought using the sources mentioned in chapter 3.

However, as Fr. Hellmann makes clear, the deliberate focus on the social aspect of Catholic theology is a fairly recent development in the broad sweep of Church history. For that reason, the sources described in the previous chapter on moral theology, whose scope encompasses contemporary ethical/moral issues, many of which have a social component, may also be useful.

However, what you really need for the subject matter of this chapter is a reference tool that focuses specifically on the social aspect of ethical issues, that is, on social justice. You could, therefore, try your luck with another keyword search (Skill Key #2d), using the phrase "social justice and encyclopedias" to see what relevant reference sources your library might have. (What keywords other than "social justice" might you use?) Your search might turn up an item such as the following:

Title	Encyclopedia of American social movements / Immanuel Ness, editor.
Published	Armonk, N.Y. : M.E. Sharpe, 2004.
Description	4 v. : ill. ; 29 cm.
Bibliography	Includes bibliographical references and indexes.
Subjects	Social movements—United States—History—Encyclopedias.
	Social change—United States—History—Encyclopedias.
	Social justice—United States—History—Encyclopedias.

(Notice the other subject headings "Social movements" and "Social change" that might give you additional points of access in the library catalog.)

None of the subject headings included in the catalog record for the *Encyclopedia of American Social Movements (EASM)* appears to focus specifically on the religious or theological aspects of these topics (though they could encompass coverage of such aspects along with other aspects—check the index, synoptic outline, and so on of the *EASM* to find out).

Student: So what good are nontheological subject headings in researching topics related to theological subjects?

Remember what you learned about "floating" subdivisions in the previous chapter. You can always try to focus on the religious/theological aspect of a subject by using either "Moral and ethical aspects" or "Religious aspects" as subdivisions with any subject, including nonreligious/theological ones. Another useful subdivision for social justice issues is the subdivision "Social aspects." (Remember that a "floating" subdivision can be used with various subject headings for various topics. This does not mean that such subject headings will always be valid, but you will not know until you try them out, and neither will most librarians.) Using all the possible combinations of the three subject headings in the previous record with the three "floating" subdivisions, I was able to find the following two subject headings in my own catalog (what you find in your own library's catalog will vary depending on what your library actually owns).

Search Format:

Subject heading	"Floating" subdivision
Social conflicts	—Religious aspects
Social justice	—Religious aspects

Student: What I find in my library catalog when I use these subject headings isn't what I'm looking for. What can I do now?

Even if what you find under such headings does not look promising, don't give up. Remember, you are doing research. Time and effort are often required to find what you want. The computer makes things a lot easier, but you still have work to do. What at first appears to be an unprofitable search may, in fact, prove very profitable indeed. For example, the heading "Social justice—Religious aspects" produced the following record of a book in a language most of us probably cannot read. You may recognize the author's name as one mentioned by Fr. Hellmann.

Author	Gutiérrez, Gustavo, 1928–
Uniform title	Dios o el oro en las Indias. French.
Title	Dieu ou l'or des Indes occidentales, 1492–1992 / Gustavo Gutiérrez ; traduit de l'espagnol (Pérou) par Lucile et

	Martial Lesay.
Published	Paris : Cerf, c1992.
Description	161 p. ; 24 cm.
Series	Théologies.
Note	Translation of: Dios o el oro en las Indias.
Bibliography	Includes bibliographical references.
Subjects	Casas, Bartolomé de las, 1474–1566.
	Indians, Treatment of—Latin America.
	Indians—Missions.
	Social justice—Religious aspects.

Even if I cannot read this book (a French translation of a book originally in Spanish), I can use the other subject headings assigned to it to continue searching. Note the subject heading "Indians, Treatment of—Latin America." If that strikes me as an interesting topic, my library catalog lists no fewer than sixty-three titles under that heading. In this way, you can discover both subject headings (and possible topics for papers) that might not otherwise have occurred to you and what books your library owns on the particular topic.

What do you think the subject heading would be for the treatment of Indians in the United States? We will learn more about the use of geographical descriptors as both subdivisions and as subject headings in their own right in a later chapter.

Student: Is there a reference tool specifically on social justice issues from a theological perspective?

Indeed, there is. As always, you can consult the *New Catholic Encyclopedia* on various social justice issues. (Look at the column of entries under "Social justice" in the index, for example.) The following reference tool, however, is dedicated entirely to social issues from a Catholic theological perspective:

Judith A. Dwyer, ed. *The New Dictionary of Catholic Social Thought*. Collegeville, MN: Liturgical Press, 1994.

The New Dictionary of Catholic Social Thought (*NDCST*) will treat many of the same issues covered by the reference sources mentioned in the previous chapter but will do so from the perspective of social justice; for example, the article on abortion appears under the rubric "Abortion, Social Implications of."

The *NDCST* contains most of the helpful features of encyclopedic reference works we have been emphasizing, such as article bibliographies, cross-references, and an index. There is also an alphabetical "List of Entries" you can scan to identify relevant articles.

Let's say you want to research social justice as it pertains to economic life. Scanning through the list of entries, your eye will fall upon a number of possible research topics, ranging from such specific items as "Association of Catholic Trade Unionists" to broader areas such as "Banks and Banking," "Capitalism," "Corporations," "Economic Order," and so on.

Once you have found an article that interests you, you can proceed to use it to acquaint yourself with the topic and to collect further possible sources of information in your library catalog, as we have been describing.

One important matter to keep in mind is that social justice issues touch just about all areas of human life and endeavor, including many complex issues of science, technology, economics, business, political and military activity, and so on. As Fr. Hellmann states, many of these areas involve complex technical issues that require Christians to be "well prepared, educated, and competent to address [them]."

Thus, with respect to economics, it may not be enough just to consult an article on "Economic Order" in the *NDCST*, for example, but, to make sure that you have an adequate understanding of the economic issues involved, you may have to consult reference and other sources whose focus is from the perspective of economics. I hope by now that you have a good idea of how to get started doing research on a topic that may be unfamiliar to you (hints: start by locating relevant reference sources; enter "economics and encyclopedias" in your library's catalog to see what your library has). The library skills you have been learning in the context of studying theology work the same way in any other subject.

Student: How do I find official pronouncements for ecclesiastical bodies mentioned by Fr. Hellmann, such as CELAM or the United States Conference of Catholic Bishops (USCCB)?

Both organizations have websites where you can find much information, including the full text of some (not all) official pronouncements or documents. (Note the .org extension on the URL, indicating the nonprofit nature of these organizations.)

http://www.celam.org

http://www.usccb.org (see especially the link to "Social Justice Issues" on this page)

However, you will discover at least one major problem with each of these websites. First, the CELAM website is entirely in Spanish (not surprising for an organization based in Latin America). Second, although the USCCB website does have the full text of many pronouncements, news releases, and so on, the official documents such as those mentioned by Fr. Hellmann are offered for sale only.

Student: So how can I get access to documents from either of these organizations?

Your library may own publications of both groups in its collection. Some CELAM documents have been translated into English. You can do an author search in your library's catalog using CELAM as a corporate author to see if your library owns any of them (you do not have to spell out the full name because your library's computer should automatically refer you to the full form of the name). If it doesn't, remember that you can still get CELAM publications through your library's interlibrary loan service (this assumes that you already know the title of the CELAM document you want).

You can find publications of the USCCB using the name of that organization for your corporate author search in the library catalog. Unfortunately, the name the U.S. bishops have chosen for themselves has changed several times throughout the twentieth and the beginning of the twenty-first centuries. So, it may be possible to find listings in your library catalog under each of the following corporate author entries. The dates refer to the years when each name was used:

National Catholic Welfare Council (1919–1922)

National Catholic Welfare Conference (1922–1966)

National Conference of Catholic Bishops (1966–2001)

United States Catholic Conference (1966–2001)

United States Conference of Catholic Bishops (2001–)

Library catalogers prefer to maintain consistency in the names of both persons and organizations, so only one form of the name is used at any one time. Do you know how many ways William Shakespeare's name can be spelled? To ensure that users of library catalogs can always find his books in the catalog, only one form of "Shakespeare" is actually used, and anyone who enters an alternate spelling ("Shakspeare," "Shakspere," etc.) will automatically be directed to the form of the name actually used in the catalog.

Names of organizations can change over time (more readily than names of persons), so when searching for publications produced by a particular organization, it is necessary to know the name of the group at that particular time. You need to keep this in mind when searching for publications of the Catholic bishops in the United States.

The actual forms of names used by libraries for two of these are as follows (your library catalog should automatically direct you to these without your having to type "Catholic Church" at the beginning):

(Corporate) author

Catholic Church National Conference of Catholic Bishops
Catholic Church United States Conference of Catholic Bishops

You can also use the following forms of the names (your library catalog should automatically redirect you to the form just given):

(Corporate author)

National Conference of Catholic Bishops
United States Conference of Catholic Bishops

You may wonder why the bishops had two names for themselves from 1966 to 2001. The reason was to distinguish the bishops' actions and statements regarding internal church matters—liturgy, priestly life, ministry, and so on—from their actions and statements regarding external matters, or relations with the secular world, as to social concerns, education, public policy, and so on. The name "National Conference of Catholic Bishops" was used for the former, while the name "United States Catholic Conference" was used for the latter. Which corporate author entry do you think is likely to be most useful in finding official publications about social justice issues for the years 1966–2001?

Fortunately, the bishops decided to do away with the dual nomenclature; the single organization name "United States Conference of Catholic Bishops" will make searching for bishops' statements in the twenty-first century a little easier. Just remember to use the correct corporate author name, depending on when the document was published.

We can now add the following to our Library Skill Keys that unlock the doors to knowledge:

Skill Key #1

Use the library's reference collection to begin your research.

a) Use a subject-specific encyclopedia to acquire specialized knowledge about a subject.

b) Use a subject-specific encyclopedia whose scope is appropriate for both your topic and the approach you want to take to that topic.

c) Use encyclopedia bibliographies to identify subject headings for your topic.

d) Use a concise subject-specific dictionary to look up the specialized vocabulary of a particular field.

e) Use an encyclopedia's index to locate information on subjects (including persons) for which there is no separate article.

f) Examine the synoptic outline of contents (or however it is designated) in an encyclopedia (1) to get a quick overview of the contents and (2) to get topic ideas for research.

g) Use an encyclopedia's index to get ideas for research topics.

h) Use cross-references to locate additional relevant material in an encyclopedia.

Student Tasks

1. Using *The New Dictionary of Catholic Social Thought* (or some other encyclopedia), find an article on a social justice issue of interest to you.

2. Use the bibliography of the article you found in #1 to identify relevant Library of Congress subject headings for your topic of interest.

3. Add the following "floating" subdivisions to the subject headings identified in #2 to see what you can find in your library's catalog.
Moral and ethical aspects
Religious aspects
Social aspects

[Note: Write down the complete subject headings (with subdivisions) that resulted in finding relevant titles.]

Skill Key #2

Use the library's catalog to locate sources of information.

a) Use subject headings to locate precisely books on your topic.

b) Use subject headings whose scope fits your topic as closely as possible, then adjust your search with a broader or narrower subject heading as necessary.

c) As an alternative to using encyclopedia bibliographies, use keyword searching to identify subject headings for your topic.

d) Combine one or more subject headings in a search to retrieve books on a topic for which no single subject heading exists.

e) Use the floating subdivision "encyclopedias" in combination with a keyword to identify encyclopedias on a subject.

f) Use the floating subdivision "moral and ethical aspects" to identify material, whether "pro" or "con," related to the ethical aspects of a subject.

g) Use the floating subdivision "religious aspects" to search for religious/theological aspects of nonreligious/nontheological subjects.

h) If necessary, use all the subject headings assigned to a book to identify material on a particular subject.

i) Use the name of an organization or group as an author to search for documents produced under the aegis of that particular group. Be aware of the possibility of changes in the group's name over time.

4. Search your library's catalog to see if you can find any documents from the United States Catholic Conference. Find a document the U.S. Catholic bishops published in the 1980s.

5. See if you can find anything relevant to your topic at the website for the United States Conference of Catholic Bishops.

IV

THE ABRAHAMIC FAITHS: CATHOLICISM AND RELATIONSHIPS WITH JUDAISM, ISLAM

8

Judaism, the Jewish People, and the Church

From the Editor

Christianity, Judaism, and Islam share a common origin that goes back to Abraham. Theology often refers to the three "Abrahamic traditions" because all three trace their roots to Abraham in their sacred scriptures. Theologically, many questions arise about our relationship to these other religious traditions—more questions than answers. To go further, many questions abound about all the major religious traditions. As an introductory theology text, it is beyond the scope of this book to examine the complex relations with every major world religious tradition, but chapters 8 and 9 will examine Judaism and Islam because of their Abrahamic connection and affiliation with Christianity. By doing so, we are providing a method for examining and understanding any other religious tradition. We certainly hope that the Reference Librarian skills you learn from these chapters will provide you with the research capability to delve deeper into other religious traditions.

We have already learned a good deal about Judaism in chapter 1 on the Old Testament (OT), so this chapter will build on that foundation and go more deeply into some of the historical relations between the two.

These two chapters demonstrate the significant role of theology in answering questions and seeking understanding about the relationship of the Abrahamic faiths. Sometimes, it means we agree to disagree until we know more. Sometimes, it means we inch our way along by listening and learning from the faith experience of others and how God is with them. Why are there other religions? Probably there are a million reasons. In the end, we do not have an answer to that question—we have one another, and it seems that God is inviting us into the mystery and that we have to listen carefully and in new ways. Christians are called to love everyone, no matter the religion, as everyone is our neighbor and we all are God's family.

This chapter examines the situation of Judaism at the time of Jesus, the developments within Judaism, events that shaped Rabbinic Judaism, traditional Jewish prayer and ritual (spirituality), modern Judaism confronting a changing world, and finally, the ongoing Jewish–Christian relations. While it would be best, of course, to walk with someone from Judaism for days or weeks or even a full faith year and attend synagogue with that person, here we can at least take a step along the path to understanding the why, what, when, where, and how of Judaism. Theology is an important part of that understanding because it has a broader perspective than a single person's understanding of his or her faith.

Judaism, the Jewish People, and the Church

Ronald Modras, Dr Theol

Overview

Necessarily, as an introduction to Catholic theology and not an encyclopedia, this book cannot be exhaustive. So why is an entire chapter devoted to Judaism? Because we cannot fully understand Christianity without understanding Judaism.

With good reason, Pope John Paul II described the Jewish people as the Church's "elder brothers" during his 1986 historic visit to the synagogue in Rome. Both Judaism and Christianity, as practiced today, grew out of Second Temple Judaism, the religion practiced by Jesus and the first Christians. The Hebrew scriptures constitute the first and longest part of the Christian Bible. The roots of the Catholic Mass are found in the prayers of the synagogue and Jewish feast of Passover. Even the most familiar words *Amen* ("so be it") and *Halleluia* ("praise Ya[weh]") are Hebrew words taken from Judaism. Moreover, as the latter word indicates, Yahweh, the God of Israel, is the God of Christianity. Out of reverence for that name, observant Jews do not even speak it but instead say *Adonai*, the Hebrew word for Lord. So when Christians or Jews pray, "The Lord is my shepherd," or when the priest at Mass says, "The Lord be with you," standing behind that English word *Lord* is the Hebrew name for God, *Yahweh*.

Just as Hinduism refers to the religious beliefs and practices of the people of India, Judaism refers to the religious beliefs and practices of the Jewish people. As one should expect with any people, there is a wide diversity among Jews, ranging from the devout to those who are completely nonreligious. Judaism refers to the religion of the Jewish people, but the Jewish people are also an ethnic group and, since 1948 and the modern state of Israel, once again a nation. Given their wide-ranging diversity, which will be demonstrated in greater detail, one should be wary of ever referring to the Jewish people as if they were some homogeneous entity. Their differences make it difficult to ever simply say "the Jews"—just as there is great diversity among the beliefs and practices of Christians, which makes it difficult to lump all of them together under this one term.

With a religious history that goes back more than three-thousand years, the beliefs and practices of the Jewish people have undergone significant evolution.

One can see this in the pages of the Hebrew Bible itself. Dramatic changes took place after Roman armies destroyed the Second Temple in 70 CE. Jews became a diaspora people without a country, living wherever they went as a religious minority. Surviving centuries of hostility and periodic persecution, Judaism continues to evolve today as Jews address the challenges of modernity as once their ancestors addressed the challenges of worshipping without a temple.

A Christian consideration of Judaism must necessarily look at the thorny, often painful history of Christian–Jewish relations. In the two-thousand years that Jews and Christians have been relating, it was in 1965, less than fifty years ago at the Second Vatican Council, that a sea change took place. One of the beneficial consequences of that change is a more unbiased perspective of how, in the first century CE, Jews and Christians first came to see one another as alien to each other's interests. Christians, in particular, forged their identities both with regard to and in contradistinction to the Jewish people.

First-Century Judaism

Jesus was born, lived, and died a Jew, an obvious fact from the gospels but one often overlooked. One cannot understand who Jesus was and what he was about without first understanding the Judaism of his day. Much like Judaism in our own day, it was marked by widespread diversity.

Divisions in Jewish Society

Jews in Jesus' day were an occupied nation. Under the domination of the Romans, they were compelled to pay taxes to the empire or else suffer the consequences. Those unable to pay had their property confiscated and, when that was gone, they lost their freedom. Slavery was at the heart of the empire's political-economic system, enforced by state-sponsored terror. Any slave who attempted to run away, as well as anyone tempted to rebel against Roman rule, faced the likelihood of capture and condemnation to a slow, agonizing death by crucifixion. Crosses were a regular feature of the landscape in Roman-occupied Judea.

For the sake of peace and order, the Romans did not interfere with the religious practices of the peoples they subjugated, so they allowed Jews to continue offering sacrifices at the Temple in Jerusalem (rebuilt after the return from exile in Babylon in the sixth century BCE and splendidly ornamented by Herod the Great in the first century BCE). They also permitted Jews to manage their own internal and religious affairs by way of a Supreme Council or Sanhedrin, with the high priest of the Temple at its head. Controlling the Sanhedrin were the Sadducees, a small group of leading priests and wealthy aristocrats. It was from their numbers that the Roman governor selected the high priest, recognizing that the Sadducees were committed to the status quo, which is to say the survival of the Temple, the Sanhedrin, and their own favored position.

Jews in Jesus' day worshipped not only at the Temple in Jerusalem but also in synagogues, gathering places for the reading and study of the Torah, the first five books of the Hebrew Bible. Attributed to Moses, the Torah was often referred to simply as "the Law" because of the hundreds of commandments it contains. The Pharisees were a movement focused on understanding and interpreting the Torah to achieve holiness through exact observance of God's commandments. Emerging about a century before the time of Jesus, the Pharisees viewed it as the vocation of every male Jew to live as if he were a priest, presiding at the most everyday, ordinary meal as if it were a sacrifice. The Pharisees developed these ideas in an oral tradition of Torah interpretation (the so-called "oral Torah"); this included belief in an afterlife, which, remarkably enough, receives no mention in the written Torah. The more conservative Sadducees rejected the oral Torah and the Pharisees' belief in an afterlife as innovations. As one can imagine, there was no love lost between the two groups.

Also prominent in the first century were the Zealots. Originating in Galilee shortly before the time of Jesus, Zealots were consumed with a sense of religious outrage that God's chosen people were being compelled to take from the fruits of their holy land and pay taxes to the heathen Romans. They considered this no less than a blasphemy that called for violent resistance; to lead them in that struggle, they looked for a military leader like their great king David, eleventh century BCE, as the promised messiah. The Zealots abhorred the Roman occupation and just as much, if not more, the Sadducees and Jewish tax collectors, whom they saw as collaborators. Though in the view of the Romans they were dangerous revolutionaries and terrorists, the Zealots considered themselves freedom fighters for the cause of God.

A fourth faction was a group of radically pious Jews called the Essenes, not mentioned in the gospels but better known today because of scrolls discovered near the ruins of a monastery at Qumran on the shore of the Dead Sea. From these Dead Sea Scrolls, we learn that the Qumran community also detested the Sadducees for their collaboration with the Romans. They regarded the Temple leadership, and in some instances Jewish society altogether, as corrupted. They were sure that the time was coming soon for a cosmic confrontation between good and evil, more specifically, between righteous Jews and idolatrous pagans.

Yeshua ha Notzri

All of these various groupings within first-century Jewish society were sure that theirs was the right way of doing God's will in response to the Roman occupation of Israel. Amid this welter of diverse Jewish opinion came Jesus of Nazareth (*Yeshua ha Notzri* in Hebrew) and his movement out of Galilee. Nonviolent but in essence more revolutionary than the Zealots, Jesus preached a countercultural way of life that he described in terms of an impending "reign" (which can also be translated as "empire") of God. He drew the contours of this way of life from the Hebrew scriptures and its faith in a God who cares about widows and orphans, a Jewish way of describing the most marginal and defenseless persons in a patriarchal culture. He called for trusting in a God who provides "daily bread" and for imitating God's compassion by forgiving debts and even enemies.

Like his fellow Jews, Jesus focused on life here and now ("on earth as it is in heaven"). When he and his followers came to Jerusalem for Passover (a freedom festival), Pilate, the Roman governor, and the Sadducees had reason to be apprehensive. Jesus was from Galilee (the home of the Zealots), preached about an "empire of God" (an alternative to the Roman Empire), and was popular with the Jewish masses. If not a Zealot, he was perceived as close enough to being one and, in any case, clearly a potential troublemaker. Nonviolent resistance is still resistance. With the collaboration of the Sadducees, Pilate had him executed.

Jesus was but one among countless Jews who died as victims of Roman terror. He would have been forgotten, not even a footnote in history, had it not been for the fact that his disciples began experiencing him as raised up, exalted at "God's right hand." The Jesus movement did not die out with Jesus' death but instead exploded as his former disciples experienced the power and presence of God (described as God's "Holy Spirit," another symbol drawn from the Hebrew scriptures—e.g., it is God's Spirit who "inspired" the prophets).

Jewish Christianity

Under the influence of this power and presence, the Jesus movement saw itself as gifted with prophets who spoke in the name of the Risen Jesus. But how should they describe him? By what titles? During his lifetime, Jesus appears to have been called *rabbi* ("teacher") and "a prophet," but now, in a community filled with teachers and prophets, those titles were not enough. The Jesus movement began referring to him as "Messiah" ("Anointed One" in Hebrew, a metaphor for "King"), *Christos* in Greek. A word that in Jesus' lifetime would have denoted a sword-wielding king like David was now used to describe the Risen One "enthroned" at God's right hand. Jesus had become "the Christ," and his followers came to be called Christians.

Not surprisingly, this new community drew regularly from the rich symbolism of its Jewish heritage. They baptized new members into their community and partook of a common meal they called the Lord's Supper, but they were all still Jews, observant of the Mosaic laws, circumcising their male children, and worshipping at the Temple. Their fellow Jews accepted them as Jews, despite their peculiar belief that Jesus of Nazareth had been exalted after his death and was God's Messiah. For Jews then, as in our own day, religious beliefs mattered but not so much as practice.

So long as they maintained observance of the Mosaic laws, their fellow Jews tolerated the Jewish Christians as just one more sect or faction within Judaism. However, when Gentiles began professing faith in Jesus and asking to become Christian, the inevitable question of whether these Gentiles had to be circumcised before they were baptized arose among the nascent Church. In other words, did they have to become Jewish before becoming Christian? No, answered Paul of Tarsus, himself a former Pharisee. The question was a crucial one for the early Church, and contentious. Nevertheless, Paul's thinking eventually prevailed, and he became the "apostle to the Gentiles."

Because of Paul's answer to the question of Christian observance of the Mosaic laws, the Church went on to become increasingly Gentile and less Jewish. Only because of that answer could Christianity become the world religion it is today. However, Paul agonized over the fact that, while Gentiles were accepting Jesus as the Messiah, his fellow Jews were not (Rom 9:2–3). Why that was the case, he ultimately left to the inscrutable and mysterious will of God (11:33). Nevertheless, of one thing he was sure: Though his fellow Jews rejected Jesus as God's Messiah, God had not rejected them. Jews were still heirs of God's promise, "for the gifts and the calling of God are irrevocable" (11:29).

The Christian church originated within a first-century Judaism that was fractured into diverse, competing, and mutually antagonistic groups. The Pharisees were further divided into two major schools of Torah interpretation: the followers of Rabbi Shammai contending with those of Rabbi Hillel. The Zealots were also divided among themselves, as became clear when their long and eagerly awaited rebellion against Rome finally broke out in the Great War (66–70 CE).

At the beginning of the war (66 CE), the Jewish Christians fled Jerusalem, an act viewed by other Jews as disloyalty to Jewish national aspirations. By the year 69, the Roman legions had retaken the countryside and laid siege to Jerusalem. Internal fighting among the Zealots weakened the resistance, and in the summer of the year 70, the Romans finally breached the walls. Jerusalem and the Temple were demolished, and perhaps as many as a million Jews perished. In Rome today, one can still see the Arch of Titus depicting Roman legions carrying the Temple's massive seven-branched candlestick in triumph as the spoils of war. Neither Judaism nor Christianity would ever be the same.

Rabbinical Judaism

The destruction of Jerusalem and the Second Temple saw the demise of the Sadducees, Zealots, and Essenes. The priestly class no longer had an altar on which to sacrifice. Among the competing factions within first-century Judaism, only two groups survived—Christians and Pharisees.

Judaism without a Temple

The story is told of Rabbi Yohanan ben Zakkai, leader of the Hillel school of Pharisees. Shortly before the fall of Jerusalem, he had himself smuggled out of the city and went to Vespasian, the general of the Roman legions. Yohanan knew Vespasian would soon become emperor, and Vespasian knew that the Hillel school of Pharisees was opposed to the rebellion. At Yohanan's request and for the sake of restoring order in Judea, Vespasian allowed the Hillel Pharisees to re-establish the Sanhedrin in the village of Jamnia (Yavneh), west of Jerusalem. There, the Pharisees set about recreating Judaism without a Temple.

The task was daunting but not impossible because the Pharisees had already developed a way of life centered on the Torah and synagogue. Observance of the Torah and its commandments would serve to substitute for Temple sacrifices. As to the challenge of interpreting the Torah and its many commandments, the Pharisees already had an oral tradition of interpretation that went back for centuries (the oral Torah). Now that they dominated the Sanhedrin, the Pharisees were in a position to make those interpretations official. As members of the Sanhedrin, they came to be called rabbis.

Judaism after 70 CE was much more defensive than it was before. The rabbis at Javne felt compelled to impose uniformity upon Jewish thought and practice. In the year 80, they inserted a prayer into the synagogue service (into the *Shemone Esreh*) that called for God to punish the *minim* ("heretics"). There is no doubt that this was meant to include Jewish Christians and was tantamount to excommunicating them from the synagogue. Jews and Christians began viewing each other with animosity as hostile outsiders.

It is at this time that the gospel according to Matthew was written, its description of Pharisees marked by a bias more commensurate with the Church's situation in 80 CE than of the Jesus movement in the year 30. In the same gospel, we find the Christian interpretation of the destruction of Jerusalem. Under the influence of the Torah's teaching that God punishes misdeeds with calamity (Deut 28:15–68), the rabbis themselves agonized over what terrible sin Israel could have possibly committed to warrant the destruction of its Temple a second time. Influenced by the same assumptions, Christians concluded that the calamities of the year 70 must have been divine punishment for the death of Jesus: "His blood be on us and on our children!" (Mt 27:25). Jesus had been the victim of Pontius Pilate and the Roman occupation of Judea with the collaboration of the much-despised Sadducees. Based on the destruction of Jerusalem and the Temple, however, Christians came to place the blame for Jesus' death almost exclusively upon Jews, primarily the Jewish leadership but by extension all Jews who refused to accept Jesus as the Messiah.

In 135 CE, the Romans put down another Jewish rebellion. Thousands more Jews lost their lives by believing Simon bar Kochba to be the messiah who would restore Israel to independence. The rabbis responded to the loss of Jewish life by insisting that any restoration of Israel and its temple would be at the end of the world, at a time when justice and peace would reign universal. That day could be hastened only by perfect observance of the commandments, indeed, by one perfect Sabbath. The rabbis' new interpretation of "messiah" served both to quell further use of arms to gain Jewish independence and to answer claims being made by the Christian church. If Jesus is the messiah, why are violence and bloodshed still rampant? Why is the lion not yet lying down with the lamb (Isa 65:25)?

From Oral Torah to the Talmud

The rabbis continued to adapt to new situations and answer questions about Jewish observance by resorting not only to the written Torah but also to their oral tradition. According to that tradition, there were hundreds more commandments beyond the usual ten, commandments about prayer, diet, property, marriage—in fact, 613 commandments in all. In the early years of their movement, including during Jesus' lifetime, the Pharisees had resisted writing down their legal opinions, but by the year 200, rabbinical leadership decided that the oral Torah would be lost if it were not recorded. The result of that decision was the Mishna, a compilation of rabbinical legal opinions up to that time.

In the Mishna, one finds the basic ethical principles of rabbinical Judaism, particularly in a tractate called the "Ethics of the Fathers" (*Pirkei Avoth*). There we read, for example, of the centrality of Torah, prayer, and the practice of charity. The very word for commandment in rabbinical tradition, *mitzvah* (*mitzvoth* in the plural), also means good deed or favor. How altruism or compassion relates to self-interest is expressed in a famous saying: "If I do not care for myself, who will? But if I care only for myself, what kind of person am I? And if now is not the time to do good, when is?" (Here, evidently, simplistic claims identifying Christianity with charity and Judaism with justice do not survive scrutiny.)

The Mishna emphasizes the importance of Torah study; ignorance of the law is no excuse for transgressions. (Rooted in the commandment requiring Torah study is the high regard Jewish tradition has for scholarship altogether.) However, just as important as study is making "a fence around the Torah," by which the Mishna means drawing up regulations that act against even those transgressions that are not deliberate. Thus, to protect against breaking the commandment that prohibits using Yahweh's name in vain, Jewish legal tradition forbade using Yahweh's name at all, even in prayer. As mentioned previously, when coming upon the name Yahweh in reading the Torah, the word *Adonai* ("Lord") would be spoken instead.

Jewish legal tradition continued to develop and evolve, as rabbis focused now not on the written Torah but on the Mishna. They argued questions such as how was the Sabbath day to be kept "holy," that is, "separate" from the other days of the week? Clearly, by resting, not working, but what kinds of activity constitute work? The rabbis decided that, among other activities, cooking, carpentry, and even writing were prohibited as being labor. (Note that writing was the professional work of a scribe.) And how was one to "make a fence" around those activities to avoid coming even close to transgressing the commandment? By not lighting a spark; by not even picking up a hammer, pen, or pencil. But what if some sort of work was a matter of life or death, for example, lifting up a weapon in self-defense? The rabbis had long held that the Sabbath rest could be broken to save life. Jews were to live by the law, not die by it.

Arguing all sides of questions like these, the rabbis continued to develop a legal tradition around the commandments of the written and oral Torah. According to the Mishna, both were given by God to Moses at Mount Sinai and had equal weight and validity. Finally, around the year 500, the amount of rabbinic commentary (called *Gemarra*) grew so massive that it too came to be compiled together with the Mishna. Rabbis in present-day Iraq created the Babylonian Talmud, a virtual encyclopedia of rabbinic legal discussion, its many volumes comprising some six-thousand pages and capable of filling three feet of space on a bookshelf.

One often sees depictions of rabbis with long, white beards dressed in prayer shawls and pondering heavy books. The books being portrayed are those of the Talmud. To be regarded as a scholar in rabbinic Judaism requires mastery of the Talmud and the ability to make judgments based on its ethical and legal principles. Some parts of the Talmud (called *Haggadah*) consist of inspirational stories, ethical sermons, and illustrations. Most of it by far (called *Halakha*, from the Hebrew word "to walk") consists of rabbinic legal discussion on how Jews are to live a Torah-centered life.

Although a small fraction of Jews rejected the Talmud and rabbinic tradition (so-called Karaites, quite possibly descendents of the Sadducees), for the vast majority of Jews, the Talmud became the foundational document for Jewish thinking, attitudes, and behavior. Whether in North Africa, Europe, or the Middle East, in Christian or eventually Muslim lands, Jews were everywhere a minority, tempted to assimilate to the religion and culture of the majority population. The fact that they did not, the fact that they survived as a distinct people, can be directly attributed to the influence of the Talmud and the distinctively Jewish way of life it created.

Traditional Jewish Faith and Practice

Though Judaism is often described as "ethical monotheism," the more accurate descriptive would be "monotheistic ethics," with the emphasis on ethics. Judaism is more a way of living than of thinking. (With its roots in Judaism, Christianity also began as a way of life, but under the influence of intellectual Greek culture, it came to emphasize correct thinking or orthodoxy in expressing its faith.)

Talmudic Judaism does have doctrines and a theology too, however; they simply were not formalized until rabbis in medieval Spain felt themselves challenged by Christian and Muslim cultures. There, the great twelfth-century Talmudic scholar and philosopher, Rabbi Moses ben Maimon (Maimonides), formulated the most widely recognized list of Jewish doctrines in his so-called Thirteen Principles.

God

In Jewish theology, as formulated by Maimonides, God exists and is uniquely one. Judaism had always held Yahweh to be *ehad*, a Hebrew word that can mean "alone" or "one." In opposition to the gods of other nations, biblical Judaism originally emphasized that Yahweh alone was their God. Eventually, Judaism came to emphasize the oneness of God. In either case, central to Jewish worship is the classic statement of Jewish faith taken from the Torah (Deut 6:4), the *Shema*: "Hear (*Shema*), O Israel: the Lord (*Adonai*) is our God, the Lord alone (*ehad*)."

God has no body, Maimonides continues, no material parts. Biblical references to the face or hand of God are to be taken not literally but as metaphors. Moreover, God is eternal, existing before all else, and alone is to be worshipped. The rabbis took literally the prohibition against idolatry and disallowed any physical images of God, but they developed a rich literature that abounds in verbal images of God. Not surprisingly, given the patriarchal cultures in which both biblical and rabbinic Judaism originated, virtually all those images are male. The one major exception is Shekinah, a feminine image for God's indwelling. Originally the cloud and pillar of fire that traveled with Israel in the exodus out of Egypt, the symbol of the Shekinah functions within Judaism in a way analogous to the Holy Spirit within Christianity, as a way of speaking of God not as transcendent in some seventh heaven but mysteriously close and present.

JOHN RENARD

Shown here is a statue of the great medieval Iberian rabbi Moses Maimonides (1135–1204), which sits in the old Jewish quarter of his hometown, Cordoba, Spain.

Torah, Covenant, and Israel

Central to Maimonides' account of Jewish faith are doctrines relating to God's actions with respect to Israel: God's word has been communicated to Israel by way of prophets. The greatest of these prophets was Moses. To him, God communicated the entire Torah (written and oral). The Torah is immutable; nothing may ever be added to or subtracted from it.

The focal point in any synagogue is the "holy ark," the receptacle that contains the central symbol of rabbinical Judaism, the Torah scroll. Specially trained scribes can spend as long as a year painstakingly making a single copy of the Torah, scrupulously following rabbinical regulations as to how and where to place the Hebrew words on specially prepared sewn-together pieces of parchment. Revered in Jewish tradition as the very word of God, Torah scrolls are regularly dressed with decorated cloth covers and elaborate crowns.

The word *Torah* in Hebrew means "teaching" or "instruction" but came to be translated into Greek (the Septuagint) as *nomos*, which means "law." This was because, besides the creation stories, patriarchal narratives, and chapters on the life of Moses, the rest of Torah consists of laws and regulations. As noted earlier, the Torah is only one part of the entire Hebrew Bible (the Tanach, an acronym for Torah, Prophets, and Writings). Whereas Christians read the entire Hebrew Bible as equally inspired, rabbinic Judaism gives pride of place to the Torah (written and oral); the rest of the Tanach is commentary.

For Judaism, the Torah and its commandments are Israel's part of the covenant (*B'rith*) or "sacred contract" that God made with Moses and the Jewish people at Mount Sinai. Variously compared by the prophets to a marriage or an adoption, the covenant was the agreement whereby Israel became Yahweh's chosen people. By this covenant, Yahweh would provide Israel with protection, freedom, and a land. Israel, in return, was to worship Yahweh alone and obey the commandments.

The idea of a chosen people was not unique in the ancient world, in which various gods were seen as adopting various peoples, but when monotheism came to replace polytheism, the idea of Jews seeing themselves as the chosen people of the only God, the question arises of whether Jews saw themselves as superior to everyone else.

Rabbinical Judaism explains the covenant in terms of Israel being chosen to receive and observe all 613 commandments of the Torah. This does not make Jews more favored. Even less does it mean that only Jews can be saved, that is, have a place in "the world-to-come." In rabbinic tradition, Gentiles come under the covenant God made with Noah. Under the Noahide covenant, non-Jews are required to observe only seven (not all 613) commandments. To have a place in the world-to-come, Gentiles need only to keep the commandments prohibiting actions like idolatry, blasphemy, murder, and adultery and requiring establishment of a just society, that is, courts of law.

The Messiah and the World to Come

Maimonides' final doctrines have to do with the future: After death, God, who is aware of all human deeds, will reward the good and punish the wicked. God will send the messiah, and there will be a bodily resurrection of the dead.

The concept of the messiah originated in Judaism with the promise to David of an eternal dynasty (2 Sam 7:16). When David's descendents fell short of the ideals that should have guided them as monarchs of God's chosen people, Israel's prophets began to look forward to a better future under a better son of David, when swords would be beaten into plowshares (Isa 2:4). The concept of a messianic age has had tremendous impact, first on Jewish and then Christian thinking and ultimately on western civilization and culture.

With its implied criticism of the status quo, messianism has sparked revolutions (the first-century Zealots), the idea of a New World (the Pilgrims and Puritans of New England), and, in a secular form (messianism without God), a faith in the future, in scientific and technological progress (modern Western culture after the Enlightenment). The main point here is that the concept of a messiah was never unambiguous. After the fall of Jerusalem in 70 CE, rabbinical Judaism maintained faith in a future personal messiah but insisted that all attempts to calculate or speed up the coming of the messianic age be resisted. Today, many Jews see the messiah not as a person but as a symbol for the Jewish people.

Belief in an afterlife is not mentioned in the written Torah. The oral Torah recorded in the Mishna of the Talmud professes faith in what it calls "the world-to-come," when God will reward good deeds and punish evil, but Jewish tradition never dwells on it. Instead, it provocatively maintains that even a few minutes in the here and now are better than the entire afterlife. In those few minutes, one can perform good deeds (*mitzvoth*). The world-to-come is in God's hands, not ours, the rabbis reasoned, so there is no need to think much or speculate about it. Emphasis is always on life here and now. Hence, the traditional Jewish toast when raising a glass of wine is *l'chaim*, "to life."

Daily Prayer and Life-Cycle Rituals

Rabbinic Judaism does not leave prayer to happenstance. Following a minutely detailed order, Jewish men put on a prayer shawl (*tallit*) and pray three times a day—morning, afternoon, and evening. In the morning, they also strap on to their right arm and forehead leather boxes (*tefilin*) holding small pieces of parchment containing verses from the Torah. Blessings or prayers of gratitude to God are to be said throughout the day, most of them beginning with the same formula: "Blessed be thou, Lord our God, Ruler of the Universe . . ." The positive regulations ("thou shalt") determining prayer are directed only to Jewish men; women and men alike are bound to observe the negative commandments ("thou shalt nots").

In addition to the daily prayers incumbent upon Jewish men as individuals, rabbinical Judaism surrounds life-cycle rituals with communal prayer. Eight days after the birth of a baby boy, the ceremony of circumcision (*bris milah*) is performed, marking the child as a son of Abraham. At the age of 13, the boy assumes the rights and responsibilities of adult Jewish males as a "son of the commandment" (*bar mitzvah*). The rite of passage is marked by the young man ascending to the pulpit in a synagogue sanctuary and reading a portion of the Torah in Hebrew. He now counts in any *minyan*, a quorum of ten or more Jewish males required for certain forms of Jewish worship. Women in rabbinic tradition do not count for a *minyan*.

Marriage is also surrounded with distinctive Jewish ceremonies: the signing of a marriage contract (*ketubah*) and standing under a canopy (*huppa*) where the bride and groom share a cup of wine, symbolic of the life they will share under a common roof. The most striking part of a traditional Jewish marriage ceremony is the breaking of a glass immediately followed by the assembled family and friends shouting "*Mazel tov*" (literally "good luck" but meaning one has *had* good luck; hence, congratulations). Though it is commonly claimed that breaking the glass is meant to remind the assembly of the destruction of the Temple and the trials Jews have had to suffer over the centuries, the more likely explanation for the custom is that the noise (like honking horns, tin cans, or rice at a non-Jewish wedding) is meant to distract evil spirits.

Traditional ceremonies surrounding death are also distinctively Jewish. Rabbinical Judaism calls for burial within a day if possible, without public viewing or embalming of the body. After that, the immediate family remains at home, refraining from customary activity for seven days (sits *shiva*), as mourners bring food and gather to pray and express their sympathy. Central to the rituals surrounding death is the recitation of the *Kaddish*, a mourner's prayer that blesses God's name and does not even mention death. At the death of a parent, a son is expected to gather with a *minyan* (usually at a synagogue) and recite the *Kaddish* prayer every day for a year.

Dietary Laws and Holy Days

The Torah lays emphasis on Israel's responsibility to be "holy" in the Hebrew sense of that word, to be "set apart." Certainly, the life-cycle rituals set Jews apart from other religious traditions, but Jewish dietary laws and holy days separate Jews from their Gentile neighbors even more so.

Among the kosher dietary laws, the prohibition against eating pork is certainly the most well known. Also forbidden, however, is shellfish, indeed any fish without fins and scales (not only shrimp, crab, and lobster but also catfish and shark). To be kosher (which means "fit" for eating), meat has to be ritually slaughtered, that is, with a prayer, the animal's throat is slit quickly with a very sharp knife, and its blood poured out completely. Blood is also not kosher, making a rare steak forbidden, as is the mixing of meat and dairy products, meaning there is no such thing as a kosher cheeseburger. Moreover, to make a fence around the law that prohibits mixing meat and dairy, Jewish law calls for separate dishes and cooking utensils for each.

Judaism also has its own calendar of holy days, each beginning with sundown of the day before. Thus, the Sabbath begins with sundown on Friday evening and ends with sundown on Saturday. Jewish tradition calls for the lighting and blessing of candles before sundown, followed by a festive meal prepared that afternoon. No lights or fires can be made (no lighting of a spark) on the Sabbath, although modern technology has eliminated much of the inconvenience with central heating, automatic timers, and thermostats. Prayer at the synagogue, study, and rest are the order of the day (though tradition allows and even encourages married couples to make love on the Sabbath).

The cycle of Jewish holy days is determined by a lunar calendar, beginning in early autumn with the New Year (*Rosh Hashanah*), the onset of the High Holy Days that culminate ten days later with the Day of Atonement (*Yom Kippur*). The New Year is marked by a festive meal that customarily includes apples dipped in honey. The synagogue service includes the blowing of a ram's horn (*shofar*) and an attitude of serious reflection on how one is living one's life. *Yom Kippur* is marked by a complete fast (food, drink, sexual relations) accompanied by prayers of repentance (*teshuva*).

Following the High Holy Days is the autumn feast of Tabernacles (*Sukkot*), a harvest thanksgiving festival at which traditional Jews are required to eat at least one meal a day in a kind of shed or booth (*sukka*) decorated with harvest symbols. In December, Jews celebrate *Chanukah*, commemorating the rededication of the Second Temple after it was defiled by enemy forces. In memory of the relighting of the menorah, the seven-branched candlestick that stood in the temple, Jews light a nine-branched *Chanukah* menorah, eat food prepared with oil (traditionally *latkes*, potato pancakes), and exchange small gifts. Although originally a minor feast in the Jewish calendar, *Chanukah* has grown in importance under the influence of Christmas, with both holidays in the December darkness constituting a "season of lights."

Passover (*Pesah*) is the spring festival when Jewish families and friends gather for a ritual meal (*seder*) and recall the exodus from Egypt. (As one wry observation about Jewish life puts it: They tried to kill us, they didn't succeed, let's eat.)

The ritual part of the meal consists of eating certain foods, most notably *matzo* (unleavened bread), and connecting them with Israel's escape from bondage. Ordinary leaven (yeast or baking powder) is strictly not kosher during the weeklong celebration, just as forbidden as pork. Hence, to put a "fence" around the law, rabbinic tradition calls for a Jewish household to have separate dishes and cooking utensils for Passover.

There are other holidays and observances in Jewish life beyond the limitations of an introduction. Suffice it here only to point out once again that everywhere in the world, for almost two thousand years, Jews were ethnic minorities with a distinct religious subculture. Whether in Spain, North Africa, or Turkey where Sephardic Jews (from *Sepharad*, the Jewish name for Spain) spoke Ladino; or in Europe, where Ashkenazic Jews (from the Jewish name for northern France and Germany) spoke Yiddish (a mixture of

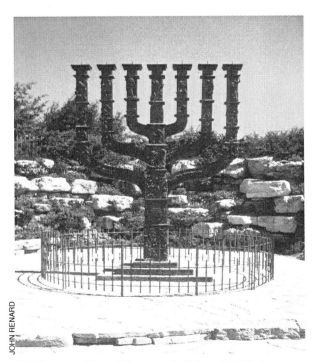

JOHN RENARD

This Monumental Menorah is engraved with low-relief biblical scenes and sits near the Israeli Parliament (Kenesset); twentieth century.

Hebrew, medieval German, and Polish), Talmudic observance enabled Jews to resist the temptation to assimilate to Christian or Muslim cultures. The challenge to assimilate intensified, however, with the onset of modernity and secular culture.

Modern Judaism

Among the tenets of modern culture is the separation of church and state, making religious faith and practice a matter of conscience and personal choice. This was the freedom of conscience written from the beginning into the U.S. Constitution and Bill of Rights. When the French Revolution (1789) made church–state separation a matter of civil law, it led to the emancipation of France's small Jewish community. French Jews became French citizens with rights equal to French Catholics and Protestants. Napoleon and his armies carried this secular form of government to other nations in Europe, including Germany. There, German Jews, who for centuries had only read and written Yiddish, began to learn to speak modern German, read German script, and assimilate into German culture. The result was the break-up of the hegemony enjoyed for centuries by Talmudic tradition and the origin of Reform Judaism.

Reform Judaism

The rabbis responsible for the rise of Reform Judaism saw themselves as equal in authority to those who determined Jewish practice at the demise of Second Temple Judaism. Originating in Germany and the United States, the Reform movement declared that Jews were citizens of their homelands, belonging to a separate religion but not a separate nation. Reform Judaism embraced the Enlightenment principle of individual rights, which included the right of Jews as individuals to decide how they would live and practice their Judaism. In practice, this amounted to the disavowal of Talmudic tradition, particularly those laws that separated Jews from Gentiles, like strict observance of the Sabbath or complete adherence to the kosher dietary laws.

Today, if Reform Jews keep any dietary prescription, it is the prohibition from eating pork. If they attend a synagogue service on Friday night or Saturday morning, they will drive to a temple for what looks very much like a Lutheran service, about an hour in length with organ, choral singing, and a sermon by the rabbi, much of it in the vernacular. (This is obviously quite different from traditional Judaism's three-hour service, to which the congregants walked, all of it in Hebrew.)

One of the most noticeable innovations of Reform Judaism is mixed or family seating at the temple. Rabbinic tradition calls for women to sit separately from men, in some synagogues behind a wall, up in a balcony, or separated by a screen going down the middle of the aisles. The Talmud calls for celebrating the birth of a Jewish boy with a *bris* and his coming of age with a *bar mitzvah*; for girls, there was nothing. Reform Judaism has embraced women's equality and rights as part of its very self-definition. It celebrates the birth of baby girls and boys with naming ceremonies and has created the *bat mitzvah* (daughter of the commandment) ceremony. When Reform Judaism began to allow women to stand at the pulpit and read publicly from the Torah, it was only a small step to allow women to be ordained rabbis.

What is being described here is Reform Judaism (not reformed, as if the reform was something in the past, now over). Under the influence of women rabbis, the reform of Judaism is continuing today, particularly in the area of language. Although the Hebrew terms are maintained as they are, new English translations of the prayers and sacred texts are being rendered in more-inclusive, gender-neutral language, with terms like *Lord* and *King* being translated as "Eternal One" and "Sovereign."

Conservative Judaism

Many Jewish immigrants to the United States, especially those from Eastern Europe, found some of the Reform movement's changes from rabbinic tradition (like family seating at worship) attractive but other changes too extreme. Thus, there arose Conservative Judaism, which is really a middle-of-the-road form of Jewish practice; not the individual but the community decides what to change in the tradition. Conservative Jews are more likely than Reform Jews to adhere strictly to the kosher dietary laws but will drive on the Sabbath to a three-hour service in Hebrew. In the last several years, Conservative Judaism has come under Reform influence and allowed both the *bat mitzvah* and the ordination of women to the rabbinate.

Orthodox Judaism

About 90 percent of religious Jews in the United States today are either Conservative or Reform. Only a small minority adhere completely to the tenets of Talmudic tradition. Although usually referred to as Orthodox Jews, the term is something of a misnomer because, as pointed out, it is not correct thinking (orthodoxy) that is most at issue but correct Jewish practice (*halacha*). Yet orthodoxy is not altogether a nonissue, because Reform Jews accept modern scientific scholarship about the compilation of the Torah centuries after the time of Moses. For Orthodox Jews, that is a heresy running contrary to the rabbinic dogma that God communicated the entire Torah to Moses.

Although they all adhere to classical rabbinic tradition, Orthodox Jews are no more monolithic than their Conservative or Reform counterparts are. So-called "Modern Orthodox" Jews strive to observe all 613 commandments while living in the modern world. They work alongside and socialize with Gentiles, attend movies and concerts, and send their children to public schools. At most, the men and boys stand out by wearing a *yarmulka* or skullcap (*kippa* in Hebrew).

Quite different from the modern orthodox are so-called ultraorthodox Jews who avoid socializing not only with Gentiles but with nonorthodox Jews, thus creating their own self-imposed ghettoes. Most conspicuous among the ultraorthodox are the Hassidic Jews (*Hassidim*), a movement going back to villages of eighteenth-century southern Poland and Ukraine. The Hassidim early on treated their rabbis (called *rebbes*) more like spiritual masters or gurus than as mere scholars, and the movement fractured into splinter groups. The largest ultraorthodox group is the Lubavitch Hassidim, conspicuous for the men wearing long sideburns, black coats, and black hats (or fur hats on occasion). Centered mostly in the Williamsburg area of Brooklyn and in Israel, the Lubavitch Hassidim educate their children in completely separate schools, prohibit them from watching movies or television, and are intent on converting the rest of American Jews to their separatist way of thinking and practice.

On the Sabbath, however, even Modern Orthodox Jews drop out of the modern world with its wide assortment of high-tech gadgetry. When Thomas Edison first closed an electrical circuit, the rabbis had to decide if doing so constituted lighting a spark, thus being forbidden on the Sabbath. Demonstrating the extraordinary influence of religious authority, the Orthodox rabbinate decided that yes, it did. Ever since that time, the Sabbath for Orthodox Jews has become a day for escaping from the world of automobile ignitions and elevator buttons, computers, iPods, and e-mail. Some of them get around the prohibition of using electricity by having their lights on timers on the Sabbath so they do not need to do the work of switching on lamps.

Christian–Jewish Relations

No introduction to Judaism would be complete without at least some consideration of Christian anti-Judaism that eventually led to anti-Semitism. Many, perhaps most, Christians are blissfully unaware of the malice and violence that Jews have suffered over the centuries and that those hostile attitudes have often been excused by appeals to the New Testament (NT). There is no discounting the fact that for two-thousand years, Christians and Jews have largely looked upon one another with antagonism, nor is there any denying that, because of that longstanding alienation, Nazi Germany was more easily able to perpetrate the genocide of European Jews that we know as the Holocaust.

Bitter Beginnings

The mutual animosity that has marked Christian–Jewish relations goes back to the first century. As we learned, Pharisees and the infant Church presented rival views of the kind of life God wanted Jews to live. Pharisees stressed the Torah and obedience to its commandments; Jewish Christians emphasized the prophets, whose words they interpreted as fulfilled in Jesus. An intrafamily quarrel became increasingly bitter as Jewish Christians began accepting and eating with Gentiles. Shortly after the destruction of Jerusalem and the Second Temple, the rabbis excommunicated as heretics nonconformist Jews, including Jewish Christians.

The Church interpreted the destruction of the Temple as historical proof of God's displeasure with the Jewish people. Israel must have committed some terrible crime, and Christians were quite sure they knew what it was. Jews were being punished for the death of Jesus; God had come to reject the Jewish people because of their rejection of Jesus. Despite the gospel evidence that Jesus was popular with the Jewish masses, Christians began viewing not just a handful of Sadducees but all Jews as Christ-killers. The Church began seeing itself and its covenant as the new Israel, replacing the old Israel with its "old" covenant. (The technical name for this replacement theory is *supercessionism*.)

It did not help matters that John's gospel (20:19) describes Jesus' Galilean Jewish disciples as locking doors for fear of the *Judaioi*, a word that makes sense as "Judeans" but has traditionally been translated as "the Jews." The infant Church was in fact a persecuted minority, and there is no lack of historical evidence that in its early years, Christians suffered at the hands of Jews, most notably during the

Bar Kochba revolt (135 CE). Christians would harbor those memories for nearly two-thousand years as proof of unwavering Jewish hostility.

Christian Ambivalence

Christian fortunes changed markedly, however, in the fourth century. First, the Emperor Constantine conceded toleration to the Christian church (313 CE). Then, the Emperor Theodosius the Great declared Christianity to be the sole official religion of the Roman Empire, decreeing both paganism and heresy to be crimes against the state (380 CE). As happens so often in history, the formerly oppressed became themselves oppressors. A series of repressive measures legally forbade Jews to make converts, to own Christian slaves, or to hold public office. In a series of sermons notorious today for their inflammatory rhetoric, Saint John Chrysostom (d. 407) preached against Christians visiting synagogues or having anything to do with Jews.

Yet both in imperial and later medieval church law, the basic Christian posture toward Jews was one of toleration. Why Jews were tolerated, while pagans and Christian heretics were not, can be credited largely to the influence of Saint Augustine (d. 430), who interpreted the Jewish people as marked with the "sign of Cain" (Gen 4:15). Jews, like Cain, had blood on their hands for the death of Jesus, but their punishment was to wander the earth; they were not to be killed.

Offensive as it appears to us today, the metaphor of Cain lay at the root of traditional Christian ambivalence toward Jews. On the one hand, it allowed Jews to survive in medieval Europe. On the other hand, it explains why Catholic monarchs could drive Jews out of England, France, and then, most painfully, Spain, without any qualms of conscience. They were simply demonstrating the superiority of Christianity and God's righteous judgment upon a people now rejected and accursed.

The situation of Jews in the Middle Ages was not one of uninterrupted abuse. There were good times as well as bad. (No people, Jews included, want to see themselves as the objects of unrelenting hostility.) They constituted a kind of middle class in the feudal system, serving as merchants and tradesmen. Though subordinate to the land-owning gentry, Jews were permitted by law to travel. That made them analogous to the knights but superior to the great masses of peasants who were tied to the land. Jews were also permitted, unlike Christians in the Middle Ages, to engage in moneylending, an occupation that easily prompted resentment and more than once led to anti-Jewish riots for the purpose of destroying debt records.

In Norwich, England, shortly before Easter in 1141, the discovery of a dead boy's body led to the accusation that Jews had killed him in a ritual murder meant to mock Christ's crucifixion. This was the origin of the so-called "blood libel," which in various forms spread throughout Europe, stereotyping Jews as murderers who use Christian blood to make Passover matzos or wine. Knowing the strict rabbinical prohibition against consuming blood, popes, kings, and emperors denounced the blood libel repeatedly. That it persisted well into the twentieth century is testimony to the fact that a lie, no matter how outrageous, if told often enough, will be believed.

The popular identification of Jews as murderers made them likely scapegoats during the fourteenth-century epidemic known as the Black Death. Two centuries later, having been driven out of England and France, Jews then found themselves caught between warring Catholics and Protestants in German-speaking lands. Martin Luther maintained the traditional medieval stereotype of Jews. He wrote a particularly venomous tract or pamphlet "Against the Jews," which came to be widely quoted by the Nazis. Increasingly, Jews moved eastward into Poland and eventually Ukraine, where the Polish aristocracy used them as agents and tax collectors among the much more numerous peasantry. Jews enjoyed more self-governance in Poland than in anywhere else in Europe. It became their land of refuge. For that reason, many Jews were concentrated there when Nazi Germany invaded Poland in September 1939.

The Holocaust and Vatican II on Jews and Judaism

Understandably, the Holocaust has made an indelible mark on the consciousness of Jews today. Christians too have reason never to forget it. Nearly six-million Jews, including a million and a half children, were murdered in the heart of what once was called Christendom. Moreover, virtually all the perpetrators had been baptized Catholic or Protestant. To be sure, there were tens of thousands of Christians among the so-called "Righteous Gentiles" who made attempts to save Jews, risking their own lives and those of their families, but most Christians were unwilling to take such risks and stood by passively, sometimes even complacently, influenced by a tradition that for centuries had characterized Jews as hostile to Christian interests.

The term **anti-Semitism** was first coined by Wilhem Marr, a nineteenth-century German atheist who hated Jews and Christians equally—too vast a topic to be treated here. Suffice it to be said that it was rampant in nineteenth-century Eastern Orthodox Russia and existed in the United States up to and during World War II.

One Christian who did not stand by passively was Archbishop Angelo Roncalli, later elected Pope John XXIII. As a papal diplomat to Turkey and Greece during World War II, he was personally responsible for saving tens of thousands of Jews through the issuance of false baptismal certificates. That experience obviously stayed with him, as when he convened the Second Vatican Council (1962–1965), he expressed the hope that the Council would make a statement about the Catholic Church and Judaism. That hope was realized on October 28, 1965, when his successor, Pope Paul VI, promulgated *Nostra Aetate*, the Council's Declaration on the Relation of the Church to Non-Christian Religions.

Nostra Aetate was a watershed document that not only impacted Catholics but also challenged other Christian churches to look at their thinking and attitudes toward Judaism and the Jewish people. In its wake, the Vatican has issued documents on how to preach about Jews and Judaism, how to interpret the Jewish scriptures, and how important it is to remember the Holocaust. In December 1993, Pope John Paul II approved the establishment of diplomatic relations between the Vatican and the state of Israel, pressing for Israelis and Palestinians alike to acknowledge one another's rights to live in peace and security in their own homelands. This constituted official recognition by the Vatican that attachment to the land of Israel is one of the defining hallmarks of Judaism.

Today, Christians and Jews collaborate on any number of peace and justice issues, socialize as friends, celebrate at one another's weddings, and attend one another's funerals. Today, Christian theologians give greater attention to the Jewish roots of Christianity. Indeed, hardly a chapter or a topic in this book has not been affected by the rethinking initiated by *Nostra Aetate*.

Jewish leaders have likewise begun a reconsideration of Christianity. In a statement entitled *Dabru Emet* (Heb., "Speak the Truth"), prominent rabbis and Jewish scholars have acknowledged, for example, that Jews and Christians worship the same God, that Christians accept the moral principles of the Torah, and that Nazism was not a Christian phenomenon. Not all Jews have endorsed that statement, but neither have all Christian churches endorsed *Nostra Aetate* or the dialogue between Christians and Jews that it initiated. Jews and Christians are not monolithic faith communities; they never have been.

The important question is can you, the reader, endorse *Nostra Aetate*, and what does that imply for you? Moreover, what does it imply for your attitude toward members of other faith communities? Jews and Christians once lived side by side and yet remained strangers to one another. It was not until they began sharing conversations with one another that walls began breaking down. Who are the strangers in your midst? When is the last time you had a conversation with someone outside your "comfort zone"?

With *Nostra Aetate*, Christians began a long-overdue conversation in 1965. It is still going on. Consider yourself invited to join in.

This document needs to be read with the heart because it is from and to the hearts of two religions seeking to be faithful to the same God. The following is an excerpt:

> As the sacred synod searches into the mystery of the Church, it remembers the bond that spiritually ties the people of the New Covenant to Abraham's stock.
>
> Thus the Church of Christ acknowledges that, according to God's saving design, the beginnings of her faith and her election are found already among the Patriarchs, Moses and the prophets. She professes that all who believe in Christ—Abraham's sons according to faith—are included in the same Patriarch's call, and likewise that the salvation of the Church is mysteriously foreshadowed by the chosen people's exodus from the land of bondage. The Church, therefore, cannot forget that she received the revelation of the Old Testament through the people with whom God in His inexpressible mercy concluded the Ancient Covenant. Nor can she forget that she draws sustenance from the root of that well-cultivated olive tree onto which have been grafted the wild shoots, the Gentiles. Indeed, the Church believes that by His cross Christ, Our Peace, reconciled Jews and Gentiles making both one in Himself.
>
> The Church keeps ever in mind the words of the Apostle about his kinsmen: "theirs is the sonship and the glory and the covenants and the law and the worship and the promises; theirs are the fathers and from them is the Christ according to the flesh" (Rom 9:4–5), the Son of the Virgin Mary. She also recalls that the Apostles, the Church's main-stay and pillars, as well as most of the early disciples who proclaimed Christ's Gospel to the world, sprang from the Jewish people.
>
> As Holy Scripture testifies, Jerusalem did not recognize the time of her visitation, nor did the Jews in large number, accept the Gospel;

indeed not a few opposed its spreading. Nevertheless, God holds the Jews most dear for the sake of their Fathers; He does not repent of the gifts He makes or of the calls He issues—such is the witness of the Apostle. In company with the Prophets and the same Apostle, the Church awaits that day, known to God alone, on which all peoples will address the Lord in a single voice and "serve him shoulder to shoulder."

Since the spiritual patrimony common to Christians and Jews is thus so great, this sacred synod wants to foster and recommend that mutual understanding and respect which is the fruit, above all, of biblical and theological studies as well as of fraternal dialogues.

True, the Jewish authorities and those who followed their lead pressed for the death of Christ; still, what happened in His passion cannot be charged against all the Jews, without distinction, then alive, nor against the Jews of today. Although the Church is the new people of God, the Jews should not be presented as rejected or accursed by God, as if this followed from the Holy Scriptures. All should see to it, then, that in catechetical work or in the preaching of the word of God they do not teach anything that does not conform to the truth of the Gospel and the spirit of Christ.

Furthermore, in her rejection of every persecution against any man, the Church, mindful of the patrimony she shares with the Jews and moved not by political reasons but by the Gospel's spiritual love, decries hatred, persecutions, displays of anti-Semitism, directed against Jews at any time and by anyone.

Besides, as the Church has always held and holds now, Christ underwent His passion and death freely, because of the sins of men and out of infinite love, in order that all may reach salvation. It is, therefore, the burden of the Church's preaching to proclaim the cross of Christ as the sign of God's all-embracing love and as the fountain from which every grace flows.

Questions about the Text

1. Draw a timeline of events and people in this article from Alexander the Great (333 BCE) to Bar Kochba (135 CE).

2. Explain what you think are the three most important relationships between Judaism and Christianity in the first century.

3. How did the destruction of the second Temple in 70 CE change Judaism, and how did rabbinic Judaism help form that response?

4. Explain one topic by the twelfth-century Talmudic scholar Maimonides that most interested you, and explain why you chose it.

5. How do rabbinic Jews pray daily, and how do they celebrate weddings in their religious ritual?

6. On what calendar are the Jewish holy days set? Make a list of five holy days and what event they celebrate.

7. What three major groups make up Modern Judaism? How do they differ?

8. What are the three major points of *Nostra Aetate*?

Questions for Discussion

1. What kind of relationship exists between Christians and Jews, according to this chapter?

2. What does this chapter say about responsibility for the death of Jesus?

3. Without using the term, what does this chapter say about *supercessionism*, that is, the theory that the Christian church has replaced the Jewish people as God's chosen?

4. What does this chapter say about anti-Semitism?

5. What are the implications of this chapter and this statement for you and your life?

For Further Study

An easily accessible insight into Hassidic life and thinking can be found in the novels of Chaim Potok, especially his first, *The Chosen*.

Bishops Committee for Ecumenical and Inter-Religious Affairs, ed. *The Bible, the Jews, and the Death of Jesus: A Collection of Catholic Documents*. Washington, DC: U.S. Conference of Catholic Bishops, 2004.

This text is a collection of Catholic statements on responsibility for the death of Jesus.

———. *Catholics Remember the Holocaust*. Washington, DC: U.S. Conference of Catholic Bishops, 2004.

This collection of Catholic statements on the Holocaust implements the Vatican document, *We Remember*.

Boys, Mary, ed. *Seeing Judaism Anew: Christianity's Sacred Obligation*. Lanham, MD: Sheed & Ward/Rowman & Littlefield, 2005.

This is a survey of Jewish–Christian relations and a Christian theology of Judaism.

Fisher, Eugene. *Faith without Prejudice: Rebuilding Christian Attitudes toward Judaism*. New York: Crossroad, 1993.

A leader in Christian–Jewish dialogue looks at such issues as Jesus' Jewishness, alleged anti-Semitism in the gospels, and who is responsible for the death of Jesus. The text contains key Vatican and U.S. bishops' statements up to 1993.

Wylen, Stephen M. *Settings of Silver: An Introduction to Judaism*. New York: Paulist Press, 1989.

This text was popularly written by a rabbi on Jewish faith, practice, and history.

From the Reference Librarian
The Encyclopedia Index in Research—Judaism

Student: How do I locate sources of information on a non-Christian religion? Do the same library skills apply?

Absolutely. For example, try the search format "Judaism and encyclopedias" to see what encyclopedias on Judaism are in your library's reference collection. Remember for the future that the library skills you are learning in this book are transferable to *any* subject, theological or not.

Where you start researching a topic in Judaism depends, in part, on which one of the three broad divisions of Judaism described by Dr. Modras is your main area of interest; that is, you want to match your topic with an encyclopedia of appropriate scope. For example, there are encyclopedias focusing on Biblical Judaism or on Modern Judaism, and so on.

Pride of place for researching *any* topic in Judaism goes to the second edition of the *Encyclopaedia Judaica* (twenty-two vols.), published in 2007. (Some libraries may still have the first edition of sixteen volumes, published in 1973.) Not only is the coverage of all aspects of Judaism exhaustive but also those responsible for the encyclopedia made this vast amount of material even more accessible by the care they gave to the index. The index is an indispensable tool for using the encyclopedia. "Only by consulting the Index will [the user] grasp the full treatment of any subject" (Preface). This is so because the editors planned the overall structure of the encyclopedia to avoid articles overlapping with one another; different aspects of a particular subject are treated in different articles. Therefore, it is essential that users of this encyclopedia consult the index to see where various aspects of the subject are dealt with in the text. To emphasize the importance of the index, the editors of the first edition even decided to take the unusual step of making it the first volume of the encyclopedia. However, the second edition follows the usual custom of the index comprising the last volume.

Let's illustrate the use of the index with a biographical example mentioned by Dr. Modras: Maimonides. You will find an article on Maimonides in volume 13 of the *Encyclopaedia Judaica*. However, if you look in the index under "Maimonides," you will see dozens of subentries referring you to articles throughout the entire encyclopedia.

For an example of a conceptual topic, look at the index entry for "Reform Judaism." Following the reference to the main article on Reform Judaism, you will find, among other things, subentries for various countries, significant individuals, and important concepts referring you to almost every other volume in the encyclopedia.

Doing research on the Talmud can be a daunting exercise for the uninitiated, but using the index can help to bring order to a complex subject. The subentries in the index under "Talmud" extend across five printed pages. At a glance, you can locate several articles related to such Talmudic topics as "civil law," "*halakhah,*" or "punishments."

The example of the *Encyclopaedia Judaica* (EJ) underscores the importance of making use of indexes in all encyclopedias. Not all encyclopedia indexes are prepared with as much care or desire for comprehensiveness as the one in the *EJ*; nevertheless, an encyclopedia index will almost always help you to find things you would have missed otherwise, and the more experience you have with encyclopedias and indexes, the more you will appreciate a high-quality index.

The *EJ* is a standard reference tool and should be in most libraries. A somewhat less exhaustive reference source on Judaism is *The Encyclopedia of Judaism*:

> Jacob Neusner, Alan J. Avery-Peck, and William Scott Green, eds. *The Encyclopedia of Judaism*. Second ed. (5 vols.). Boston, MA: Brill, 2005.
>
> The organization of this encyclopedia differs significantly from that of the *Encyclopaedia Judaica*, being comprised of a series of longer topical essays alphabetically arranged (from "Art and Material Culture of Judaism—Medieval through Modern Times" to "Zionism and Orthodox Judaism"). Use of the index is necessary for locating specific (factual) information. If your library has both the *Encyclopaedia Judaica* and the *Encyclopedia of Judaism*, compare the index entries for "Maimonides" in the two encyclopedias.

Additional standard reference sources on Judaism are listed next, but none of these is as comprehensive as those just discussed.

> Louis Jacobs, *The Jewish Religion: A Companion*. Oxford, UK: Oxford University Press, 1995.
>
> R. J. Zwi Werblowsky and Geoffrey Wigoder, eds. *The Oxford Dictionary of the Jewish Religion*. Oxford, UK: Oxford University Press, 1997.
>
> Geoffrey Wigoder, ed. *The New Encyclopedia of Judaism*. New York: New York University Press, 2002.

Specialized reference works focusing on particular aspects of Jewish religion and history include the following:

Dan Cohn-Sherbok. *A Dictionary of Judaism and Christianity*. Philadelphia, PA: Trinity Press International, 1991.

> This reference work explores "in direct and simple language" the "important connections" between Judaism and Christianity.

Israel Gutman, ed. *Encyclopedia of the Holocaust*. 4 vols. New York: Macmillan, 1990.

Edward Kessler and Neil Wenborn, eds. *Dictionary of Jewish-Christian Relations*. Oxford, UK: Cambridge University Press, 2005.

Tzvi M. Rabinowicz, ed. *The Encyclopedia of Hasidism*. Lanham, MD: Jason Aronson Inc., 1996.

Robert Rozett and Shmuel Spector, eds. *Encyclopedia of the Holocaust*. New York: Facts on File, 2000.

Student Tasks

1. Go to your library and use the keyword search "Judaism AND encyclopedias" to see what encyclopedias your library has on this subject (are there other terms besides *Judaism* you could use?). Check the indexes in at least two of the encyclopedias. How do they compare? Is one index more detailed than the other? Pick a particular topic in Judaism and compare the index entries. Does one of the indexes prove to be more useful?

2. Choose one of the persons mentioned in this chapter, and find an encyclopedia article on that person. Now look at the index entry for that person. Is there more information in the encyclopedia or in the article you looked up?

3. Choose a conceptual topic from the chapter, and use an encyclopedia index to locate information on that topic throughout the encyclopedia.

4. Search the Internet for information on the same person you looked up in #2. Do the same for the conceptual topic you looked up in #3. How easy is it to find authoritative information? How many different ways can you search for this kind of information on the Internet?

Here is the latest addition to our set of Library Skills:

Skill Key #1

Use the library's reference collection to begin your research.

a) Use a subject-specific encyclopedia to acquire specialized knowledge about a subject.

b) Use a subject-specific encyclopedia whose scope is appropriate for both your topic and the approach you want to take to that topic.

c) Use encyclopedia bibliographies to identify subject headings for your topic.

d) Use a concise subject-specific dictionary to look up the specialized vocabulary of a particular field.

e) Use an encyclopedia's index to locate information on subjects (including persons) for which there is no separate article.

f) Examine the synoptic outline of contents (or however it is designated) in an encyclopedia (1) to get a quick overview of the contents and (2) to get topic ideas for research.

g) Use an encyclopedia's index to get ideas for research topics.

h) Use cross-references to locate additional relevant material in an encyclopedia.

i) **Use an encyclopedia's index to locate all (or as much as you want) relevant material on your topic. Note especially how detailed the index is and whether the editors of the encyclopedia make any special comments about it.**

Skill Key #2

Use the library's catalog to locate sources of information.

a) Use subject headings to locate precisely books on your topic.

b) Use subject headings whose scope fits your topic as closely as possible, then adjust your search with a broader or narrower subject heading as necessary.

c) As an alternative to using encyclopedia bibliographies, use keyword searching to identify subject headings for your topic.

d) Combine one or more subject headings in a search to retrieve books on a topic for which no single subject heading exists.

e) Use the floating subdivision "encyclopedias" in combination with a keyword to identify encyclopedias on a subject.

f) Use the floating subdivision "moral and ethical aspects" to identify material, whether "pro" or "con," related to the ethical aspects of a subject.

g) Use the floating subdivision "religious aspects" to search for religious/theological aspects of nonreligious/nontheological subjects.

h) If necessary, use all the subject headings assigned to a book to identify material on a particular subject.

i) Use the name of an organization or group as an author to search for documents produced under the aegis of that particular group. Be aware of the possibility of changes in the group's name over time.

9

Islamic Religious Experience: Foundations, Scripture, and Spirituality

From the Editor

Walking down the street, a person of another faith might see a church or a mosque and know something general or have an impression about the believers who go there. A person might also decide to attend a service and observe more of what these believers do. This knowledge, while important, would be the result of only a superficial observation. It would fall short of understanding why these religious people form their lives, worship, perform ceremonies, and pray the way they do. It is the difference between knowing about it and living it. It is the difference between a journey for sightseeing and a pilgrimage for the soul.

From the other chapters in this book, we can see that the wellsprings of religion are deep and orient the direction of people's lives, individually and communally. Even the word *religion* means "to tie or bind again" (Lat.: *ligare*, meaning "to tie or bind"; and *re*, meaning "again"). Religions bind themselves to God by their commitment and actions. Islam is a particular religious tradition that ties believers continuously in their particular relationship with the one God, Allah (Arabic for "the Deity"). Muslims understand that this invitation was offered by Allah through divine revelation to his prophet Muhammad.

As Islam is the most recent of the three Abrahamic religions, some commonalities might be expected. Islam and Christianity share with Judaism the religious tradition that goes back to Abraham ("The Father of Faith"), as well as the prophets sent by God. Islam shares with Christianity a high regard for Jesus as a prophet, with deep respect for his mother Mary. Theologically, it seems clear that the three religious traditions pray to the same God.

We shall read more on this shortly, but for now, theology has to start somewhere deeper than superficial observations, impressions, or general ideas. It must move to understanding tied to respect and desire to know the other's religious experience. The appreciative understanding of listening and learning is the same method used in the previous chapter on Judaism and is applicable for understanding any religious tradition.

This chapter will help us in a special way. It is not a typical explanation with facts and dates about Islam. It challenges us to step beyond merely knowing intellectually about Islam to appreciating its religious experience—the why beneath the what. It prompts us to ask what their experience is and why that experience forms their lives. By the time you finish this chapter, we hope you will have an appreciation of and an insight into the Islamic believer's world.

The chapter discusses Islam in four parts. (1) Our journey toward the soul of Islam begins with God, not in an abstract way but in the concrete images of God that people pray with every day. (2) Then, we will examine what God has revealed to humanity in the sacred scripture of the Qur'an (or "Book"), which binds Muslims to God in their daily lives. (3) Next, we will look to the sacred role of God's human collaborators. (4) Finally, in exploring scriptural themes in Islamic spirituality, we will explore the soul itself, that inner center where the different ways in which we worship, pray, and live in the world come alive. To provide a better appreciation of concepts, terms, and the Qur'an itself, we include key Arabic words and their translations in the chapter.

Islamic Religious Experience: Foundations, Scripture, and Spirituality

John Renard, PhD

Overview

Islam as a religious tradition developed in the rich religious and cultural matrix of the Middle East. With its three foundational theological elements, Islam stands firmly in the line of the Abrahamic monotheistic faiths. Belief in an omnipotent creative deity, in the centrality of a revealed sacred scripture, and in the necessity of prophets to communicate the mind of the deity to humankind links Islam explicitly to Judaism and Christianity. We will investigate how images of God as creator and guide, of the Qur'an as light and guidance, and of Muhammad as prophet inform an Islamic spirituality—or approach to life.

Non-Muslims are often surprised, even shocked, to hear that Islam's central spiritual and ethical presuppositions are virtually identical to those of Judaism and Christianity. Why then, many people ask, do Jews, Christians, and Muslims not get along better, especially in the Middle East? Perhaps the best response to that and similar queries is that strife is simply endemic to the human race. Why do the Catholics and Protestants of Northern Ireland hold so tenaciously to their ancient rivalries and hatred? They are, of course, all Christians. Most Christians and Jews will find it simple enough to distinguish between what individuals or groups do and the ideals and values for which a faith tradition stands—at least when it comes to their own. However, non-Muslims too often and too readily equate the behavior of a minority of Muslims, generally identified as extremist, fundamentalist, revolutionary, or right-wing fanatics, with the whole of a tradition and the generality of its adherents.

A sad fact of human history has been that communities of persons—ethnic, political, economic, or religious—tend to become closed systems bent on defending themselves against the threat posed by other such communities. That their religious affiliations are more often blamed for factionalism and intolerance than are other equally liable forces is really only a testimony to the intensity of the emotional responses that religious language and imagery can elicit.

What if one could approach the study of Islam (or any religious or cultural tradition, for that matter) free of the prejudices and suspicions that so easily cloud one's vision and skew one's judgment of other persons? Though none of us can claim true objectivity, we can at least begin with the assumption that the qualities we have the greatest difficulty accepting in another reflect in large measure what we cannot accept in ourselves.

Much of the allegedly objective journalism that has fed American curiosity about the Middle East in recent years reeks of condescension and thinly veiled bigotry. One television correspondent, reporting on the aftermath of the Persian Gulf conflict of 1991 (also known as "Desert Storm") but not limited to that war, characterized Saudi Arabia's policy as "Pray and pay: pray to Allah, and pay anyone who can provide" necessary services and protection. The tone of his remark was inherently demeaning, but beyond that, it seemed to suggest that Christian America and Jewish Israel would of course never rely on such a strategy.

One could cite numerous examples of that peculiar attitude. Just after the cease-fire in the first Persian Gulf hostilities, another reporter interviewed a young soldier who had secured as souvenirs an AK-47 rifle and a Qur'an. Asked what he intended to do with the book, the soldier replied that he would spend some time reading about what sort of being "this Allah" was. He clearly expected the worst, but he did not find it strange to be fighting shoulder to shoulder with coalition troops who read the same scripture as the enemy.

Islamic Images of God

But who is "this Allah" of whom Muslims speak? Many non-Muslims have the impression that the term *Allah* refers to some despotic deity with a taste for violence and infidel blood. Perhaps that is because so many television and movie images of Muslim soldiers depict them screaming, "Allahu Akbar!" ("God is supreme") as they attack or celebrate victory. How is it, some may wonder, that Muslims seem so readily to associate Allah with violence? In Arabic, the word *Allah* is simply a compound of *al-* (the definite article, "the") and *ilah* ("god," "deity"). Joined together, they signify "God." You may find this a bit shocking, but it is very significant that nearly all Arabic speakers, including Iraqi Jews and Syrian Christians, refer to their Supreme Being as Allah.

Images of God are central to virtually every religious tradition and crucial to one's understanding of how religious motivation works. For example, most of us tend to believe that God is on our side—even those who do not believe in God except when it suits their purposes. Hence, proprietary ideas of who God is, what God likes and dislikes, and how God deals with human problems make it challenging indeed to open one's mind to the images of God that other people hold dear—never mind that if God is as big as most religious traditions claim, God has the option of being on everyone's side. That little piece of logic soon gets swept under the rug, for it wreaks havoc with the human penchant for sanctifying divisions and enmities with claims to divine favor.

Images of God prevalent in one religious tradition inevitably overlap with those of another, but each tradition has its distinctive tone and emphasis. Christians, for example, who find it quaint and dangerous that Muslims believe God has prepared rewards in paradise for those who die a martyr's death, might well recall that Christianity too has had its own tradition of martyrdom from the beginning. If Jews and Christians take offense at the idea that the God of Islam sanctions certain forms of violence, they would do well to recall not only the Just War theory but also the shockingly bloody images of God in Deuteronomy and other early sections of the Hebrew scriptures, and even in the New Testament (NT) (cf. Lev 20:9–14, 26:7–8, 21–39; Deut 20:10–14, 21:10ff, 21:18–21, 22:20–21, 23–24; Ps 58:6–9, 64:7–10, 69:22–27, 139:19–22; Mt 10:34; Lk 12:49, 20:9–18). Religious persons understandably gravitate to those images of God already embedded in their traditions that help explain the circumstances in which they find themselves. Similarly, if asked to reflect on the matter, most of us would likely assume that their most cherished (or dreaded) images of God are very close to those of the person next to them on the synagogue bench or the church pew. We might be surprised to discover that, in fact, our images of God bear a greater likeness to those of the Muslim in the mosque across town than to those of our coreligionists.

Most Jews and Christians are convinced their God is loving and kind, provident and generous, as well as thirsty for justice and equity; most Muslims believe the same. Of the "Ninety-Nine Most Beautiful Names" of God, the two by far most frequently invoked are "Gracious or Compassionate" and "Merciful." All but one of the Qur'an's 114 *suras* (chapters) begins with the phrase, "In the name of God, the Gracious and Merciful." One might say these two names are as important for Muslims as are the names Father, Son, and Holy Spirit heard in so many Christian invocations. Virtually every Muslim public speaker begins with that Qur'anic phrase and goes on to wish the audience the blessings and mercy of God.

The opening chapter of the Qur'an sets the tone of prayer for Muslims and lays the foundation for our present consideration:

In the Name of God, the Compassionate and Merciful: Praise to God,
Lord of the Universe.

> The Compassionate, the Merciful,
> Master of the Day of Judgment.
> You alone do we serve; from you alone do we seek help.
> Lead us along the Straight Path,
> the path of those who experience the shower of your grace,
> not of those who have merited your anger
> or of those who have gone astray. (Qur'an[Q] 1:1–7)

Here, we find clues to several of the principal divine attributes. Compassion and mercy top the list and receive an emphatic second mention. In addition, God rules the "two worlds" (seen and unseen, i.e., the universe), takes account at Judgment, offers aid and grace, and manifests a wrathful side to those who prefer arrogant independence from the origin of all things. At the center of the prayer, the Muslim asks for guidance on the Straight Path, a path laid out and marked as the way of divine graciousness.

Not one of the Ninety-Nine Names of God, on which Muslims meditate as they finger the thirty-three beads of the rosary, will sound a dissonant note in the ear of Christian or Jew. All of those names conjure up images of God. Islamic tradition has divided the names into those that express an awareness of God's beauty and approachability (*jamal*) and those that evoke a sense of the divine majesty and awe-inspiring power (*jalal*). These references to the two sides of God recall the theological distinction between immanence and transcendence. God is both near and accessible—closer even than the jugular vein, according to Qur'an 50:16—and infinitely beyond human experience and imagining. Rudolf Otto's classic definition of the "holy" can further clarify the matter. The great German thinker calls the "sacred" or "holy" "the mystery both terrifying and fascinating" (Otto, 1958). *Mystery* refers to irreducible, unanalyzable meaning, before which one can only stand silent. Paradoxically, one who experiences mystery cannot but be filled simultaneously with intimations of both irresistible attractiveness and sheer dread (Otto, 1958). Think, for example, of Moses' curiosity at the sight of the burning bush and of his terror at finding himself in the presence of the Living God. He is riveted between the desire to flee and wanting to stay forever. Or think of Peter, James, and John, who go to the mountain and are frightened to find Jesus transfigured in glory before them, speaking with Moses and Elijah, yet in their fear is the awe that results in Peter wanting to build three tents to keep the sanctity of their presence earthbound.

Though all religious traditions ultimately strive to give expression to the total experience of divine mystery, each has its distinctive ways of emphasizing one or the other aspect. Whereas Christianity's central doctrine of Incarnation tips the scale toward divine immanence, Islamic imagery tends to interpret the experience of God rather in terms of transcendence and majesty. This is only a rough and relative characterization, however; Christians also view God as beyond human grasp, and as we shall see later, Islamic tradition has also known God as an intimate companion. It is fair to say that most images of God both enjoy seasons of prominence and suffer periods of relative disuse in the history of every religious tradition. On balance, however, the Islamic tradition has generally preferred images of divine majesty.

One fascinating image that is both highly instructive and easily misinterpreted is that of the divine trickster. One occasionally hears non-Muslims characterize Islam's God as wily or cunning, as though God delighted in cruel hoaxes. Not so. The Qur'an refers to God as the "best of those who devise schemes" (e.g., Q 3:47, 8:30, 13:42, 27:51) to indicate that no human being can know the mind of God. Al-Ghazali (d. 1111), one of Islam's greatest pastoral theologians and one of the most famous citizens of medieval Baghdad, develops the idea further. Partially because of its shock value, Ghazali sees in the divine stratagem (*makr*) the ultimate reminder that human beings are better off not trying to second-guess their creator. Ghazali tells the story of how once when the angel Gabriel was with Muhammad, the two acknowledged to each other that they felt stark terror in the presence of God. God then spoke to them to reassure them; they need not be afraid, for He had made them secure. Should they indeed be unafraid, Muhammad wondered? Had not God Himself told them not to tremble? Gabriel cautioned that they ought not banish their fear too casually, regardless of the apparent meaning of God's words; they were, after all, in the presence of *God*. There, only a fool would know no dread (McKane, 1952, pp. 57ff). This arresting image

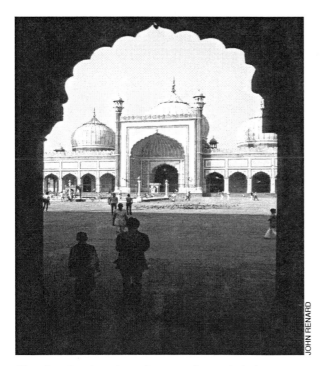

Shown here from the archway of a surrounding portico is the seventeenth-century Congregational Mosque in Delhi, India. Note the reflecting pool in the courtyard and the three domes over the prayer hall.

JOHN RENARD

is meant to emphasize God's utter transcendence of human imagining. A human being who thinks he or she has God down to a pattern has wandered from the Straight Path into the realm of presumptuousness. Let no one imagine that God is so boring as to be predictable.

Numerous verses of the Qur'an emphasize God's sovereignty and power. Two such texts come to mind. The first, called the "Throne Verse," appears as an inscription around the interior of domes in dozens of major mosques across the world:

> God—there is no deity but He; the Living, the Everlasting. Neither slumber nor sleep overcome Him. To Him belong all that heavens and earth encompass. Who can intercede with Him, except by his leave? He knows all that surrounds [created beings], while they can grasp nothing of what He knows, except as He chooses. His Throne stretches across heaven and earth; sovereignty over them tires him not, for He is the Exalted, the Magnificent. (Q 2:255)

God is thus the beginning and end of all things, the Creator, the Sustainer, the Provider, the Lord of space and time. According to a saying of Muhammad (part of a body of literature called "Hadith"), the Throne Verse, like all the Qur'an, has existed eternally in the mind of God and was known to earlier prophets. Anas ibn Malik (c. 612–712), a well-known companion to the Prophet Muhammad, said:

> God revealed to Moses, "Whoever continues to recite the Throne Verse after every prayer, on him will I bestow more than that granted to those who are ever thankful. His reward shall be as great as that of prophets and that granted the righteous for their good deeds. I shall spread over him my right hand in mercy. Nothing would hinder him from entering Paradise."
> . . . Moses said, "My Lord, how can anyone hear this and not continue to observe it?" God said, "I grant this to no one except a prophet, a righteous person, a man I love. . . ." (Ayoub, 1984, p. 248)

Later in this chapter, we will return to this text briefly to discuss some issues related to the interpretation of scripture.

One of the great writers who have elaborated on the theme of God's transcendence is the Persian Sana'i of Ghazna (d. 1131, in what is now Afghanistan). Addressing God, he writes in the preface to his mystical didactic epic, the *Garden of Ultimate Reality*:

> O you who nourish the soul and ornament the visible world,
>> And you who grant wisdom and are indulgent with those who lack it;

> Creator and sustainer of space and of time,
> Custodian and provider of dweller and dwelling;
> All is of your making, dwelling and dweller,
> All is within your compass, time and space.
> Fire and air, water and earth,
> All are mysteriously within the scope of your power.
> All that is between your Throne and this earth
> Are but a fraction of your handiwork;
> Inspirited intelligence acts as your swift herald,
> Every living tongue that moves in every mouth
> Has but one purpose: to give you praise.
> Your sublime and exalted names
> Evidence your beneficence and grace and kindness.
> Every one of them outstrips throne and globe and dominion;
> They are a thousand plus one and a hundred less one.
> But to those who are outside the spiritual sanctuary,
> The names are veiled.
> O Lord, in your largesse and mercy
> Allow this heart and soul a glimpse of your name! (From the Persian
> of Sana'i's *Hadiqat al Haqiqat*, I:2–11)

A second Qur'anic text, perhaps even more important as an architectural inscription than is the Throne Verse, offers a magnificently imaginative glimpse of the unimaginable. The "Verse of Light" provides another ingredient in our complex of imagery:

> God is the Light of Heaven and Earth. Picture His light as a niche within which there is a lamp, and the lamp is within a glass. And it is as though the glass were a glittering star lit from a sacred olive tree neither of east nor west, whose oil would fairly radiate even without the touch of fire. Light upon light, and God guides to his light whom He will. (Q 24:35)

That text has inspired marvelous designs on prayer carpets and on the niches (*mihrab*, a recess in the wall that orientates the worshiper toward Mecca) of mosques all over the world. It suggests several relevant issues in this context. First, it recalls the symbolism of the revelatory cosmic tree, one that glows without being consumed and is so large it spans the universe (being, therefore, exclusive of neither east nor west). On the level of imagery, the text has functioned as a kind of summary, like the Throne Verse, of divine qualities.

Second, the last line brings to mind a question that has been significant in shaping Islamic intellectual history, namely, the matter of divine ordination of events or predestination. If God guides whom He will, then does He also not will to guide others? And if so, could those others truly be held responsible if they lose their way? The issue is complex. Suffice it to say for the moment that Islamic tradition has generally striven to strike a balance between God's unlimited power and the human person's limited freedom and commensurate accountability. It is useful to think of the apparent predilection for some form of divine predetermination as an analogy to the Biblical phenomenon of God's "hardening the heart" of Pharaoh and of even some of the people of Israel.

Finally, the Verse of Light alludes to that crucial divine function of guidance, which in turn brings us back to the image of journey. "Guide" is one of the ninety-nine names, and the Qur'an often speaks of God in that capacity. Just after the Throne Verse, the scripture continues: "God is the Guardian of those who believe; He brings them forth from darkness into His light. Those who choose not to believe in their arrogance will be led from the light into darkness, there to become companions of the fire forever" (Q 2:257). The irony, in view of the Verse of Light, is striking. Those who rely on themselves cannot discover the authentic light but come only to that fire that is darkness itself.

According to some interpreters, God's relationship to journeying goes beyond the function of guidance. A widely influential and prolific thinker named Ibn Arabi (born in Spain, d. 1240) elaborates on the connections. He discerns sixteen journeys in the Qur'an. God begins by taking the primordial journey from the utter transcendence and inaccessibility of Sublimity downward to His Throne. From there, God dispatches Creation on its journey from nonbeing into being and sends down the Qur'an. God sends Adam on the Journey of Calamity from paradise to earth. Noah embarks on the Journey of Safety, and Moses on the Journey of Divine Appointment to meet God (we will shortly recall how Moses' chief attribute is that he conversed with God).

In Ibn Arabi's view, and in that of other important mystics before and since, every spiritual journey is one of three types directly related to God. There are journeys away from, toward, and in God. The first occurs when God banishes a fallen angel, when shame drives a sinner away, or when God sends a prophet or messenger into the world. Second, though all beings travel toward God, not all reach their goal. Unrepentant sinners experience the frustration of endless wandering; those who have obeyed but remain imperfect in their acknowledgment of the absolute unity and sovereignty of God arrive in the divine presence but are veiled from the divine vision; and the elect find the ultimate goal. Of those who journey in God, some (known as philosophers) falter along the way because they rely on the rational faculty; the elect, saints, and prophets make easy progress (Ibish, 1971, pp. 441–446. For more on the subject and on Ibn Arabi's "prophetology," see Chittick, 1990; and Austin, 1980).

As we will see shortly, the essential mediating role of prophets is to lead people from darkness to light. Speaking of the mission of Moses and his brother Aaron, Qur'an 37:117–118 says: "We [God speaking] gave them the Book that clarifies, and led them to the Straight Path." We turn now to consider first, Islam's scripture within the context of the larger history of revelation, and second, the place of Muhammad within the history of prophethood.

The Qur'an and the History of Revelation

> It is He [God] who sent down [revealed] to you the Book, confirming in truth all that preceded it; and before that He had sent down the Torah and the Gospel as guidance to humankind. . . . (Q 3:3)

Among the many foundations of Islamic religious tradition that intrigue and often puzzle non-Muslims, the Qur'an surely ranks high. First-time readers with some knowledge of Biblical narratives are invariably struck by the frequent allusions to familiar tales of Adam and Eve, Abraham, Moses, David and Solomon, and Jesus and Mary. Christians, especially, marvel that an entire chapter (sura 19) is named after Mary and that Jesus' mother is actually mentioned more often by name in the Qur'an than in the Greek Testament (the Christian scripture).

More careful examination of the scriptures, such as a comparison of the story of Joseph in sura 12 with the account in Genesis 37–50, inevitably raises numerous questions for Muslims and non-Muslims alike. When Christians and Jews discover a Qur'anic Moses or Joseph, or Jesus or Mary, who do and say things evidently at variance with the Biblical narratives, they often conclude that the Qur'an must be a slightly modified "borrowing." Muslims, on the other hand, explain discrepancies as evidence that Jews and Christians have obviously tampered with the original revelation to make it more palatable and less demanding. In fact, some argue, had the earlier "Peoples of the Book" not altered the record, God would not have needed to restore the revelation to its pristine purity by sending Muhammad with a corrective message. Besides, Muslim tradition adds, Muhammad was illiterate and therefore could not have plagiarized Biblical material.

Neither point of view is helpful, for both conclusions arise out of a spirit of partisan competition rather than out of a desire to deal openly with the data of history. The arguments seek only to defend the integrity of one scripture at the expense of the other. True, a great deal is at stake here, but only to the degree that we are unable to take the larger view of God's communication with humankind.

One possibility Christians and Jews might profitably explore is this: Just as stories of the great religious figures do not belong exclusively to any people or culture, so their capacity to reveal divine truth belongs to all whom God wishes to have access to them. Stories are a free-floating possession of humanity. If variations on narratives that some associate with the Bible occur in the Qur'an, they are there for an important purpose that transcends the rights of Christians and Jews to claim exclusive ownership of "their" stories and truths.

Muslims, for their part, might well understand the Qur'an as bringing a new perspective, reinforcing the ancient message, and enhancing and multiplying the opportunities for human beings to respond in faith. More than one Muslim author has suggested that Muhammad's "illiteracy" functions in Islamic theology much the way Mary's virginity functions in Christianity. In neither case does the human being strive to initiate. In both instances, it is God who effects the wonder of sending His word into the world. For Christians, Mary is the medium for the Word made Flesh; for Muslims, Muhammad serves as the instrument by which the Word is made Book. (See, for example, S. H. Nasr, *Ideals and Realities of Islam* [London: Allen & Unwin, 1966] for related observations.) The "Inlibration" thus parallels the "Incarnation."

The Qur'an itself suggests an explanation for the controversy at hand here:

> Humankind were once a single community. God sent prophets with news and warnings, and through them revealed the Book in truth that He might judge between people when they disagreed with one another. But, after the clear indicators had come to them, it was only out of self-centered stubbornness that they differed among themselves. God guided those who believed to the truth over which they argued, for God guides to the Straight Path whom He will. (Q 2:213)

Before considering further such important issues as the place of the Qur'an in Islamic life and various modes of interpretation, it will be helpful to sum up briefly some of the Qur'an's most important formal qualities and themes.

As a historic event, the revelation of the Arabic Qur'an defined a community of faith as its fundamental source of authority. Unlike either the Hebrew or the

Greek testaments, the Qur'an unfolded over a relatively short period of time, and its articulation is attributed to only one human being. Beginning in about 610 CE, when he was about 40 years old, Muhammad began to experience, in mostly auditory but occasionally visual form, what he would come to identify as divine revelations. Muhammad initially delivered the message orally, somewhat in the form of homiletical material. Not until more than two decades after the Prophet's death would a definitive text be compiled and written. Tradition has divided the text into two main periods, the Meccan and Medinan, corresponding to the years before and after the Hijra, the move to Medina in 622 CE. Scholars have more recently further divided the Meccan period into early, middle, and late periods, on the basis of the form and content of the suras.

During the Meccan Period (610–621), five themes appear most often in the earliest suras: (1) Evidently presuming belief in some deity on the part of their hearers, they emphasize God's creative power, providence, and guidance. There was at first no emphasis on belief in only one God. (2) They speak of accountability at judgment in a rather general way, without specific reference to particular reward or punishment as motivation for upright behavior. In view of these two, the suras suggest that the appropriate response for the individual is a combination of gratitude and worship. (3) This response flows out of an inner recognition of one's total dependence on God expressed formally in prayer. (4) Two parallel social consequences are also acknowledged in the need for generosity, as expressed in giving to those in need and seeking a just distribution of wealth. (5) Finally, the early message includes the theme of Muhammad's dawning awareness of his own prophetic mission and all that it would demand of him.

During the middle Meccan period, both the tone and the content of the suras began to change. Stories, first of indigenous Arabian and then of Biblical prophets, illustrated graphically the disastrous consequences attendant upon refusal to hear the prophetic message. Here, one finds a growing insistence on monotheistic belief and forthright condemnation of idolatry.

Toward the end of the Meccan period, emphasis on the rejection of past prophets grew apace with Muhammad's own experience of local opposition.

During the Medinan period (622–632 CE), both the style and the content changed dramatically. Whereas the Meccan suras tended to be poetic in tone, a quite dramatic form called rhymed prose (*saj'*), the later message became more prose-like. Its content reflected the growing need to regulate the daily life of the expanding community of Muslims, and the reality of increased contact with

Spread of Islam

Christians and Jews (of whom several large tribes played a major part in the life of Medina) (see Watt, 1953, 1956).

Over a period of twenty-three years or so, the divine interventions would come upon Muhammad in a variety of circumstances, often at times when he was struggling with a particular problem or issue. For example, for a while after the Hijra, the Muslims faced Jerusalem when they prayed, as did the local Jews. Apparently, some friction caused a falling out with the Jewish community, causing Muhammad concern over the continued symbolic statement of the prayer orientation. Thus came the revelation, "We have seen you turning your face about toward the heavens. We shall now turn you toward a direction (*qibla*) that you will find satisfying. Turn your face toward the Mosque of the Sanctuary [site of the Ka'ba in Mecca]; wherever you are, turn your faces toward it" (Q 2:144). That verse sometimes serves as a decorative inscription over the *mihrab* (niche) in mosques.

Ka'ba

One of the sacred sites of Islam, situated in Mecca in present-day Saudi Arabia, the city of the pilgrimage (one of the five pillars of Islam), this one-room, cube-shaped stone structure is believed to have been built by Abraham and his son Ishmael, and the nearby well called Zamzam is believed to have been used by Ishmael's mother, Hagar. Each year, millions of pilgrims come to visit Mecca and the Ka'ba as part of their spiritual journey.

The Qur'an forms the core of all Islamic worship and devotional activity. As part of the daily ritual prayer, Muslims regularly recite the opening sura quoted earlier, as well as several other short pieces. An example is the very brief sura 112 *al-Ikhlas* (Sincerity or Purity of Faith): "Proclaim: He is One God, God the besought of all; He does not beget; He is not begotten; and there is none like Him." It is an unmistakable reminder to Muslims that they are different from Christians with their belief in Father, Son, and Spirit. However, perhaps just as important as the theological content is the sheer physical experience of reciting and/or hearing recitation of the Qur'an. The effect on listeners is often profound, for the mode of delivery combined with the extraordinarily earthy sound of Arabic make for an intensely moving experience. One commentator has likened the recitation to the Christian practice of Communion, in that in both instances, one has the Word on the tongue (Cragg, 1973, 1971).

Qur'an recitation is also part of many religious occasions outside the five daily prayers. After a funeral, families of the deceased often hire a reciter to come and grace the time for condolence with appropriate scriptural texts. During the fasting month of Ramadan, Muslims make a special place for recitation. They commemorate the twenty-seventh day of that lunar month as the "Night of Power," when Muhammad received the first revelation. In addition, the entire Qur'an is recited during the thirty nights of Ramadan. For that and other such "liturgical" purposes, the text of the scripture has been divided into thirty sections, each of which is further halved, and those halves further quartered, yielding a total of 240 divisions. One can easily keep track of how far one has to go during each period of recitation.

There are social dimensions to be considered as well. All across the Islamic world, the art of Qur'an recitation is highly prized. One can almost always tune to a radio station that broadcasts recitation and commentary all day. In some places, such as Malaysia and Indonesia and even on a smaller scale here in the United States, the art has become very competitive. National contests draw huge crowds to sports stadiums, and winners look forward to going to a grand final meet in Mecca. In virtually any large mosque, for example, one can find people sitting alone and chanting their recitation quietly to themselves or engaging in lively discussions about the text.

On the level of individual devotion too, the Qur'an functions prominently. Some Muslims still strive to memorize the entire book, whose approximately six-thousand verses make it roughly the length of the NT. Memorizing the text means having it in one's heart and "keeping" it there. Paralleling the memorization of the Qur'an is what has been called the Qur'anization of the memory. The phrase originally referred to the intensely scriptural way of thinking manifested by some of the great Muslim spiritual writers and mystical poets, but there are further implications as well. Especially throughout the Arabic-speaking world, phrases from the Qur'an have become so much a part of ordinary speech, particularly among traditional-minded Muslims, that many people no longer know where the sacred ends and the profane begins.

Methods of Exegesis

Islamic tradition has known several important varieties of scriptural interpretation, or exegesis. In the last section, we looked at two of the Qur'an's premier texts, the Throne Verse and the Verse of Light. We shall return to them shortly for some insight into how Muslims have interpreted their scripture. The Qur'an itself makes a foundational observation as to the two principal ways human beings might understand its verses:

> He it is who has revealed the Book to you. Some of its verses/signs are categorical in meaning. They are the mother [i.e., essence] of the Book. Others are open to interpretation [i.e., metaphorical or allegorical]. Those whose hearts harbor ill-will pursue its metaphorical verses, in their desire for disharmony and esoteric interpretation [ta'wil]. None but God knows the inner meaning. (Q 3:7)

That short text is remarkable in its succinct articulation of the central difficulty all scripture-based traditions must face. The text clearly comes down on the side of clarity and literal meaning. Unfortunately, it leaves unanswered the question of why it contains the ambiguous at all.

Legal

We will call the first type of interpretation the "legal" or juristic. For all Muslims, Qur'an is at the heart of all religious law, followed in short order by sayings attributed to Muhammad, called Hadith. It is the task of the legal scholar to search the text for the clearest, least ambiguous references to a given regulatory matter (from dietary law to family inheritance to criminal sanctions). What the jurist wants is to interpret the scripture so as to extend its applicability to present needs and circumstances, even if those were not obviously foremost at the time of the revelation.

Theological

A second type of exegesis is the theological. Ever since at least the late seventh or early eighth century, Muslims have been asking difficult questions about how the sacred text communicates the divine mystery. The imagery of God seated on the Throne has been at the center of much discussion in classical Islamic theology, for it raises the question of whether and to what degree one ought to interpret scripture literally. Taken literally, the text conjures up anthropomorphic pictures of the deity: There is a Throne and God actually sits upon it, and so forth. Taken metaphorically, the text becomes a colorful reference to divine sovereignty and transcendence. Islamic tradition has on the whole considered the latter option a dangerous invitation to water down the meaning of the sacred text.

Two of the principal positions in the theological debate are those of a group called the Mu'tazilites (emerged in the eighth century CE, literally means "those who keep themselves apart") and the school of a man named al-Ash'ari (d. 944). A fundamental tenet of the Mu'tazilites was that the Qur'an was not uncreated, as the traditionalists argued, but created and therefore subject to the critique of human reason. It sounds perhaps like so much hair splitting, but it had the import of Christian theological debate around the divinity and humanity of Jesus. Basing all their arguments on reason (doing theology from below, one could say), the Mu'tazilites believed that taking literally such texts as the Throne Verse made no sense at all, for the anthropomorphism thus entailed would bring God down to human scale. It was simply not rational to speak that way about the transcendent. In his classic Mu'tazilite commentary, Zamakhshari says of the *kursi*, or footstool, attached to the Throne: "It is no more than an image expressing God's greatness. In reality, there is neither *kursi*, an act of sitting, nor one who sits" (Ayoub, 1984, p. 251). The verse therefore uses a "fanciful image" to communicate the idea of God's extensive power, knowledge, and sovereignty (Gatje, 1976, pp. 146–147).

Al-Ash'ari had been a member of the Mu'tazilites in his youth and became disaffected with their inability to rein in their own rational arguments. He countered that, on the contrary, what made no sense was any attempt to limit God in any direction whatsoever. He concluded that one simply ought not to speculate about what God has in mind. If the Qur'an says God sits on a throne, one must take the statement at face value and let it be. He quotes, with utmost approval, the Hadith of Muhammad, "The *kursi* is the place of the two feet [the footstool of God]. It has a squeaking sound like that of a new saddle" (Ayoub, 1984, p. 249). His now-famous methodological formula, *bila kayf* ("without a how"), sums up the notion that one simply ought not to speculate on these things. Ash`ari's opinion has carried the day, for the most part, with its emphasis on divine mystery.

Allegorical

The Shi`a or Shi`ite Muslims were especially partial to a third type of exegesis. Just as the jurists read scripture with any eye for regulatory items and the rationalists went for the anthropomorphisms, Shi`ite interpreters have been keen to focus on any text that might support the religious and political legitimacy of Muhammad's son-in-law Ali and his descendants. Shi`ite exegesis is therefore highly allegorical. Recall, for example, the Verse of Light. One classic reading of it likens God's light to Muhammad, the niche to Muhammad's breast, the lamp to the knowledge of prophecy, and the glass to Muhammad's prophetic knowledge passed along to Ali. That the tree is of neither east nor west means Ali was neither Jew nor Christian. Just as the tree nearly glowed even untouched by fire, so Ali would nearly utter the prophetic knowledge, even if Muhammad had not passed it on. And the phrase "Light upon light" refers to the succession of one Imam (spiritual descendent of Ali) from the previous Imam (Gatje, 1976, pp. 243–245).

Mystical

Finally, the fourth type is mystical exegesis. Islamic mystics have read the sacred text for any hint of the possibility of an intimate relationship between human and divine. Traditionalists often found such talk at least slightly blasphemous, and rationalists regarded it as sentimental at best, but the rich mystical tradition has mined every reference to divine love and concern, every suggestion of divine immanence, discerning at least two levels of meaning in each tidbit. The outward meaning is apparent to most everyone: to arrive at the hidden meaning requires *ta'wil*, the very thing some would say the Qur'an counsels against (see Q 3:7, quoted previously).

Some examples of the Qur'anic phrases dearest to the mystics include the following:

> To God belong the East and the West; wherever you turn, there is the face of God. (2:115)

> I am truly near: I answer the prayer of the petitioner who beseeches me. Therefore let them respond to me and have faith in me, that they might receive guidance. (2:186)

Everything on earth perishes; but the face of your Lord remains, majestic and most revered. (55:26–27)

While the mystical tradition was not loathe to interpret such texts metaphorically, they did so without in any way deflating them of their mystery, as the Mu'tazilite approach ran the risk of doing. In his reading of the Throne Verse, for example, the mystic Ibn 'Arabi considers the *kursi* to be the center of knowledge on the cosmic scale, as is the human heart on the microcosmic level. He goes on to say that God does not tire of keeping all things in existence, "because they have no existence without Him . . . Rather the realm of the ideal form is His inner dimension and the realm of forms is His outer dimension. They have no existence except in Him. Nor are they other than He" (Ayoub, 1984, pp. 250–251). Such statements, liable as it may seem to the charge of pantheistic monism, that is, where everything is one and is God, were the sort of utterances for which many a mystic ran afoul of more than traditional thinkers.

Before we move on to the Prophet, two other beautiful short texts will help to reinforce the sense of power and inexhaustible grandeur that Muslims experience in their scripture.

The first text and its parallel emphasize the infinitude of God's revelation, extending impossibly beyond creation's capacity: "If all the trees on earth were pens and all the oceans ink, with seven more seas besides, they would not suffice to record the words of God" (Q 31:27; see also 18:109). Christian readers may be reminded of the text with which John's gospel ends: "But there are also many other things that Jesus did; if every one of them were written down, I suppose that the world itself could not contain the books that would be written" (Jn 21:25). The second is reminiscent of a theme associated with Mount Sinai. Sinai swooned when God gave Moses the Torah and, according to the mystics and rabbis, exploded into many pieces, each of which fell

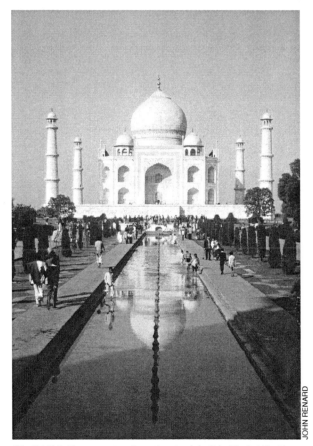

JOHN RENARD

The Taj Mahal is a seventeenth-century tomb built by Mughal Muslim ruler Shah Jahan as a burial place for his favorite wife in Agra, North-Central India. Passages from the Qur'an are etched throughout the tomb and surrounding buildings.

upon and blessed a part of the earth. "If we had sent this Qur'an down upon a mountain, you would have seen it crumble to pieces and humble itself for fear of God" (Q 59:21).

Muhammad and the History of Prophethood

> Say "We believe in God and what has been revealed to us and what was revealed to Abraham and Isma`il and Isaac and Jacob and the tribes, and what was given to Moses and Jesus and what was given to the prophets from their Lord. We make no distinction among them and to Him do we surrender gratefully [lit., "we are Muslims to Him"]." (Q 2:136; see also 29:46)

Jewish and Christian readers will already have some familiarity with the notion of prophets and prophetic mission. Since time immemorial, prophet-types have played a major role in the religious history of the Middle East. In the Hebrew scriptures, prophets receive a mandate to speak on God's behalf. Their mission often requires that they stand up to the high and mighty, posing the divine challenge of justice for the powerless of the earth. The problem of how to discern true prophets from charlatans has exercised religious minds for millennia as well. In addition to the full-fledged prophets, lesser characters have also played a part. These include sages, oracles, and soothsayers.

All of these religious types were familiar to many people in the Arabia of Muhammad's day, but as Muhammad would discover, the majority of the populace welcomed the advent of a prophet no more enthusiastically in the seventh century CE than they would have in the seventh century BCE. A brief summary of the major events of Muhammad's life will provide the necessary immediate context for our consideration of his paradigmatic role in the life of the Muslim community.

Muhammad was born in the trading town of Mecca around 570 CE to a rather poor family of the clan of Hashim, one of the branches of the Quraysh tribe. His father died before Muhammad was born, and the boy's mother died when he was 6 years old. According to Arabian custom, the youngster was sent to be reared among the Bedouin tribes of the desert regions. Tradition names his nurse Halima. After his mother's death, Muhammad grew up first in the custody of his grandfather, Abd al-Muttalib, and later in the house of his uncle, Abu Talib, whose son Ali we have already mentioned briefly. Tradition has it that the young Muhammad traveled with his uncle on business. One story tells how in Syria they met an old Christian monk named Bahira, who discerned the marks of prophetic greatness in the boy.

At this time, pre-Islamic Arabian religion was mostly a kind of "polyde-monism," with multiple spirits, mostly associated with natural features such as stones (e.g., the Black Stone in a corner of the Ka'ba), springs, groves of trees, and so on. When Muhammad was about 25, he married a widow fifteen years his senior. Khadija ran her own caravan business, and Muhammad went to work for her. Apparently, Muhammad liked occasionally to retreat to mountain solitude to meditate and seek within the source of life. Around 610 CE, when Muhammad had reached the age long considered in the Middle East a necessary precondition for the imparting of wisdom and ministry, he began to experience troubling visitations that sent him, in turmoil, to ask Khadija's counsel.

On the "Night of Power" now commemorated on the twenty-seventh day of Ramadan, the earliest message commanded him to "Recite!" (lit., "make qur'an, recitation") that which no human being could know unaided. The encounter left him confused and uncertain. Not until as much as a year later did Muhammad hear a follow-up message of confirmation: "Indeed your Lord is the one who best knows who has strayed from His path, who best knows those who are guided" (Q 68:7). Assured that he was not losing his sanity, Muhammad persisted in his attitude of attentiveness to the messages from the unseen world. From then on, revelations came more frequently. During the next several years, Muhammad slowly gathered a circle of converts who would form the nucleus of a faith community. Leaders of the Quraysh (rulers of Mecca) grew increasingly unhappy at the effects of Muhammad's preaching on caravan and pilgrim traffic to the Ka'ba and at the prospect of a rival leader in their midst. Around 615 CE, under growing pressure and amid threats to the safety of his community, Muhammad sent a group to seek asylum across the Red Sea with the Christian rule of Abyssinia (Ethiopia). Muhammad remained in Mecca.

Tradition reports that on the twenty-seventh night of the month of Rajab (late August) in the year 621 CE, Muhammad underwent a two-fold mystical experience. In the first part, God "carried his servant by night, from the Mosque of the Sanctuary to the Farther Mosque" (Q 17:1). Later interpreters would equate the first site with the shrine of the Ka'ba in Mecca, the second with the southern end of the temple platform in Jerusalem, where now stands an early eighth-century structure called "the Farther Mosque" (*al-masjid al-aqsa*). This "Night Journey" (*isra'*) was already clearly a kind of otherworldly experience, for ancient narratives place Muhammad in the company of earlier prophets in the Farther Mosque, who naturally asked him to lead them in the ritual prayer. The second part of the journey, however, called the "Ascension" (*mi'raj*), finds the Prophet riding a winged human-faced steed named Buraq and led by Gabriel toward the very throne of God. Marvelously embellished tales have developed around this experience. Vivid descriptions of Muhammad's excursion follow him through the various levels of heaven, where he meets all of his major prophetic forebears, down to the dark circles of hell, where Gabriel shows him the horrors of the damned. This is truly the picture of a heroic journey of initiation in the mysteries of the unseen world. Many Muslims believe the journey involved physical locomotion, but a strong tradition of nonliteralistic interpretation has always regarded it as a spiritual and inward experience. It is considered a paradigm of the individual Muslim's spiritual path.

During the year of the Night Journey and Ascension, and perhaps also during the previous year, Muhammad had been investigating the possibility of moving his community from the increasingly hostile environment of Mecca to a safer haven. Hopeful prospects arrived in 621 CE with a delegation from Yathrib, a city several-hundred miles north of Mecca. Looking for someone to help them negotiate a peaceful settlement to factional problems in their city, the representatives invited Muhammad to come and apply his already renowned talent for arbitration. Arrangements were finalized, and in 622 CE, the Muslims headed north to Yathrib, whose name would soon change to Medinat an-Nabi ("City of the Prophet"), or simply Medina. That crucial journey was called the *Hijra* or Emigration. It marked the birthday of Islam, so to speak, and the beginning of the Muslim calendar (with dates marked AH, "after the Hijra"). This journey developed in Islamic piety and as a metaphor for the Muslim community's relationships with the world at large.

Muhammad's years in Medina, as reflected in the text of the Qur'an as well as in later historical writing, witnessed major changes in his style of leadership and in the shape of the community of believers. Muhammad's prominence in the new setting gave prestige to the community. As the group increased, so did the demands on Muhammad's administrative time and skill so that what began as spiritual leadership gradually grew into a more comprehensive oversight. During the Medinan period, the Muslims also took up arms against the Quraysh, who had carried on a continuous campaign against the Muslims after the Hijra and fought a number of serious military engagements with the Meccan forces. After nearly eight years of bitter conflict, the two sides struck a truce. Muhammad returned there in 630 to claim the city for the Muslims, and by that time, the Quraysh had decided not to resist, so the city was taken without significant military effort. In 630, Muhammad led a triumphal band to claim the city for the Muslims. Two years later, Muhammad returned to Mecca for what would be his farewell pilgrimage to the Ka`ba: the *Hajj* ("pilgrimage"), as a religious symbol and experience of return to the center and as a metaphor around which to understand Islam as a unique community of faith.

Given this brief overview of the key events in Muhammad's life, it remains for us to try to understand how Muhammad saw himself within the larger sweep of God's use of prophets to reveal the Word to humankind. Both the Qur'an and the Hadith are replete with references to earlier prophets, from Adam to Jesus. Islamic tradition numbers over two-dozen figures sent to particular peoples, including David, Solomon, Noah, and Jonah, as well as the Arabian figures Hud, Salih, and Shu`ayb. All of them are "prophets" (*nabi*, pl. *anbiya'*) commissioned to warn their people; some are in addition "messengers" (*rasul*, pl. *rusul*) to whom scriptures are revealed. All of the prophets and messengers experienced rejection at the hands of their people, and some were killed. In every instance, God dealt harshly with the people.

Muhammad readily identified with several of the prophets in particular, especially with Abraham, the "Friend of the Merciful" (*Khalil ar-Rahman*), and Moses, "God's Conversant" (*Kalim Allah*). In Islamic tradition, Abraham was neither Jew nor Christian but a *hanif*, a seeker after the one true God. As the Qur'an says:

> Truly Abraham was a model [lit., an *umma*], obedient to God, and a seeker [lit., *hanif*] who assigned no partner to God. He responded in gratitude to the bounty of the one who chose him and guided him to the Straight Path . . . So We have revealed to you [*Muhammad*] that you should follow the believing ways [lit., *milla*] of Abraham the seeker. . . . (Q 16:120–121, 123)

It was Abraham who had prayed that God would "send among them a messenger from their midst who will unfold to them your signs and teach them the Book and the wisdom." (Q 2:129)

Moses' importance in the Qur'an is equal to that of Abraham:

> We sent Moses with Our signs: "Bring your people out from profound darkness into the light and make them mindful of the days of God." Truly in that are signs for all who are long-suffering and grateful. (Q 4:5)

Qur'an 73:15 likens Muhammad especially to Moses. Islamic tradition likewise sees a reference to Muhammad in the words of Deuteronomy 18:18, in which God says to Moses, "I will raise up for them a prophet like you from among their own people; I will put my words in the mouth of the prophet, who shall speak to them everything that I command" (Corbin, 1978, pp. 121ff.). Curiously, one text of the Qur'an (7:155–157) has God speaking approvingly to Moses of "those who follow the Apostle, the unlettered Prophet [i.e., Muhammad] whom they find written of [in their own] Torah and Gospel. . . ." The allusion is apparently first to the text of Deuteronomy just mentioned, and second, to references in the gospel of John (14–16) to the Paraclete.

Medieval Muslim theologians interpreted the Johannine text in a fascinating manner. This is an important opportunity to exemplify how languages differ. Speakers of Semitic languages such as Arabic become accustomed to finding basic meanings in consonantal roots of words that, when written, are without their vowels. Transferring that way of thinking to Greek, scholars reasoned that Christians had misread Jesus' term as *parakletos*, "advocate or counselor," interpreted by Christians as the Holy Spirit. A simple insertion of the correct vowels would yield *periklutos*, "the highly praised one," and thus a meaning more acceptable to Muslims. The name *Muhammad* in Arabic derives from the root *HaMaDa*, "to praise." To intensify a root meaning, Arabic doubles the middle consonant, hence *HaMMaDa*, "to praise highly." In order to express the idea that a particular individual has been praised highly, Arabic forms a passive participle by prefixing *mu-* and producing the word *muHaMMaD*, the "highly praised one."

What is most important to note in all this is the Muslim conviction that God sends a message to suit every circumstance perfectly. As the Qur'an says, "We (God) have sent no messenger except with the language of his people, that he might give them clarity. God allows to wander off whom He will, and He guides whom He will" (Q 4:4).

All prophets have been wayfarers, as have all human beings. But what distinguishes prophets, from Adam to Muhammad, from the rest of wandering humankind is that God's messengers come with the explicit mission of helping the rest find their way amid the confusion, the maze of possible paths and goals, the plethora of markers and way stations. Islamic tradition offers a wide range of imaginative models of spiritual progress. One model associates various stages along the way with individual prophet–guides. The latter are in turn associated with particular colors, degrees of spiritual achievement, levels of the cosmos, and such human faculties as heart, spirit, and innermost secrets. Using such a model, one can speak of spiritual progress as a process of encountering a succession of the "prophets of one's own being" as the traveler proceeds upward through the spectrum of colors and from the gross to the subtle.

Distinctive Scriptural Themes in Islamic Spirituality

Qur'anic themes are central to any appreciation of Islamic spirituality. It is to such thoughts as these that Muslims instinctively advert as they reflect on their deepest religious values. This section will begin with (1) the theme of prayer in the Qur'an and Qur'an as prayer, then (2) move to several of the fundamental interior attitudes Muslims are called to cultivate, and finally (3) cover the outward responsibilities where the tradition challenges believers to put those attitudes into action.

Prayer in the Qur'an and Qur'an as Prayer

One of the principal difficulties non-Muslims encounter in reading the Qur'an is that of finding a focus that can help them trace the scripture's basic message. The foregoing section on Qur'anic interpretation has noted that what one sees in the Qur'an depends a great deal on what one is looking for. For our purposes, it is essential to bear in mind that the Qur'an, as all sacred texts, seeks to communicate an experience. One way to focus on the heart of that experience is to read the Qur'an as both a sourcebook of prayer and as a prayer in itself.

As a sourcebook of prayer, the Qur'an lays the conceptual and practical foundations for all subsequent developments in the history of Islamic spirituality. Here, I am speaking of the scripture as a word spoken by God and addressed to human beings. As a prayer in itself, the Qur'an becomes a divinely initiated word addressed back to God. I will return to the latter aspect later in this chapter, in the context of experiencing the Qur'an in memory and recitation. For the moment, let us look at prayer as a theme in the sacred text, both as divine instruction in how humans ought to respond to God and as concrete prophetic example.

Some of the earliest texts suggest that night vigil and recitation were at the heart of the matter. References to "prostration" and to various daily times for prayer also occur in early suras. For example, a sura dated to about 615–616 CE says: "Therefore glorify God when evening comes and when you awake; for to Him belongs praise in the heavens and on the earth; and in late afternoon and as dusk begins to fall" (Q 30:17–18). Such suggestions of what eventually developed into the five daily prayers receive more detailed attention in later suras, especially those of the Medinan period, when the growing Muslim community needed increasing communal discipline and instruction.

Examples of personal prayer, or what would come to be known as the prayer of invocation or supplication (*du'a*), also abound in the Qur'an. During the middle and later Meccan periods, when Muhammad was experiencing growing opposition from influential members of the Quraysh tribe, stories of previous prophets and the enmity of their peoples toward them become crucial to the scripture's message. Those prophets naturally serve as models of prayer, suggesting both when and how one ought to address God from the heart. The years 615–622 were times of particular hardship for the small Muslim community, and the praying of the pre-Islamic prophets reflects and comments on that experience. Abraham's extended prayer at the core of sura 14 is a prime example. He intercedes for the people of Mecca:

> My Lord, make this city secure, and protect me and my children from worshipping idols. My Lord, truly have they misguided many people. One who follows me is with me, but the one who rebels—but You are the Forgiving, the Merciful . . . My Lord, cause me and my descendants to be given to regular communal prayer, O our Lord, and receive my supplication. Our Lord, be forgiving to me and my parents and all believers on that Day of Reckoning.

From the Medinan period comes another, more generic prayer as an example of the sentiments a community of believers such as the one by then more firmly established might express:

> Our Lord, not in vain have You created this, may You be glorified! . . . We have heard the call of one inviting to faith, "Believe in Your Lord," and so we have believed. Our Lord, forgive our sins, cover our evil deeds, and let us die among the righteous. Our Lord, give us what You have promised through your Messengers and let us not be put to shame on Resurrection Day. (Q 3)

The Qur'an and the Inner Life

Among the various essential attitudes the Qur'an recommends, the following four deserve special mention: attentiveness, intention, striving, and gratitude. The theological equivalent of the attitude of attentiveness is uncompromising monotheism—belief in and acknowledgement of one God only, called *tawhid* in Arabic. Its opposite is carelessness, laziness, a spiritual torpor born of self-absorption, a most basic and destructive form of denial. Attentiveness means seeing things as they really are, with the eyes of faith; it means discerning in creation and in oneself, as well as in the revealed scripture, the "signs" of the Creator and Revealer.

Without that mindfulness and heedfulness, no divine–human relationship is possible. Directly related to that attentiveness is right intention. Any action merely performed by rote loses its fully human character and hence produces no spiritual benefit. I will discuss later some of the more subtle aspects of intention in relation to the performance of religious observances and in relation to the need for high vigilance regarding one's general state of soul and motivation. Suffice it to note here that explicit intention precedes all fully human acts.

At the center of the human condition lies the need to struggle, to strive against one's baser tendencies and against the spiritual entropy born of the heedlessness endemic to the human race. Here lies the core of that most misunderstood of Islamic themes, *jihad.* The Arabic root *JaHaDa* (with the three consonantal root letters in upper case) means "to exert oneself." Believers must struggle against whatever stands between the self and its origin and goal, and strive to overcome injustice and oppression. Battle against the fiercest of all enemies, the enemy that resides "between one's two sides," as Hadith puts it, ancient tradition calls the Greater Jihad. To the Lesser Jihad, combat against outward foes, we will come shortly.

What could possibly motivate the hard work of rigorous spiritual discipline? One often hears Islam characterized as a religion of submission, whose adherents operate largely out of fear of a cold, capricious deity. While the Qur'an's emphasis on divine majesty and power has indeed sometimes given rise to a resigned fatalism, the scripture in no way recommends passivity. Prayer for forgiveness occurs often in the Qur'an, but a sense of gratitude to God is at least as significant a motive for ethical action as is fear of punishment. "God has given you all you have asked for; and were you to attempt to add up the kindnesses of God, you would fall short. Indeed, humanity is prey to injustice and ingratitude" (Q 14:34).

All positive virtues flow from the awareness that God is the beneficent and unstinting source of all good, who expects that those most blessed will in turn share their gifts most generously with others. As a means to the attainment of gratitude, one must be purified of any delusions of grandeur or self-sufficiency, as well as of selfish motivation in giving. The term that came to mean "almsgiving," *zakat,* derives from a root meaning "to purify oneself."

> If you give alms in public, for others to see, it is well; but if you conceal your alms, and give them to the poor, it is better for you . . . Whatever of good you spend in alms shall be for your souls and you should not spend except out of longing for the face of God. (Q 2:271–272)

Gratitude ultimately flows over into praise of God, an attitude that suffuses both the Qur'an and ordinary Arabic speech. We turn now to the implications of these interior qualities for human action.

The "Five Pillars" of Islam

The following is a summary of the basic minimum beliefs and practices that are part of a larger religious reality.

Daily practices

1. The profession of belief (*Shahada*): "There is no deity but God and Muhammad is the Messenger of God." God is otherness yet oneness; God relies on the truth-telling of human messengers who are called "prophets."

2. Five brief but regular ritual prayer times from early morning to late evening (*Salat*): The prayer can be performed anywhere but must be oriented toward the Arabian city of Mecca. Before the prayer itself, one begins by ritual cleansing with water, but if necessary, sand, or even earth, is acceptable.

Occasional practices

3. Almsgiving (*zakat*): One's wealth, which is of this earth and temporary, comes from Allah, and almsgiving is meant to purify oneself of any sense of ownership, so this act is to remind the donor of the source of all good gifts.

4. Fasting: While most religions recommend fasting in some form, Islamic practice is more rigorous partly because the ninth lunar month of Ramadan rotates through all the seasons. Abstaining from food, drink, and sexual gratification from dawn to sunset every day for thirty days is a sharp reminder to focus on the more important dimensions of life, a need that only God can fill. Among the desired effects is a deepened compassion for the poor and hungry, the will to counter one's own baser tendencies, and a clearer sense of one's relationship to the Creator.

5. Pilgrimage (*hajj*): While some other major world religious traditions emphasize pilgrimage, the practice is perhaps more central to Islam than to others. Muslims are enjoined to visit Mecca once in a lifetime, thus maintaining a strong sense of being members of a community on pilgrimage, and they formally fulfill their duty of the Hajj only between the eighth and thirteenth days of the twelfth lunar month.

The Outward Dimensions of Qur'anic Spirituality

The human spirit does not suffer isolation gladly; it naturally seeks expression in relationships to other persons and to the world. Generosity, personal responsibility, and diligence in the Lesser Jihad are three manifestations of healthy engagement of the individual with his or her surroundings. (1) Generosity is the outward result of inner gratitude: one can be truly generous only to the degree that one acknowledges God's primacy in giving.

> Give to kin, to the poor and the traveler what they need; that is best for those who seek the face of God.... What you give in the hope of profiting at the expense of other people will gain you nothing in God's sight; what you give as purifying alms [zakat] as you seek the face of God—that will produce abundant return. (Q 30:38–39)

All beneficence thus points not to the individual, who serves really as a broker, but to God. Generosity in turn is linked to a heavy emphasis on social responsibility (see e.g., Q 2:177). The scripture condemns those who hoard their wealth in the hope that it will save them from their mortality (Q 104:1–3). Equally condemned are those "who do not treat the orphan with dignity nor encourage each other to feed the poor . . . [and who] greedily devour their inheritances" (Q 89:17–19).

One of the Islamic ethical and theological issues most discussed over the centuries, from the earliest times, has been that of the (2) tension between divine omnipotence and human responsibility and moral freedom. In attempts to preserve God's transcendent sovereignty from the slightest hint of dilution, parties to the debate have sometimes gone to the extreme of virtually denying human freedom. On the other side, an overriding concern to safeguard individual moral responsibility has led some to the opposite extreme of suggesting that it is God whose choices are limited. As we have seen, one can interpret the Qur'an in a wide variety of ways, but it maintains a paradoxical balance. God's power knows no bounds, but human beings both enjoy a wide array of options and must shoulder responsibility for their choices. Repeatedly, the scripture makes it clear that "God does not change a people's condition until they change the thoughts of their own hearts" (Q 13:11).

That responsibility leads to the final outward dimension, willingness to engage actively in the hard work of (3) stewardship over creation. Acceptance of the divine charge of accountability for the shape of things here on earth, Islamic tradition calls the Lesser Jihad. One cannot authentically enter into this often-mundane striving without first joining the battle within, the Greater Jihad. In practice, the struggle involves acting on one's convictions about everything, from the environment to human rights to local school board elections. Muslim authors speak of the jihad of the pen, of the tongue, and, more recently, of the ballot box. Wherever human beings work for peace and justice, there is jihad. There is also the jihad of the sword. As a last resort, when all other means have been exhausted, jihad may also include the use of force, but the use of violent means is carefully hedged with prohibitions against terrorism, mistreatment of prisoners, and wanton destruction of natural resources. War against an aggressor is justifiable because "aggression is more despicable than killing" (Q 2:193).

Questions about the Text

1. What are the root words and name for God in Islam?

2. What is a *sura*?

3. How long did it take for the Qur'an to be written? How did the tone of the Qur'an change from the Meccan to Medinan period?

4. What are the four exegetical types used to interpret the Qur'an? What does each emphasize?

5. What is the "Night of Power"?

6. What is the *Hijra*?

7. What does the name *Muhammad* mean?

8. What are the four "essential attitudes" for the inner life?

9. What three qualities are needed for the "outward" relationships to persons and the world? Explain them.

Questions for Discussion

1. How can a religious person's images of God influence the individual's overall approach to life? What image is dominant for you?

2. How can the divine names offer insight into Islam and other traditions? What names do you find most helpful?

3. After reading the chapter, what aspects of Islam were new to you? What would you like to know more about, and why?

4. From the reading of the text, in what ways have you found that Muhammad's life served as an exemplar for Muslims?

5. What similarities and differences do you see in the essential attitudes and outward relations between Islam and your religious experience?

For Further Study

Austin, R. W. J., trans. *The Bezels of Wisdom*. Mahwah, NJ: Paulist Press, 1980.

Ayoub, M. *The Qur'an and its Interpreters*. Albany: State University of New York, 1984.

Bloom, Jonathan, and Sheila Blair. *Islamic Art*. London: Phaidon, 1997.

This text is a beautifully illustrated and engaging introduction to the various visual expressions associated with major Islamic societies for nearly a millennium and a half.

Chittick, William. *The Sufi Path of Knowledge*. Albany: State University of New York Press, 1990.

Corbin, Henry. *The Man of Light in Iranian Sufism*. Boulder, CO: Shambhala, 1978.

Cragg, K. *The Event of the Qur'an*. London: Allen & Unwin, 1971.

———. *The Mind of the Qur'an*. London: Allen & Unwin, 1973.

Ernst, Carl W. *Following Muhammad: Rethinking Islam in the Contemporary World*. Chapel Hill: University of North Carolina Press, 2003.

This is an excellent approach to unmasking some of the prevalent stereotypes about Islam and Muslims.

———. *The Shambhala Guide to Sufism*. Boston: Shambhala, 1997.

This text is a very readable introduction to the literary, social, and institutional dimensions of a phenomenon often identified as the "mystical" approach to Islam.

Gatje, H. *The Qur'an and its Exegesis*. Berkeley and Los Angeles: University of California Press, 1976.

Ibish, Yusuf. "Ibn Arabi's Theory of Journeying," in Y. Ibish and P. L. Wilson, eds., *Traditional Modes of Contemplation and Action*. Tehran: Imperial Iranian Academy of Philosophy, 1971.

McKane, William. *The Book of Fear and Hope*. Leiden, MA: Brill, 1962.

Nasr, S. H. *Ideals and Realities of Islam*. London: Allen & Unwin, 1966.

Otto, Rudolf. *The Idea of the Holy*. New York: Galaxy, 1958.

Renard, John. *Seven Doors to Islam: Spirituality and the Religious Life of Muslims*. Berkeley: University of California Press, 1996.

> The author provides a thematic look at the vast range of literary and visual expressions of the Islamic tradition.

Renard, John, ed. *Windows on the House of Islam: Muslim Sources on Spirituality and Religious Life*. Berkeley: University of California Press, 1998.

> This is an anthology of primary source material translated from a dozen languages and organized according to the major thematic categories of *Seven Doors to Islam*.

Sells, Michael. *Approaching the Qur'an: The Early Revelations*. Ashland, OR: White Cloud Press, 1999.

> This text offers beautifully translated texts of the scripture, along with a CD illustrating various styles of formal recitation by professional Qur'an reciters from across the globe.

Watt, M. *Muhammad in Mecca, Muhammad in Medina*. Oxford, UK: Oxford University Press, 1953, 1956.

From the Reference Librarian
Synoptic Outlines of Contents for all Topics—Islam

Student: How do I find topics for research in Islam (or any religious tradition)?

The simplest way is to find an encyclopedia whose scope includes the particular religion of interest and that also has a synoptic outline of contents. (How would you locate in your library catalog an encyclopedia on Islam? On religion in general?) We have already described the use of such synoptic outlines in a previous chapter, but they are a helpful feature that many encyclopedias provide, so it is worthwhile to look at another example. The synoptic outline is prepared by professionals who understand the relationship of the various topics within a field and who try to present that field in an organized way.

Fortunately, the major English-language encyclopedia for the study of all religion(s), the fifteen-volume *Encyclopedia of Religion* (first ed., 1987; second ed., 2005) contains such an outline along with a detailed index in volume 15.

The synoptic index in the *Encyclopedia of Religion* is organized into forty-four broad divisions, including major world religions ("Christianity," "Jainism," etc.), as well as historical (e.g., "Greek Religion," i.e., ancient Greek religion), geographical (e.g., "Caribbean Religions"), and ethnographic (e.g., "African American Religions") categories. Within each of these broad divisions are listings of "Principle Articles," "Supporting Articles," and "Biographical Articles." Certain categories have unique lists: The entry for "Islam" also lists articles under the heading "Schools, Groups, and Communities." Thus, it is possible to tell at a glance what is contained in the encyclopedia about a particular religious tradition.

Browsing through the list of articles may also be a way of discovering a topic for research if you are having trouble identifying one. In this case, the various kinds of topics for which the encyclopedia facilitates research include biographical and conceptual articles. Conceptual articles would include such topics mentioned by Dr. Renard as "Free Will and Predestination (Islamic Concepts)," "Shiism," or "Qur'ān: Tradition of Scholarship and Interpretation." You may also discover such unexpected topics as "Islamic Calligraphy" or "Ecology and Islam." The list of biographical articles is also helpful, especially because systems of transliterating Arabic names into English can vary. For example, the author identified by Dr. Renard as Ibn Arabi appears in the list as "Ibn al-ʿArabī," while Al-Ghazali appears under "Ghazālī, Abū Hāmid al-."

As useful as the synoptic outline is, it may not tell you everything you want to know. For example, let's suppose that you are interested in the question, "What is the Islamic understanding of God?" The synoptic outline tells you that there is indeed an article on "God in Islam." But what if you are particularly interested in the "Ninety-Nine Most Beautiful Names (of God)"? Dr. Renard mentioned two. What are the other ninety-seven? What is their significance?

To begin locating information on these kinds of questions, you will need to use the index. Fortunately, the editors of the *Encyclopedia of Religion* have provided a very detailed one. An index entry for "Names and naming" tells you that there is an article on that subject on pages 6406–6412 (vol. 9) of the encyclopedia. Furthermore, the index indicates that the naming "of God and other sacred beings" is discussed on pages 6406–6409. Under "of God and other sacred beings" appears an entry "in Islam," indicating that material can be found on pages 619–620, 621, 3562, and 6407.

Remember, there is often more than one way to look up a subject in an index. Sometimes, it can be useful to experiment with a different approach. For example, instead of searching the index with the concept of "names and naming," you could look under "Islam" (you could look under "God" too, but, in this case, the entry gives you a cross-reference telling you to look under individual religions). The subentry "God in" under "Islam" has a lengthy list of sub-subentries, including one for "names of" that lists even more pages than those we found in the "Names and naming" entry.

Here is one to try on your own. How would you find information in the *Encyclopedia of Religion* (or some similar reference work) regarding Islamic views of non-Muslim figures such as Abraham, Moses, or Jesus?

Such synoptic outlines as contained in the *Encyclopedia of Religion* are included in the following reference works:

Gordon D. Newby. *A Concise Encyclopedia of Islam*. Oxford, UK: Oneworld Publications, 2002.

> Here designated as a "Thematic Index" on pp. 233–244, that is, entries are grouped by categories such as "Beliefs," "Terms and Concepts," "Persons," "Places and geographic locations." However, it includes no detailed index.

John L. Esposito, ed. *The Oxford Encyclopedia of the Modern Islamic World*. 4 vols. Oxford, UK: Oxford University Press, 1995. Vol. 4, "Synoptic Outline of Contents," "Index."

What does the word *modern* in the title tell you about the kinds of subjects you can expect to find?

Richard C. Martin, ed. *Encyclopedia of Islam and the Muslim World*. 2 vols. Woodbridge, CT: Macmillan Reference USA, 2004.

See "[alphabetical] List of entries," "Synoptic outline of entries," "List of maps," "Glossary," "Appendix: Genealogies and Timelines," "Index."

The following titles are all useful for quickly looking up terms, definitions, and basic factual information; that is, they fall into the category of "concise" dictionary:

Ludwig W. Adamec. *Historical Dictionary of Islam*. Lanham, MD: Scarecrow Press, 2001.

E. van Donzel. *Islamic Desk Reference: Compiled from The Encyclopaedia of Islam*. Boston, MA: Brill, 1994.

John L. Esposito, ed. *The Oxford Dictionary of Islam*. Oxford, UK: Oxford University Press, 2003.

Ian Richard Netton. *A Popular Dictionary of Islam*. Atlantic Highliands, NJ: Humanities Press International, 1992.

The most extensive reference work on Islam in English is the twelve-volume *Encyclopedia of Islam*. However, the following title is more likely to be useful for undergraduates:

Cyril Glassé. *The New Encyclopedia of Islam*. Lanham, MD: Rowman & Littlefield, 2001.

Contains a number of helpful features, including color photographs, several appendices containing maps, historical synopses, charts, genealogical tables, chronology, and so on.

The following reference works are useful for research focused on the Qur'ān:

Oliver Leaman, ed. *The Qur'an: an Encyclopedia*. Oxford, UK: Routledge, 2006.

Jane Dammen McAuliffe, ed. *Encyclopaedia of the Qur'ān*. 5 vols. Boston, MA: Brill, 2001–2006.

The material presented in this chapter should allow you to solidify the library skills you have learned in previous chapters.

Skill Key #1

Use the library's reference collection to begin your research.

a) Use a subject-specific encyclopedia to acquire specialized knowledge about a subject.

b) Use a subject-specific encyclopedia whose scope is appropriate for both your topic and the approach you want to take to that topic.

c) Use encyclopedia bibliographies to identify subject headings for your topic.

d) Use a concise subject-specific dictionary to look up the specialized vocabulary of a particular field.

e) Use an encyclopedia's index to locate information on subjects (including persons) for which there is no separate article.

f) Examine the synoptic outline of contents (or however it is designated) in an encyclopedia (1) to get a quick overview of the contents and (2) to get topic ideas for research.

g) Use an encyclopedia's index to get ideas for research topics.

h) Use cross-references to locate additional relevant material in an encyclopedia.

i) Use an encyclopedia's index to locate all (or as much as you want) relevant material on your topic. Note especially how detailed the index is and whether the editors of the encyclopedia make any special comments about it.

Skill Key #2

Use the library's catalog to locate sources of information.

a) Use subject headings to locate precisely books on your topic.

b) Use subject headings whose scope fits your topic as closely as possible, then adjust your search with a broader or narrower subject heading as necessary.

c) As an alternative to using encyclopedia bibliographies, use keyword searching to identify subject headings for your topic.

d) Combine one or more subject headings in a search to retrieve books on a topic for which no single subject heading exists.

e) Use the floating subdivision "encyclopedias" in combination with a keyword to identify encyclopedias on a subject.

f) Use the floating subdivision "moral and ethical aspects" to identify material, whether "pro" or "con," related to the ethical aspects of a subject.

g) Use the floating subdivision "religious aspects" to search for religious/theological aspects of nonreligious/nontheological subjects.

h) If necessary, use all the subject headings assigned to a book to identify material on a particular subject.

i) Use the name of an organization or group as an author to search for documents produced under the aegis of that particular group. Be aware of the possibility of changes in the group's name over time.

Student Tasks

1. Do a keyword search on "Islam AND encyclopedias" in your library catalog. If your library does not have any encyclopedias specifically on Islam, try a broader search: "religion AND encyclopedias."

2. If your library owns the *Encyclopedia of Religion*, look at the entries under "Islam" in the synoptic outline of contents in volume 15. Then, look at the index entries under

"Islam." How does the list of articles in the synoptic outline compare with the index entries? Is there a topic that looks interesting and that you would like to pursue?

3. If the library does not have the *Encyclopedia of Religion*, find an alternative (using the technique given in #1). If you can, find an encyclopedia with a synoptic outline (or however it may be designated).

4. Choose one of the persons mentioned in the chapter by Dr. Renard, and find an encyclopedia article on that person. Now, look at the index entry for that person. Is there more in the encyclopedia about the person than in just the article you looked up?

5. Choose a conceptual topic from the chapter, and use an encyclopedia index to locate information on that topic throughout the encyclopedia.

6. Search the Internet for information on the same person you looked up in #3. Do the same for the conceptual topic you looked up in #4. Did you find information you would regard as authoritative? What leads you to think so? How many different ways can you search for this kind of information on the Internet?

V

CATHOLIC THEOLOGY IN
A GLOBAL CONTEXT

10

Catholic Theology in a Global Context: A World Church

From the Editor

To love God implies that we can expect many surprises in our lives. As a classic humorous remark puts it, "If you want to make God laugh, just tell God your plans." Perhaps a way of describing a "God of surprises" is this: Just when we think we have all the answers, when we have put them in a box, closed the flaps, and tied the pretty red bow around it neatly and tight, God smiles at us, unties the nice petty bow, opens the box, takes out the answers we have packaged so nicely—and gives us a bigger box! This chapter explores some of the questions that need a bigger box.

After the Resurrection, Jesus' "final command" to his disciples is "Go, therefore, and make disciples of all the nations. . . ." So, the Church as the community of disciples did precisely this; they went out into the world, spreading the Good News.

Twenty centuries later, the Church is still preaching this good news. The world, however, keeps changing and presenting new opportunities to follow Christ. As we will read in this chapter, new challenges arise as the people in the Church have moved from a predominantly western Eurocentric population to a fast-growing population throughout a global context. We are becoming a world church. This means that the necessary functions of the Church, such as decision making, theology, liturgy, governance, and so on, will be done on a wider scale, in different ways, with different insights, and with increasing global awareness. God seems to be leading us to a new way of being a church.

This chapter introduces us to many Christian communities around the world. The chapter is not one with finished answers. God has untied our bow, opened our little box, and handed us a bigger one and is telling us that we think too small for the workings of the Holy Spirit. We must realize in a new way again that God really is the God of all people and loves us all.

This chapter finishes our book with a realization of the future that is occurring before our eyes. In the Reference Librarian's section, we will find more skills to probe this world context and to find resources to help us understand it. This chapter concludes our research skills. Remember, a skill needs to be used and reused. It can be applied to any academic discipline, for our own wonder, or for curiosity. Please practice it often; a world of knowledge and education can be opened up for a lifetime.

Catholic Theology in a Global Context: A World Church

Angelyn Dries, OSF, PhD

Overview

> "How is it that we hear, each of us, in our own native language . . . about God's deeds of power?" (Acts 2:8–11)

For much of the nineteenth and twentieth centuries, the theological "greats," such as Karl Rahner, Yves Congar, Hans Küng, Edward Schillebeeckx, and David Tracy, grew up, were educated, and taught either in Europe or in North America. North Americans often studied in Germany, France, Rome, and Belgium to learn from these and other theologians. During the same time period, many of the immigrants to North America were from Europe, Eastern Europe, or the Mediterranean countries. However, since at least 1970, the theological picture has opened in new geographic directions, as is true for immigrants coming to North America.

We often find ourselves working or attending class with Asians, Africans, Europeans, Latin Americans, and even Oceanians. The U.S. census in 2000 highlighted the diversity of ethnic and racial backgrounds in this part of North America. At the same time, global statistics indicate a numerical shift in Catholic and Christian populations from Europe and North America to Asia and the southern hemisphere. We also once again became aware of the worldwide scope of the Church with CNN's almost nonstop coverage of the events following the death of Pope John Paul II. The cameras panned over the many faces of Catholics in India, Kenya, and the Philippines. In the last twenty years, scholars began to use the term *World Christianity* or *world church* to characterize a new awareness of the Church's diversity. However, a world church is more than geography.

Growth in Catholicism by Continents, 1975–2000

Continent	Catholic Population 1975	Catholic Population 2000	Change
Africa	48,528,000	130,018,000	168%
America	341,290,000	519,391,000	52%
Asia	52,589,000	107,301,000	104%
Europe	261,924,000	280,144,000	7%
Oceania	5,227,000	8,202,000	57%

Source: Froehle and Gautier, 46, 71, 86, 103, 116.

Meaning of Terms: World Christianity, World Church

The fall of the Berlin Wall and the massacre of students in Tiananmen Square, both happening in 1989, drew our attention to globalization as one of several megatrends that affect us all. We are impacted by a "world culture," which has been developing due to the growth of capitalism, free-trade agreements, instant communications, economic interdependence, and technology, among other things. The idea of a church reaching to the "ends of the earth" has been part of Roman Catholic history, beginning with the apostles and with Saint Paul. More recently, several theologians have used the term *World Christianity* or *world church* as a way to speak about the impact that local churches are having on all Catholics.

In 1945, a Maryknoll, New York, priest named John Considine wrote a small book, entitled *World Christianity*. Considine had many years of experience working in Rome, where he interacted with missionaries and local church leaders from all over the world. He also traveled extensively in Latin America and Africa to see firsthand the Catholic peoples in what at that time were considered mission countries. He observed that the immense post-World War II changes had made it imperative that Catholics have a knowledge, an understanding, and a regard for the peoples of the Church Universal.

At the Second Vatican Council (1961–1965), bishops from all over the world gathered in Rome, where, for the first time, they themselves realized in a graphic way the diversity and particularity of the Church, represented by indigenous Church leadership. This included the presence of bishops from the Eastern Rite Churches, which historically were shaped in a different theological culture than the Roman Catholic Church. Karl Rahner, a *peritus* (theological expert) at the Council, noted the gathering as "the Church's first official self-actualization as a world Church" (Rahner, 1979, 717). He noted that, to some extent, the theology that had been exported from Europe carried with it a particular culture and civilization, which Europe considered superior to others. Such exportation had practical as well as theoretical problems. For example, in African cultures where polygamy was the practice, did a man need to give up all his wives except one to be baptized as a Catholic? What would

> **Definitions of Globalization**
>
> "Convergence of a multipolar world, global capitalism, and communications technologies." (Robert Schreiter, *The New Catholicity*, 8)
>
> "The intensification of worldwide social relations which link distant localities in such a way that local happenings are shaped by events occurring many miles away and vice versa." (Anthony Giddens, quoted in *Magesa*, 2004, 150–151)

become of his other wives, who would thereby lose their social and economic identity in the close-knit community?

Rahner's experience of the Second Vatican Council led him to identify three theological eras in the Catholic Church:

1. The period of Jewish Christianity, when the proclamation of the saving message of Jesus was first given among the Jewish people.

2. The period of the Church in the distinct cultural region of Hellenism and Europe. The apostle Paul introduced a radically new direction for the church in the context of the "pagan," "gentile," or Roman religion. At the same time, however, Eastern Christianity took its own path with a different philosophical and theological emphasis.

3. The present period, after the Council, when "the sphere of the Church's life is in fact the entire world." (Rahner, 1979, 721)

Rahner suggested, "Either the Church sees and recognizes these essential differences of other cultures for which she should become a world church and with a Pauline boldness draws the necessary consequences from this recognition, or she remains a Western Church and so in the final analysis betrays the meaning of Vatican II" (Rahner, 1979, 724).

That the gospel is "translatable" within cultures is itself an important consequence of the doctrine of the incarnation. This point has been made by Lamin Sanneh, a Gambian-born Yale professor who first converted to Islam and then to Catholicism. Christianity "translated itself out of" Aramaic and Hebrew into Greek and Latin and eventually into most of the languages of the world (Sanneh, 1). Islam has proven itself adaptable in many places, but it holds Arabic as central to its prayer, sacred literature, and law. Christianity, however, has seen new cultures and languages as potential sources for the expression of the central Christian message. This concept is identified theologically in the expression called "inculturation." Inculturation is the interaction and adaptation of the gospel in various contexts, a practice modeled on the incarnation, that is, the Word of God become flesh in Jesus, revealing God's saving love to all. This reality is dynamically and critically "incarnated" in specific cultures and situations and involves both a critique and affirmation of a culture.

Theological Aspects of a World Church

Just before the Second Vatican Council, voices of local churches and of missionaries around the world were beginning to find expression, not just in vernacular languages in Eucharistic liturgies but also in the area of theology. Women and men in Latin America, Africa, and Asia were highlighting new emphases, themes, and methods in theology.

All theology, according to Saint Anselm (1033–1109), is "faith seeking understanding," but theology unfolding in different parts of the world has a different context. Theology in western countries came to rely heavily upon scholastic philosophy for the clarification of revelation and religious truths. Scholastic methodology tended to rely on reason and to work deductively; that is, general principles were logically applied to specific issues or questions. By the 1960s, "emerging subaltern voices," as Sri Lankan theologian R. S. Sugirtharajah has called them, began to be heard (Fabella and Sugirtharajah, 2000, 2). In general, much of this theology developed in an ecumenical environment and was based strongly on the Bible, with men and women theologians noticeably connected with their local church communities.

Much of world theology is being done in communitarian fashion. That is, theologians are crossing denominational boundaries to work together to shape a theology that explores the gospel in their particular cultural context. Nevertheless, we will briefly note two representative theologians from three areas and identify their context, methodology, sources for theology, and major themes/issues. We will see that local contexts affect the reception of the gospel and interaction with various Catholic traditions and thus give a particular "flavor" to a specific theology.

Latin American Theology

Catholic life and teaching entered Central and South America as part of Spain and Portugal's colonial empire, beginning in 1492. Some of the theological issues of that time with respect to the colonial empire centered on the development of international law, the identification of the "others" (i.e., indigenous peoples) as persons in their own right, and establishing whether Native Americans could be admitted fully into the Church through baptism. Latin America remained an "official" Catholic region politically, culturally, and religiously for most of its post-1492 history.

In the 1960s, theologians from Latin America addressed the great economic and social disparity they found in most of their countries. They were assisted by a large body of Catholic social teaching, beginning with Pope Leo XIII's *Rerum Novarum* ("On the Condition of Workers," 1891) and supported by the Vatican Council II's *Gaudium et Spes* (1965) and later, the World Synod of Catholic Bishops' statement, *Justice in the World* (1971).

> The joy and hope, the grief and anguish of the people of our time, especially those who are poor or are afflicted in any way, are the joy and hope, the grief and anguish of the followers of Christ, as well. (*Gaudium et Spes* 1)

> Action on behalf of justice and participation in the transformation of the world fully appear to us as a constitutive dimension of the preaching of the Gospel, or, in other words, of the Church's mission for the redemption of the human race and its liberation from every oppressive situation. (*Justice in the World* 6)

Many people suffered because of oppressive governments, the presence of crushing poverty, the murder and disappearance of citizens, a chasm between the poor and the rich, and widespread illiteracy. Oftentimes, Catholic Church leaders tended to side with the political leadership. Communism and Marxism seemed a viable alternative for people, especially those who were poor. Within this situation, local church leaders and some missionaries from abroad began to form small groups where people reflected upon their lives and poverty in light of the Jewish and Christian scriptures. They then took action to rectify injustice, as they saw it. The method was a "liberative *praxis*" (Gk., "action"). The groups came to be known as *communidades de base* ("base communities"). In the 1960s and 1970s, many such groups sprang up in Latin America, forming one of the foundations for liberation theology.

Rather than using a philosophical framework to analyze religious truth, liberation theology tended to rely on social sciences to critically reflect upon social and political realities. Theologians worked inductively, rather than deductively, starting with people's experience and then examining the scriptures and Church teachings in light of them. Theologians based their theology on the experience of many poor people, so liberation theology was sometimes thought of as "theology from below," in contrast to "theology from above" (i.e., theology done by "experts").

Several themes surfaced, all of them scripturally based. Jesus is portrayed as the liberator not only from personal sin but also from the structural sin of poverty and conditions that kept people oppressed. The Exodus paradigm highlights God as the God of the poor and the work of the people as hastening the reign of God. Reflecting upon the words of the Jewish prophets, especially Isaiah and Micah, liberation theologians challenged the Church to be a church of the poor.

The growth of liberation theology, the strength of the base communities, the development of literacy programs, and the criticism of unjust government or church structures together began to have social and political consequences. Lay people were gaining confidence and new skills and demanding justice. Some politicians and other groups that perceived these developments as a threat to their power began murdering their own people and missionaries who were helping to "conscientize" the people. Probably the most well-known of those martyred are those in El Salvador: Archbishop Oscar Romero, the four U.S. Catholic women (1980), and the six Jesuits teaching at the University of Central America and their housekeeper and her daughter (1989).

Some North Americans heard about liberation theology from missionaries who wrote back home to tell family and friends what was happening in Latin America, but Gustavo Gutiérrez, a Peruvian theologian, presented the first full treatment in his groundbreaking *Theology of Liberation: History, Politics, and Salvation* (1973). Theology is a critical reflection upon praxis. The starting point for theology is engagement with people in their situation, which is where the Word of God is revealed. In particular, situations need to be judged from the perspective of those who are on the margins of society and the Church. He highlighted key biblical themes:

(a) The Exodus—a passage to liberation in order to make them a holy people

(b) The eschatological promise of the reign of God—How does the vision of God inform the present?

(c) The prophetic—both denounces injustice and transforms the present reality to reflect the values and reality of the reign of God

Gutiérrez sees Jesus Christ as the liberator and salvation as liberation from the broken relationships found personally and structurally in society. Several of the key themes of liberation theology found their way into the Latin American bishops' pastoral statement when they met in Puebla, Mexico, in 1979. Gutierrez writes:

> The most important instance of [the process of human liberation] in our times, especially in underdeveloped and oppressed countries, is the struggle to construct a just and fraternal society, where persons can live with dignity and be the agents of their own destiny. It is my opinion that

the term *development* does not well express these profound aspirations. *Liberation*, on the other hand, seems to express them better. Moreover, in another way the notion of liberation is more exact and all-embracing: it emphasizes that human beings transform themselves by conquering their liberty throughout their existence and their history. The Bible presents liberation—salvation—in Christ as the total gift, which, by taking on the levels I indicate, gives the whole process of liberation its deepest meaning and its complete and unforeseeable fulfillment. Liberation can thus be approached as a single salvific process. This viewpoint, therefore, permits us to consider the *unity, without confusion*, of the various human dimensions, that is, one's relationships with other humans and with the Lord, which theology has been attempting to establish for some time; this approach will provide the framework for our reflection. (p. x)

Theologian Maria Pilar Aquino, whose parents were Mexican immigrant workers, emphasizes many of the same themes of early liberation theologians from Latin America, but she particularly focuses on the theological contributions of women's lives and perspective in the process, highlighting the strong role Mary, mother of Jesus, continues to hold. Important principles underlying her methodology are the faith of the people, option for the poor and oppressed, and a "liberating praxis" of accompaniment with people in their struggle for dignity, peace, and humanization.

Her methodology arises from the centrality of the faith of the people, the option for the poor and oppressed, a close relationship between spirituality and theology, and a "liberating praxis" of accompaniment with people in their struggle for dignity, peace, and humanization (see Aquino, 1993). Women's experience corrects an androcentric (or "male-centered") position of liberation theology and provides a sense of realism for theology. Theology is "realist," treating human nature with its conflicts, contradictions, hopes, and struggles, so that those situations and tendencies that create death might be transformed into life.

African Theology

Catholic life in Northern Africa traces itself back to almost the beginnings of Christianity. The apostle Mark influenced the Coptic Church in Alexandria, Egypt, a church that continues today. The Acts of the Apostles tells the story of the Ethiopian who was converted by Philip the apostle (see Acts 8:29, 39), and there has been a consistent Christian presence in Ethiopia (the area was called Abyssinia at the time), since at least 500 CE, after the arrival of nine Syrian missionaries twenty years earlier. North Africa was well represented in the theological formulation of key aspects of the relationship of the members of the Trinity and Jesus' nature. In the twentieth century, many African countries are postcolonial nations, which also have a history of Muslim and Christian slave trade and Muslim and Catholic interaction, especially in sub-Saharan Africa. Africans retain a strong community orientation, tribal identity, and oral traditions. The spirit world is present and active, intervening in daily life. Africans still widely practice polygamy and retain traditional sacrificial rites.

Africans have been reclaiming their early Church and patristic roots, as well as their cultures. Several theologians employ "narrative" theology, using the dynamics of African proverbs, songs, myths, African rituals, and life experiences as the basis for reflecting upon current experience and the gospel. With a vibrant song tradition among many tribes, it is not surprising that Africans are calling for more vibrant liturgical rituals, which encompass or intersect African rituals, worldview, and spontaneity. Themes and issues theologians address are inculturation, peace, and reconciliation between and among tribes, as well as a criticism of "anthropological poverty," an internalization of the mentality of dominated and exploited peoples. African ecclesiology suggests strong and active participation of all members of the Church.

We will look at two theologians who explore what inculturation means for Africa. A biblical scholar from Nigeria, Teresa Okure plumbs the meaning of New Testament (NT) passages, which show Jesus among the people of his day. A key concept she notes is his "self-emptying" (Gk.: *kenosis*; see Phil 2:6–11; Jn 1:1c, 14) in the Incarnation. In his humanity, Jesus emptied himself of a "divine mode of operating" and took on our humanity. Jesus was born into a Jewish culture in the eastern part of the Mediterranean, when Israel was dominated by the Roman Empire, but he also critiqued his culture, especially its attitudes toward riches; the impoverished; socially unacceptable people; and religious practices and laws, which were seen as ends in themselves. Okure cites the resources Jesus drew upon in his inculturation:

- His certainty that he was doing the will of the One who sent him;
- His conviction of his mission to transform people's lives and cultures;
- His own personal integrity.

Okure challenges the Nigerian Church, in particular, to be self-emptying: to examine new theological paths arising from the experience and fabric of African lives, rather than to cling to those inherited theological and liturgical structures foreign to African life. The Church needs to be "self-emptied" of a kind of tribalism that excludes some people and discriminates, to the detriment of the building up of the body of Christ. Self-emptying means addressing the personal fears people might have as they work to transform the African Church and society.

> In the Incarnation, therefore, it is not only humanity that tends towards God in Christ and becomes one with God, but it is God also, who tends towards humanity and becomes one with humankind. Paul would regard this as a great mystery (see Eph 5:32).

> Our effort to understand inculturation in the Nigerian and other African contexts, thus requires us to identify the two realities, that must needs be united and mutually enriched. These two realities are our Christian faith—the Good News of Jesus Christ, and our African reality of peoples in their different cultures. (Okure, 1990, pp. 57–58)

Tanzanian priest and theologian Laurenti Magesa combines a pastoral sensitivity, theological sharpness, and a social science methodology to examine and challenge elements of Catholic life, such as moral traditions and marriage, in Kenya, Tanzania, and Uganda.

MARYKNOLL FATHERS AND BROTHERS

The painting of The Pentecost shown here is by Tanzanian artist Charles Ndege. Fr. Joe Healey and other Maryknollers have commissioned a number of Ndege paintings, and Christmas cards with his paintings are published by Paulines Publications Africa.

He follows the now-familiar methodological path of an examination of the experience of African Catholics in the three countries mentioned. He brings to light the process of "religious–cultural symbiosis," that is, how the faith has actually been received by Africans, and considers what the Church of the future might look like, especially in liturgy and pastoral practice. Of particular note is the description of Jesus, common among other African theologians. African sensitivities see Jesus as the Brother–Ancestor–Healer in the Church as Family. Each of the nouns arises not only from scripture but also from important African values. Much of indigenous African worship bonds the present generation with their ancestors. Ancestors share blood with descendents, are viewed as sacred, mediate the visible world and that which is unseen, and possess spiritual powers. So, too, does Jesus. This "ancestral ecclesiology" flows over into sacramental and moral life, healing, and hospitality.

Asian Theology

Asia includes a vast amount of territory and almost two-thirds of the population on the earth, so it is difficult to generalize about so many groups. There is a longstanding tradition that the Catholic Church has been in India since the preaching of the apostle Mark, who came to the Malabar coast of South India in 52 CE, though more probably a sustained Catholic presence has been in that area since the fourth century. Nestorian missionaries, followers of an early bishop of Constantinople, brought Christianity to China in 635 CE. Franciscan missionary John of Monte Corvino traveled from Persia to India in 1291, where he preached and baptized a number of people and then proceeded to Beijing, where he was joined by another Franciscan and spent many years in Cathay (the name for China at the time). John noted at the time the strong presence of Nestorian Christianity in the area.

Asian Catholics continue to live among followers of the ancient religions of Hinduism and Buddhism. These religions see no disconnection between "religion" and the rest of life, as people in North America often do. Catholics are a significant minority in all Asian countries, except the Philippines, where Catholicism is the predominant religion. Catholics are making their theological way partially in dialogue with those religions. Asian philosophical traditions differ from the reason and logic of western philosophy in that they assume that a harmony undergirds all of daily life. The *Yin* and *Yang* of Taoism, for example, are "true" together, sometimes in different practices or perhaps in opposite realities (i.e., hot and cold). Harmony is the constant balancing of these unifying forces. These traditions understand the nature of truth as being multiform, rather than monoform.

Asian theological methodology and sources are related, as we find in the poetry and dramas of a Catholic South Korean layman, Kim Chi-Ha, imprisoned, tortured, and in solitary confinement for many years between 1960 and 1970. The experience of unjust suffering and oppression forms the basis of *Minjung* ("the Korean people") theology, which uses folk tales and community identity to reflect upon the gospel as it intersects with a fundamental Korean concept of *han* ("suffering"). *Han*, a complex Korean word, describes a basic "suppressed vitality" or existential pain arising from suppression (cf. Ahn, 1997).

Jesuit Aloysius Pieris, a Sri Lankan theologian, also employs an Asian "style" as he explores theology against the backdrop of Buddhism and within the fundamental concept of harmony in Asian culture and thinking. For example, he suggests that a harmony exists between the Word and Silence. In a dialectical relationship, Silence is the unspoken Word and the Word is Silence heard. Theory and praxis are one and the same for Asian theologians.

RÉUNION DES MUSÉES NATIONAUX/ART RESOURCE, NY.

Shown in this photo is the Nestorian Monument (or Stele), which was discovered in 1625 in Xi An. The inscribed Chinese characters tell us that the monument was built to commemorate the introduction of Christianity in China in 781 CE, and they note the arrival of a Nestorian missionary in the, then, capital city of China. 1907–1908, Photo: Thierry Ollivier. Musée des Arts Asiatiques-Guimet, Paris, France.

Here let me refer to the current trend of using "Buddhist techniques" of meditation in "Christian Prayer" without any reverence for the soteriological [salvific] context of such techniques. For the naïve presupposition is that the (Buddhist) *Way* could be had without the (Buddhist) *Truth*. It is time to impress on our theologians that in our culture the *method* cannot be severed from the *goal*. . . . *Technē* [the Greek word from which derives the English word, *technique*] is not a mechanical action, but a skill, an art. In our traditions, the art of doing a thing is itself the thing done. The *goal* of life, in Buddhism, is the *art* of living it. The perfection to be achieved is the style of achieving it! The obvious corollary is that the Asian method of doing theology is itself Asian theology. *Theopraxis* is already the formulation of Theology. (Pieris, 1979, 447)

Karl Rahner, in his *Theological Investigations* (Vol. 8, 1971, pp. 66, 86), and more recently the Asian Synod of Bishops (1999) have drawn attention to the critical role that women have in addressing significant social, political, and cultural problems in Asian countries. Prostitution, trafficking in women and children, and violence against women are identified as key realities affecting women's dignity and worth. Such horrendous situations are often supported by myths and proverbs related to women. These and other pastoral concerns form the basis of much of the theological development in Asia. In 2002, fifty-five Asian Catholic women theologians met to reflect theologically upon the 1999 Asian Bishops Synod meeting. The theme of their gathering, "Ecclesia of Women in Asia: Gathering the Voices of the Silenced," highlighted six major areas affecting women: violence, the Bible, church structure, spirituality, ecofeminism, and world religions. If a practice toward women denies their dignity or voice, the result will affect how we see their role in the community and in the Church, but it will also be revealed in an implicit Christology. We see this clearly in this excerpt from the keynote address given by Evelyn Monteiro at the conference:

Women and the Bible

The Bible has been one of the most misused books against women. The silence, invisibility and trivialization of the role and experience of women within the Bible are misread as divine principle rather than recognizing it as the work of men written in an ethos of patriarchy. The image of women as the "weaker vessel" "created for the sake of man," as "inferior," "temptress," "gateway to hell," etc., is misinterpreted as deigned by the Creator rather than recognizing her as a being created in the image and likeness of God. Consequently, not only are women silenced but also the biblical notion of gender equality remains hidden within the pages of Scriptures.

Women and Church Structure

Does the Church structure lend itself to be supportive of the place and role of women in the life and governance of the Church? Is the Church of Asia women-friendly? Is the Church, the Body of Christ, in solidarity with women through participatory opportunities and through empowering and entrusting women with full and creative leadership responsibilities? These are some questions that perhaps need to be addressed especially in view of the Synodal document that states, "[T]he Church should be a participatory Church in which no one feels excluded, and judge the wider participation of women in the life and mission of the Church in Asia to be an especially pressing need." (Monteiro, 2005, p. xxi)

The World Church in North America

About the same time the world theologies were developing, major ethnic or racial groups in North America (some of whom had been here prior to the colonial empires) developed a consciousness about their specific religious and theological identities. In the late 1960s, James H. Cone began to develop a "black theology," and by the early 1980s, Hispanic theology developed against the background of Cesar Chavez, Dolores Huerta, and the Farm Workers' boycott movement. Theologians Cone and Diana L. Hayes critiqued racism, the residual effects of slavery, and unjust social and ecclesial structures.

An Overview of Selected Theologies in the World Church

	Latin America	Africa	Asia
Context	Colonial remnants remain in culture; large gap between rich and poor; situations of violence, especially in the 1970s and 1980s	Animism, tribal cultures, strong community orientation	Catholics live as a minority among Buddhists, Hindus, Confucianists; in some countries, Catholicism considered a foreign religion
Theological emphases	Liberation; situations need to be judged from viewpoint of marginalized people	Inculturation	Inculturation
Method	Observe, judge, act; done in "base communities"; use of social sciences	Use of symbol (i.e., sacramental), narrative, music	Ecumenical; done in dialogue with other religions
Emphases in sources	Scriptural passages that highlight liberation, release from injustice: Exodus, prophets in the Jewish scriptures	Attention given to tribal myths, music, ceremonies, "folklore," and indigenous traditions	Interaction with Asian philosophy of harmony

In the 1970s, Asian immigrants began to enter North America in large numbers, especially from Vietnam and Laos. Peter Phan, a Vietnamese priest and theologian, draws on the cultural and spiritual riches of Asian American immigrants and Asian culture to suggest a Vietnamese American theology.

The U.S. Catholic bishops have been aware of intercontinental connections in the world church in their pastoral letters on "Call to Solidarity with Africa" (2002) and on immigration (written in conjunction with the Bishops of Mexico, 2003). Thus, we can see that each local church needs to think globally, as well as locally.

Some Commonalities in Theologies from around the Globe

Theology being done by local churches throughout the world exemplifies the rich ways in which Catholic faith is "seeking understanding." Several commonalities in theological development are easily discernible. Theology and a world church have been impacted by women's voices and by particular situations that create injustice or affect the dignity and worth of human beings. The theologies have a strong biblical base and are done in a context of living in longstanding, multireligious relationships. Almost all start with praxis or experience, rather than with theory, and pursue transformation of individuals, society, and the Church. The theologies tend toward the practical but seek "the face of Christ" in a particular cultural context. The areas of greatest theological exploration are found in the chapters and topics we have discussed in this book: scripture, Christology, ecclesiology, sacraments, morality, social justice, and religious traditions of Judaism and Islam.

Diversity and Unity, a World Church Theological Issue

Several broad theological questions are raised in the experience of a world church: What is the relationship between unity and diversity? What holds everything together if we have so much difference? Wouldn't it be easier if Catholic theology were the same all over the world?

From its origins, Christianity has had diversity, beginning with multiple Gospel traditions and varieties of church structures in the patristic period. Eastern Rite Churches, including the Ukrainian Church (Byzantine Rite) and the Maronite Church (both of which are also found in North America), have tended to highlight the mystery of God, the need to entrust oneself to that mystery, and a harmony between the mind and experience. We do need to "test the spirits to see whether they are from God . . ." (1 Jn 4:1), but perhaps it is not a matter of either diversity or unity, but of *both* diversity and unity. As Laurenti Magesa and others have noted, the Incarnation is the model. Jesus Christ, like us in everything but sin, is the point or nexus of unity and diversity for us all. As noted in the beginning of this chapter, Catholicism is a world church: one body with many members but with the differences that inculturation invariably brings.

The theological constructions, which we have examined in various ways through this chapter and this book, are not ends in themselves but are gifts for the growth of the Body of Christ, as the Church continues its journey as pilgrim people. In many ways, world church theology is the act of preaching the gospel of Jesus, or evangelization.

> Theological language contains much that is approximate; it must therefore always be open to renovation from new perspectives, further precision of concepts, and the correction of formulations. Similarly, there is the permanent emergence of new paths in our speech about God which seeks to express revealed truth in appropriate terms. All this is required along with the clear conviction that—according to a traditional affirmation— no theology can be identified with the faith. Theological pluralism within the unity of faith is an old fact in the church. In this context different theologies are useful and important efforts but on condition that they do not consider themselves unique or indispensable and they be aware of their role of modestly serving the primary tasks of the church. (Gutierrez, cited in Nickeloff, 1996, pp. 271–272)

Questions about the Text

1. What are Rahner's three theological eras in the Church? What are his reasons for these divisions?

2. What is inculturation? Give an example.

3. What is globalization? Give an example.

4. What is one characteristic of Latin American theology?

5. What is one characteristic of African theology?

6. What is one characteristic of Asian theology?

Questions for Discussion

1. What situations, events, or media have made you aware of a "world church" or "World Christianity"?

2. Compare the samples of theologies from around the world. What do they have in common? What is unique to each?

3. Suggest specific ways in which different socioeconomic, religious, and cultural contexts around the world affect how one does theology.

4. What contributions do you think these diverse theologies make to the world church?

5. Which of the theologies mentioned in this chapter finds a resonance with you? Why? What difference would they make in the world?

For Further Study

Print Sources

Ahn, Byung-Mu. "Korean Theology," in Karl Muller, Theo Sundermeier, Stephen B. Bevans, and Richard H. Bliese, eds. *Dictionary of Mission, Theology, History, Perspectives*. Maryknoll, NY: Orbis Books, 1997.

Alangaram, A., SJ. *Christ of the Asian Peoples. Towards an Asian Contextual Christology*. Bangalore, India: Asian Trading Corporation, 1999.

The author explores what Christology looks like in "Asian clothes," using as a background the documents published by the Federation of Asian Bishops Conference.

Amaladoss, Michael, SJ. *Making All Things New: Dialogue, Pluralism, and Evangelization in Asia*. Maryknoll, NY: Orbis Books, 1990.

A leading Jesuit from India explores the issues of the Church in Asia as it intersects with long-established religions older than Christianity.

Aquino, Maria Pilar. *Our Cry for Life: Feminist Theology from Latin America*. Maryknoll, NY: Orbis Books, 1993.

Bellagamba, Anthony. *Mission and Ministry in the Global Church*. Maryknoll, NY: Orbis Books, 1992.

A missionary with experience in several countries provides a challenge to Christians who have an interest in understanding and living a sense of mission, even though they never leave their own country. Two chapters especially provide an overview of the changing social and political realities that impact the Catholic Church worldwide: "Megatrends Affecting the Church" and "The Emerging Global Church."

Bosch, David J. *Transforming Mission: Paradigm Shifts in Theology of Mission*. Maryknoll, NY: Orbis Books, 1991.

See also the companion volume with primary sources: Norman Thomas, ed. *Classic Texts in Mission and World Christianity*. Maryknoll, NY: Orbis Books, 1995. This now-classic text provides a synopsis of mission from historical and thematic perspectives.

Considine, John Joseph, *World Christianity*. Milwaukee, WI: Bruce, 1945.

While Protestants had begun in the 1920s to think in terms of the *missio Dei* as the foundation for mission, Roman Catholics did not identify this emphasis until the Second Vatican Council. Considine was a forerunner in suggesting the idea among Roman Catholics.

Gutiérrez, Gustavo. *Theology of Liberation: History, Politics, and Salvation*. Maryknoll, NY: Orbis Books, 1973.

The classic text on liberation theology became a significant way for American Catholics to learn about the theological response of the Latin American Church to the problems of poverty and oppression.

Irvin, Dale, and Scott Sunquist. *History of the World Christian Movement*. 2 vols. Maryknoll, NY: Orbis Books, 2001, 2007.

This history provides a picture of the Western Roman Catholic Church, the Eastern Rite Churches, and the Churches of the southern hemisphere, several of which date back to the first decades of Christianity.

Magesa, Laurenti. *Anatomy of Inculturation: Transforming the Church in Africa*. Maryknoll, NY: Orbis Books, 2004.

Monteiro, Evelyn. "Ecclesia of Women in Asia, A Forum for Catholic Women Doing Theology in Asia," in Evelyn Monteiro, SC, and Antoinette Gutzler, MM, eds., *Ecclesia of Women in Asia*. Delhi, India: ISPCK, 2005.

National Council of Catholic Bishops. "Strangers No Longer: Together on the Journey of Hope." A pastoral letter concerning migration from the Catholic Bishops of Mexico and the United States, January 22, 2003. Available online at http://www.uscc.org/mrs/stranger.htm.

Nickoloff, James B., ed. *Gustavo Gutiérrez: Essential Writings*. Minneapolis, MN: Fortress Press, 1996.

Okure, Teresa. "Inculturation: Biblical/Theological Bases," in Teresa Okure, Paul van Thiel, et al., eds., *Inculturation of Christianity in Africa*. Eldoret, Kenya: AMECEA Gaba Publications, 1990.

Phan, Peter C. *Many Faces, One Church: Cultural Diversity and the American Catholic Experience*. Lanham, MD: Rowman & Littlefield, 2004.

The author explores the implications of global Catholicism as immigrants made their way to the United States.

Pieris, Aloysius, SJ. *Love Meets Wisdom: A Christian Experience of Buddhism*. Maryknoll, NY: Orbis Books, 1988.

———. "The Asian Sense in Theology," *Dialogue* VI, nos. 1, 2 (January–August 1979): 447.

Rahner, Karl, SJ. "Towards a Fundamental Theological Interpretation of Vatican II," *Theological Studies* 40.4 (December 1979): 716–727.

Sanneh, Lamin. *Encountering the West: Christianity and the Global Cultural Process: The Africa Dimension*. Maryknoll, NY: Orbis Books, 1993.

U.S. Catholic Bishops. "A Call to Solidarity with Africa." November 14, 2001. Available online at http://www.usccb.org/sdwp/africa.htm.

Reference Works

Froehle, Bryan T., and Mary L. Gautier. *Global Catholicism: Portrait of a World Church*. Maryknoll, NY: Orbis Books, 2003.

See selected charts for comparison of statistics on Catholicism across the continents.

Fabella, Virginia, MM, and R. S. Sugirtharajah, eds. *Dictionary of Third World Theologies.* Maryknoll, NY: Orbis Books, 2000.

Selected Websites

U.S. Catholic Conference of Bishops. Available online at http://www. usccb.org.

Sixteen percent of the departments relate to some aspect of the diversity of North American Catholicism or to the relationship between U.S. Catholics and people around the world. See especially the following departments: African American Catholics, Catholic Relief Services, Church in Latin America, Hispanic Affairs, Migration and Refugee Services, Social Development and World Peace, World Mission.

Africa Faith and Justice Network. Available online at http://www.afjn. edu/.

U.S. Catholic China Bureau. Available online at http://www.usccb.net.

Dictionary of African Christian Biographies Project. Overseas Ministries Study Center, New Haven, CT. Available online at http://www. dacb.org/.

Videos

Voices of Women. Available from Mission Education Office, Columban Fathers. St. Columbans, NE.

This video shows a good example of liberation theology with women in the Philippines in a "base community" setting.

In the Shadow of Dabajian Mountain. Available from Mission Education Office, Columban Fathers. St. Columbans, NE.

This video shows the interaction between missionaries and the indigenous Atayal in the mountains of Taiwan, both working to conserve the local culture.

Walking from the Shadows. Available from Mission Education Office, Columban Fathers. St. Columbans, NE.

This shows the work of missionaries among exploited migrant workers in Taiwan, most of them women. It also illustrates some of the effects of globalization.

From the Reference Librarian
Geographical Descriptors—World Christianity

Student: What resources are available for researching the global context of Christianity?

In one sense, everything you have learned throughout this book about reference sources and research techniques has prepared you for researching Christianity in its global context. For example, as Sr. Dries states, globalization raises issues of social and economic justice, the status of women, "liberation," and so on, so much of what you learned in the chapter on social justice will also be applicable for researching these issues in their global setting. Viewing Christianity in its global context also raises new issues for more traditional theological topics such as Christology and ecclesiology, so the resources and techniques described in the chapters on those topics will also be of use. You have been prepared to research the encounter of Christianity with other world religions by your previous study of Judaism and Islam. The effects of indigenous contexts on the Church's liturgical life can be studied using the resources of the chapter on sacraments. Even the issue of "inculturation," so much discussed in connection with the global setting of Christianity, is the modern version of what took place in the encounter of ancient Christianity with its own "global" setting—the world of Hellenistic, Greco-Roman culture. The chapters on the New Testament and Judaism have, among other things, prepared you for the study of inculturation in that ancient setting in which modern concerns are foreshadowed.

Student: So are there no reference sources or techniques I can use for research specifically in this area?

There are, indeed, a number of reference sources of varying scope that focus in some way on issues related to Christianity's global impact. These include encyclopedias and dictionaries relating to Christian missions (e.g., *Dictionary of Mission: Theology, History, Perspectives*), Christianity in a particular geographical area (e.g., *A Dictionary of Asian Christianity*), and particular theological issues (e.g., *Dictionary of Feminist Theologies*). Doubtless, more such reference works will be published in the future. (See the reference bibliography at the end of this section.)

However, one reference tool's scope is much broader than any of these and takes pride of place for researching global Christianity:

Fahlbusch, Erwin, et al., eds. *The Encyclopedia of Christianity*. 5 vols. Grand
Rapids, MI: William B. Eerdmans, 1999.

The preface of this encyclopedia declares explicitly that it was written with the
intention of "describing Christianity in its global context," that is, its scope is truly global. To that end, scholars from many countries and various cultural backgrounds have contributed articles, including articles about Christianity on every
continent (so there are articles on "Asia," "Africa," etc.) and articles on Christianity
in over 170 individual countries.

If your library does not own *The Encyclopedia of Christianity* (although it
should; this is a standard reference source), *the New Catholic Encyclopedia*, first or
second edition, is a good alternative.

Student: "World Christianity" is a big topic. How can I narrow it down?

The term *World Christianity* is perhaps a little misleading. The main point of
Sr. Dries's chapter is the diversity to be found in the various expressions of Christianity throughout the world, a diversity created by the variety of indigenous customs, patterns of thought, cultural expressions, and so on. Rather than a single
"World Christianity," there are, rather, "World Christianities." One way of studying "World Christianity," then, is to focus on a particular expression of it found in
a specific geographical/cultural location.

To see how this works, let's start with the article on Brazil from *The Encyclopedia of Christianity*. After noting the titles in the bibliography at the end of the
article, we might discover the following records in the library catalog:

Author	Bruneau, Thomas C.
Title	The political transformation of the Brazilian Catholic Church [by] Thomas C. Bruneau.
Published	[London, New York] Cambridge University Press [1974]
Description	xiv, 270 p. map. 23 cm.
Series	Perspectives on development ; 2.
Note	Based on the author's thesis, University of California, Berkeley.
Bibliography	Bibliography: p. [253]–264.
Subjects	Catholic Church—Brazil.
	Church and state—Brazil.

Author	Mainwaring, Scott, 1954–
Title	The Catholic Church and politics in Brazil, 1916–1985 / Scott Mainwaring.
Published	Stanford, Calif. : Stanford University Press, 1986.
Description	xv, 328 p. ; 23 cm.
Note	Includes index.
Bibliography	Bibliography: p. [297]–319.
Subjects	Catholic Church—Brazil—History—20th century.
	Church and state—Brazil—History—20th century.
	Brazil—Church history.
	Brazil—Politics and government—20th century.

As you examine the list of subject headings for these two books, you will notice that the geographical designation "Brazil" is used in two ways. In the first record, "Brazil" appears after the subject headings "Catholic church" and "Church and state." These are two examples of subject headings that can be subdivided geographically. This works with many (though not all) subject headings, so one way to "particularize" your search (assuming you have a subject heading to start with) is to add a geographical descriptor as a subdivision.

In the second record, the geographical designation "Brazil" itself appears as a subject heading, which is then further specified by the addition of the subdivision "Church history." After all, a book on Brazil could be about many other things besides Church history.

Student: How do I know whether to use a geographical descriptor as the main subject heading or as a subdivision?

Sometimes, you can use either one (or both) and it will not make any difference. (See the second catalog record just shown.) The main reason for knowing both ways of using geographical descriptors in subject headings is that not all subject headings subdivide geographically. But, you can still give a geographical focus to your search using subject headings that cannot be so subdivided in combination with a search using a geographical descriptor that may appear in another subject heading for the same book.

Let's say you are interested in ecclesiological structures in Africa. From what you learned in the chapter on ecclesiology, you know (or could find out) that the subject heading for ecclesiology is "Church." But "Church" does not subdivide geographically; you cannot use "Church—Africa" as a subject heading. However, if you begin with a search on "Church" and then combine that with a search on

"Africa" as a subject term, you might retrieve a record such as the following (if you do not know how to combine searches in this manner, ask your librarian to show you):

Author	Rweyemamu, Robert.
Title	People of God in the missionary nature of the church. A study of concilian ecclesiology applied to the missionary pastoral in Africa.
Published	Rome, 1968. (Delivery: Neue Zeitschrift für Missionwissenschaft, Schöneck/Beckenried.)
Description	xiv, 132 p. 21 cm.
Note	Issued also as thesis, Urbanian University, Rome.
Bibliography	Bibliography: p. v–xiii.
Subjects	Church.
	Mission of the church.
	Christianity—Africa.

Notice that "Africa" appears as a subdivision of "Christianity," which does subdivide geographically (giving you another potential subject heading to use). You might also be able to find records where "Africa" is the main subject heading.

Let's try another one. This time you are interested in researching Christological views in Latin America. One subject heading for Christology you may have learned in the chapter on Christology is "Jesus Christ—Person and offices," another subject heading that does not subdivide geographically. Beginning with this subject heading and combining it with a search for "Latin America" as a subject term might produce a record such as the following:

Uniform title	Jesús, ni vencido ni monarca celestial. English.
Title	Faces of Jesus : Latin American christologies / edited by José Míguez Bonino ; translated from the Spanish by Robert R. Barr.
Published	Maryknoll, N.Y. : Orbis Books, c1984.
Description	vi, 186 p. ; 24 cm.
Note	Translation of: Jesús, ni vencido ni monarca celestial.
Bibliography	Includes bibliographies and index.
Subjects	Jesus Christ—Person and offices.
	Theology, Doctrinal—Latin America—History—20th century.

"Latin America" appears after another subject heading, "Theology, Doctrinal," and this gives you an additional point of access for researching this topic. (Question: Why would the heading "Theology, Doctrinal—Latin America" be useful for researching Christology?)

Student: What if my library doesn't have anything on my topic?

Don't despair. Library collections are complex, and even librarians sometimes need to spend time locating what they are looking for. It would be a poor library indeed that did not have anything on your topic. Usually, however, it is just a matter of finding the right key to unlock the door to the library's riches. There are many keys available for your use because there are many ways of gaining access to your library's collection. In this book, you have been introduced to some of them. There are other keys, such as using periodical indexes and databases to locate articles, with which your librarian can assist you. If you have used up all your "keys," don't be afraid to ask librarians to share their "key rings." That is why they are there.

Reference Bibliography

Fahlbusch, Erwin, et al., eds. *The Encyclopedia of Christianity*. 5 vols. Grand Rapids, MI: William B. Eerdmans, 1999.

Each volume has an alphabetical "List of Entries" for that volume, as well as bibliographies and cross-references. The explicit aim of this reference work is to describe Christianity "in its global context." It includes articles by scholars from many countries and cultural backgrounds, articles on Christianity in every continent and over 170 individual countries, articles on Christianity in its "various regional expressions," and so on.

Müller, Karl, SVD, Theo Sundermeier, Stephen B. Bevans, SVD, and Richard H. Bliese, eds. *Dictionary of Mission: Theology, History, Perspectives*. Maryknoll, NY: Orbis Books, 1997.

See the "Contents" on pp. vii–xii for a list of articles. Also contains extensive bibliographies.

Russell, Letty M., and J. Shannon Clarkson, eds. *Dictionary of Feminist Theologies*. Louisville, KY: Westminster John Knox Press, 1996.

Sunquist, Scott W., ed. *A Dictionary of Asian Christianity*. Grand Rapids, MI: William B. Eerdmans, 2001.

> This volume contains no index, but see the alphabetical list of entries on pp. ix–xix. Contains bibliographies and focuses on one of the three major "areas" mentioned by Sr. Dries. Unfortunately, there is no equivalent (yet) for either Africa or Latin America, but the *Encyclopedia of Christianity* mentioned previously provides excellent coverage of all such areas.

U.S. Catholic Mission Handbook 2000. Washington, DC: U.S. Catholic Mission Association, 2000.

> This source contains a "Mission Inventory 1998–1999," "Analytical Charts," and "Mission Articles Marking the Millennium." See the U.S. Catholic Mission Association website available online at www. uscatholicmission.org for a more recent version of the handbook and much more information.

Library Skills

Here is our final list of library skills. You may want to copy them and keep them handy with you as you master the ins and outs of research. You can use them for any subject—the skills are transferable—so put them in a notebook, written or electronic, that is readily accessible and with you. There are many other library skills besides these, but if you have mastered these, you are well on your way to becoming an expert library user. Remember, practice makes perfect, and these skills can help you for a lifetime. Use them wisely and well.

Student Tasks

1. Choose a country. Find out if your library has a dictionary or encyclopedia on Christianity in that country. If it does not, find an encyclopedia that does tell you about Christianity in that country.

2. Choose a country. Search your library catalog using the name of the country as a subject heading. Scroll through the list of subject headings. What subdivisions do you see after the name of the country that would be relevant for studying theology or Christianity in that country?

3. Use the name of the country you selected for #2 as a subdivision following the subject heading "Church history" or "Christianity" (e.g., Church history—Brazil; Christianity—Great Britain). How do the results compare with what you found in #2?

4. Choose a country or region. Try to find a website for the organization of Catholic bishops for that country or region. What problems do you encounter in trying to do this?

The Librarian's Guide to Solid Research

Skill Key #1

Use the library's reference collection to begin your research.

a) Use a subject-specific encyclopedia to acquire specialized knowledge about a subject.

b) Use a subject-specific encyclopedia whose scope is appropriate for both your topic and the approach you want to take to that topic.

c) Use encyclopedia bibliographies to identify subject headings for your topic.

d) Use a concise subject-specific dictionary to look up the specialized vocabulary of a particular field.

e) Use an encyclopedia's index to locate information on subjects (including persons) for which there is no separate article.

f) Examine the synoptic outline of contents (or however it is designated) in an encyclopedia (1) to get a quick overview of the contents and (2) to get topic ideas for research.

g) Use an encyclopedia's index to get ideas for research topics.

h) Use cross-references to locate additional relevant material in an encyclopedia.

i) Use an encyclopedia's index to locate all (or as much as you want) relevant material on your topic. Note especially how detailed the index is and whether the editors of the encyclopedia make any special comments about it.

Skill Key #2

Use the library's catalog to locate sources of information.

a) Use subject headings to locate precisely books on your topic.

b) Use subject headings whose scope fits your topic as closely as possible, then adjust your search with a broader or narrower subject heading as necessary.

c) As an alternative to using encyclopedia bibliographies, use keyword searching to identify subject headings for your topic.

d) Combine one or more subject headings in a search to retrieve books on a topic for which no single subject heading exists.

e) Use the floating subdivision "encyclopedias" in combination with a keyword to identify encyclopedias on a subject.

f) Use the floating subdivision "moral and ethical aspects" to identify material, whether "pro" or "con," related to the ethical aspects of a subject.

g) Use the floating subdivision "religious aspects" to search for religious/theological aspects of nonreligious/nontheological subjects.

h) If necessary, use all the subject headings assigned to a book to identify material on a particular subject.

i) Use the name of an organization or group as an author to search for documents produced under the aegis of that particular group. Be aware of the possibility of changes in the group's name over time.

j) Use geographical descriptors either as subject headings or as subdivisions to focus research on a subject as it relates to a particular geographical area, such as "local" expressions of Christianity.

Acknowledgments

The scriptural quotations contained herein are from the New Revised Standard Version of the Bible, Catholic Edition. Copyright © 1993 and 1989 by the Division of Christian Education of the National Council of the Churches of Christ in the United States of America. All rights reserved.

The expert staff at Pius XII Memorial Library, Saint Louis University, provided much support for the creation of the research sections of this text. Electronic catalog excerpts contained herein were provided by Pius XII Memorial Library. Catalog software at Pius XII Memorial Library was created by Innovative Interfaces, Inc., a library automation company in Emeryville, CA.

The excerpts that reference the *Catechism* are from the English translation of the *Catechism of the Catholic Church* for use in the United States of America. Copyright © 1994 by the United States Catholic Conference, Inc.—Libreria Editrice Vaticana. Used with permission.

Cover image: Raphael (Raffaello Sanzio) (1483–1520). Allegory of Theology. Detail from the ceiling of the Stanza della Segnatura. Stanze di Raffaello, Vatican Palace, Vatican State. Photo Credit: Scala / Art Resource, NY.

Chapter 9, "Islamic Religious Experience: Foundations, Scripture, and Spirituality," is abridged excerpts from Renard, John. *Seven Doors to Islam: Spirituality and the Religious Life of Muslims*. Berkeley: University of California Press, 1996. Used with permission. All rights reserved.

Index